Cities Made of Boundarie⌐

Cities Made of Boundaries

Mapping Social Life in Urban Form

Benjamin N. Vis

First published in 2018 by
UCL Press
University College London
Gower Street
London WC1E 6BT

Available to download free: www.ucl.ac.uk/ucl-press

ISBN: 978–1–78735–107–3 (Hbk.)
ISBN: 978–1–78735–106–6 (Pbk.)
ISBN: 978–1–78735–105–9 (PDF)
ISBN: 978–1–78735–108–0 (epub)
ISBN: 978–1–78735–109–7 (mobi)
ISBN: 978–1–78735–110–3 (html)
DOI: https://doi.org/10.14324/111.9781787351059

'One could spend a lifetime on nothing but boundaries.
This would be a worthwhile work.'
Edward T. Hall, 1996: viii

Acknowledgements

The research that led to this book started life destined to provide a better understanding of functional classifications applied to Maya cities, evaluated through the lens of contemporary urban geography. Undertaking my PhD at the University of Leeds, I encountered the flexibility to change course dramatically and ended up working through the development of a social comparative methodology to contribute to understanding urban form across time and space within the same frame of reference. My doctorate was supported by the Prins Bernhard Cultuurfonds to start doctoral research abroad, and Leeds University Research Scholarship. Without the sustained security of these grants the present book would simply not exist. My Research Fellowship at the University of Kent, supported by the Eastern Area Research Consortium (EARC), helped its refinement and development into a monograph in subsequent years. Boldly seeking to innovate on fundamental grounds within an overtly interdisciplinary position, leaning on a great diversity of discourse, I am grateful that UCL Press was brave enough to take on this project. Their fees waiver for early career researchers means that the ideas in this book will now be available to all without impediments, and through sharing these ideas may fulfil more promises than would otherwise be possible.

Institutions facilitate, but environments enable. Even though both my parents pursued research, I needed the encouragement and reassurance of my father, Jan Vis, to take on the PhD. Soon after, he set his example. It was for me to follow. Throughout, I could count on the unwavering support of Rianne Dubois. Holding ground when what you have let yourself in for unfolds inexorably, has to be admired. It isn't over yet. Every day, my daughter Thule, has the presence of mind to remind me persuasively that there is life away from the screen. I have fond memories of G.12, the graveyard view lending perspective, and the people who shared that space and process with me: especially Andy Newing, Nik Lomax and, regretfully briefly, Mikkel Bojesen. I went from a school with brutalist prospects to brutalist incarceration. Yet, I can now release these ideas into the world, which were first met by the open gazes of Andrew Evans, David Bell and Penelope Goodman. They met my intellectual charges with ardour and trust, and offered guidance to my unceremonious stretching of disciplinary perspectives. The quantitative outcomes to this research were ensured by Andrew Evans' foolhardy effort in constructing the initial geocomputational tools. His perverse pleasure is something I still benefit from and, by means of this book, is now yours for the taking. While at Leeds, further structural advice and support from John Thorp, Dominic Powlesland, Paul Waley and Mark Birkin broadened horizons. Critiques and cautions accompanied by unreserved endorsement from Ray Laurence and Martin Purvis consolidated my confidence to make this book.

Except when browsing, I am not one to keep an open tab. Yet, I feel indebted to a great number of people, projects and institutions, many of which have proven indispensable to shaping and completing this research. Manifesting progressive spirit, Scott Hutson, on behalf of the Pakbeh Regional Economy Program, shared the original map of Chunchucmil years ahead of publication. He tenaciously engaged in correspondence to explain and clarify particulars, compensating for my inexperience and untrained eye. Derek Keene played a much similar role for his medieval city plans of Winchester. I am beholden to Martin Biddle and Katherine Barclay of the Winchester Excavations Committee and the Winchester Research Unit in particular for granting me access and reproduction fees for Keene's original Winchester city plans. I was selflessly assisted by Geoff Denford (Winchester Museum Service), Katherine Barclay and David Sherren in obtaining initial digitisations of the Winchester plans. Furthermore, Ian Scrivener-Lindley and Tracy Matthews of Winchester City Council shared Winchester's spatial and digital heritage and monuments records. Nick Millea aided me in accessing important historical maps and records on Winchester. The GIS specialists at the Leeds School of Geography, especially Helen Durham, Nick Malleson and Rachel Oldroyd, are thanked for their patient replies and smart resolves, while Rachel Homer refreshed my perspective on statistical possibilities. Mark Gillings navigated me through a key impasse in the conversion of spatial data, solving in minutes what had stifled me for weeks. Anna Clough and Alison Manson provided significant support to my use of spatial and graphical software respectively. Humble gratitude is owed to Ioanna Stavroulaki and Lars Marcus from the Spatial Morphology Group at Chalmers University of Technology, Ed Parham of Space Syntax Ltd and Bill Hillier, Jeremy Whitehand of *Urban Morphology*, Karl Kropf, Scott Hutson, Andrew Sayer, Polity Press, and Michael Conzen and Peter Lang for permitting me the use of images from their research and publications. Lloyd Bosworth jumped in to maintain the best standards across visual material.

A large number of individuals have offered critical advice, comments, challenging views and supportive conversation. This has helped me in making important decisions, pursuing promising directions and avoiding dead ends. An undoubtedly non-exhaustive list includes Keith Lilley, Michael E. Smith, Elisabeth Graham, Reinout Rutte, Ad van Drunen, Karl Kropf, Akkelies van Nes, Lars Marcus, Gareth Dean, Tim Bisschops, Sam Griffiths, April Beisaw, Andrew Brown, David Wheatley, Paul Wright and Siân Horan Smith. I have troubled yet many others with a pressing need for data and case studies at an exploratory stage, and I trust yet more may jog my memory of when they were called upon.

As the work for this book advanced, my thinking became articulated within the international and cross-disciplinary groups assembled with the support of two separate grants. The ESRC-NCRM Digital Social Research grant for the *Assembly of Comparative Urbanisation and the Material Environment* (ACUMEN) enabled me to launch the first platform to contextualise and test my ideas. The Arts and Humanities Research Council (AHRC) Research Network grant for *Pre-Columbian Tropical Urban Life: Placing the past in designs for sustainable urban futures* (TruLife) gave new impetus to situating the significance and timeliness of my work. I continue to appreciate the collaboration with my co-applicants Andrew Evans, Penelope Goodman and Keith Lilley, and co-investigator Christian Isendahl, TruLife steering group members Elizabeth Graham and Karsten Lambers, and all network members, speakers, participants, guests and affiliates, on these initiatives respectively. While these grants may not have been intended as direct support to this book, these opportunities and communities have made its core message both more cogent and palatable.

All of these people placed faith in me and my endeavour and showed courage in spite of its uncertain destination. The nature of help is such that the providers often have only an inkling about their impact on the receiver. The nature of research is such that the author carries the risk of not knowing where or how it will end. Now that I have converted their willingness and kindnesses into this achievement, I sincerely hope all will enjoy at least aspects of this work.

Contents

LIST OF FIGURES

LIST OF TABLES

LIST OF ABBREVIATIONS

1550s	Refers to the sixteenth-century Winchester time-slice based on the 1550s plans drawn up in Keene (1985)
ANT	Actor Network Theory
BLT	Boundary Line Type
dGPS	Differential Global Positioning System
geoTIFF	Raster image in TIFF format with georeferencing information embedded
GIS	Geographical Information System
HGIS	Historical Geographical Information System
ISUF	International Seminar on Urban Form
LCP	Least-Cost Path
MM	Ordnance Survey's MasterMap, used as shorthand for the twenty-first-century time-slice of Winchester which is based on it
OS	Ordnance Survey, mapping agency of the UK
OS1872	Refers to the nineteenth-century Winchester time-slice based on the first edition large-scale Ordnance Survey town plan published over 1871–1872
PEMY	Economic Foundations of Mayapan project
PST	Place Syntax Tool
RMS error	Root mean square error, used for the residual error for georeferencing in *ArcGIS*

INTRODUCTION TO *CITIES MADE OF BOUNDARIES*

The rationale

We live in a time when over half of the world's population resides in cities, a proportion that is expected to grow rapidly. A thorough understanding of this way of inhabiting the world has never been more pertinent. Alongside consideration of how to promote the ecological sustainability of urban life, social scientific concern with the societies inhabiting urbanised landscapes has understandably been preoccupied with the actuality of city dwelling, current governance and future planning. Due to this temporally narrow scope, the problems we are confronted with as populations build and reside in cities are often regarded as particular to our present-day predicament. In addition, this confined perspective results in research efforts being almost exclusively absorbed by cities belonging to a western or globalised urban tradition. This comes at the expense of understanding historically and culturally indigenous city building.

It is generally accepted that the spatial design of cities (their physical construction and form) is a determinant of the social life in, and subsequent development of, cities. Simultaneously, people are quick to point out the apparent inaptitude or inability of contemporary urban design ideas to effectively improve the many societal and sustainability issues revolving around urban life. In order to make positive contributions to the continued development of cities and urbanised ways of life, a better understanding is needed of the relationship between society and space and the nature of inhabiting an environment of our own making. Seen in this light, it is peculiar that urban academic discourse is inclined to such narrow perspectives, ignoring many known alternative patterns attesting to the versatility of urban possibilities.

Granted, the vast majority of the non-western or non-globalised urban traditions are a fixture of the past. Archaeological research teaches us that human beings have manifested a proclivity to urbanise for many millennia, and that the resulting settlements took widely varying forms. Although the disappearance of these alternative urban forms could be taken as a sign of general inadequacy, archaeological evidence is mounting that demonstrates many examples have been remarkably resilient, successfully persisting as a city or tradition for numerous centuries. Much of the current global urban paradigm finds its roots in the historically compact cities of Europe – but were the Spanish invaders not marvelled by the overall sophistication of the Aztec capital Tenochtitlan?

It applies to all previous urban traditions that they, to various degrees of success, accommodated inhabitation by an urban society, their physical form standing in support of the everyday functioning of urban social life. In spite of differing technological abilities, environmental requirements and cultural, economic or political ideas, cities of the past, as in the present, share that they need to function as spaces that are being inhabited. In all their morphological variety and complexity, cities in every respect are part and parcel of the fundamental human process of inhabiting the world. Given the openness of this developmental process it is extraordinary that, out of the spectrum of feasible opportunities to manipulate and transform the environment for all kinds of societal organisation, so much resemblance exists amongst protean urban forms.

The similarities resulting from the essentially human process that produces cities is easily acknowledged. Yet, social scientific research on urbanism and urban form exhibits a certain reluctance to overcome the limitations on the transferability of interpretative knowledge that are imposed by working on isolated examples of cities materialising in time-space specific socio-cultural contexts. Accordingly, the knowledge acquired on urbanisation and urban life remains relevant only within the particularity of that context. Indeed, glancing over urban landscapes other than those roughly pertaining to the influence of global standardisation clarifies that one cannot assume the general validity of theoretical frameworks employed for narrowly focused urban academic discourse.

If we desire a deeper and commonly relevant social understanding of the breadth of alternative traditions of building and inhabiting urban form, we need frames of reference that allow socio-cultural diversity to arise from fundamental principles. This requires a comparative approach built on concepts and analytical units from which particular meaning can emerge. Conducting radical comparative research can supply the evidence-base for emancipating knowledge that critically articulates the contrasts and consistencies in geographically separate cases and their development through time. Through interpretively unrestricted radical comparisons that exploit ubiquitous data on built form, we could learn about the mechanisms of how cities function socially. We may assess how inhabitants are restricted and enabled in creating diverse urban landscapes and developmental trajectories that accommodate degrees of social coherence and resilience, and their successes and failures in long-term sustainability. From a critical context that consists of optimally diverse and versatile knowledge we may approach current practice directing urban design interventions and strategies with greater confidence.

This book is tasked with making that first step: to devise an appropriate means for the radical comparative social study of the rudimentary material and spatial characteristics of urban built environments as they are inhabited across all urban traditions and throughout the full history of cities' existence.

The questions

Presenting the background of my rationale elucidates that this book has been developed from a particular premise. I see urban life and development as part of the fundamentally human process of inhabiting the world. This causes a change in perspective as to what research on cities should address, emphasising a need for radical comparisons. To devise an appropriate means to enable such research, it is clear this book embarks on an endeavour of integral methodological development. That is, building a methodology from the bottom up, grounded by appropriate theorising and conceptual frameworks. Here that means a grounding that empowers and informs radical social comparisons of cities, seen through a lens that highlights the ubiquity of people inhabiting urban built environments. In establishing this methodological goal, this book will contribute to the realms of the man-environment paradigm and society-space relations at large.

My route of methodological development is guided by the pursuit of two main questions. The first addresses the grounding of the endeavour. How can we improve our understanding of the role of the built environment as emergent from the human process of inhabiting the world, and the functioning of urban life and development? The second addresses the subsequent need for a workable research process and the practical operationalisation of comparing urban built environments. How can we recognise and study inhabitation of urban built environments comparatively across geographical areas, societies, cultures and through time?

The consequence of these main questions is that an appropriately conceived object, field and method of research need to be determined. To clarify what causes the particular structure of this book, I have broken the consecutive developmental steps down into further questions that specify the ones above. The entire sequence follows consequential logic, because addressing each question introduces the next.

1. How can the urban built environment serve as an object for radical comparative social research, and what level of social interpretation is comparatively viable? (Chapter 1)
2. How can it be ensured that the development of method is appropriate to the ideational and empirical understanding of the research object, and how should a research process to this effect be designed? (Chapter 2)
3. What is an appropriate theoretical framework for understanding the specific structuring role of the built environment in the human process of inhabiting the world? (Chapter 3)
4. Which information contained in the built environment is key to characterising and explicating its structuring role in the human process of inhabiting the world, and which meaningful constitutive element can be derived to operationalise in research? (Chapters 3 and 4)
5. How can our understanding of that constitutive element that informs us of the built environment's role in human inhabitation (especially urbanised) be conceptualised to fit the widest possible range of data on the urban built environment to suit a comparative frame of reference? (Chapter 5)
6. How can such conceptualisations be operationalised in (empirical and technical) research practice on actual urban built environment datasets of different origins, to cover both maximum contrast between urban traditions and the diachronic process of urban development? (Chapters 6 and 7)
7. Which are valid and viable directions for analysis with radically comparative potential for social interpretation, and how can such analytical measures be formulated and put to work? (Chapters 8 and 9)

Each reader may have particular interests in how any one of these questions is addressed, which may result in the inclination to take different approaches to reading this book. This especially can be expected from the division between theory and method, and concepts and observation, or is simply informed by disciplinary divides. To aid one's way through the consequential logic that structures the sequence of chapters, this book is punctuated with cross-references. These act as sign-posts and markers for both what is to come as well as where and how present issues are grounded or previously introduced.

The content

Knowing how integral methodological development causes the structure of this book, I will now briefly look at what can be expected to be presented in reply to the questions in each chapter. Chapter 1 pitches just how interpretive social investigations in comparative urbanism can effectively be positioned. When evaluating previous thought on the nature of cities (i.e. what they are), it transpires that there has been a preoccupation with classification and the origin of cities. The dominant discourse, which is to pinpoint which requirements must be met to designate a settlement a city, results in static views and categories that prevent a critical assessment of how cities function and compare as socially emergent places. At the same time, the widely available data on the physical form of cities throughout human history comes to the fore as the constant point of reference. In reply, then, I formulate a working definition of the city as urban life in an urbanised landscape to establish an intellectual setting for the methodological development. On this basis, Chapter 1 determines at which level of detail interpretive efforts can be pitched to overcome the limitations of socio-cultural and historical particularism. Only when accepting an appropriate level for interpretations can truly comparative contributions to the social knowledge of urban life and development be made. A 'low-level' interpretation on the recursive relationship between human beings and the material manifestations of their environment is defined.

Having paved the ground for a social take on radical comparative urban studies, Chapter 2 discusses how a critical realist philosophy of science can be adapted for this purpose. This adaptation establishes both my base assumptions captured in metaconcepts for theorising, and designs the research process through which ideational understanding and empirical observation become structurally linked. A critical realist consideration of archaeological reasoning proves a cogent advocate for redefining 'the material' as an emergent entity that directly incorporates its human and social origin. Materiality discourse, in both archaeology and human geography, currently seems unable to achieve a similarly synergetic conceptualisation. Critical realist discourse in human geography usefully distils the research processes through which 'the material' could become part of social scientific research. In addition, critical realism helps define the other metaconcepts of 'the social' and 'spatial (in)dependence' that inform my theoretical groundwork, and so comes to direct my course in methodological development.

Chapter 3 presents a constitutive theoretical framework through which we gain a precise understanding of the role of the built environment as emergent from the human process of inhabiting the world. I theorise a number of conditional statements. First, I determine what it means to be a human inhabitant of the world. Second, I introduce a series of abstractions framing the contingent consequences of inhabiting the world that are necessary conditions for the occurrence of city emergence, or rather, as we come to understand, inhabited urban built environments. The bottom-up reasoning of this constitutive theoretical framework reveals that differentiation is key to the intelligibility of habitability in the social and spatial world. Consequentially, differentiation also causes the transformative making-habitable of the socio-spatial world. Making-habitable captures the process through which eventually cities are built. The recognition and introduction of differentiations as materialised physical properties that constitute the spatial subdivisions which compose the built environment complex, become denoted by the flexible notion of boundaries. The affective and affording physical properties of materialised boundaries so assume their socio-spatial significance for urban inhabitation. The book subsequently focuses on this phenomenon.

The three preceding chapters install three distinct theoretical platforms. These theoretical platforms constitute a conceptual premise that is comprised of a disciplinary, scientific, and phenomenological nature respectively. Together, these platforms advance an interdisciplinary synthesis that grounds the launch of a targeted methodological development, fulfilling three specific theoretical tasks. Thanks to Chapter 1 we know exactly on which level a radical social comparative contribution to urban studies should be pitched. Thanks to Chapter 2 we have adapted the social scientific critical realist tools (processes and metaconcepts) to pave an original path for research design. Thanks to Chapter 3 we are in possession of a precisely articulated multidisciplinary and conditional theoretical framework of understanding the phenomenon of the inhabited (urban) built environment.

From this point, we can appreciate that the inhabited urban built environment is made of boundaries. Regarding the built environment as a composite complex of boundaries demands a new look at how spatial data truly represents the spatial and material characteristics that urban built environments comprise. Therefore, Chapter 4 first critically evaluates (social scientific and philosophical) boundary theory to select those ideas that can crucially relate to how we understand the representative nature of spatial data. It transpires that the boundaries' operation of seclusion is a determinant for the spatial subdivisions of the built environment. Accepting the nature of boundaries as secluding sites of difference, I introduce the fiat and bona fide boundary distinction to navigate us through a sequence of abstractions. This sequence is designed to better appreciate how abstract spatial data refer to the concrete social empirical reality of the material presence of the built environment to its inhabiting society. Through these abstractions, the notion of types of boundary lines to create a built environment ontology of analytical units that are at once ideational and empirical is introduced. Ultimately, we gain a thorough understanding of what happens to spatial data on boundaries at each stage, from the original input data through to an analytical mapping practice.

Chapter 5, then, forms a pivotal point in the methodological development, because it presents the ontological Boundary Line Types (BLTs) with fully illustrated definitions.[1] To formulate effective formal definitions I first argue the requirements for an ontology that ensures comparative applicability is maximised. This includes a review of the level of detail and material-spatial principles that guide how spatial data representing the built environment should be approached. Equality of information assures parity in applying the ontological BLTs, so spatial data must comprise an equivalent outline selection forming the contiguous complex of subdivisions. On this basis BLTs can be identified. The chapter then turns to introducing the iteratively abstracted BLT definitions themselves. In addition, I reason through the consequence of investing spatial data with a formal BLT redescription. This redescription produces the socio-spatial ontology intrinsic to a city, or its socio-spatial signature of inhabitation.

---

1. Towards the back of this book a supplementary table of abridged BLT definitions can be found, serving as a quick and easy reference throughout all chapters.

A city's intrinsic BLT ontology can be approached from three levels of socio-spatial significance that comprise distinct contexts, which both restrict and inform possible social interpretations.

At this stage in the development, our attention turns to the practical operationalisation of BLTs. Even though applying BLTs will follow a completely original theory and interpretive purpose, it is important to acknowledge that the vantage of analytically (re)mapping built form is not an intellectual vacuum. While readers from different backgrounds may find a review of existing methods welcome, Chapter 6 serves a more constructive purpose. By taking cues from existing research methods that previously developed practices to adapt urban plans, map urban space, and carry out spatial analysis on urban form and built configurations, the implementation of a new but related method will prove more effective. Naturally, running through the foundations of these precursors it becomes undeniable that none of the existing methods will be suitable outright for work on boundaries as broadly proposed, and BLTs in particular. As an analytical mapping practice the shared reference to urban built form means that research techniques of existing methods, including data preparation, basic terminology and analytical pointers, can greatly benefit a BLT-based method. Notwithstanding the existence of related urban design philosophies and architectural typologies, Chapter 6 focuses around three strongly represented relevant fields that emphasise urban layout and structure: urban historical GIS (Geographical Information System, HGIS), urban morphology and space syntax. To support and continue BLT method development, the practice of historically reconstructive mapping, the terminology of urban morphology and the empirical analytical rigour of space syntax are especially of value.

Chapter 7 is dedicated to the practical operationalisation of BLT Mapping. The application of BLTs to prepared spatial data of urban built environments plans in a GIS environment is called identification. To demonstrate the radical comparative ability of BLTs, first two contrasting case studies are selected: sixth-century Chunchucmil (Classic Maya, Mexico) and medieval to contemporary Winchester (western historical, UK). Together these case studies fulfil a demonstration of great variety in urban situations and involve a diverse set of associated legacy spatial datasets. To be precise, legacy data consisting of: urban maps derived from archaeological topographical surveys, reconstructed maps of historical situations, historical cartography and contemporary national mapping agency standards. Chapter 7 provides a rationale for the selection of these cities to exemplify two dramatically divergent urban traditions: tropical dispersed low-density urbanism, and temperate climate compact high-density urbanism. The chapter then uses test case areas to demonstrate the practical and technical stages of data preparation. By providing an overview of key technical details and pragmatic decisions adapted to the specific treatment that the origin of each legacy dataset commands, it can virtually serve as a manual for creating BLT data and overcoming inevitable limitations to our knowledge about urban spatial datasets.

Since BLT identification is carried out in a vector GIS software environment, Chapter 8 first needs to address the particularities of the spatial data structure that is created by BLT Mapping. While the BLT data structure opens a vast array of analytical opportunities, there are also limitations to how well they can be exploited. The complications of working effectively on this rich vector data in diachronic perspective is discussed. Simultaneously, the heuristic value of the primary analytical unit of single BLTs and the derivative analytical unit of the topological segment (co-located BLT combinations) is recognised as it emerges from the BLT data structure. Most of the chapter, then, is dedicated to presenting rationales for hypothetical spatial analytical measures. These measures remain hypothetical due to the lack of dedicated geocomputational tools to work with BLT data, yet their functioning and potential can be confidently projected and this sets an agenda for software development. The interpretive value of such measures is at once inherently ensured and restricted through the lens of the three levels of socio-spatial significance introduced in Chapter 5. Therefore, the analytical measures are explicitly proposed within the overlapping realms of each correspondent interpretive context. It will be shown how the efficacy of applying analytical units and the relevant scope of interpretive analyses is highly susceptible to improvement from original geocomputational software development. While many of these analytical extensions and composite complications remain directions for future research, a selection within computational reach is carried forward in the next chapter.

Now BLT Mapping has become fully invested and enabled in a GIS working environment, Chapter 9 presents preliminary analytical explorations and their interpretive potential as applied to my two test cases of Chunchucmil and Winchester. My aim is not to dive into the intricacies of full-fledged particular case studies, but to carry out targeted tests to demonstrate what BLT Mapping presently enables. In exploring valid and viable directions for spatial analysis and radical urban comparisons, this chapter introduces a number of innovations. First, some original basic geocomputational functionality was sourced in support of developing BLT Mapping in the format of an *ArcGIS* plugin.

These computational functions regard a broad sweep approach to first, visualising BLT maps, and second, generating global statistics on BLT datasets. Alongside, I utilise native GIS geoprocessing functions to aid visual data exploration. Furthermore, I introduce the manual production of 'clock diagrams' that graphically standardise complex boundary morphologies in support of detailed topological and morphological intra- and inter-city comparisons. As a demonstration of the general functionality, compatibility and applicability of the BLT Mapping method, Chapter 9 offers a positive conclusion to the methodological development of this book. The value of the interpretive insights derived from the relatively small, data-driven, test case areas will accordingly be limited. The purpose of showing the analytical tenets and promise that result from my initial explorations, innovations and demonstrations is to provide a compellingly broad proof of concept and foundation for future applications and adaptations. My methodological endeavour thus ends with some evidence, techniques and guidance for taking on a wide-ranging body of case studies to start acquiring a radically comparative evidence-base for the inhabitation of urban built environments.

The book

This book begins a journey. So as to ensure that journey is off to a good start, it makes the first step. Exactly how that first step is made is just as important as the discoveries along the way. Rather than just proffering the reader an empirically applicable method, it is the express purpose of this book to be as explicit as possible about how BLT Mapping is conceived. Presenting BLT Mapping in this way not only enables applications, but empowers researchers to meticulously construct alternative (radical) comparative methods with similar rigour. By exhibiting the methodology at its different stages of development, it welcomes engagement on all of these stages. A strong conviction in the benefits of structurally linked and causally tighter integration of ideational concepts and empirical observations lies behind this particular methodological development. Ultimately, by writing this book I seek to strengthen and better equip the field of comparative urban studies to generate deeper understandings of the fundamentally human phenomenon of the experience and development of settled and urban life. The long-term benefits of such profound understanding are wide ranging.

Coming up with the most responsible and locally appropriate ways of developing landscapes supportive of long-term human inhabitation is recognised as one of the great challenges of our time (see Weller et al. 2017). My contribution comes from one specific perspective: the rudimentary social understanding of inhabiting urban form. Understanding the characteristics and dynamics of the social aspect of cities' material structure is only one constitutive part of meeting the challenge for an evidence-base to improve our decision-making on continued urban development. The examples featured in this book highlight the tremendous potential that appropriate comparative frames of reference have in bringing urban trajectories of entirely different cultural, temporal and environmental contexts in direct relation to each other. This is significant, because I am certain that we should learn from the diversity of human life and indigenous responses to our social, cultural, economic and ecological environment. We must make a critical effort to understand the intricacies of how this plays out in the greatest variety of cases if we are going to be better informed and more aware of the many alternative ways we can plan and design for inhabiting the world.

On one level, the research towards BLT Mapping this book contains can simply facilitate the production of particular cultural, archaeological and historical knowledge about urban societies and explicate the developmental processes of (past) urbanisation. On another level, its foundational concepts and interpretive insights could eventually become reified in urban design and planning interventions. Employing BLT Mapping may support or challenge the socio-spatial implications of hypotheses formulated on urban form in the past, present and future. Systematic critical comparisons open our eyes to better appreciate alternatives to our own contemporary experience and the risks of trusting that the technological solutions of 'smart cities' will supply socially sustainable, ecologically conceived urban futures (cf. Colding & Barthel 2017). In other words, this work's proclaimed trait is the pursuit of making fundamental research thresholds more accessible and attainable. Its more silent ambition is a contribution to the future of inhabiting our planet.

CHAPTER 1
TOWARDS RADICAL COMPARATIVE URBAN STUDIES

Introduction

In this book I focus on a particular situation that may occur in the broad, long-term process of human inhabitation of the world. When people settle in a particular location and the population starts to rise, the landscape becomes increasingly manipulated through human-environment interactions that accommodate how that residency functions. Simply put, within this book, living in a landscape of our own making will be referred to as the 'inhabited built environment' (see Chapter 3 for a theoretical treatise). Furthermore, my focus is directed to situations that are considered 'urban'. Because 'urban' characterises the life, activities, provisions, and all things to do with cities, it is a problematic term. Cities and therefore urban life have existed for millennia. Currently over half the world's population is considered to reside in cities. Yet, no single definition of the city is agreed upon. Disquietude over the lack of such definition has certainly not impeded cities as a substantive field of research. This even applies to the extent that having a categorical definition of the city could be counterproductive for some research in the first place (e.g. Smith 1989). Currently, the city or urbanism is a research theme in several disciplines and is increasingly represented by the field of urban studies.

Taking urban landscapes as the result of ongoing *essentially human processes of inhabitation* makes them a deeply historical phenomenon. Consequently, we must heed archaeological and historical thought on the origins of 'urban situations', alongside a social theoretical position towards urbanisation as a general process in human social life. Urban 'inhabited built environments' can only become a concept informing comparative methodological development within a context that explicitly defines my particular perspective on urbanism. This chapter will therefore lay the groundwork for studying the urban comparatively by anthologising disciplinary approaches which characterise the nature of urbanism, and by offering a process-based working definition of the city which centres on the practices of urban life. Subsequently, I will explain how comparative urbanism, broadly conceived, initially requires low-level interpretation instead of high levels of particular contextualisation. This groundwork then enables new theoretical and methodological work supporting research on the urban landscape as a social process.

Urban studies

For the foreseeable future the rapid urbanisation of the world is widely recognised as one of the major humanitarian global challenges (Dittmar 2013). It is therefore no surprise that urbanism should be at the forefront of research development. Urban studies is not a traditional academic discipline. Despite representation in many institutions and specialised research journals, its core area of interest is still fragmented over many academic disciplines. Nonetheless, Bowen et al. (2010) demonstrate that there is considerable coherence amongst the intellectual pursuits associated with urban studies. Importantly, Harris & Smith (2011) point out that Bowen et al.'s (2010) analysis of the field overlooks the significant presence of, and contributions made to, urban research from historical vantage points.

The deep historical nature of the processes of human inhabitation of the world was already recognised, so with the advancements in this book I deliberately intend to include all of human history: from prehistory to the present. The settling process that keeps on increasing the world's urbanised population is fundamentally human. Therefore, to contribute a comparative understanding of the conditions and characteristics of urban life requires a perspective that accommodates the fundamentally human diversity in settlement patterns across cultures and through time. Any single piece of work is unlikely to accomplish a satisfying cross-section representing all instances of urban life. Instead, my investigations centre on how to start a body of research based on commensurable foundations which could come to encompass the diversity of cities.

To achieve commensurable research we must first establish the availability of equivalent information on urban places across time and space. Any archaeologist would be quick to point out that the material record, which their discipline is based upon, is probably the best preserved information source throughout the deep past of human life. Furthermore, no anthropologist would deny that material culture is part and parcel of continuing human life, society and culture (see Miller 1998, 2005). The material record naturally includes the dimension, shape and material composition of inhabited landscapes or urban built environments. Kropf (2009: 117) states: 'The tangibility, ubiquity and persistence of physical form make it the most suited to act as the point of reference for co-ordinating and comparing aspects.' The same is asserted by Harris & Smith (2011: 103), who note:

> arguably the most enduring characteristic of cities, one that almost invariably forms the basis of their definition, concerns their physical presence. They are dense, well-populated settlements with considerable investment in the built environment, and other infrastructural components. We can, and do, debate exactly how large, or how dense, a place has to be to count as urban, but hardly anyone doubts that size matters.

All of Parr's (2007) 'spatial definitions' of the city initially refer to the developed area, the physical entity, before characterising three kinds of socio-functional city. So it becomes a reasonable expectation that to embark on a methodological development for the social interpretations comparing the full range of urban possibilities throughout human history, our first port of call comprises the physical transformation of the landscape. Intense and relatively large-scale inhabitation of the landscape is accommodated by such physical transformations, even though we may not always be able to retrieve all modifications.

The notion of comparative urbanism already exists in urban studies and urban geography. However, Smith (2009b) draws attention to the fact that considering the breadth and depth of urban traditions, comparative urban geography displays a severely limited historical scope (see Briggs 2004 for an exception). Urban studies with explicit reference to the physical and architectural characteristics of the built environment regularly demonstrate historical interest (e.g. Bastian 1980; Daunton 1983; Lawrence 1996; Rotenberg 1996; Jenkins 2002). Yet, they rarely penetrate deeper than about two centuries' worth (the medieval underpinnings of urban morphology (Conzen 1960) and Kostof's (1991, 1992) well-known historically descriptive classifications of urban form are exceptions). This apparent historical myopia has been noted in both human geographical urban and planning interests (Nijman 2007; Smith 2009b; Harris & Smith 2011; York et al. 2011) as well as historical geography in particular. Often the early modern period acts as the earliest starting point (Jones 2004; Lilley 2011b). The particular field of urban historical geography (see Dennis & Prince 1988; Denecke 1988, discussing British and German research practice respectively), which maintains an allegiance with urban morphology (Conzen 1960; Moudon 1997), did cautiously venture into the early medieval period (e.g. Denecke & Shaw 1988). Yet, this has not resulted in a more structural presence of historical depth. There is no clear reason why this preoccupation with recentism should prevail. On the contrary, from the perspective of human or society-space relations and the ongoing processes of urbanisation, there is much to gain by structurally engaging the building processes composing the urban *longue durée*.

Urban studies and urban geography not only suffer from temporal myopia; they have culturally favoured western and globalised examples of urban form (Wheatley 1969; Graham 1996; see Edensor & Jayne 2012 for a recent attempt to intervene). The urban alternatives (cf. Smith 2012) that different areas of the world, undergoing their own environmental and cultural evolution, have known before industrialisation and globalisation have been neglected or brushed aside, together with all ancient or 'pre-industrial' urban traditions (see Graham 1996) in several seminal texts on urbanism (e.g. Mumford 1961; Sjoberg 1960; Fox 1977).[1] This cultural preoccupation could in part be explained by the desire to formulate successful planning policies, acting as a driver for inquiry in practice. When accepting that urban planning today takes place amidst the stage of, and in response to, political and economic globalisation (Massey 2007; Newman & Thornley 2011; Knox & Mayer 2013; Faulconbridge & Grubbauer 2015), there is the temptation to apply the unifying structure of globalism to highlight urban individualism, which stands in the way of improving our understanding of cities (Scott & Storper 2015). Habraken (2000: 10) concedes:

> The necessity of a disciplined and detached stance, so self-evident in the natural sciences, is by no means self-evident in studies of the built environment. We are fully immersed in the object of our inquiry – in fact, we are part of it – and value judgments color our every observation.

---

1. Rather worryingly, some myopia persists even now. In Clark's (2013) *Oxford Handbook of Cities in World History* the presence of Pre-Colombian cities is severely marginalised and in so doing misrepresented.

While I will not join Habraken in his recommendation to advance in a natural scientific fashion, I call to supersede the western embedding of urban scholarship. This is not to favour postcolonial particularism, but to inform comparative methods with the essentially human and social phenomenon of urbanism as occurring in geographically and culturally separated traditions (cf. Scott & Storper 2015; Peck 2015). Planning and design professionals have much to gain from trading normative assertions or particularism and 'difference-finding' (see Peck 2015) for analytical insights derived from common frames of reference with appropriately defined units of analysis. From this vantage, comparison permits difference to emerge and becomes articulated and meaningful (Scott & Storper 2015). Such more rigorous and radical comparative work could open our eyes to the lessons concealed in the alternative solutions humanity has lived through, emanating from the common developmental processes of settling and cohabitation. Only recently signs are emerging that deeply historical and radical comparisons may be welcomed for applications in sustainable development policies (Barthel & Isendahl 2013; Simon & Adam-Bradford 2016).

Coming from an archaeological perspective, Fletcher (2010: 253) remarks that to suppose the world's wildly varying urban traditions 'had equivalent socialities would strain the contextual uniqueness of human social life'. Yet, also in archaeology it applies that to launch research from specific culture historical contexts (cf. the ideographic tendencies of comparative urbanism in human geography) would grind insights to a halt, resulting in isolated statements on particularities (contextual interpretation will be discussed later). A fuller appreciation of ancient urban traditions as examples of the same social processes as current urbanisation holds great potential for increasing our understanding of urban challenges today (see Smith 2010a, 2012). The challenge for (archaeological) research is to come up with rigorous comparative frames of reference and critical analytical methods or measures to make this holistic process-driven approach productive (Smith 2012; Smith & Peregrine 2012).

In fact, it has long been recognised (Pollard 1977: 46) that '[a]rchaeologists, in particular, have much to offer to increase our understanding of the structure and functioning of urban settlements'. Yet, data constraints and the specificity of disciplinary foci have made efforts to structurally address this potential scarce. More recently, however, it could be argued that technological advancements and accumulated archaeological data have made it much more feasible to undertake comparative research on the deeper functional history of urbanism (Smith 2012). To date, most archaeological efforts have addressed urbanism at the level of urban origins and the scale of settlement patterns. In part, this is undoubtedly due to the overwhelming influence of Childe's (1950) pivotal proposal of the 'Urban Revolution'[2] (Smith 2009a) and, in part, by the fragmentary and limited nature of archaeological data.

Urban origins

The debate on the origin of cities is closely tied to defining the city as a category and classifying different kinds of cities (e.g. Wirth 1938; Fox 1977). Even though this research is little to do with demarcating the principal nature of the city – accepting that the urban is an extant mundane situation – much foundational and deep historical urban thought has sprung from these concerns. In order to explain the principles of a low-level interpretive comparative urbanism based on a process-oriented working definition of the city, one should be aware of the wider context in which cities emerge as both a phenomenon and a research concept.[3]

Childe's contribution to urban research was part of a much larger body of thought, which included an economic critique and reimagining of the prehistoric three-age system and an influential position on the culture-historical approach as applied to material culture. His socio-economic evolutionary concepts went on to find wide appeal and form a major influence across historical disciplines into the 1990s (Greene 1999). He coined the term the Urban Revolution (amongst others, such as the Neolithic Revolution, inspired by the quick changes of the modern Industrial Revolution) to mark the process of transformation from primarily agricultural societies into more complex, state-based, urban societies. Adam T. Smith (2003) emphasises that Childe was more directly concerned with state formation (cf. Smith 2009a on complex societies) than with urbanism as a concurring phenomenon, in spite of the ordinary

2. Smith (2009a) discusses how Childe's first presentation of this term appeared in his 1936 book *Man Makes Himself*, but how his more accessible paper from 1950, 'The Urban Revolution', went on to become one of the most widely cited papers published by an archaeologist. The latter is generally recognised as the full-fledged discussion of his ideas on urbanism, though these should be seen as part of a wider appreciation of the emergence of complex societies characterised by many traits which are also of importance as urban features.
3. It should be noted here that Scott & Storper (2015) opened the debate on the questions of 'what cities are' and 'why they are' as a critique of the current state of theorising in urban studies and the aforementioned particularism of comparative urban research (Peck 2015; Mould 2016; Walker 2016; Storper & Scott 2016). The vantage and definitions developed in this chapter could be seen as a stance in this unresolved debate. However, despite the

archaeological reading of his work emphasising the emergence and traits of urbanism. In addition, Wheatley (1972: 612) points out that Childe (1950) isolated only one primary dependent variable in the generation of urbanism: 'the progress of technology, resulting in the augmentation of food surpluses'. Consequently, according to Wheatley, Childe succeeded in demarcating a stage of development rather than establishing the process of the Urban Revolution.

Childe's persuasive fascination with the origin of urbanism is better served by an inter-city than an intra-city scale. The coarser nature of evidence required for discussing urban systems and settlement patterns relieves some of the pressure on archaeological resources for more intensive mapping and excavation. Coincidentally, crude data is an adequate fit for purely quantitative empirical spatial analyses, whilst remaining relevant for addressing questions on why cities appear at certain locations and in specific relation to each other.

The relative placement and assessment of the importance of sites within settlement patterns have often been tackled by applying size-rankings and spatial pattern analyses (e.g. Kowalewski 1990, 2003; Falconer & Savage 1995; Savage 1997; Drennan & Peterson 2004; Algaze 2005; Smith 2005). Christaller's (1933) economic 'central place theory' stays influential in the development of such supra-city quantitative analyses in archaeology. Wheatley (1972) anthologises research in central place theory when it was still very much in development. Contemporary urban research on the internal structure of metropolitan regions and multiple nuclei are related to the same family of economic urban thought. Central place theory in archaeology is currently influencing predictive modelling for settlement patterns (Vaughn & Crawford 2009; Fletcher 2008), which bears relevance to rank-size rule methods. Increasingly, history and archaeology are advancing along lines akin to relational geographical theory, knowledge and policy transfer, and network thinking (e.g. Newman & Thornley 2011; McCann & Ward 2011; Faulconbridge & Grubbauer 2015) to conceptualise regional and global urbanity and urban systems (e.g. Verbruggen 2007; Brughmans et al. 2012; Raja 2017; and globalisation more generally: Hodos 2017). In contrast, Smith

fundamental nature of my arguments, I will stress that this book is structured by a particular research purpose and therefore does not purport to offer a unifying theory that is adequate and practicable to serve the full breadth of urban research represented in this debate. By going back (in this chapter and Chapter 3) to how human being and human action may transform landscapes into cities my point of departure is not rooted in cities of the global North as a *fait accompli* (see Robinson & Roy's (2016) critique), but will appeal to the essential universality of the 'human condition'.

(2006) presents a concise overview of interpretive concepts and models that combine types of cities including several ways in which, including those artificial, cities are founded.

Quantitative approaches alone cannot appreciate the complexity of urban origins. Evidence of origins is indicative of much more diversity and plurality in the processes of urban emergence than Childe's historically influential 'revolution vocabulary' (Greene 1999) suggests (Blanton 1982). Criteria for the definition and classification of urban settlement are problematic and, except for certain statistical studies, not necessarily informative (cf. Grove 1972; Smith 1972). Nonetheless, a rank-size based approach indicated that the view that Mesopotamian urbanism respects similar principles as dense western urban conventions might be in need of revision to accommodate the sheer variety of settlements (see Falconer & Savage 1995). Classificatory and quantitative approaches thus can aid the formulation of further questions and research.

Distinguishing city types and providing classifications results directly from the attempts to identify or disentangle the variables and characteristics that constitute a city. Indeed the definition of what a city constitutes has been a matter of debate for the better part of a century. One of the pivotal positions in this debate came from Louis Wirth (1938). He was the first to make apparent the lack of a sociological definition of a city. Introducing a sociological definition of the city would immediately take into account that urbanism is not confined to the city locus. He envisioned a definition relying on four characteristics: population size, density, heterogeneous individuals, and settlement permanence, which are still of relevance in much contemporary thought on this subject.

Categorical cities

Paul Wheatley (1972) categorised Wirth's (1938) take on urbanism as a trait-complex approach, 'converting a simple aggregate of features into an ideal type construct' (Wheatley 1972: 608). He presents the reader with an overview of the types of strategies recognised within the elusive term 'urbanism', in fashion at the time. Trait-complex approaches exist next to: ideal-type constructs, which dichotomise urban society to non-urban counterparts such as the urban-rural divide; ecological theories of urban development, which posit urban society and social organisation as responses to pressures of the environment, broadly including measures of biological determinism and the origins of urbanism; cities as centres of dominance, which view the role of the city as a power phenomenon, leading from the city as generator of effective space to Christaller's economical central place theory, producing hierarchies within city regions; and expediential approaches, relying on definitions based on numerical size for classification. Wheatley (1972: 621–622) concludes that these types of strategy are not mutually exclusive:

> [A]lthough the *strategies* are complementary [...] they are jointly directed towards four seemingly contradictory *conceptions* of urbanism in terms of (i) an interactional model which emphasizes the growth and structure of specialized networks of social, economic, and political relationships focused in cities; (ii) a normative model in which urbanism is viewed as a way of life. [...]; (iii) an economic model, concerned primarily with productive activities in a spatial context; and (iv) a demographic model, which treats urban forms essentially as aggregations of population in restricted areas.

Classification is relevant because effectively it would be impossible to pinpoint the emergence of cities if it cannot be defined what a city is. This problem permeates the continuing discussions on the origins of urbanism. Outside archaeology Jacobs (1969) is often credited as the one to adopt the case of Çatalhöyük (southern Anatolia, Turkey) as the earliest city in the grand narratives devised to explain the emergence of urbanism. Although archaeologists cannot quite agree on whether Çatalhöyük can qualify as a city, town or village (Taylor 2012), simply on the basis of size, Fletcher (2010) sees reason enough to dismiss its potentially urban status. Emberling (2003) denies Çatalhöyük this status on the basis of a missing hinterland. Taylor (2012) adapts the disagreement in archaeology in his revamped progressive model of urbanism where the city comes first. So, Çatalhöyük becomes reputed for showing the first features, but not all traits of 'city-ness'. As opposed to this functional placement, Soja (2010; also Blake 2002) still uses Çatalhöyük as an urban case study to support certain arguments around the progress and acceleration of innovation as part of the urban origin narrative.

Importantly, although the authors mentioned here acknowledge alternative urban traditions to differing degrees, this grand narrative approach seems counterproductive with regards to understanding the common formative processes of urbanisation. Meanwhile archaeologists seem to have become more pragmatic. From an infatuation with ideal type categorical typologies of differing cities (see Fox 1977; e.g. Sanders

& Webster 1988), Cowgill (2004) suggests replacing typologies with more flexible variables placed along axes or dimensions. Smith (2007, 2010a, 2010b), in turn, privileges a functional definition of the city (as in fulfilling urban functions), which then can be employed usefully in framing the case studies of others (e.g. Fernández-Götz & Krausse 2013). More recently Smith (2016) specified his functional definition approach by suggesting a polythetic set of attributes to determine the intensity of early urbanism instead. For contemporary cities Parr's (2007) interrelated 'spatial definitions' display a similar concern with the social functions of the city as a physical entity (the built city, cf. Scott & Storper 2015), bringing consumptions of goods and service provision in connection with employment opportunities and requirements.

These categorical concerns are relevant because identifying urbanism and classifying places as cities have not only been problematic with regards to the earliest known cities. The overall futility of a single grand narrative is also exemplified by the debate on Maya urbanism. When Sanders & Webster (1988) cast doubt over the urban status of Maya cities – an opinion voiced earlier by Coe (1961) – they were criticised by Smith (1989) and Chase et al. (1990) for overgeneralising Mesoamerican urbanism as a whole, and failing to recognise the variability and complexity of urban functions and possibilities. Smith (1989; also McCafferty & Peuramaki-Brown 2007) points out that archaeological data in the region is too scant to make such all-encompassing statements, while with regards to Aztec settlements archaeological evidence becomes generally more productive when viewed as part of an urban tradition (see also M.E. Smith 2008).

Depending on the criteria one uses, Maya cities could be classified as urban, which is the way they were approached by many before anyway (e.g. Andrews 1975). Fortunately, Mayanists have since moved on, retaining the urban vocabulary (Grube 2000; Sharer & Traxler 2005; Joyce 2009) and leaving the debate behind. In the light of the recent discoveries of urbanised sprawl for a multitude of Maya cities (e.g. Chase et al. 2011a, 2011b, 2016; Golden et al. 2016; Hutson 2016), this corrective seems fully justified. It was conceded that such discussion is not necessarily helpful in the understanding of the nature of urbanism and how it functions as part of a societal structure, regardless of how state-like or urban that is (Graham 1999; McCafferty & Peuramaki-Brown 2007).

Acknowledging the urbanised nature of such settlements, the notion of 'tropical urbanism' has been suggested (Graham 1996, 1999). Alternatively the Maya tradition has been categorised as featuring a 'low-density (agrarian)' pattern of urbanism (Fletcher 2009, 2010, 2012; Peuramaki-Brown 2013). This is also applied to the ancient Khmer of Angkor Wat, whose culture, Coe (1961) equally asserted, does not feature cities. Arguably similar traditions existed in e.g. eighteenth- to nineteenth-century Africa (Smith 2011a; also Storey 2006). None of these are current urban settlement patterns. This does not withstand that agrarian and dispersed urban traditions thrived and were remarkably resilient over long periods (Fletcher 2010; Isendahl & Smith 2013).

Unfortunately, without an equivalent in today's western and globalised paradigms of urban planning, these traditions have yet to receive the scholarly scrutiny they deserve. Meanwhile the extant categories used to characterise urbanism can only be flexibly applied (M.L. Smith 2003a; Cowgill 2004) and even then the 'problem is that these categories are [...] insufficient, cross-culturally problematic, and too protean. Something more rigorous is needed to adequately define urbanism and incorporate low-density urbanism both in the industrial and in the agrarian worlds' (Fletcher 2010: 252). Consequently, in 2016 I started a research network (*Pre-Columbian Tropical Urban Life*, TruLife) to explore interdisciplinary shared concerns and research potential between Maya cities and sustainable urban design, so that Maya cities may contribute to the global challenge of urbanisation. Furthermore, this book builds on an example of Maya urbanism demonstrating this very purpose and future potential.

It is clear that no agreed-upon resolution on early urbanism has been reached (see Smith 2016). Moreover, the debate on formulating a unifying and appropriate definition of the (early) city has continued (Smith 2003a; Fletcher 2010) and is being revived. The validity of several of the old concepts and models are being revisited (see Gaydarska 2016; Christophersen 2016; Andersson 2016; Raja 2016) at the same time that contemporary urban studies have started questioning what a city is and why they exist (Scott & Storper 2015; Peck 2015; Mould 2016; Walker 2016; Robinson & Roy 2016; Storper & Scott 2016). In these debates, the ideas of Wirth and Childe remain catalytic beacons.

The cultural myopia on western urbanism – the direct historical relation with antiquity and Mesopotamia usually unquestioned (but see Wheatley 1969; Graham 1996) – has tainted the discussion on defining 'the city'. This makes it difficult to study alternative urban traditions as part of a common human phenomenon. The ongoing debates demonstrate that when going beyond time-space specificity, the context of policy and administration, or any historically documented decrees that determine and ascribe city status and inhabitants' civic rights, the picture of what constitutes a city remains muddled. We can all concur with Fletcher (2010: 253) that: 'The study of urbanism currently does not have an agreed basis for rigorous worldwide comparison.' Ultimately all this suggests is that, when laying the foundation for comparative studies, no single (static) definition would result in an appropriately equal basis for selecting and studying cases. In contrast, the suggestion for a focus on *how cities function as a process* (cf. Graham 1999; also Christophersen 2015) is something to subscribe to when a deeper understanding of urban life and development as part of the inhabitation of landscape is sought.

Comparative urbanism

Fortunately, in both urban studies and archaeology, research overall has not been deterred by the disagreement over definitions. Each project either explicitly or implicitly chooses its own perspective, albeit generating broader understandings is hampered by the lack of appropriate and rigorous frames of reference (Yoffee 2009; Fletcher 2010; Smith 2012). Nevertheless, urbanism and ancient cities have received a lot of attention in archaeology during the past decade or so. A non-exhaustive representation of archaeological work on ancient cities without a single cultural emphasis can be found in seven recent volumes: Smith's (M.L. 2003b) *The Social Construction of Ancient Cities*; Atkin & Rykwert's (2005) *Structure and Meaning in Human Settlements*; Storey's (2006) *Urbanism in the Pre-Industrial World*; Marcus & Sabloff's (2008) *The Ancient City*; Gates' (2011) *Ancient Cities*; Clark's (2013) *Oxford Handbook of Cities in World History*; and Creekmore & Fisher's (2014) *Making Ancient Cities*.

Yoffee (2009) notes that several of these volumes do not go through the effort of critical synthesis nor do they all constructively live up to their intellectual foci. '[T]he cities portrayed in these volumes for the most part seem abstractions, lifeless, and unconcerned with the lived experience of citizens' (Yoffee 2009: 282). While the latest volume certainly works towards rectifying this (e.g. Magnoni et al. 2014), this realisation is surprising. A further concern is that these volumes inadvertently assist in dichotomising the field of comparative urban studies by juxtaposing the 'ancient' or 'pre-industrial' city with 'contemporary' cities. Within this book no such distinction shall be made. Furthermore, despite the initial decontextualisation necessary for a comparative approach, emplaced lived experience (see Chapter 3) will be a significant component of my low-level interpretive approach (discussed below).

Yoffee (2009: 282) remarks that 'any comparison of early cities with modern ones needs to be taken seriously. We can learn from our colleagues in historical archaeology [...] and in urban geography.' Even though he upholds the view that ancient cities are predominantly not like modern cities, he reasons 'comparison will lead us to explain why this is the case'. Vice versa, Smith (2012; also Smith 2010a; Isendahl & Smith 2013; Barthel & Isendahl 2013; Vis 2016) cogently argues why and how studies of ancient urbanism could be of relevance to urban studies today (see also Smith et al. 2012, on archaeology's contribution to social science debates). So, what is considered to be a city today can serve as a basis for ancient-modern comparisons without presuming their differences and similarities or questioning and defining the exact nature of urbanism.

A preoccupation with 'ancient cities', or the equifinality of city origins and the nature of urbanism, risks obstructing and restricting comparative investigation into the functioning of cities and the processes from which cities emerge. Therefore, my aim is not to present yet another version of a grand narrative explaining the urban phenomenon in general. As Wheatley (1972: 602) put it: 'it is not particularly profitable for a social scientist to attempt to discuss the nature, the essential quality, of urbanism. That is a metaphysical question more amenable to philosophical enquiry than to the empirical methods of the social sciences.' Instead, I propose to accept that cities exist: not as a *fait accompli*, but in necessary relation to the general ongoing processes of humans settling and modifying the landscape. Cities are for living in and continue to be developed in that process of inhabitation. When inhabited, cities are always changing. There is no reason to distinguish *a priori* between types of cities or time periods, because the basic principles of how urban landscapes function as inhabited environments remain. Only from a position of understanding fundamental similarities can the specificities articulated by comparison become meaningful (*sensu* Scott & Storper 2015).

Yet, to contextualise my methodological agenda, it cannot be denied that clarity is desirable on how I regard the quality of urbanity of a place. The preceding literature-based discussion conveys that a methodological contribution can be achieved based on a rigorously conceptualised comparative frame of reference. The definition that determines urbanity as the quality of any place affords cities equifinality (i.e. the same developmental outcome reached through different trajectories). Yet, as comparative urban studies emphasise, the characteristics of each instance of this quality are pluriform. In other words, to compare rigorously, our understanding of basic principles must account for all imaginable diversity among end states which have attained the same (urban) quality. The following working definition (cf. Smith 2007), which is based on the social practices of urban life, is intended to lend my comparative frame of reference this flexibility. Because it is not intended to be applied or tested as a classification measure, the test cases in this book demonstrating the methodological developments (see Chapter 7) are assumed to function accordingly.

Social practice based definition of cities

Highlighting social practice, my working definition is based on urban life, accepting that the ordinary existence of cities is a prerequisite for this.

A city is a contiguous locus positioned in the physical landscape, which has been developed for human inhabitation through social-environmental interaction, and is resided in to such extent that for a predominant number of the population there is no unavoidable need to leave its confines. All of everyday life's necessities can be met through social relations, either directly or indirectly (i.e. using relations to agents and (resource) locations external to the contiguous locus' confines), which can be found within its confines. The interactions of everyday life, in turn, are constitutive of, accommodated by and mediated by the environment. The environment has become physically transformed in such a way as to permit dedicated occupation by such social processes, which in themselves are also constant negotiations with their social and physical environment. This dynamic situation is expected to meet basic requirements for permanency within the locus' confines on the level of human life.

There are a few things to note with regards to this process-oriented definition.[4] First, it avoids identifying any specific traits *a priori*. That is, what is entailed by the necessities of everyday life is not prescribed. Nevertheless, it can be conceded that permanence must be delimited at the least by the requirements for survival.

Second, the aspects of the urban landscape that qualify as contiguity are not prescribed. This is dependent on the processes of everyday life, though it does require the features of the developed landscape to serve (unspecified) purposes within everyday life.

---

4. Ley (2010) offers a preliminary attempt at a phenomenological systemic basis for a *morphological* definition of the city. The definition here departs from the process of inhabitation of which built form is an outcome (see Chapter 3 for theoretical grounding, and Chapter 6 for urban morphology).

Third, no claims are made towards thresholds of size and density or intensity. This is dependent on the population and the way the population developed the landscape for inhabitation.

Fourth, inhabitants are not made 'urban prisoners'. That is, they may not *have to* leave to uphold their everyday functioning, but still can do so for other reasons. Vice versa, non-residents can enter and partake in the city. In this way structural yet autonomous placement within the wider landscape, including external relations, are ensured. In addition, the predominant proportion of residents cannot be reliant on direct external relations controlling subsistence, as is literally the case in prison complexes.

Fifth, any difference between urban-rural becomes a transitional and flexible distinction. It could be expected that beyond the city's confines, people increasingly lead an everyday life in which they are not reliant on the relations within the city's contiguously developed locus to provide. Simultaneously, this leaves open the possibility that the existence of cities 'urbanises' the whole landscape to some extent (see Blake 2002).[5]

Sixth, the definition supposes a measure of social complexity that should be sufficient to allow everyday life for individuals to unfold within the locus' confines by using all relations and interactions (including some that may be external) that take place there.

Seventh, this definition requires that cities are viewed as being contingent on the processes of inhabitation and development taking place accordingly. This means we must be aware of the distinction between studying cities as social phenomena and employing a purely empirical focus on the physical characteristics of cities. Archaeologists typically encounter cities as abandoned, derelict and disturbed developed loci. Empirical recording alone cannot *comprehend* the constituents of the city. Studying cities socially should entail studying urban life, and therefore rely on the assumption that all urban built environments are inhabited environments.

Eighth, this definition renders certain intensively developed loci non-urban when it cannot be established that everyday life could unfold within the city's confines. This may include excesses of monumentality and (political or cosmological) planned idealism, which may display physical characteristics almost impossible to distinguish from the

---

5. In current large-scale urban consideration of planning for megacities and urban agriculture, the regionality of cities and the blurring of urban-rural distinctions, building on McGee's desakota-model in Soja's post-metropolitan era (see Kasper et al. 2015), is becoming an accepted and potentially productive view, especially for peri-urban development (see Simon & Adam-Bradford 2016). Here it is employed as a general perspective.

complex composite of places with 'true urban life'. Indeed, a physically developed environment may hold the potential to accommodate urban life even though it has not taken place.[6] Although, for their subsistence, elaborate religious and palatial complexes may have relied on a hinterland, which is only developed to a lesser extent, these are examples of monumentality rather than full-fledged cities.

Finally, however, the main admonition with this definition, and what will restrict effective classification of any place, is the probable impossibility to confirm with certainty that any developed landscape could fulfil all requirements for everyday life to take place within its confines. Furthermore, many places that are currently not commonly regarded or treated as cities may fulfil these requirements. Contemporary multinuclear city-regions might hypothetically fulfil the requirements as both separate cities and a single one. Consequently, this definition provides the grounds for studying elaborate places of settlement in their own right and on the basis of their intrinsic characteristics. Conversely, it leaves open the question of which exact traits are unique to cities as opposed to settlements that are not cities, and how these might differ from society to society. Therefore, it becomes contingent upon the comparative framing of research respecting this process-oriented definition whether such questions can be answered in the future.

Ultimately, it is my premise that sociality is at work in spatial contexts of cohabitation constructed by humans. Thus, whatever information we use to study urbanism requires a social theoretical understanding. While not exactly a 'sociological' definition (cf. Smith 2016), the notion of developing an urban perspective based on 'social practice' is not without precedent, as Joyce (2009: 192) exemplifies:

> [S]ocial and political formations like ancient cities and polities are instantiations of ongoing social relations simultaneously embedded in and both producing and reproducing historical traditions [...]. Rather than integrated and coherent, societies are fragmented and contested to varying degrees such that there is never complete closure to any system of social relations. Practices and the cultural and material conditions that constitute landscapes

---

6. China is reported (Rapoza 2015; Jacobs 2016) to have planned and built huge urban areas that nonetheless, to date, have never been occupied. They are intended to and hold the potential to fully accommodate the processes of urban life in the future, but some may fail to achieve this stage.

are always negotiations among differently positioned actors – socially embedded individuals and groups – distinguished by varying identities, interests, emotions, knowledge, outlooks, and dispositions. As locations characterized by a 'greater concentration of social relationships' (Southall 1983: 10), cities are places where these negotiations are perhaps most concentrated, intense, and unrelenting.

With these words Joyce similarly steers the study of urbanism according to Graham's (1999) suggestion that it is more productive to shift interests from what a city is to how a city works.

A deeper theoretical grounding for my definition can be found in Pred's (1984, 1986) conceptualisation of place as a historically contingent process. 'Places are a kind of historical micro-geographies [sic], in which many individual territories interact and biographies collide. The crossings of behaviour and movement generate spatial transformations and localise structures. The historical construction of place involves the appropriation and transformation of space as well as the reproduction and transformation of society in time and space' (Vis 2009: 75). Thus, in spatial-material terms, the city is merely an intensively developed place, which conditions the everyday life that is simultaneously responsible for its formation. A contextualisation based on process permits generating understandings of the dynamics and functioning of places. Many of the static categories necessary to classify a variety of city types are contingent upon these processes.

Ancient-to-modern comparisons are most useful for how they can elucidate the ways in which places functioned and have been developed whilst being constitutive effects of social life themselves. Cities and their structures are emergent from the social-environmental interactions of locally residing urban life. Such social practice based perspective can exist next to other explanations of urban existence. Following Joyce (2009) these include: (1) cultural evolution: based on a model of linear progression typically assuming a relation to complex social organisation; (2) functional: including the many city types following from a main functional characterisation, e.g. political, religious, regal-ritual, administrative, and mercantile (see Fox 1977), but also the city-state (e.g. Hansen 2000) as opposed to cities in territorial states (Trigger 2003); (3) elitist: an authoritative power drives the settlement, e.g. the concepts of synoikism[7] (see Blake 2002), where an authority may force

7. Also known as synoecism or sinecism.

relocation so an amalgamation of residency develops as a single urban unit (for an example see Bakirtzis 2003); (4) action theoretical[8]: a catalytic and/or innovation based explanation; (5) environmental: emergence of settlements based on natural factors and resilience (see Trigger 1972). Seeing urbanism as social practice actually underlies all of these explanations for city foundation or urban development without predetermination. In the end, all urban landscapes are caused by a common societal process.[9]

What to study comparatively

The notion of the 'inhabited urban built environment' opened this chapter. The urban context of the present work is now explained. This notion simultaneously incorporates the logical object of study or the information source for a broadly comparative methodology in urban studies: the built environment, due to its physical endurance and ubiquity (Harris & Smith 2011). Despite a variety of views on comparative urbanism in urban studies over the years (e.g. Robinson 2004; Dear 2005; Nijman 2007; Ward 2010), it is important to note that urban geography (like urban sociology) has become more concerned with society as taking place in the context of the city than the life of the city itself (Zimmermann 2012). In no small part this is the influence of the Lefebvrian (Lefebvre 1991) proposition to view space as socially produced and imagined.

Ward (2010) shows that comparative urbanism has been around in various guises, notably with quantitative beginnings using the city as a pre-given bounded locality, for several decades. Recently it has shifted towards fashionable socially produced and relational strands of social theoretical thought. In so doing, cities are not themselves the object of study. The focus has become fixed on the socio-culturally contextualised activities that take place within it. These activities are part of much more fluid and transient, far-reaching, social structures. The implication of this is that comparative urbanism is currently not well-equipped to elucidate how cities function in their own right (cf. Yoffee's (2009) remark on the lack of lived experience in archaeological urban work). For example, in

---

8. This should not be confused with Weber's social action (Campbell 1981), Von Mises' (1998) purposeful action, Giddens' (1984) purposive action or agency, and De Certeau's (1988) resistance within everyday life, all of which qualify (inter)action generally.
9. Chapter 3 presents a conceptualisation of the causal processes in human and social life leading to the generic construction of inhabited (urban) built environments.

Robinson's (2004) work cities become cogwheels in a global postcolonial narrative (see Clarke 2012), while in Dear's (2005) work urban life and city-regions receive their meaning from specific socio-political and cultural contexts. Instead, the low-level interpretive approach that I pursue in the remainder of this chapter makes use of empirical information on each (physical) city itself. This information remains decontextualised from specific social implications to empower comparative understanding beyond segregative particularities.

Recently, German urban sociologists in particular have proposed to refocus research on the city itself, without letting it become immediately subsumed by cultural contexts – as is the case in current social research on cities (see Löw 2013). Their approach is based on what they call the *Eigenlogik* (intrinsic logic) of cities (Zimmermann 2012; Löw 2013) and seeks to redress social urban research to regard the city-specific characteristics. It propagates, in tandem with architectural sociology or anthropology (Delitz unpublished), the pursuit of a sociology *of* the city rather than a sociology *in* the city (Zimmermann 2012; also: Löw 2008). Architectural anthropologist Yaneva (2012: 4) states:

> The danger is that when we talk about *different* cities (Cardiff, Sydney, Paris, London), *different* social contexts and *different* urban cultures, we tend to describe local treatments of the universal. Too often we assume that cities have common features such as infrastructure, markets, transport networks and city authorities. Culture is taken as a variable that is relative and situated.

Whereas early adoptions of the *Eigenlogik* perspective (Löw 2013) seem to focus on a city-specific cultural history with a minor role for the particular material properties of the spaces that compose the place, architectural anthropology repositions that interest.

Delitz (unpublished) proposes a scheme of major architectural properties by which to broadly characterise cities. Material properties, or the actual substance of cities, are part of the *Eigenlogik* of cities. However, relational, imagined and contextual approaches to urban research tend to overlook this substance as a ubiquitously present, yet uniquely formed, object of study. Griffiths (2013) notes that the same is happening in the humanities. Unsurprisingly, the spatial turn in history (e.g. Arnade et al. 2002) is influenced by the same socially constructivist thought – e.g. Briggs (2004) places cities as part of historically specific larger designs for society. Yet, approaching cities as social practice in space, *sensu* society-space relations (Griffiths 2013) and emplaced inhabitation (cf. Ingold 2008a; Howes 2005a, see Chapter 3), has much to gain from direct engagement with what places were physically really like for the inhabitants. The physical shapes composing 'the urban built environment' complex embody a cogent comparative source of information on the functioning of particular cities, because practice is an inherent part of their presence and significance.

This argument positions research on an intra-city and individual inhabitant scale, requiring quite intricate details on the way space has been built up. While this may be relatively easy to achieve for contemporary cities, further back in time (archaeologically) it is a challenge to retrieve a similar level of data. Where urban historical research can often roughly distinguish which sectors of a city were developed when, further evidence is typically scant and piecemeal. This results in area or zonal maps, the resolution of which is too coarse to enable discussions on the experience of the inhabitants (e.g. Historic Towns Atlas series (Lobel 1969; Speet 1982); Conzen 1960). Increasingly, there are mathematical and agent-based-modelling approaches that seek to express the evolution of the intrinsic shape of cities in law-like formulas (e.g. Batty & Longley 1994; Bettencourt 2013; Longley & Batty 2003; see Sayer 1979 for a modelling critique), which are argued to incorporate social factors in formalisations. Though such methods may both steer investigations and inform planning through isolating abstracted factors in city development comparatively, they are far removed from comprehensively addressing the human experience of inhabitation or understanding the opportunities for social interaction and development.

The open-endedness and complexity of real social systems and processes, as emphasised in complexity theory (Bentley & Maschner 2003, 2009a), suggests that such models and formulas will never be able to fully account for how processes take place in the real world. Yet, the critical application of modelling makes an interesting specialist research tool. It should be acknowledged that actual understanding in social science is subjectively limited to one's own frame of reference. Inter-subjective understanding even restricts direct linguistic communication (vs. Zierhofer 2002; cf. Vis 2009: 105–7). Learning processes and emplaced experience, such as geographically delimited inhabitation and acculturation, may converge individuals' biographies and enable improvements in inter-subjective understandings. Nonetheless, uniquely positioned and situated individuals (cf. Hägerstrand 1975, 1976; Pred 1977, 1981; Thrift & Pred 1981; Vis 2010) cannot achieve an equal understanding for immediate exchange.

The same rational actions[10] and the same language are likely to mean slightly different things and be intended slightly differently. '[I]t cannot [...] be safely assumed that the words a community uses to refer to the actions are a sufficient description of what is happening, or why. Nor can we assume that the social actions that are concurrent with a material assemblage are necessarily compatible with it' (Fletcher 2004: 111). Similarly, the understanding, interpretation, and appreciation of intent and outcome will inherently differ between individuals, even if the individuals can be said to generally adhere to an overarching scheme. This intrinsic individualism alone gives social processes openness and therefore the flexibility to *change* at the hand of individual (inter)actions with the social and physical environment. Moreover, it stringently confines the potential for *comprehensive explanation* to historically and culturally specified contexts.

Even with detailed contextual knowledge it applies that 'similarities between individual plans, building forms and decorative elements do not necessarily imply that they have the same meaning. [...] '[C]omparable shapes and plans can easily be considered representations of different realities' (Mekking 2009: 35). Given this individuality and arbitrariness of the 'meaning' of intentional acts and communication – be that cultural, ideological, cosmological, religious, political or other – it is surprising that built form and architectural styles and traits have readily sparked research and interpretation on exactly that level.

Even when this kind of meaning and intention underlie the decision to build space in a particular way, the primary effects of its physical occurrence take place on a more fundamental level of experience and potentiality, notwithstanding its presumed meaning. With regards to style, architect and Mayanist Andrews (1975: 32) asserted:

> [I]t can be argued that style is a secondary indicator of cultural tradition, since the larger Maya area appears to be fairly homogeneous when more basic factors are considered. Style as such has very little to do with determining the physical organization and spatial order of the centre as a whole and can be thought of as a superficial overlay which is subject to change at will [...].

10. Rational actors should not be confused with conforming to normative rules. Decisions to act are ordinally reached (see Von Mises 1998; Vis 2010) – one prefers to do something rather than something else with the expectation that it will improve one's position and situation. It is not prescribed that any action will have the intended effect nor can it be generally prescribed what is considered to be an improvement. Rational actions are subjective and may therefore seem irrational to other individuals.

Rather than first considering the basic (common) causal effects of spatial-material construction to structure a particular complex – which has immediate implications for restricting and enabling opportunities of encounters, interactions, and framing the outcomes of interactions – archaeologists and anthropologists tend to be seduced by their ability to order and organise according to (visual) traits and decorative patterns. Interpretation in these cases is often aided by coarse analogies with other (not spatial-material) data which operate on high levels of particular specificity, instead of comparative information.

Representation and meaning

Representational thinking for interpretation as relevant to specific contexts is both favoured and well-explained by Mekking (2009: 25).

> Transversal thinking always and everywhere enables anybody to relate people, events and other aspects of life, irrespective of their being causally related or not. [...] Because building is an identifying act of positioning oneself in public space, the mental horizon of the patron-builder will inevitably be part of a worldview, a religion, a political ideology, or even the marketing strategy of a multinational. [...] If we focus on the built environment, this means that someone orders an urban structure [...] according to a chosen tradition, which represents, by its formal and material aspects, precisely those things one would like to have others understand as being characteristic for oneself or for one's living conditions. What can be concluded from all this is that the logic of representation obviously requires a direct comparison between products, like buildings or architectural designs [...].

The use of comparison in this quote is suggestive of a learning process. This appears concurrent with constitutive phenomenology (Schütz 1967) and can be replicated in interpretive research. Nevertheless, Mekking (2009: 44) also claims that 'never before [globalisation] has it been so difficult to understand the built environment without using a comparative analysis. The signalled, alarming lack of knowledge about the different cultural traditions that architecture forms a part of, has made a meaningful analysis of the built environment as such all the more urgent.'

The analytical challenge of comparison alluded to here regards the 'discrete' separation and identification of cultures and societies (rather than comparing urban built environments per se). This then echoes Dear's (2005: 247) statement, concerning the conceptual conflicts between the specificity of a place and generalising understandings, that 'Everyone knows that comparative urbanism is difficult.' To his credit, Mekking (2009: 33–34) is mindful of the counterproductive effects of periodisation in historical comparisons as it obstructs dynamic temporality. 'Since it consists of sheer projection and has nothing to do with historical analysis as such, one should never use it.' In contrast, Robinson's (2004) design for comparative urban research focuses around a specific historical period. This has the logical consequence that rather than learning about cities, we learn about societies taking place in cities around that time. However, whether culturally or historically specified, it is generally neglected that the complications with comparisons might result from the highly specific contextual frames of reference that are used without question (cf. Scott & Storper 2015). According to Mekking (2009), to interpret representative reality one has to know the specific social group who built the architecture, their background and ambitions. Their preferred specific forms and materials relate to the function and architectural product they realise. In other words, his interpretive analysis becomes framed within the symbolism and meaning of shape and material, rather than what its *material presence* implies in terms of social interaction (see Chapter 2) and thus the practices of inhabitation and development.

Clearly, Mekking's analytical resolution on the basis of culturally embedded architectural traditions operates on the shape itself. This is a rather different premise than to analyse the structuring properties of shape within the inhabited built environment as advocated here. Comparative or generalising understandings of the historic context in which cities occur and, arguably, according to which entire cities are shaped can be beneficial. However, I argue that understanding cities as a phenomenon occurring within a common, fundamentally human, process of settling, would lay a strong rudimentary foundation upon which such contingent specific meaning could be better understood. Any traits conveying messages and communication inextricably cohere with how shapes structure and accommodate inhabitation first. As Kropf (2011: 398) recognises: 'First and foremost, it is our habitat. The built environment is an essential part of day-to-day life.'

It can be agreed that 'a person who is busy creating a dwelling place, uses his or her coordinates and body parts to structure, to proportion, and to orientate this structure[, which is] how people make a meaningful place out of their structure. It is meaningful because one's own body is the bearer of what any place in time means to each builder and inhabitant' (Mekking 2009: 36). Consequently, the researcher is provided with a conceptual framework with which schemata of meaning in the shape of architectural complexes can be uncovered comparatively. However, Mekking's three clusters (anthropomorphic, physiomorphic, sociomorphic) that form the basic meaningful stratum of built environments forego the solid causal psychological theory to truly substantiate such a proposal on a generic human level.

The archaeological proclivity to focus on architectural traditions and (building) typologies to interpret the built environments of cities, often constructing speculative analogies about the potential symbolic meaning being communicated, assumes, *sensu* Mekking (2009: 26), that 'expressing something about one's identity is always the goal of ordering or creating an artefact'. Rather than always being the intention of creating and ordering, it is an inescapable truth that, just like any human action, creating and ordering are expressive of identity. This principle, however, explains the readiness in archaeology to ascribe meaning to the ordering of places (see examples in Zedeño & Bowser 2009; Bowser & Zedeño 2009). Furthermore, using symbolism (influenced by Eliade) in the explanation of physical city characteristics has long been a mainstay of comparative urban discourse, as initiated by Wheatley (1969: 9). '[C]osmo-magical symbolism […] informed the ideal-type traditional city in both the Old and New Worlds, which brought it into being, sustained it, and was imprinted on its physiognomy.' For example, in the Maya area the patterns of urban planning have tentatively been interpreted as 'cosmogrammes' (Ashmore & Sabloff 2002, 2003; Špracj 2009). Although my proposition is not to reduce urban built environment comparisons to environmental determinism, neither can the high-level interpretation of contingent culture-specific expression readily support comparative work.

Environmental determinism

To compare built environments, I suggest there is a more rudimentary or essential social significance to the inhabitation of urban built environments than the contingency or arbitrariness of cultural and contrived communication schemes. One would be forgiven for thinking this alludes to a reduction to law-like determinism following either social or environmental models. Such *sensu stricto* functionalist perspectives would test explanatory hypotheses instead of leading to (inter)subjective understandings of inhabiting urban built environments.

This does not withstand that the local geography, topography, climate, material physics, availability of resources and other natural factors will – as society comes to learn about its requirements for inhabiting that environment successfully, sustainably (initially meeting necessities for biological survival) and comfortably – increasingly determine certain aspects of urban form. Moreover, the state of technological knowledge and advancement will enable and restrict physical construction and modification in particular ways. So clearly, neither social practice nor meaningful contexts in isolation or combined will fully determine urban built form. There are physical and environmental limitations determining the (im)possibilities of material construction to how and which features can be built and shaped (see also Chapter 2 on 'the material'). In other words, there always is a certain level of environmental determinism at play in the processes of urban settling and developing the landscape.

Kropf (1996) acknowledges that natural features and geographical location are of importance in the constitution of the physical properties of how urban form determines the character of a town. After all, anyone visiting a town or looking at their plans will recognise the enormous influence natural features have on its general layout, feel and functioning (investigable by comparative positivist measures). Conzen (1968) argues that it is important to include contour lines in town plans, which is common practice in archaeological mapping, because natural features may result in 'inherited outlines' (i.e. persisting shapes) in the pre-urban layout of a developing place. It is essential to realise, however, that despite the influence environmental determinism will exert on the shape of the urban built environment, its social practice opportunities are dependent on the basic properties of the material and spatial configuration constructed as a result. This configuration will incorporate any adaptations to natural topography or other (im)possibilities posed by (bio)physics.

As a consequence, no matter the restrictions imposed by environmental determinism, the specific configuration of the built environment is necessarily socially significant. Any built environment is the product of constitutive human and social interactions. Moreover, Deligne alerts us to the risk of overestimating the restricting influence of the natural environment in the development of cities and new towns (PhD thesis 2003, cited in Taverne 2008: 184). It is thus suggested that building according to will, in whatever way man pleases, is quite resourceful and resilient. This supports the view that all built form is emergent from and constitutive of the social (see Chapter 2 on 'the social').

Even if due to environmental factors there are true impossibilities imposed on e.g. the orientation, location or specific composition of any built feature, the spatial results of dealing with that are socially constitutive all the same. The features that are eventually built and the environmental features that are eventually incorporated are still part of a socially significant built environment with a view to accommodate (restrict and enable) social (inter)actions as a contiguous locus. As soon as anything is built it becomes a social reality within the inhabited (urban) built environment. Building is immediately a social act and therefore any shape resulting from it is instantaneously a social reality. The social significance of the basic properties of the material and spatial configuration of an urban built environment can therefore always be studied without having to consider the exact nature (influence) of the environmental determinism at play, although a full narrative explaining the development of a place (a city history as described by Rutte 2008) would be expected to take this into account.

Low-level meaning (avoiding conflation)

Now we can return to the kind of interpretive analysis implied by the process-oriented and social practice perspective within the definition of cities as urban life presented earlier. I have just argued that within environmental determinism and the biological sustenance of its inhabitants, i.e. pure (rational) functionalism, the effects of designing and shaping one's environment are nonetheless socially significant. Furthermore, I have exposed the problems arising from launching comparative research from highly specific contextual perspectives. It is paramount that all building affects how the landscape is experienced and is conducive to subsequent interactions within it. In material records of the built environment (in the archaeological sense) we have a record of performed actions, but no direct means to access the psyche[11] and the contingency of cultural understandings. Yet, the reality of the existence

---

11. Although it is possible that psychological functioning eventually is the primary determinant of spatial and social behaviour, the individual circumstances that lead to decisions could still not be fully known and taken into account. Psychology limits insights to individual cases and situations, while a social perspective can assume the constitutive relevance of individualism in decision-making processes, but is able to assess and appreciate the complex of outcomes within socio-spatial contexts. In the words of Merton (1936: 896): 'Psychological considerations of the source or origin of motives, though they are undoubtedly important for a more complete understanding of the mechanisms involved in the development of unexpected consequences of conduct, will thus be ignored.'

of intentions and socio-culturally specific backgrounds cannot be denied. Indeed, this existence necessarily plays a role in the decisions to act and to appropriate a landscape for inhabitation. Such contextual approaches represent a distinct level of investigation. These contexts are contingent on the opportunities created by the more basic spatial-material structuring of the life-world within which the conditions (determining the flexibility of the foundations) for the emergence of the imaginative productions of space (see Lefebvre 1991) and representational traditions are accommodated.

The comparative interpretive objective of this research is therefore positioned between vulgar empiricism or law-like functionalism (based on assumed objective measures) and representational meaning. It looks for the constitutive implications of material presence on inhabiting a landscape that is being developed according to human design. This interpretive focus roughly corresponds to what has been called 'low-level meaning' in Rapoport's (1988, 1990) work on the built environment. This level mainly conveys recursive human-environment relationships (Smith 2007). In addition, here this level intends to incorporate the experiential knowledge such interactive practices acquire. The way material presence conditions opportunities to develop a 'sense of place' (cf. Tuan 1977; Pred 1986), and an inhabited identity as subsequently introduced in place formation, are always included *implicitly*. Experiential knowledge and the 'sense of place' better correspond to Rapoport's 'middle-level meaning'. Finally, 'high-level meaning' refers primarily to cosmovision and the supernatural. It should be noted that representational meaning, as promoted in Mekking's (2009) work, and indeed regularly seen in archaeological interpretations of urban planning and architecture (e.g. Ashmore & Sabloff 2002, 2003; Atkin & Rykwert 2005; Šprajc 2009; critique: M.E. Smith 2003), concentrates on middle- and high-level meaning. Importantly, the specificities of power, communication and ideology placed in the realm of 'middle-level meaning' are subject to such research. As Smith (2007) reflects, except for a slowly increasing engagement with techniques that are primarily empiricist in nature, especially some types of spatial analysis originating in other disciplines (see Fisher 2009; Cutting 2003, for adaptations of architectural built environment methods), low-level meaning has received little attention in studies on ancient urbanism or long-term comparisons.

A potential caveat in Rapoport's (1988, 1990) levels of meaning is its predominant focus on design and planning, since it does not discuss what the spaces created by built form are actually used for. It could be argued that the use of space, in a utilitarian sense of particular functions, is part of the response to and intentions for space within the three levels of meaning. Alternatively, we turn to Mekking's (2009: 24) discussions on what the built environment represents once again to understand how this is also intrinsically different and rather elusive on the level of space and shape.

> [N]ew functions are initially always represented by architectural shapes which were not explicitly designed for it. [...] Referring to the functional side of architecture is nothing more than mentioning just another reality represented by the medium. Trying to discriminate between building types on the grounds of their functional aspect means using the term 'building type' in an improper way, since all architectural typology is exclusively based on formal aspects. In some cases, the function of a specific group of buildings and its (formal) typology seem to match so perfectly that one would be tempted to see it as a 'natural' and 'unavoidable' combination.

This sharp statement brings us to realise a significant difference in the type of information we are presented with. Our responses to and contextual understandings of the shape of built form do not necessarily also prescribe how it was used, since there are many utilitarian opportunities enabled by the same spatial-material framing of interaction opportunities (see also Fletcher 2004; Sayer 2000; Chapter 2 will develop this notion of 'spatial independence' further). Yaneva (2012) argues similarly that too often cities are assumed to have common utility features within differing cultural contexts. What actually occurred in specific spaces is only accessible through other types of information. Such information is different from the basic material and spatial properties of the complex composite that a built environment's configuration offers researchers. Mekking's 'formal aspects' of architecture articulate this difference, which incidentally concurs distinctions made by Rapoport (1990). It should be repeated, however, that material properties to do with style or adornment, which may provide clues on use, are not included in this research, because they are essentially secondary aspects of constructing a spatial composition (see Andrews 1975).

Spatial composition has a constitutive structuring role of which Batty (2009: 194) recently said: 'Currently there is considerable confusion about the way that the physical structure relates to human behaviour.' Mekking (2009: 41) explicates just such a fundamental role of built space: 'All over the world and for ages now, people have found their own ways to distinguish between "them" and "us". In architectural terms, it mainly means erecting walls to include "those who belong to us" and exclude "those who do not belong to us".' This role of *seclusion as a primary operative* for conceptualising the built environment will be elaborated on in Chapters 4 and 5. It forms the tenet of unifying a way to discuss spatial organisation (cf. Rapoport 1994). Separating use from a fundamental structuring role not only clarifies the information we are after, it also increases comparability across datasets. This especially applies to working with mapped representations of original empirical data, which is important for accomplishing comparative interpretation.

Placing a non-utilitarian limitation on interpretation will help explicate how the interpretive objectives are commensurate with the empirical information employed in research. Lynch (1981) noted that using commonplace (often cultural) terms for architectural objects leads to conflation in understanding. He uses the example of a church to demonstrate that a church is at once an architectural template and a function. The word church may be associated with the particular building, once built with the intention of fulfilling religious expectations, and taking on a predetermined socio-cultural role. However, the way it frames interaction socio-spatially – a 'socially positioned spatiality' in its built environment context (see Vis 2009) – permits wider possibilities. In order to clear up the confusion signalled by Batty (2009) we need to carefully disentangle which information allows for interpretive claims on which level. Disentangling our information source so it fits the interpretive aims may prevent the conflation caused by the uncritical use of commonplace and lay terms (see Chapter 2, especially Sayer 1985). Disentangling effectively means devising conceptualisations that are able to account for the breadth of diversity of the human settling practices under scrutiny, here comprising all urban traditions. Establishing an appropriate level of interpretation will facilitate spatial practice analysis of society-space relations constitutive of cities through cross-cultural and diachronic comparisons (see Griffiths 2013). When applied broadly this can yield profound understandings of differences and similarities in patterns and processes.

Yet, conflation is not only confined to the cultural embedding and scope of the interpreter. The framing of the objectives of research can also cause research outcomes that are themselves conflated or at least confused. When Wheatley (1972) identified the fashionable approaches to urbanism (discussed above), he also noted how these appeared to concur exactly with Tilly's (1967) categorisation of contradictory conceptions of urbanisation. Where Tilly comments on the lack of attempts to define urbanisation as a process, Wheatley condemns the lack of attention to urbanity as an overarching context or phenomenon. In the absence of clarity on and the uncritical use of terms like urbanism and urbanisation researchers had included too much in their concepts (Tilly 1967). The resultant research perspectives inhibit the development of comparative urban studies (Wheatley 1972). Rutte (2008) demonstrates that urban historians have been particularly prone to be unselective in their research objectives. Unselectiveness often leads to indiscriminative totalising explanatory narratives (see also Diederiks & Laan 1976; e.g. Speet 2006) in which inadvertently various aspects of urban life and the city itself are neglected or overlooked. Consequently it becomes difficult to connect interpretive claims to relevant information sources. 'Purposive conflation' as found in urban history has had similar effects on urban morphological accounts of cities (see Kropf 2009).

Research practice

An interpretive approach based on low-level meaning is intended to prevent these kinds of conflation. One is required to understand the information source, must identify the commensurate interpretive scope, and institute appropriate conceptualisation. For that reason investigation can neither start from the objectification of analytical empiricism as contrasted against and discussed through conceptual frameworks, nor can it start from uncritical culturally embedded empiricism using conflated (commonplace) terms to frame research.

However, overcoming this requires a process of knowledge production which allows the empirical record on the basic material and spatial properties of built environment configurations to speak for itself. Our interpretation cannot rely on elusive high-level representational contexts or positivist measurements awaiting contingent meaningful ordering. Both have undeniable uses for the construction of the full narrative of the life and development of cities, but here I make the conscious choice to limit my approach to comparative urbanism to a social practice perspective.

While in archaeology the empirical, functional and representational interpretive paradigms seemingly have been going hand in hand, they do so somewhat unawares. On the one hand this may be due to purposive conflation, possibly resulting from other urban disciplinary influences. On the other hand, this is due to a lack of intra-city and wide coverage datasets on ancient cities appropriate for comparison. There is no justification for comparative urban geographical discourse to ignore the data that archaeology has been assembling on cities all over the world for decades (Smith 2009b). Yet, we should acknowledge that only in the last decade technological advancements and traditional long-term field mapping projects are producing datasets at such resolutions that everyday urban life and development can be studied properly (see e.g. Evans et al. 2007; Marcus & Sabloff 2008; Hutson et al. 2008; Sinclair et al. 2010; Chase et al. 2011a; Arnauld et al. 2012). The diversity on display in tropical cities now is huge and ever increasing. This emphasises the enormous potential for broadening and contextualising our contemporary knowledge of urbanisation and urban life.

Perhaps unsurprisingly, it is in archaeological discourse that appeals are made for developing systematic and rigorous comparative frames of reference with direct relevance to social scientific issues. Here attempts emerge to come up with methodologies with wide comparative merit to the built environment on various scales (e.g. Smith 2010a, 2010b, 2011a, 2011b; York et al. 2011; Stanley et al. 2012, 2015; Isendahl & Smith 2013; Dennehy et al. 2016). Currently comparative analytical tools and measures are predominantly adopted from other disciplines, such as architecture and geography (see selected examples in Chapter 6). Alternatively comparison is driven by juxtaposing an increasing number of urban cases – i.e. exclusively empirically informed comparison. Regardless, current discourse shows that we can overcome previous obstructions caused by archaeology's meticulous and particularist empirical research processes. No longer are we detracted from formulating the frameworks, questions and perspectives to guide the analysis of these datasets beyond crude quantitative variables on small selections. Archaeology can now stretch research to city-wide (recent attempts e.g. Magnoni et al. 2012; Richards-Rissetto 2012; Hare & Masson 2012; Richards-Rissetto & Landau 2014) and comparative scales (e.g. York et al. 2011; Stanley et al. 2015; Dennehy et al. 2016).

Hägerstrand (1976: 332) gave us an insightful view on the importance of everyday individual lives in relation to understanding case studies of bounded wholes, here cities. These wholes display a complex of togetherness in occurring features across time and space.

> Actually what is at stake here is not in the first place the understanding of unique areas of the world but a deeper insight into the *principles of togetherness* where-ever [sic] it occurs. But these

principles, as I see it, can only be derived from a careful study of actual individual cases. Such cases need not be of any particular scale, but [...] I believe that the small settings – say the daily range of people – is of crucial importance to look into for revealing insights that can later be applied to wider areas. More important than the spatial scale is the treatment of process. Togetherness is not just *resting* together. It is also *movement* and *encounter*.

Against this background quantitative analytical tools should be used in an exploratory and directly interpretive way for individual cases, which due to their formal nature can later be used for systematic comparisons. This requires a basis of careful theorisation of data (Chapter 4) as well as human phenomena (Chapter 3). The influx of theoretical criticism in Geographical Information System (GIS) science (Leszczynski 2009; Kwan & Schwanen 2009) is leading to an increasingly balanced conduct of hypothesising and exploring landscape perception in GIS applications (Wheatley & Gillings 2000), aimed at generating e.g. human sensory (e.g. Llobera 2003; Paliou & Knight 2013; Smith & Cochrane 2011), affordance and phenomenological (Gillings 2012; McEwan & Millican 2012), and socio-political (Lemonnier 2012; Kosiba & Bauer 2013) understandings. In this book I work towards quantitative GIS tools and consider appropriately defined comparative measures. The practice of this is discussed in Chapters 7–9.

Exciting possibilities are emerging. The perspective sketched in this chapter is in desperate need of a method especially devised as appropriate for the resultant comparative interpretive objective. This cannot forego a commensurate social theory, as suggested by Yoffee (2009), but will at least need to satisfy Smith's (2011b) *empirical theoretical* requirements to be applicable at all. Neither should the methodology follow any particular disciplinary discourse, possibly finding its home most comfortably in the inherently interdisciplinary space of urban studies. After all, the aim is to *stop thinking about cities and in cities, but start thinking on cities and engaging with cities* as they occur to us and are developed through inhabitation (cf. Zimmermann's (2012) and Löw's (2012) aforementioned *Eigenlogik*). The material and spatial information contained in the built environment is both the most enduring and ubiquitous source available to us to start this comparative pursuit. The first focus of comparative understanding (low-level interpretation) available to the researcher refers to the occurrence and presence of built environments in the urban life-world. That is, how its emergence from, existence within, and accommodation of social practice is significant to societal structuring and development. The omnipresence of the material reality of built environments as a constitutive part of social practice merits further attention, whether its shape is partially or primarily driven by either measurable environmental, functional or communicable ideational factors. My aim is to enable research in the remit of comparative urbanism determined by Nijman (2007: 1), which is to develop 'knowledge, understanding, and generalization at a level between what is true of all cities and what is true of one city at a given point in time. [...] Comparative urbanism [...] is the systematic study of similarity and difference among cities or urban processes.'

The potency, cogency, reliability and relevance of a new method for radical comparisons all depend on a foundational philosophy of science which is capable of providing the basis for both theory building and an appropriate epistemology. This is the topic of the following chapter, which appropriates a critical realist view for the conceptual purpose of creating knowledge about the world.

CHAPTER 2
ADAPTING A CRITICAL REALIST RESEARCH PROCESS

Introduction

The preceding chapter specified the distinct scope for a methodological contribution to comparative urbanism. To develop a proper methodology for the comparative social study of urban built environments now requires appropriate theoretical grounding and conceptualisation. Low-level interpretation was proposed to ensure productive comparative contributions, in accordance with a fundamental view on urbanism as a human and social process as opposed to the pitfalls of reductionism and particularism.

This chapter will therefore perform two main tasks. On the one hand I will take an epistemological stance to structure a research practice to theorise and conceptualise the substantive field of interest. This requires establishing a workable link between the external reality and conceptual understanding of the world, because through empirical information on the built environment experiential understanding is not immediately accessible. On the other hand I will define a number of metaconcepts which determine how and on which level of detail fundamentally human and social processes are understood. Subsequently, Chapter 3 introduces a theoretical framework on the (urban) built environment respecting these metaconcepts, which departs from the Heideggerian existential premise of human being-in-the-world.

This chapter will first discuss how a critical realist philosophy of science helps us to define the metaconceptual realms of 'the social', 'the material', and 'spatial (in)dependence'. These metaconcepts act as premises to formulate concepts appropriate to urbanisation and urban life as a human and social process of inhabitation. The process of inhabitation replaces the static notion of the city as a category, or the concrete specificities of social life in a particular place. As such it must refrain from separate exclusive considerations of the physical, spatial or social in historical process. Defining the social, the material, and spatial (in)dependence clarifies how these are *necessarily* incorporated as constituents of the temporality and composition of our human life-world, while we change and develop that world for inhabitation through experience and affect.

Ultimately, this chapter contains ideas inspired by critical realism that lay the basis for theorising *a priori* conditions of human being-in-the-world and human experiential knowledge of the inhabitation process. Chapter 3 will develop and use these conditions to reveal the essential socio-spatial role the built environment plays in the process of inhabitation. Here I will articulate a research practice of immanent theoretical critique and iterative abstraction. This practice will determine how we can progress from conceptualisation to the empirically retrievable aspects of the built environment relevant to inhabitation. Accordingly, the current chapter also forms the philosophical grounding for Chapters 4 and 5. These explicate concepts to unlock the information concealed in the built environment (our research object) to guide the study of concrete instances of urbanity for a deeper comparative social understanding. In other words, here it will transpire how concepts and analysis can be devised to operationalise low-level interpretation in method and technique (Chapters 6–9).

Philosophical position

Some lines of conceptualisation for methodological development were well underway when I discovered the remarkable resemblance and resonance with research practice adapted from critical realist philosophy. My fortuitous introduction to Pratt's (1995) human geographical recapitulation alerted me to the social study of spatial phenomena through this philosophy of science. The logical effect of this timely realisation is that critical realism now permeates the stages of methodological development as the philosophical 'underlabourer' it positions itself as (see Pratt 1995). Critical realism presents cogently developed ideas, especially processes and methods, for research that are suitable for substantive social sciences (Yeung 1997). In particular, the way that critical realism helps to navigate the space between interpretive aims and empirical enquiry inspires structure here. Therefore, I will reflect on my position towards, and my use of, critical realist thought, especially as adapted within the discipline of human geography. In so doing, this chapter presents not only the skeleton of the research process adhered to, but importantly it also clarifies what is and what is not part of the remit of knowledge production through the new methodology. In other words, what can come to be known, respecting the aforementioned metaconcepts.

As an archaeologist it is relatively easy to acknowledge that there are many processes in the world that pre-exist us (both personally and as a species). Extending that notion logically leads one to accept the existence of an external reality. That is, a reality external to ourselves. Knowledge of things that pre-exist us, however, is restricted to our own empirical reality. This argument is often used in discussions of knowledge in 'postprocessual' archaeology (see e.g. Fahlander 2012; Wallace 2011). Knowledge, therefore, is only ever limited, and it is questionable whether external reality is ever fully knowable because this would demand of us to transcend the limitations of our own being. Conceding to the existence of an external reality, as first assumed in archaeological empirical practice, confirms this work is placed in the realm of realist philosophy. Yet, realist philosophy exists in various guises with its respective qualifiers.

Previously (Vis 2009), I have concurred with the reasoning of Putnam's (1981, 1990) internal realism as a moderate version of relativism: things can be true within conceptual confines, opening the way to formulating multiple truths about things that exist side by side. For developments here, this needs further specification. Critical realism's stance represents the conviction that although multiple truths and outcomes may exist, the validity of these truths is not equal. The 'practical adequacy' of knowledge will be more enduring when applied in real life if it approaches external reality closer (Sayer 1993; Pratt 1995; Yeung 1997). Putnam later shifted his internal realist position to a 'direct realism' inspired by an advanced interest in human perception (Farkas 2003). Critical realism leaves open the possibility of a 'direct awareness' (Yeung 1997), which seemingly concurs with this idea of the direct perception of external reality. In turn, critical realism rather comments on the adequacy of conceptualisations and how they inform research.

For the purposes of this research, which was *not predetermined* by any of these ideas, it appears that *internal* realism could be said to be of relevance in the way that it refers to the substantive domain this methodology studies. The substantive domain is necessarily an abstracted and partial knowledge of the world. *Critical* realism provides a philosophical ontology which facilitates the formulation of epistemologies of substantive disciplines (Yeung 1997; Sayer 2013; Cox 2013b). The conceptualisation of the substantive domain delimiting the discipline – here the social science of the inhabited built environment – identifies and informs which aspects to study. This creates an internal realism of sorts, which can be criticised for its practical adequacy.

Furthermore, how I conceptualise human *being* phenomenologically (see Chapter 3) concurs to an extent with 'direct realism' or 'direct awareness'. Direct awareness could be defined as the origin of our experiential knowledge: what we self-referentially and experientially know to be true. It thus forms part of the condition of human being and all associated causalities, but the knowledge within direct awareness cannot directly be recognised as empirical phenomena externally. In the case of the inhabited urban built environment, it could be said that we know cities to fulfil the expectation of social life in flux as it occupies its spatial form. A deeper, emancipating understanding of the nature of the inhabited built environment depends on a practically adequate conceptualisation of it, rather than such situated understanding (see Sayer 1985, 1993). Thus, all of our knowledge cannot be reduced to experiential knowledge, but it would be misleading not to acknowledge its instrumental position in everyday life.

Geography and archaeology

The substantive domain of the inhabited built environment places this research firmly between relevant academic disciplines. The following are especially worth mentioning: the spatiality of social life as studied in human geography and applied in planning; and the materiality of social life as studied in archaeology (and anthropology) and formally applied in architecture and urban design. In my pursuit to improve understanding and analysis, my first allegiance is to human geography and archaeology.

Roy Bhaskar's realism was originally intended to ground both natural and social sciences. Its adaptations in social science logically spurred on debates in human geography with Andrew Sayer as its most notable proponent (Sayer 1981, 1985, 1993; Layder 1988; Duncan & Savage 1989; Cox & Mair 1989; Lawson & Staeheli 1990, 1991; Chappell 1991; Pratt 1995; Yeung 1997). Critiques targeted postmodern and Marxist traditions in interest fields such as labour and capitalism, whilst methodological pointers typically took on the vestiges of traditional social scientific research, such as interviewing techniques (e.g. Pratt 1995). After over a decade of silent existence, critical realism is making an open resurgence in geograph-ical theorising (e.g. Massey 2005; Jessop et al. 2008; M. Jones 2009). Recently even old paradigmatic debates reappeared (Cox 2013a; and comments and reply: Sayer 2013; Pratt 2013; Cox 2013b).[1] These debates do not contravene that, in social sciences in general, critical realist influences have become a mainstay (e.g. Archer 1995; Sayer 2000; Groff 2004; *MIS Quarterly*, 2013), while the renewed human geographical discussion highlights (Sayer 2013; Pratt 2013) that there is still ample scope to produce knowledge through critical realist engagements.

In contrast to human geography and sociology, archaeology has steered clear of broader engagements with critical realism. Sandra Wallace's (2011) *Contradictions of Archaeological Theory* appears a first notable exception. Human geographical discourse ties crit-ical realism to postmodernist critique, and to the development of social scientific methods and emancipatory knowledge (Sayer 1993, 2000; Pratt 1995; Yeung 1997). It seems too early to tell whether Wallace's critical realist corrective of archaeological theory will spur on development distinct from relational, new material, and non-representational theory (cf. Alberti 2016), but it certainly presents an opportune match.

The archaeological discipline has been caught in post-modern (and possibly what is sometimes called 'post-post-modern') tribulations for a few decades, taking a relativist stance of acceptance (Fahlander 2012). This appears to have grown out of 'processualist' concerns with the particular. Communicating dispersed ideas without overarching epistemology was aptly dubbed 'the tolerance trap' by Wiseman (2011; *sensu* Dervin 1993). Bintliff & Pearce's (2011) poignant title alludes to a 'death' of theory, but actually shows how tolerance leads to the some-what uncritical embrace of theoretical eclecticism (see Vis 2012). So, archaeological theory and associated practice mirrors the situation of relativism and irrealism in the social sciences (Groff 2004; Byers 2012; also Sayer 1993); indeed a time ripe for an intervention. In archaeology

---

1. This discussion instigated by Cox (2013a) is particular to scientific conduct from a capitalist perspective. Vis (2010) shows how prevalent assumptions about capital combined with the subjective motivation to act (economically) challenge mechanisms assumed by Cox (2013a) without his historical materialist explanations for change. The conception of the acting subject (Vis 2010) is much closer to premises in this research. In turn, the comparative aims pursued here have nothing to gain by adopting a prescriptive capitalist view of societies. Change is pro-pelled by the mismatch of expectation and outcome due to inescapable limited knowledge of reality (cf. Vis 2010), added to everyday resistance in subjective participation in society's imposed spiel and accumulative experience of this (cf. Vis 2009), despite the deceptive con-formism of much human action.

the theoretical preoccupation with paradigmatic discourses and metaphysics (cf. Bentley & Maschner 2009b; Bintliff & Pearce 2011; Fahlander 2012) is detaining the discussion on how we actually proceed to work with archaeological material *sensu* Smith's (2011a) empirical theory. Wallace's (2011) plea is welcome. She argues how archaeology can be opened to a more comprehensive alternative to counterproductive postmodern tendencies beyond their useful critiques (e.g. Sayer 1993; Fahlander 2012) within a critical philosophy of science, which directly engages with empirical information.

Wallace's (2011) efforts to correct archaeology's position as a social science result from recognising archaeology's fallacies and contradictions stemming from development in a split discipline: empirically bound with social interpretive aims. Deeper engagement with her philosophical critique will not serve the methodological programme of this research. Instead, I deem it more productive to explain how tenets of critical realism have facilitated the methodological development process.

Critical realism has proven itself to be particularly strong at constructively bridging the divide between conceptual and empirical scientific conduct. This makes archaeology's material nature a suitable fit for the operationalisation of critical realist notions of knowledge creation. Acknowledging that methodologically the inhabited built environment only serves as an object of study translated into a material record indeed supports the suggestion for archaeology's return to its material foundations (Webmoor 2007), though care should be taken to not recreate the fallacies addressed by Wallace (2011).

Materiality

There have been long and avid debates on the nature of space in human geography and social sciences (e.g. Blaut 1961; Giddens 1984; Sayer 1985; Granö 1997; Blake 2002; Jessop et al. 2008; M. Jones 2009), and more recently in the humanities (Arnade et al. 2002; Griffiths 2013). Despite this, active engagement with its material properties – the matter that shapes space – is strangely subdued. Archaeology is the discipline with most structural traction on the purview of materiality. However, its potential purchase to inform other disciplines of materiality's importance in spatial debates is arguably crumbling under the influence of relational and imagined (constructivist) approaches to thinking space (see Blake 2002). Materiality is not completely absent from human geography, however. This is shown by research concerned with 'repopulating' the world inhabited by humans with the things in our everyday lives (e.g. Jackson 2000; Anderson & Tolia-Kelly 2004).

It is easily recognised that giving material culture a structural position in social and cultural geography resonates well with archaeological adaptations of Actor Network Theory (ANT) into 'symmetrical archaeology' (e.g. Webmoor & Witmore 2008).[2] ANT leads suggestions to take full account of a 'more-than-human world' to incorporate the technical intricacies of human life (e.g. Whatmore 2006). On a landscape scale, allowing a role for material features in the experience of landscape leads to subjective geographical research (e.g. Wylie 2005) which almost replicates what has come to be known as 'archaeological phenomenology' (Tilley 1994). This relates to research on sensory responses and making sense of objects' materiality in making place in human geography (e.g. Hetherington 2003). The affective dimension of the landscape as restricting and enabling of movement across (designed) spaces with technological objects is studied with more pragmatic aims (e.g. Bissell 2009). Usually, however, these approaches appear to rely on the nonhuman elements of the life-world to be encountered as already constituted objects (cf. Hinchcliffe 2003), despite claims towards a more dialectic understanding (e.g. Wylie 2005).

As Anderson & Tolia-Kelly (2004) show, geographers are clearly undecided and still debating the epistemological position of the material. It is virtually always framed in immediately meaningful (i.e. produced, as in the Lefebvrian sense of space (Lefebvre 1991)) cultural and political perspectives. Meaningful production of space largely prevents the material from speaking for itself, despite acknowledging its 'capacities and effects'. The integral perspective on materiality and what it does in the social (cf. Anderson & Tolia-Kelly 2004) is a useful vantage point. Yet, it achieves little beyond reacquainting geographical accounts with the mass or matter involved in human–nonhuman relational accounts of the world.

Amidst current attention on materiality in the form of connectivity and relations in performance, choreographical, embodiment and non-representational oriented geographies (see Anderson & Tolia-Kelly 2004; Anderson & Wylie 2009), Rose & Wylie (2006: 477) express an

2. Actor Network Theory, originating from Science and Technology Studies (STS), proposes that nonhuman objects can partake in social systems, which are envisaged as connected-up networks. It studies relations as simultaneously material (things) and semiotic (conceptual), hence *symmetrical* archaeology. While I pursue a similar position, the conceptualisations in Chapters 4 and 5 are differently nuanced, as is my position on permitting nonhuman objects agency (see below).

opinion derived from landscape geographies which is arguably most susceptible to an approach giving the material a more active voice.

> [L]andscape is entanglement. [...] But we still have the feeling that, here, a certain topographical richness is being sacrificed for the sake of topological complexity. [...] And the result, it can be argued, is a sort of ontological overflattening. [...] To put this another way, we are left with a topology without topography – a surface without relief, contour, or morphology.

ANT adaptations in archaeology run that same risk of 'ontological flattening'. Materiality has been criticised for being poorly defined and not taking the physical matter of materials into account at all (Ingold 2007). Archaeological discussions on materiality, and Ingold's (2007, 2008a, 2008b) rather physically entangled proposals of the fluxes of which the world consists (cf. Rose & Wylie (2006) on human and non-human processes), lead to propositions for ontological mixtures on the one hand (Webmoor & Witmore 2008) and the world as a meshwork (Ingold 2008a, 2008b, 2011) on the other. The logical extreme of these 'worldviews' makes it increasingly impossible to study any object or category. Things end up being defined as indistinguishable; mixtures and entanglements of one and the other. Yet, due to the nature of archaeology's exclusively material evidence, the longstanding practice of landscape archaeology (see David & Thomas 2008) can never be completely devoid of the material properties, geometry, substance, morphology, etc. These are inherently part of the topologies we draw from them. Contrary to cultural geography, archaeology cannot choose not to be an empirical science (cf. Anderson & Wylie 2009; Fletcher 2004).

The material

Critical realism's appropriated prerogative to direct conventional social scientific methodologies may overlook the potential it holds for a social science on the basis of material evidence, as conducted in archaeology. Logically, critical realist archaeology cannot go without an initial recording of material properties in order to make inferences on the role these properties played in the social. Wallace (2011) recognises the important contribution operationalising the material could make to critical realism and, vice versa, on that basis the contribution of critical realism to archaeological thought. Fragmentation in archaeological theorising has been addressed in numerous publications (e.g. Hegmon 2003; Fogelin 2007; Webmoor 2007; Bentley & Maschner 2009b; Bintliff & Pearce 2011). Wallace (2011) constructs a strong argument for how critical realism as a philosophy of science can help overcome the uncritical plurality in archaeological theory. My interest is not with philosophical critique and debate, but with her suggestion that, following critical realist ideas, the way forward could consist of the construction of *an ontology of the material as an emergent entity*. Wallace (2011) suggests that such an ontology could resolve the contradictions in the theoretical underpinnings of archaeology's paradigms of processualism, post-processualism and, recently, the proposition of ANT inspired 'symmetrical archaeology' (see Webmoor 2007).

Critical realism does not propagate a grand theory, but facilitates the development of disciplinary theory and epistemology. Wallace (2011) points out that although critical realism does not engage with materiality as it features in the archaeological discipline (and is employed in my interdisciplinary endeavour), its philosophical role facilitates the building of archaeological theories of the material. Social scientific and human geographical applications of critical realism to research methods emphasise conventional social scientific qualitative analysis and engagements with live subjects (see Pratt 1995; Yeung 1997; Sayer 2000). Somewhat ironically, what could be called a 'material turn' in archaeological theorising is inspired by relational thinking of similar pedigree as described above for human geography (e.g. Ingold 2007; Webmoor & Witmore 2008; Fahlander 2012). Evidently material is at the basis of the discipline regardless, perhaps contrary to human geography. Yet, Wallace (2011) shows that relational influences similar to human geography keep the proposal of symmetrical archaeology from a successful treatment of the material as active and constitutive in its epistemology, because of the lack of an ontological status.

In symmetrical archaeological conduct, Wallace (2011: 96–97) remarks:

> Ontology becomes meaningless as this version [of reality] encompasses everything in an undecipherable mish-mash [...]. The amalgamation of all these into an undifferentiated whole would obviate the possibility of understanding the deep underlying workings of reality [...]. The logical problem of dichotomisation is therefore solved, but the denial of the ontological reality of the

material remains. Although symmetrical archaeology claims to take into account relationality, particularly between people and things, the logical extension of a theory of conflation is that relationality becomes untenable. If there are no separate ontological categories, there is nothing that can be related. Relationality becomes one-dimensional, as it refers only to the condition of the ontological mixture of reality.

The ontological mixture of symmetrical archaeology is a counterproductive exaggeration. In order to give materiality a constitutive place in human and social life it is not necessary to equate the material and the social. It suffices to structurally take into account that the material (and its properties) is an inherent part of human and social life. At the same time it is necessary to allow for ontological categories of the material in order to study human phenomena through material records.

'The characterisation of the material as a reflection of the social is the key error of current theorising [...]. The material is seen as a distilling or concretisation of abstract and non-physical ideas into a solid form that can then be observed and described by archaeologists' (Wallace 2011: 121). In this work, I use the concept of materialisation when discussing the built environment (see Chapter 3; also Vis 2009): physical transformation or modification is the concretisation induced by interaction and conceptual thought. A decision and idea, desire or expectation has to precede action. However, this does not remove causal agency from the material itself. Materialisation is never a complete translation, and always a transformation carried out within the affordances of the material properties previously extant. Although material cannot 'act' or 'perform agency' in the human and symmetrical sense, the *properties of its presence have restricting and enabling causal powers*. Therefore, the material necessarily imparts an influence when acted upon as emplaced within the human life-world. The resultant material shapes and features, however, are distinct in that they bear the direct evidence of human engagement with the physical properties of the world, and therefore permit more elaborate interpretive analyses.

The intentions of the performed human and social interactions constituting the inhabitation of the world have, after all, led to a material presence, however incomplete its exact expression of those intentions and relations might be. The effects of the materialisation and the subsequent role of its presence in the human and social life-world can successfully be studied as dialectic relations. 'To acknowledge only effects is limiting in its actualism and does not represent the complete range of agentive properties of the material, especially the basic onto-logical nature of the material that enables it to be an *agent without intent*' (Wallace 2011: 124, emphasis added; developed from Fletcher's (2004) material as 'actor without intent'[3]). Similarly, in social theory, the dialectics of individual-structure and human-material include both the forming or creation of structure/material and the being formed by structure/material (Wallace 2011; Archer 1995). Human beings are emplaced in a material world, which features properties that would exist without human presence also (cf. the furnished world (Gibson 1979) in flux (Ingold 2008a)). The causal powers of these properties are agency without intent (Wallace 2011), which as such can enter into human social interactions.

The agency without intent sets material ontologically apart from humans, who possess intentional agency as an emergent quality. 'One of the theoretical strengths of critical realism is the recognition that actualised or empirical events do not constitute all of reality. A deeper reality of potential or unactualised powers exists. The ontological nature of things or people include the ability, whether realised or not, to "do" certain things as a result of their essential powers and possibilities' (Wallace 2011: 129). This level of understanding is where the interpretive power within the methodology based on the material record that I develop here should be sought. Accepting the built environment as a material human creation further adds the understanding of its existence as an outcome of actions. These actions themselves are part of the same processes of settling and inhabitation that would be ongoing (dialectically) in the empirical social reality of continued inhabitation and development of that built environment.

Material information on the built environment itself only permits comments on, and analysis of, what actually occurred as that which has been realised in its construction (materialisation), but not what occurred without affecting the material nature of the built environment. The role and abilities of the material presence of the built environment when encountered and engaged with in human interactions are thus the core of investigation here. This viewpoint does not withstand the ontological reality of the built environment's physicality without human relations.

---

3. '[T]he material possesses pattern in its own right, has the effect of constraining options and creating friction, and is also potentially able to undermine viable social life[.] The material is then an "actor without intent" with which people try to engage. This would create a dynamic in which the inertial and abrasive impact of the material framework on community life is a key agency in the long-term outcomes we see in the archaeological record. [... This] would be a proper construct of archaeological theory' (Fletcher 2004: 111–112).

Though, insofar as social science aims to understand the social, my methodology will be restricted to the potential the built environment holds for human and social relations, and their mutually developmental relationship.

The physicality which imbues the material its ontological properties and agency pre-existed human interaction, which is where – from processes of modification and transformation – the material emerged. This is no different from the critical realist argument that the emergent entities of human beings and societies 'must obey the laws of physics, chemistry and biology, but as [they are] emergent [they] will also exhibit properties that cannot be explained by the natural sciences' (Wallace 2011: 148). This concurs with my argument that social science may follow an epistemology that is intrinsically different from natural scientific and positivist standards. This intrinsic difference originates from a scientific conduct regarding members of the same species studying themselves. From this perspective different (internal) kinds of understandings can be reached (see Vis 2009). This assertion incorporates the intersubjective (though necessarily incomplete) understanding that results from experiential knowledge we all hold about our (inter)actions with the physicality of the world (cf. Hägerstrand 1984; Yeung 1997).

As an emergent phenomenon (entity) time-space, human interaction and the physicality of material are internally related as that which is materialised, containing its own causal mechanisms and powers (cf. Wallace 2011: 153). This resonates with the inherent link between the construction of built environments and the formation of society along the constitutive axes of time, human action and human space (Vis 2009). Although, maintaining the same logic, not all aspects of the social can become known by its material (i.e. physical matter) constituents because materialisation is neither complete nor ubiquitous transformation.[4] 'The artefact as observed and recorded by an archaeologist is a physical element of an absent past. The analysis of the object in context can therefore lead to an understanding of the absent social and material existents whose interaction resulted in the presence of the artefact in the archaeological record' (Wallace 2011: 131). Hägerstrand's (1984: 377) suggestion of approaching things within a 'diorama' leads him to the

---

4. This incompleteness can be recognised in the social as an entity-concept (see later in this chapter) and the fact that the nature of investigation of the social, tied to the outcomes of actions and communications, is of a different nature than psychology as inner workings and feelings (cf. Vis 2010 on the outcome of action). The idea of the entity-concept resonates well with the logic of emergence, as it conveys particular causal powers which are associated with the presupposed irreducibility to its constituents.

logical conclusion that archaeologists need to try and fill out a complete story of a 'once living context' by interpreting remnants of that continuum. In other words, because the material is an emergent entity the possibility for better understanding is opened by studying aspects of it.

The material as an emergent concept, however, should not be mistaken for a reproductive (or replicative) constant. As I argued previously (Vis 2009), coupling the time-geographical idea of unique position and situation along life-paths (Hägerstrand 1970, 1975; Pred 1977, 1981) with De Certeau's (1988) broad notion of performed resistance in the practices of everyday life is the driver for change (even when outcomes of action may look conformist). To this Wallace (2011: 124) adds: 'the conditions for intentional emancipatory change exist in the potential development of a consciousness of the constraining role of the material'. Thus, socially speaking, the inhabitation of the built environment makes change a logical and necessary (inescapable) occurrence, whilst from the physical processes seen as 'agency without intent' (Wallace 2011) change grows more complex.

The material inhabited built environment

Positioning 'the material' as an emergent entity is the essence of Wallace's (2011) resolution to overcoming contradiction in archaeological theory. She concludes that the development of a full ontology of the material is needed to inform future research. Likewise, human geography is in need of an appropriate ontology of the material. It is beyond my current scope, however, to formulate a comprehensive material ontology. Nonetheless, this work relies heavily on seeing the material as an emergent entity (in addition to human beings as an emergent entity) and acknowledges its much wider relevance. In fact, the inhabited built environment could serve as an *ontological category* within the material. The exact information and conceptual understanding conveyed by the notion of the inhabited built environment will be clarified. However, this is not the place to explain how this notion differs from other potential ontological categories of the material.

Accepting the inhabited built environment's material nature, it becomes possible to take *the properties of the material articulation of spatial subdivisions* (Chapter 4 elaborates) of built environment configurations as a single information source on the human phenomenon of urban inhabitation. These properties can be studied in necessary relation to the social it is inhabited and developed by, while the physicality of the built environment itself remains independent of its inhabitation. So, this ontological category becomes determined by the consequences of the material as an emergent entity. A critical realist assessment demonstrates how its emergence productively combines conceptual and empirical reasoning. Taken as material evidence of space (Chapter 4), this offers opportunities and limitations to interpreting something that is not or, no longer, present to be observed. As a consequence, such evidence in the contemporary world becomes a candidate for an archaeology of the present. The Winchester test case presented in Chapter 7 will affirm this possibility. Indeed, basic materiality creates the principle for a comparative starting point to improve our understanding of this substantive domain through research.

The *absence* of *live subjects* and communication to observe directly delimits the interpretive reach in terms of the experiential and developmental potentialities *afforded by the physicality* of the *empirical material*. Pursuing social scientific aims requires viewing the material as if it were still part of a 'live' process of inhabitation (as usual in empirical social scientific observation). It could thus be said that comparing inhabited built-environments-based material evidence is delimited by Schiffer's (1987) c-transforms, which shape its final material presence (and not the n-transforms, i.e. the independence of physicality).[5] The focus lies on the stages of material development – including the final placement or deposit of spatial-material compositions – as bearing witness to the processes that were once going on thanks to the presence of the social. The social is currently absent or at least absent from our material evidence. Still, one should remain mindful of the physical processes within the material that are external to the human processes of interest (cf. Hägerstrand 1984).

The phenomenon of the inhabited built environment should be seen as a selective (by practice and data), contextual (by an understanding of the urban), immobile (as opposed to moveable artefacts) evidential category of the ontology of the material. This category becomes the substantive domain that this research investigates, requiring its own epistemology, ontology and methods. Although Chapter 1 situates this study within the realm of social interpretive urban studies, it becomes apparent that the inhabited built environment forms a specific social, spatial and especially material object of research of each particular urban context. The logical conclusion of critical realist ontological reasoning should

---

5. C-transforms and n-transforms refer to the cultural and noncultural processes, whereby the systemic context of societies in the material (physical) world is converted into the archaeological context of artefacts: i.e. site formation processes.

be able to determine whether cities, an everyday or commonplace category (Sayer 1985), make sense as a separate emergent entity. That is, do cities indeed have a distinct set of (material, social, and spatial) causal powers? Answering this question is to be aspired to in the future. It would explain how cities (as built environments) are validated as an intrinsically separate object of study. Regardless, presuming such validation is the vantage point assumed by the followers of the *Eigenlogik* of cities (Zimmermann 2012; Löw 2013).

My working definition of cities as urban life (Chapter 1) may offer a building block towards specifying a satisfactory answer. Along the way, the methodology formulated in this book will instead enable the assessment and identification of (emergent) properties and processes with regard to the built environment, which constitute any particular city as an entity in its own right. Subsequent comparative analysis could pull out regularities in inhabited built environment constituents that are shared across cities. It is not pre-given that the inhabited built environment contains aspects of properties that may render cities unique entities.

Embedding the research process

We now have established the ontologically material position of the inhabited built environment in terms of critical realism, which creates the empirical anchor, *sensu* archaeology. The remainder of this chapter will discuss which tenets of critical realism, 'as a philosophical argument about the ontology of reality' (Yeung 1997: 54), will be informing the epistemology and method behind my programme of methodological development. Following this research process will not only lead to a rigorous theoretical framework elucidating and exposing the inhabited (urban) built environment, but eventually allows the identification of analytical units within that phenomenon that open up routes for investigation. Consequently, a process to guide the operationalisation of such analytical units into the empirical reality of research practice is required.

Generally speaking, this research process entails the progression from selecting a broad phenomenon of interest to identification of a substantive domain of which a specified knowledge is desired. Subsequently, the route to producing such knowledge requires the precise conceptualisation of that substantive domain, and the recognition of how to study this domain appropriately. Inevitably, the empirical operationalisation will be limited to constructing knowledge that is within the scope of these initial conceptualisations. Alternative knowledge creation would require its own appropriate concepts and an ontology commensurate with that perspective. However, within a substantive domain these knowledges should always be complementary rather than a contradictory plurality, unless flaws in the initial conceptualisation of the substantive domain can be identified. As knowledge is inevitably an incomplete version of external reality, *any understanding reached is not a conclusion but a hypothesis*. The endurance of knowledge is determined by its practical adequacy (e.g. applied to emancipate and to broaden contexts critically).

This comprehensive view of the scientific process makes clear that the successful linkage between the conceptual and the empirical is paramount. This is where critical realism's meta-ideas about knowledge creation can really help and inform a path towards a constructive research process and method. So far in the process, I committed to contribute to the understanding of the everyday notion of urban life as an intensive, transformative settlement practice within a particular locus as a long-term phenomenon through comparative research. The inhabited built environment was conceptualised as the substantive domain consistently evidencing the everyday encounter and recognition of cities as a complex of physical spaces constructed by humans. Furthermore, the material nature of this substantive domain has been made explicit through Wallace's (2011) critical realist characterisation of the material as an emergent entity. Hägerstrand (1984) already acknowledged that such selection from a greater interconnected whole is an unavoidable part of geographical research processes, which is commensurate with a critical realist starting point of research on social phenomena (cf. Pratt 1995; Yeung 1997).

The first step will therefore have to consist of a conceptualisation of the presence of the inhabited built environment. In effect, this forms a theoretical understanding of logical coherence and causal necessity that will be assumed as a broad and true framework for the entire substantive domain. As the notions of the material as an emergent entity and the inhabited built environment are new, this theory consists not so much of an immanently critical review (cf. Yeung 1997), but of an immanently critical formulation of reasoning. This formulation is itself logically susceptible to critical realism's immanent critique. Therefore, following Sayer (1981), the internal realistic tendency expressed at the beginning of this chapter is vulnerable to immanent critique and empirical discoveries, on the basis of which it can be corrected.

While I concede that separate elements of the social processes captured in my broad comparative urban framework could be suitable objects of empirical enquiry themselves – in fact, many of them are, e.g. the study of planning policy and urban politics – the grand, long-term and non-society specific or culturally normative scope of comparative research would not directly benefit from concerns with particular time-space specific engagements. Direct concerns with intrinsic time-space specificity deteriorates comparative applicability (cf. Scott & Storper 2015; Peck 2015). Effectively, my initial efforts resemble the kind of grand theory or high theoretical order that Smith (2011a) appears to forego in favour of 'empirical theories' (cf. Ellen 2010 on theoretical hierarchy).

For current purposes, however, the philosophical embedding of the epistemology requires such meta-theory in order to indicate how to construct conceptualisations that can be linked to the empirical evidence. This empirical evidence can then be studied within that theoretical framework, whilst being explicit about the limitations of the perspective taken. So, although social phenomena are intrinsically meaningful (see Sayer 2000), empirical evidence on those phenomena (like the built environment) is not intrinsically meaningful in order to infer the absent social processes without such theoretical framework. My suggestion is that the subsequent empirical conceptualisation could be regarded as one of Smith's empirical urban theories in the sociological middle range (Smith 2011a; see also Trigger (1989) for a similar theoretical proposal). In one sense this will lead to a low-level thick description.

The critical realist demand for immanent critique here holds that a fundamental theoretical framework is first constructed which departs from the existential stance of 'human being-in-the-world'. Chapter 3 will deliberately keep this on a general level of human perception and experience, closing in on the key causal mechanisms (see Fig. 2.1) of our encountering and inhabiting the world. In doing so, a temporal processive perspective is installed instead of concepts as isolated conditional statements (which include e.g. the notion of man's embodiment or the importance of sensory perception in specific scenarios). This research perspective offers investigative opportunities that are highly comparable to Tilly's (2008: 2–20) historically sensitive relational realism. A focus on causal processes results in constitutive theory (cf. Vis 2009). The idea of constitutive theory in the present context is

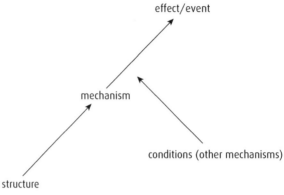

Fig. 2.1 The critical realist view of causation.

The critical realist view of causation, notwithstanding the roles played by historically time-space specific contingencies in determining the exact outcome. (Image source: Sayer 2000: 15, reproduced by kind permission of Andrew Sayer).

inspired by Schütz's (1967) constitutive adaptation of phenomenology, which enables a sociology of the everyday on the basis of how we come to know the world. The temporality of contiguous processes captured in constitutive theory is important to invite theorising that engages with the long-term.

Spatial (in)dependence

Not even the inhabited built environment as a concrete object of study can be treated comprehensively within the limitations of a single research project, *sensu* Sayer (1981: 7; original emphasis).

> [I]n order to understand this combination [of all relations], we normally have to isolate each element in thought first, even though they do not and sometimes could not exist in isolation in reality. It's important to note that whether the concrete is observable (and hence an empirical object for us) is contingent (i.e. neither necessary nor impossible). *The concepts 'concrete' and 'empirical' are not equivalent.*

This has bearing on the city as a commonplace notion rather than being fully understood, as well as the limitations of the scientific process despite Hägerstrand's diorama. Our limitation here is largely due to selecting a specified information source from a consistently observable occurrence: the built environment.

Built environment's most immediate information source is the spatial composition which is caused by its material properties (see Chapter 1). 'Matter *always* necessarily has spatial extention [*sic*] and spatial relations only exist through objects, of whatever kind. To the best of our knowledge, empty space or spaceless matter are physical impossibilities' (Sayer 1985: 52; original emphasis). In other words, our objectives are delimited by the 'difference that space makes' (cf. Sayer 1985). More particularly the research process will have to build an ontology of empirically applicable concepts. Altogether these concepts must express the causal powers of the properties of the materiality that compose spaces within the built environment 'as it happens' in inhabitation and development. (Recognising that the built environment consists of multiple spaces directly creates a focus on their separation, which is a necessary condition for spaces to exist (see Chapter 4).) Sayer (1985: 54) first asserts that '[a]bstract social theory need only consider space insofar as necessary properties of objects are involved, and this does not amount to very much'. We, however, must take full account of his continuation: 'It must acknowledge that all matter has spatial extension and hence that processes do not take place on the head of a pin and that no two objects can occupy the same (relative) place at the same time'. Therefore, in the ontological abstraction of the built environment our focus will be on the causal powers of the *spatial dependence* (Sayer 2000) of interaction and subsequent development (physical transformation) opportunities.

Logically, this spatial dependence is most strongly expressed in the restrictions and impossibilities created by the most durable and pervasive structures. In the materiality of cities that is the built environment. In terms of the availability of data this also ensures the relative ubiquity of cases. Sayer (2000: 137) argues: 'structures which are less durable (for example, cultural forms) are too influenced by geohistorical contexts for their explanation to be divorced from those settings'. Here the distinction should be made between the large degree to which what actually occurred is contingent upon spatial structures or spatially *independent* (flexible) (Sayer 2000), and the fact that whatever occurs in space is still accommodated by whatever structure space is comprised of.

Contestation of the material properties encountered is inseparable from its part in the occurrence of social relations and any physical transformations (cf. De Certeau's resistance as applied to change previously). The necessity of human encounter for materialising modification and transformation, as well as continued occupation, make the role of the material presence of the built environment a necessary causal power. Yet, material presence alone cannot account for the full causation of change from one developmental stage to another.

Furthermore, it is historically contingent which causal powers have played a role in stages of development and the restricting and enabling of interaction (see Pred's (1984, 1986) time-geographical development of systems theory in a spatial world). Yet, it is a necessity that the material presence will have had a role. Sayer (1985) explains that it is not the empirical regularity or universalism that makes events and occurrences a law, but their necessity as mechanisms. Yeung (1997: 57) says: 'It should not be expected that these abstract causal mechanisms can explain events directly without any need for empirical research into the contingency of the concrete.' Finally, in Sayer's (2000: 138) words: 'Abstraction identifies the necessary conditions of existence of phenomena, but that is different from showing how actual instances of them come into being.' In terms of the built environment these statements mean that it may be contingent which constituent element is constructed, but when it occurs it becomes a necessary constituent of interactions (events) in that locus.

In continuation, 'what theory provides us with is an understanding of the concrete by means of abstract concepts denoting its *determinations*' (Sayer 1981: 9; original emphasis). Abstractions in the theoretical framework imminently presented (Chapter 3) contain an awareness of phenomena that are not further separated and examined. For example, by assuming the existence of human beings, their biological, chemical and physical premises are not questioned. And, by restricting ourselves to that which occurred, although not what actually happened *in* space or cities (see also Chapter 6), the cognitive psychology, emotions and decision-making processes that lead to the outcomes represented by our evidence are not examined. It will thus be assumed that human beings make decisions to act in an ordinally rational way,[6] in respect of their unique position and situation with the expectation to improve it (Von Mises 1998; Vis 2010). But, why this position and situation arises from individuals' specific (historical) conditions is not questioned. Nor will a

---

6. This should not be confused for normative rationality in actors. The unique position and situation of individuals inhibit a complete understanding of their motivations, nor can their motivations ever be judged on their rationality.

comprehensive aetiology of society (e.g. Giddens 1984; Archer 1995) be provided as a constitutive explanation (more detail on my view on 'society' can be found in Vis 2009). Instead, I will use a rudimentary abstraction (understanding) of 'the social', which originated as an implicit notion before my engagement with critical realism. This abstraction holds that 'the social' concerns everything that requires and emerges out of the co-presence of more than one person.

The social

The collective adjective 'social' is often indiscriminately used to pertain to a large variety of societal understandings, which are uncritically presented as distinct. This regards what could be called *realms* of the social, such as the cultural, class stratification, politics, economics, religion, etc. Researchers usually have a certain encultured experiential knowledge about these terms, because we encounter them in our own lives. In scientific discourse these terms also describe disciplinary fields. Yet, in much social research they are used as an under-defined concept similar to Sayer's (1985, 2000) layman's and everyday concepts (cf. Fletcher's (2004) concern that generally familiar assumptions could be an inadequate basis for understanding).

The fact that there is no thorough understanding of what each of these realms entails remains concealed, despite creating a sense of general agreement over what they are as categories. One might be inclined to suggest that such categories are the constituents of the social – the social being an overarching term – but it seems to me that instead they are better regarded as potential foundations of ontological categories of the emergent entity of society. However, the meaningful narratives these categories refer to are contingent upon the social, whereas our subject of methodological development here concerns the social (interaction) opportunities that are spatial-materially afforded.

This means that the conceptualisations presented in continuation will not make an attempt at claiming to uncover meaning within the confines of such 'societal realms' in particular. Instead, the conceptualisations are significant in general for all such realms at once. Therefore, the term 'social', when used throughout this book, should be seen as an inseparable aggregate: an entity-concept (see note 4 above; cf. Vis 2010). We know of this entity-concept that all such realms may have a part to play, but we cannot distinguish the exact influence of any one.

Moreover, the theoretical embedding of our empirical information source (i.e. the spatial morphology of the built environment) will not support access to such interpretations based on a necessary connection. Imagine the construction of a wall. Labour and economy, power claims over what is being walled, a social or political sanctioning decision, socio-cultural and aesthetic norms and values may all be at play at once (and to varying overlapping degrees) in how this wall is placed and shaped, as well as the consequential developmental role it plays. By the material presence of the wall's morphology alone we cannot separate out these aspects of the social. In other words, for the purposes of this methodological effort, the potential differences between societal realms do not exist, nor is the potential for identifying such differences the subject of subsequent investigative efforts.

Nonetheless, the contributions of these respective realms are always implicitly included in any consideration of social relations and interaction. Thus, for present purposes we must subscribe to the assertion that *the social is knowable as an entity of interactional outcomes of which the composition of built environments forms part*. We accept that *the lack of discrete separation puts each societal realm beyond the reach of this research process*. As a consequence, this methodology's interpretive contributions trade persuasive meaningful narratives for more rudimentary scrutiny of the causal conditions that are created and characterised by mechanistic elements (using Sayer's (2000) explanation of historical interpretation, cf. Tilly's (2008: 2–20) relational realism).

Iterative abstraction

Iterative abstraction and grounded theory are two typical methodological pointers in critical realist research (Yeung 1997; Sayer 2000), and actually provide the best results when used in conjunction. The goal is 'to discover and conceptualise generative mechanisms' (Yeung 1997: 58) by a process of abstraction, closing in on the essential causal power of objects in relation to a concrete phenomenon and helping to distinguish the necessary from the contingent relations between them. When exercising this process here, the aim is to rationally abstract the causal powers of the material presence of the built environment's spatial morphology in the social processes it partakes in. Or, put differently, the spatial dependence of what is afforded by the causal mechanisms in relation to the built environment's spatial morphology (here: 'boundary operations', see Chapter 5 and onwards). The process of abstraction therefore needs to presuppose the object of study, which is the inhabited built environment, recorded as spatial morphology. Simultaneously, it should be recognised that abstraction can only elucidate the concrete phenomenon partially (cf. Yeung 1997). In our methodological journey there are several stages of abstraction.

The first formulates the immanently critical constitutive theory, which itself expresses the underlying understanding of the causal mechanisms leading to the development of inhabited built environments as an effect or outcome. On that basis, iterative abstraction and grounded theorising can be initiated to discover the constitutive elements of material transformation shaping the built environment for inhabitation. An additional exercise of abstraction aims to better understand the abstract representation of spatial data derived from an empirical reality. Together these abstractions provide the epistemological principles that determine what we could come to know by studying this data. Versions of these latter two abstractions were embarked on at an early stage before streamlining their structure following a critical realist interjection.

In iterative abstraction – applied here with the aim to formulate ontological elements redescribing and defining the inhabited built environment's spatial morphology – the collection of unexpected empirical evidence may give cause to revise or reaffirm the initial abstractions made. Although presented by Yeung (1997) as separate instances of typical methodological implementations of critical realism, this work's progressive structure is not served by the formal distinction between iterative abstraction and grounded theory. The process of *retroduction*, *sensu* Bhaskar (moving from describing a phenomenon to its generative aspects and conditions), which underlies the process of iterative abstraction, here also serves to elucidate the spatial data acquired from the empirical reality of cases. This, in turn, ensures that the iterative abstraction towards the elements of an inhabited built environment ontology does not occur in a vacuum according to the requirements of critical realist grounded theory (see Yeung 1997, for more detail).

Key criteria for successful abstraction (uncovering the real essence) consist of functional equivalence (causal powers) and plausibility (constituent of another knowable entity) of each element defined. The constitutive theory should therefore indicate the mechanism that holds *ontological primacy* in the conceptualisation (Chapter 5). At the same time, iterative abstraction contains the possibility of induction as necessary relations can be recognised from the outcomes of actions (cf. Yeung 1997). Minor examples of this will be revealed in the conceptualisation of the inhabited built environment.

Following the process of iterative abstraction, an ontology of empirically applicable concepts is formulated. This conceptualisation remains practically adequate for as long as these concepts can be positively and exclusively identified in the empirical evidence. This latter, applied, aspect of the process rather looks like grounded theory as described by Yeung (1997). Having established a theoretical framework for the object of interest, and conceptualised what of the spatial-material empirical reality is represented and thus what can be known from the data, it can be presupposed that the abstract concepts are empirically recognisable in the data. It should be noted here that although Pratt (1995) and Yeung (1997) claim that phenomenology is *antithetical* to critical realism, the theorising within this project will *not* concur with that assertion.

The empirical induction (from a situated perspective) of which some phenomenological research suffers (cf. the individualistic archaeological phenomenology) should be avoided. This kind of culturally embedded or historically contextual (often assumedly commonsensical) empiricism causes conflation, as can be seen in Lynch's (1981) example of the category of a church. It obstructs understanding of the concrete in which everything has a part. Church concerns a conflation of space, material, function and performance and, depending on the question of contingency and necessity, obscures the difference between spatial dependence and independence. This is what iterative abstraction attempts to avoid. However, as mentioned before, the focus on causality driving iterative abstraction fits well with the *constitutive* branch of phenomenology as devised by Schütz (1967), which in itself may be able to overcome philosophical disparity with the suggestion of a similar epistemology. Regardless of philosophical origin, the importance of methods 'cannot be exercised unless they are supported by strong philosophical claims at the ontological and epistemological levels' (Yeung 1997: 55). Here, a convergence of phenomenological ideas about knowledge production with philosophical ideas about the critical realist scientific process emerges.

The nature of the next step, the operationalisation (empirical analysis) of the conceptual stages (realist analysis) (see Sayer 2000), is suggested by Sayer's (1981: 9–10) following argument:

> Good or 'rational' abstractions should isolate necessary relationships. The concrete, as a unity of diverse determinations, is a combination of several necessary relationships, but the form of the combination is contingent, and *therefore only determinable through empirical research. As such, its form cannot be assumed to*

have already been 'taken up' into the theoretical framework in the same way that the nature of the abstract can. [...] we simply have to go and find out through theoretically-informed empirical research [original emphasis].

Sayer's (1979) own classic critique of urban modelling as a planning solution concurs with this. The consequence is that the final stages of methodological development in this book are dedicated to an exploration of the characteristics of the identified abstract concepts in cases of empirical evidence, to get to know the contingent regularities and variation in the way they are related in the whole. Only from this exploration can something be said about the ontology of a particular unique city by means of its inhabited built environment.

Exploration is little more than observing reorganised data. 'It is now widely recognised that observation is not theory-neutral but theory-laden, and that theory does not merely "order facts" but makes claims about the nature of its object. So, in evaluating observations we are also assessing particular theoretical concepts and existential claims' (Sayer 1981: 6). Despite the prevalence of qualitative critical realist research, it is conceded that quantitative methods 'are particularly useful to establish the empirical regularities between objects. Although these concrete regularities are not causal relations, they can inform the abstraction of causal mechanisms. Quantitative methods are also useful in drawing attention to the external and contingent relations between objects' (Yeung 1997: 57). The latter statement emphasises the relevance of quantitative methods for guiding correlative investigations in conjunction with 'lower order' concepts (see Chapter 6 on space syntax).

Ontological abstractions can still benefit from engagement with 'lower order',[7] more mundane, commonplace and concrete features in research: e.g. house, church, street, park, etc. 'These "lower order" concepts are certainly not "operationalisations" of "theoretical terms" (which is how empiricists would see the matter), but different aspects of the object of study' (Sayer 1981: 13). Low order concepts open the way for correlative research which could lead researchers to ask new questions, in turn accomplishing yet further insights on the concrete phenomenon in its entirety.

Studying low order concepts is part of the critical realist process of triangulation, where multiple methods are employed. Part of this

---

7. This critical realist term should not be confused with the low-level interpretation advocated in Chapter 1.

process can be correlative in either data, method, or on increasingly time-space (historically) specific grounds, while part could also make an effort to define 'common units' of investigation, thereby expanding comparative grounds for research and strengthening the data work. Given that methods require philosophy and theory, one should take Sayer's (2000: 147) warning to heart: 'In practice the attempt to combine many theoretical insights can easily become unmanageable, and the tendency to slide into ad hoc uses of unexamined concepts [...] becomes stronger than usual.' The expectation is that triangulation according to critical realist principles, or adding to the initial research outcomes and ontology critically, will eventually improve practical adequacy. The appropriation of the causal mechanism should approach more closely the concrete when different facets of the same phenomenon are complementarily integrated (see Yeung 1997). Where additional research is confined to the correlative realm, the philosophical position of critical realism as an 'underlabourer' could be extended to its operationalisation in empirical analysis.

Finally, abstraction is possible on any scale of the causal hierarchy of emergent entities, i.e. ontological stratification (e.g. from the individual to the city to globalisation), without affecting its social significance (Sayer 1981, 2000). Physical shape or spatial separation may not itself be a direct necessity for the constitution of cities – but as a consequence of material differentiation through transformation, it creates form by dividing up space into the composition (form to space, cf. Mavridou 2012) that is the built environment. This will be demonstrated to be a necessity for making space habitable, as in city dwelling, in the next chapter. However, causal mechanisms, not conditional statements, make a definition of an emergent entity. In the same way an aetiology of society (e.g. Giddens 1984; Archer 1995), containing several levels of emergent entities, is a condition for urban life (in cities). Yet, it is contingent whether a city is developed at all. The necessities of the human condition and the causal mechanisms of inhabiting the world, from which a city as an inhabited urban built environment may emerge, are given a theoretical framework in the next chapter, which respects the understanding and limitations within the metaconcepts of 'the material', 'the social' and 'spatial dependence'.

Ultimately, with regards to research practice, I broadly adhere to Bhaskar's social scientific realism as summarised by Yeung (1997: 52): 'a scientific Philosophy that celebrates the existence of reality independent of human consciousness (realist ontology), ascribes causal powers to human reasons and social structures (realist ontology), rejects relativism in social and scientific discourses (realist epistemology) and re-orientates the social sciences towards its emancipatory goals (realist epistemology)'.

Despite the solid philosophical foundation for this research process, one should be wary of its inherent risks (roughly following Sayer 2000).

First, the inescapable partial focus of abstraction could restrain analysis and understanding until a reductionist level. While abstraction is reduction, it should not become reduction to the extent that conceptualisations lose the ability to be used meaningfully.

Second, identification errors are possible in the empirical operationalisation of the abstraction and thus in the iterative process. This may entail both false positives of a concept within empirical data, or missing empirical characteristics to represent an ontologically or causally distinct pattern.

Third, one may mistake what is functional for phenomena to occur as necessary conditions. (Cf. accidental properties: e.g. this often applies to the precise building material used in construction.)

Fourth, failing to acknowledge the contingency of 'reproduction' of emergent structures could slide into structuralism. After all, something happening once does not necessitate it happening again. Combine this with the necessity of change propelled by the always unique position and situation of an individual and it is unlikely that social phenomena are reproduced in a strict sense, despite the prevalence of this turn of phrase in social theorising.

Concluding interpretations resulting from following the research process developed in this chapter should be seen as the dissemination of analytical outcomes upon which hypothetical narratives could be built. These hypotheses can serve as practically adequate knowledge until they are superseded. Now, this book will direct attention to formulating an immanently critical theoretical framework for the inhabited urban built environment.

CHAPTER 3
CONSTITUTING BUILT ENVIRONMENTS, ESTABLISHING BOUNDARIES

Introduction

The preceding two chapters form the groundwork that specifies exactly how my pursuit of methodological development will contribute to comparative urbanism. There is now an established interdisciplinary position towards urban studies, which determines the level of interpretative contribution sought. Subsequently, three theoretical metaconcepts were defined and a critical realist research process was outlined as appropriate to the material object of study: the urban built environment. Together this contextualisation provides the foundation, direction and structure for methodological development. How this elaborate embedding is determined is a direct consequence of the substantive domain in which the research objectives express an interest. Cross-cultural and diachronic social urban comparisons require one to both define the significance of inhabiting *built* environments and how this significance can be studied. Taking cue from the conceptual definitions now formulated, especially the process-oriented, social practice based working definition of the city (Chapter 1), and the metaconceptual definitions of 'the social', 'the material' and 'spatial (in)dependence' (Chapter 2), this chapter continues to develop a theoretical framework of understanding built environments based on causal mechanisms. The social theoretical tenets presented here build on an epistemological basis laid in *Built Environments, Constructed Societies* (Vis 2009) and expand on Vis (2013), which specifically introduced my take on the social systemic and time-geographical ideas progressed in this chapter.

The theoretical framework will place the spatial and physical information that built environments contain within a fundamental interpretive scope pertaining to the substantive domain defined previously (cf. Chapters 1 and 2). How this chapter will capture the functioning of the social inhabitation process directly serves as the theoretical underpinning of the empirical socio-spatial concepts formulated in Chapter 5. It sets out an immanently critical theory of the underlying sequence of causal necessities (cf. Chapter 2) of inhabiting the world, despite the development of a city and urban life being a progressive contingency. The theoretical framework reveals the constitution and process of the inhabited urban built environment. This is how we come to know the elementary rudiments of *what about* the built environment is socio-spatially significant to inhabitation, i.e., as we will find, *boundaries of differentiation*. Subsequently, in Chapter 4 boundaries are taken forward as a concept and spatial data, which leads on to a better understanding of built environment information. Through the theoretical argumentation in this chapter, boundaries become the elementary aspect that the applied method becomes dedicated to. Boundaries become the basic property of the material configuration through which the complex composition of the built environment is manifested. I will demonstrate that comparative research and a commensurate treatment of spatial data can be based on boundaries.

Reasoning towards a theoretical framework

The previous chapter explains (pertaining to iterative abstraction) that this exercise in critical reasoning, almost a thought experiment, forms a first stage in a process geared to methodological development, which will unfold in several steps of conceptualisation. It presupposes the existence of the inhabited built environment, but elucidates how this existence came about by placing it in direct progressive relation to human beings coming into and inhabiting the world as it occurs to us. On no account should this be seen as an absolute, prescriptive evolution that all human existence in the world did, or should eventually, completely move through. So, the following pages present necessary conditions as well as causal mechanisms, the operation of which is a progressive contingency.

These abstracted sequences should thus be seen as an exercise that picks up on the processes of settling, through which something we already know to exist – cities – can be more appropriately understood as continuing part of those processes. Reasoning through the processes from a necessary starting point to a known end point produces our theoretical framework. According to Yeung's (1997) assertion, such abstraction can only elucidate the concrete phenomenon of the inhabited built environment partially. Here elucidation is delimited by the common human process of inhabitation of, and settling in, the world. This theoretical framework will maintain the low-level *rudimentary understanding* established in my preceding discussions and is *susceptible to any criticism that demonstrates that the situations outlined cannot lead to the consequences suggested.*

Importantly, it should be noted that in critical realist terms, this theoretical framework consists of conditional statements without which the consequential stages of development could not be reached. This is not the same as comprehensively revealing all complete necessary causal relations between one situation and the other. As alluded to before, under no circumstance is it necessary that a(n) (urban) built environment is developed and, especially, there are no predestined determinants for how this would be developed. Recall that the world hosts relatively stable nomadic, hunter-gatherer and 'rural' village societies. The conditional statements provide the basis upon which a causal mechanism could operate, but it remains contingent on other factors whether this happens. This stage of conceptualisation is therefore not a product of iterative abstraction as explained in Chapter 2. Instead, it concerns the immanently critical formulation of a constitutive theory. Again, this should not be confused with a critical realist's immanent critique of extant literature. Instead, this reasoning builds on inevitable foundational thoughts created by others, which are reworked and placed in a framework that is itself logically susceptible to immanent critique.

Through this theoretical framework it should become clear how to understand the development of the inhabited built environment on a fundamental level, and to identify the essential (trans)formative element through which to investigate information on this object of study comparatively. That is, the urban built environment's *material morphology* as it plays an inherent role in, and allows, inhabitation. In so doing, the basis is laid for the conceptualisation of this element (boundaries) as empirical information and the process of iterative abstraction. Iterative abstraction then formulates an ontology of the constitutive characteristics through which differing occurrences of that element (boundaries) can be recognised, and contextually understood and positioned in the built environment as a whole.

The condition of being human

Although urbanisation might not be a universal necessity, it is recognised as a cross-cultural and historically repeated phenomenon resulting from the intensive development of places for inhabitation. Despite such local formations being historically contingent, cities themselves become constitutive of the development of the societies residing in them. This can be known because the condition of being human does not allow us to extract ourselves from, or escape, our being-in-the-world (sometimes expressed as our 'facticity' in philosophy). So what, in the context of a constitutive understanding of built environments, is meant by the condition of being human in the world?

The existential formulation as used above is unavoidable. I will not assert that Heidegger's (especially 1972) philosophy is *sensu stricto* followed. Yet, the foundational character of his ideas as filtered through adaptations by, especially, phenomenologists – amongst whom the constitutive phenomenology of Schütz[1] (e.g. 1967) has had the greatest influence on my thinking – is undeniable. To be in the world is manifested through structural linkages with the world (temporal and spatial relations between human being and nonhuman things). Heidegger's argument holds that we cannot exist unless we have a world to be in. Existentialist philosophy came forth from the notion that the essence of man follows his existence, captured by our condition or facticity. So, the significance of the world to our being depends on how we are in the world. The way we are in the world is first and foremost temporally and physically conditioned by our bodies, through which we occupy a position in the world. The physical properties of our body relate to the physical properties of the world, while the physical (biological) nature of our bodies intrinsically delimits our time of being through degeneration, ending in mortality.

Phenomenological adaptations in psychological and practice-theoretical anthropology have strongly developed the consequential idea of embodiment. This results from attempts to overcome the mind–body dichotomy (see Bourdieu 1977; Csordas 1990; Ingold 2000; Low & Lawrence-Zúñiga 2006), which have since gained a persuasive and influential position in social theorising. Through the anthropological proposition of embodiment the human body has become established as a site

1. In archaeology the original metaphysical (Husserl) and existential (Merleau-Ponty) branches of phenomenology have grown to become much more popular than the here prioritised sociologically inspired constitutive phenomenology of Alfred Schütz. A discussion of how these branches relate can be found in Campbell (1981). The rationale for preferring Schütz's phenomenology results from its strong action-theoretical connection, which through Von Mises (1998) is central to the theoretical arguments here. Furthermore, Schütz's (1967) cogent proposition of a social subject with social experience in an individual life-world resonates well with the social scientific aims of the present endeavour. It allows a ready connection to a social constitutive or emergent perspective of society in systems theoretical sociology (cf. Giddens 1984), while simultaneously maintaining a connection to the experiential reality of inhabiting a physical world (see also adaptations in Vis 2009).

of lived experience and embodied agency (Joyce 2005). The physical and biological nature of our embodiment is such that we have mental command over our body. This makes our psyche, which incorporates the mental capacity to decide to act, an immediate in our being.

A resultant premise is that human beings act necessarily. Human beings already act by being there, which therefore also comprises the choice not to act (Von Mises 1998). As mentioned before, human beings act rationally, which is not to say that rationality follows a normative pattern (Chapter 1, note 6). Following Von Mises' (1998) precise action-theoretical formulation of purposeful action, decisions to act are ordinal: someone acts to improve one's position and situation, and prefers to do one thing over another in the expectation of the improving nature of the action's outcome (also see Vis 2010). In Von Mises' (1998: 18) own words:

> Human action is necessarily always rational. [...] The ultimate end of action is always the satisfaction of some desires of the acting man. Since nobody is in a position to substitute his own value judgments for those of the acting individual, it is vain to pass judgment on other people's aims and volitions. No man is qualified to declare what would make another man happier or less discontented.

Von Mises therefore even proposes to reject the qualifiers rational and irrational. Of course, there is no guarantee that the outcome of action is as envisioned. One cannot foresee the outcome of action. In concert with the emergent entity of human being in critical realism, man is ultimately biologically and physically restricted in his actions.

Now we have situated ourselves in our bodies, the physical nature of which installs the mental capacity by which we can act, the perception of bodily being and the enabling effects this has is realised. 'Man is in a position to act because he has the ability to discover causal relations which determine change and becoming in the universe. Acting requires and presupposes the category of causality' (Von Mises 1998: 22). The experience of embodiment and its effects fit us into the world simply by being there, as do the actions we inevitably perform from that continuously changing position and situation.

Embodiment alone cannot fully account for our being in the world and the phenomenological bi-implication of man and environment (see Ingold 2000; Kolen 2005). Both being in the world and this bi-implication hold at its core that the body does not only physically capacitate us, it is also intrinsically part of the physical nature of the world. Howes (2005a) has proposed the concept of *emplacement* to express the immediacy of the sensuous interrelationship of mind–body–environment, which requires and presupposes sensory experience.[2] This creates an environment incorporating ourselves that is both physical and social (involving the presence of others) through our causal interactional experiences of it.

Sharing the intrinsic conditions of our nature, *a priori* we have a self-referential intersubjective or empathetic understanding of other human beings. This is necessarily limited to our divergent position and situation, and the unique knowledge and experience that are incorporated in it. Self-referential understanding implicates that it cannot be assumed that any two understandings and uses of learned concepts are exactly the same. Yet, through converging (increasingly proximate) biographies, fundamentally evolving ephemeral phases and concepts in how we live in the world can become more constant and persistent, which does not contradict the uniqueness of individuals' situatedness within it.

A human being is necessarily conditioned to be somewhere and sometime. Following the principles elucidated by time-geography, from inception we occupy a time and space through our emplaced being. The same space can only be occupied once, while time is exclusive in the sense that we cannot be in two places at once (see Hägerstrand 1975, 1976; Pred 1977, 1981; Thrift & Pred 1981). Consequently, not only because of what we do and experience but also within the world, one's position is always unique. Since our situated knowledge (see Schütz (1967) for essentials on how we acquire knowledge) frames the expectations we have about the causality of our actions, it is not only vain to pass judgment on someone else's actions, it is simply impossible to fully grasp the rationale behind someone else's decision to act. In addition, no action that seemingly conforms to or reproduces prescribed or existent patterns and structures will necessarily have been performed with that expectation or experience of it (cf. De Certeau's (1988) resistance in the practice of everyday life). Understanding and anticipating someone else's actions is limited to what is self-referentially and intersubjectively possible.

Endowed with emplacement, situated purposeful action, and the causality of this, human being is ready to be in, encounter and inhabit the world. We first perceive the space we occupy as an embodied being,

---

2. It recently transpired that Lefebvre (2014) also explored the senses more fully in subsequent, but long undiscovered work.

and our senses allow us to perceive our surroundings also. From the experience of occupation through our capacity to act, we come to know about the causality of interaction within the environment we are part of and the mutually affecting physical properties and processes. This is both immediate and inescapable. Our being is acting, and consequently each action occupies time and space. Our actions give our being time-space specific particularities. The incorporation of physicality means that any of its outcomes will affect and transform the temporal and spatial properties of the environment (cf. Pred's (1984, 1986) transformation of nature). In this way, following Richardson (2006), '[t]he world [...] does not stand apart from us and our actions, but depends on our being in. Through our actions we create the world in which we are, we create to be in our creations' (Vis 2009: 40). On the life-path we are compelled to move through (cf. time-geography), our interactions construct relationships with our physical and social environment, the outcomes of which play a constitutive role in how we subsequently act (see Griffiths & Quick 2005).

Presupposing the existence of others, the formations in which we inhabit the world together (societies) are a specific emergent bundle of human inter-personal (i.e. social) relations developing out of a constant merger of the axes of human time, human action, and human space (these axes were explicated in Vis 2009). As perceivers and producers of the physical and social properties of the temporal and spatial environment we occupy, we both encounter and experience its properties through interaction. We can create conceptions of them in anticipation of action and through transversal thinking (cf. Mekking's (2009) representation; Chapter 1). The human and social production of physical properties in this process thus results from our perceptive and experiential being-in-the-world and our emplaced or situated knowledge of causative actions (see Ingold (2008a) on inhabiting the world). From the moment of the first transformative interaction with the environment, human action as productive and perceptive can no longer be experienced as separated perspectives because they occur simultaneously. Still, human action is significant from both the productive and perceptive perspective in elucidating the role of the environment in societal development.

Now the condition of human-being-in-the-world is inextricably socio-spatially determined, we can shift our focus to the process of encountering and inhabiting the world. Regarding human beings as socio-spatial beings implies the inherent relations of human beings to the physical properties of space and other human beings. Even though our inhabitation of the world is inseparably social and spatial, it is heuristically advantageous to initially present this process as two divided sequences of constitutive (bottom-up) reasoning: human *being* in the *spatial* world and human *being* in the *social* world. It will demonstrably follow from these sequences that the heuristically separated ways of inhabiting the world are in fact merged as immediately socio-spatial. From the vantage point of the socio-spatial nature of the constitutive processes structurally relating us to the world we inhabit, it becomes possible to gain an understanding of why human beings transform their life-worlds. As the (urban) built environment consists of a complex transformation of the life-world – then the primary accommodating product and scene of social life unfolding over time – such constitutive understanding will permit the study of the significance of the physical presence of the built environment in societal development.

Essentially this is to ask just what it is that the built environment does within the inhabitation of the world. It clearly stands in opposition to a world that is not transformed and therefore does not pose a situation where we live in our creations. However, to assume that an untransformed environment is an empty environment amounts to a gross oversimplification. Hence, my theoretical framework starts with the imaginary (abstract) notion of empty space.

Human being in the spatial world

Empty space

Most people will have some idea about what empty space or emptiness[3] entails. So I appeal to the reader's imagination of being in a spatial world that is empty. Most probably this will conjure up notions of nothing on a fundamental level – the troublesome semantic concept of non-existence – through to analogies with empty boxes or empty delimited spaces (rooms, areas) at the more mundane end. The latter is contradictory as the delimitation of a space indicates the presence of something carving up the world. To maintain the thought experiment we need to assume all-encompassing emptiness. This implies there are no confines to or things within the environment we are in whatsoever. It contains no formed entities and no objects.

3. It is acknowledged that emptiness can be a philosophically laden term, but it is felt that the argument here is helped by appealing to an intersubjective or commonsensical imagination of empty space.

Such a notion of empty space cannot be made concrete and therefore only exists as a metaphysical concept. Our everyday concept of emptiness ends up being like nothing. As an imaginary construct it eludes exemplification. Ingold (2008a) takes after Gibson (1979) when he encourages his readers to think of a stark blue sky without any entities such as clouds and when he explains that the absence of textural differences creates the perception of an empty void rather than the surfaces we perceive normally. Thus, the essence of emptiness is the absence of differences and boundlessness: an endless void in which nothing exists.

The fundamental problem is that we imagine in spite of ourselves. If empty space would be something with our being in, this would refute its emptiness. Hägerstrand (1984) said that every action is for its outcome dependent on what is present and absent. We established before that humans act by being there. However, if nothing is present there is nothing to be emplaced in, let alone to act within, so action would be without consequence and causality. Accordingly, empty space contradicts the human condition of a continuously perceptive and experiencing being through our encountering the world (cf. Ingold 2008a). With no surfaces to experience, empty space would be *unintelligible*: there is nothing to inhabit, nothing to engage in interaction with or to relate to (see Table 3.1). A way to make the notion of empty space concrete is to imagine the world unaffected by human presence; a world which no human being before inhabited. This kind of emptiness will be captured in the concept of primordial space.

Primordial space

Ultimately, primordial space is an abstract notion (like empty space) because we cannot (re)construct a situation in which the world was not affected by human presence before. As soon as we place ourselves in such a world, essentially the world is affected by our presence, but we can nonetheless imagine a situation in which the world occurs to us without human presence. This can be seen as an abstracted perception of the world we would encounter in the imagination that no human would inhabit it, while it still contains everything we would otherwise perceive and experience. This idea is close to what Ingold (2008a) calls the 'as if' world. The same assumption is made every day when we think about the properties of the world as something remaining in existence when we are no longer present to experience them first hand. Primordial space is imagined, but includes all the features that set the scene for potential habitation. This scene refers to Gibson's (1979) 'furnished environment', which comprises the textures, substances, objects, etc. that 'afford' us to interact with the world from our emplaced situation.

Affordance, originating from ecological psychology, remains the subject of contestation, as differing ideas about its relevance and nature persist (Jones 2003; Costall 2006). Broadly speaking, in this work affordance appears as conceptually close to Gibson's (1979) original proposition: the opportunities offered by and consequences of acting upon the physical properties of the world. Affordance is separate from the perception of objects' substance and surface properties, because it concerns the action-centred implications of their presence.[4] The notion of emplaced lived experience (Howes 2005a) tentatively brings these two positions close together. Primordial space as a world including affording furnishings can tentatively be exemplified.

Primordial space as simply featuring affording furnishings may resemble the landscapes we normally regard as wild and natural, i.e. not cultivated and inhabited by human beings (cf. Deleuze 1984), which is usually not unlike big nature reserves. One should be careful with such assumptions, however, as what appears wild and untouched is often deceptive. Since we can understand the (deceptive) experience of not recognising human presence due to the apparent absence of (traces of) physical transformations, the primordial world as such is made imaginable and intelligible. Emplaced lived experience generates an understanding of opportunities to use, and the effects of interacting with, the furnished world's physicality and resources. Regardless of the (past) presence of others, primordial space then could encompass Ingold's (2008a) 'life in the open world'. Ingold explains that the world and all it contains is in continuous flux, a world entirely composed of comings and goings, which we get to know through lived experience (life-paths) rather than static, exiled viewpoints. As I emphasise persistently, viewing the world in flux benefits a focus on formative processes. However, both Gibson (1979) and Ingold (2008a) always include ecology comprehensively, without selecting the human or social as a focus.

As we come to know the furnished world in our imagination, we recognise how it affords our essential needs and is ready for our survival. That means that if we were to encounter such a world it would be *inhabitable*, because of the intelligibility of the affordances in its physical properties providing opportunities to survive (see Table 3.1). Comparing this

4. Operationalised views of the concept of affordance can be found in discussions on materiality, e.g. Knappett (2004, 2007) and Ingold (2007, 2008a, 2008b) and related ideas discussed by Webmoor & Witmore (2008) in material culture studies in relation to the technological focus in ANT.

understanding to geographer Appleton's (1975) evolutionary theory for the aesthetic appreciation of landscape paintings, there appears to be further grounds for the importance of landscapes to afford inhabitation.

Appleton's (1975) prospect-refuge theory focuses on the appreciation of the means for survival and opportunities for protective shelter offered by the landscape shown.[5] Before any human traces and transformation in the world, primordial space would probably have revealed its affordances to our ancient ancestors in this way. Through the experience of 'life in the open world' (Ingold 2008a) we started using caves as dwellings and gathered fruits of the land for subsistence (i.e. acting upon its furnishings). In other words, before impressing our presence on the spatial world, a furnished world already offers opportunities for inhabitation without modification.

In sharp and significant contrast to empty space, the (would be) process of emplaced inhabitation of primordial space thus includes all perceptible and experiential physical properties. These textures, surfaces, substances, and spatial distinctions (see Gibson 1979; Ingold 2008a) allow us to engage in interaction with and recognise differences between spaces in the world. Our experiential knowledge will be acquired in spatial conceptions, because our ability to perceive the differences in the physical properties of the world and experience their affordances contextually (i.e. making things discrete and giving shape to them within surroundings) is retained. It is in this way that my reasoning goes beyond the visual perception of Gibson (1979) and the aesthetic theory of Appleton (1975). Consequentially, primordial space is definitely not empty as a 'would be' inhabitable environment.

The experience of 'emptiness' should be retained for experimental psychology where voids and the absence of extrasomatic matter could potentially be tested. In our everyday encounters with the world we inhabit, it is through experiencing the spatial world as indistinct (undifferentiated) or equalitarian that we encounter the idea of emptiness.[6]

Equalitarian space

Equalitarian is used as the qualitative description of the experience of the spatial world as continuously indistinctive by repetitions of the same. Equalitarian space is therefore instinctively related to empty

---

5. Appleton's (1975) landscape analysis incorporates human-made elements also, such as a house, placed in the landscape, which often become a focal point for the scene. In his evolutionary view this is due to the refuge they offer.
6. The Euclidian or geometric space of *spatial science* replicates this emptiness in a particular way.

space in the sense that repetitions of the same occur to our entire perceptive horizon. (Technically, emptiness is incapable of letting anything occur, including things being equal, which is necessarily also indistinct.) In idealised form equalitarian space is essentially a situation consisting of a continuous binary difference delimiting equal things, which repeats itself in a constant rhythm. Concretising equalitarian space, for example, as it could occur in the primordial spatial world, its scene of features would appear to us as a sensory limitless stretch of repeated equal things. True or ideal equalitarian space is as abstract as empty space and therefore unlikely to exist (cf. Gibson's (1979) open environment). One could, however, imagine concretised examples (think of virtual reality) that come close using the commonsensical boundary of the horizon.

Taking after the image conjured by Ingold (2008a) and Gibson (1979) one could picture oneself being on a sandy plain, a level surface of sand that stretches as far as the eye can see, under smoothly overcast sky. Such a space does not inhibit life and interaction per se, but neither does it *ab initio* offer features that characteristically afford inhabitation. We can only identify all that occurs to us as an equal binary distinction: an endless body of sand and an endless stretch of sky. This likely makes us uncomfortably perplexed. It may appear to us as simple, but such a world would be beyond comprehension because we cannot distinguish anything in it. We would be in space, but could not relate our location to anything.

Complicating this example, the surface may have relief: repetitive sandy hills and slopes. Now we can distinguish the delimitation of one hill from another through perception and experience of the landscape. However, such an endless equal repetition of similar hills will still pose the same limitations as before. Establishing a location and orientation would be hard if not impossible. A dense pine forest presents an alternative example. Despite the opportunities offered by trees, the repetitive environment would remain largely unintelligible and in this case would strictly limit our horizon. All trees would be similar and we would be confused by the continuous binary difference. Even in a human-made environment something alike might occur. Imagine for example endless stretches of similar agricultural fields or an urban environment filling our field of vision with uniform blocks of flats. Despite embodying a binary distinction, equalitarian space is therefore virtually *unintelligible* (see Table 3.1).

In the concrete world we encounter and inhabit, monotonous binary heterogeneous landscapes instilling in us a perceptive condition of emptiness are usually restricted and temporary occurrences. Since we have come to know the world, our expectation is that by using our own physical capacity and command of our body, moving in any direction we will eventually reach differences from such current environment (limits). Nonetheless, people getting hopelessly lost in a forest – the famous fairy tale of *Hansel and Gretel* a case in point – illustrate the perceptive and intellectual gravity of when such situations occur. It is easily forgotten in the abstract world, and then remembered in the concrete world, how the existence and movement of celestial bodies have been old friends to navigation. These aspects are features in the nature of a concrete primordial world. That is, the world as it would occur to us through lived experience when we start inhabiting it. Since we not only occupy space (as in time-geography), but inhabit the world (Ingold 2008a), our human condition and capacities, including emplaced perception and interaction, will allow us to get to know 'primordial space' in all its complexity. The diversity added through differentiations that compose complexity in the concrete world offers the opportunities for inhabitation not just on a physical level, but by making it intelligible.

Yet, as the above suggests, when we are emplaced in equalitarian space we would not be completely helpless. When moving from the abstract into a concrete state of the world (Table 3.1 recapitulates the relation between the stages of the spatial world), we have the ability to interact and incur change in our position and situation as well as the environment. The concrete world does not inhibit our being there, nor physical interaction with the world, as is the case with the completely abstract constructs of primordial and empty space.

When we start inhabiting equalitarian space or are emplaced in the processes of the primordial world, we start to exploit its habitability either as already present or as something that may become available to us, modifying the environment through interaction. *Modification of the physical properties*

Table 3.1   The conceptualisation of the differentiation of being in the spatial world.

Spatial differentiation	Conceptual nature	Intellectual character
Empty space	Abstract	Unintelligible
Primordial space	Abstract	Inhabitable
Equalitarian space	Abstract/concrete	Unintelligible
Marked space	Concrete	Made intelligible
Filled space	Concrete	Made habitable

of the environment we inhabit can improve its intelligibility and habitability.
Upon closer engagement with the environment through interaction, the
limitations (dimensions or by distance) and characteristics (in extent or
detail) of equalitarian space would typically be revealed. It is through such
lived experience that (unique) physical properties reveal their affordances
for modification, through which they become more intelligible (regardless
of the presence of other people) in cases where the concrete world did not
itself extrasomatically offer enough differentiation.

Marked space

Being emplaced in the concrete world we immediately (involuntarily)
and deliberately interact with our environment, which usually leaves
physical traces of our presence and activities in the properties and
processes already in place. Marked space comprises the modifying effects
of our emplaced lived experience of space, including those modifications
on extant properties that enhance or improve our inhabitation. When
confronted with the perception of emptiness we may thus use our abilities to make (permanent) changes to, i.e. mark, the physical properties
of which this space consists for future reference.

Change introduces an additional or enhanced differentiation into
the environment. This improves the intelligibility and in this way the process of inhabitation (through purposeful interaction). *Hansel and Gretel*
understood this principle when they decided to leave pebbles on their
tracks through the woods. However, when at last pebbles could not be
gathered they used bread crumbs instead. As this was not a lasting physical modification, their resolve left them at a loose end (unintelligible)
once more upon return.[7] So, marked space is determined by the introduction of further lasting distinctions to the physical properties and their
contexts of the spatial world, like carvings in tree barks or flattening earth
and cobbles into paths. The differentiations created render the unintelligible space intelligible by making our previous presence and engagement
with its properties perceptible (see Table 3.1).

Modifying the physical properties of our environment has a
marking effect on the processes of formation (see Ingold 2008a on
fluxes of binding and unbinding[8]) that are already ongoing in the world

---

7. In the sense of Appleton's (1975) prospect-refuge theory they also understood perfectly well
   the potential refuge offered by the humanly constructed cottage they encountered. The risk
   they found themselves exposed to subsequently was due to social factors and not the physical
   properties of the space they inhabited.

we encounter. In various ways marked space is only a transitional concept. Marking implies that we deliberately modify or enhance the physical distinctions already there, or leave traces on surfaces involuntarily. Marked space therefore does not witness the full human construction of distinctions. It does not yet pose a full transformation of physical properties to create and subdivide space by design. Nonetheless, intellectually we can connect the dots of the processes of human interaction when we encounter its marks. For example, the traces left by a camping ground we would conceive as a continuous area of past human activity. On the basis of scattered markings we may subjectively project dividing distinctions in space following from and guiding interactions in that locus. In this transitional sense marked space conveys only the tenets of a process by which we 'fill' space that was previously unaffected by human presence (cf. Kropf's (1993) unbuilt environment).

Through the emplaced lived experience of inhabiting the landscape we introduce traces of our presence as we come to know our environment and start recognising the marks of human presence we encounter. Our experiential knowledge of inhabiting the world in this way causes its improved intelligibility. Without the perceptive and experiential understanding of the differentiation between distinct features of the spatial world, the combination of extant properties and introduced markings, it would be doubtful if human beings could function in it.

Differentiation is as complex and diverse as the properties affording the sensory perception, intelligible recognition, and experiential knowledge of cause and effect through which interactional methods can modify. All conceptual constructs that become anchored in our knowledge of distinctions that we encounter and learn about originate in perception and experience. In this way, emplaced lived experience builds up (or constitutes) a stock of knowledge (see Schütz 1967), founded upon and thus consisting of distinct (differentiated) elements of things

8. Seeing the world in fluxes of binding and unbinding may be a very accurate representation of reality. In a way this view rekindles the famous philosophical aphorism *panta rhei* (everything flows) and its associated insights. However, the resultant meshwork disallows the identification of things as discrete objects and therefore hampers any form of empirical research, whilst here the empirical reality of inhabitation appears as largely dependent on human recognition and acceptance of occurring things as distinct. In Chapter 4 the world in flux contrasts with, and thus questions, the more rigid physical nature of *bona fide* boundaries (see Smith & Varzi 1997, 2000; Smith 2001), which is instrumental to my empirical data conceptualisation. It can be conceded here that distinctions are deceptively discrete as they always retain a relation to their outside as a constitutive contrast (see the section on autopoietic systems below), but it would be counterproductive to only see zones of intermingling and mixed entanglement at the interfaces between things (*sensu* Ingold 2008a).

(or constituents of entities) that occur on our life-paths. Appreciating and understanding inhabitation of our environment in this way is a continuous subjective self-referential process, notwithstanding that also without our presence the world is not a static place, but in continuous formation. Thus, albeit from an exclusively human perspective (rather than ecological), I concur with Ingold's (2008a) assertion that we introduce human processes into the world by living and acting (participating) in that spatial formation ('open world'). One stage further: the process of inhabitation goes beyond making intelligible, to a true manipulation of the environment by introducing differentiation that delimits discrete spatial objects or subdivisions to inhabit.

Filled space

Filled space refers to a spatial world of our own making. Filled space is no longer confined to marking to make it more intelligible and thus ready for inhabitation, but comprehends a complete process of *transformation*. This entails space becoming designed and subdivided according to the effects of our interactions on physical properties for the purpose of inhabiting it. In other words, filled space is the outcome of making space habitable (see also Table 3.1 for context). As such it appears as merely an extension of (transitional) marked space. Not only can we now intellectually conceive of subdivisions in activity areas, but there is also an empirical reality of actually constructed subdivisions. While marked space results from the modification of extant physical properties of the environment, to get filled space human interaction contiguously contains and transforms its physical properties. This either literally represents an extension of previously marked space or, for a contiguous locus or place (cf. Chapter 1's definition of the city), constitutes a new process of inhabitation.

One could argue that on the basis of containment or circumscribing areas spatially, the entire contemporary world has been filled (cf. Soja's idea that most of the landscape is urbanised (Blake 2002)), but this is not the place to discuss the overall extent of the effects of human presence. It suffices to understand that there are still vast regions and scattered patches of the world in which physical properties are not fully or notably determined by human action (e.g. the aforementioned nature reserves). In filled space the spatial world is divided in partitions, including those containing 'primordial residuals' that have been created by efforts of physical transformation or building. In essence, filled space conceptualises an inhabited environment that has become a built environment: an appropriated, ultimately transient world made for inhabitation (cf. Rose 2012).

In a built environment, marking actions are replaced by building actions which *transform* space. According to architect Van der Laan (1983) the creation of architectonic structures is man's attempt at making space habitable (which presupposes the prerequisite of the intelligibility of differentiations created). Therefore it is not surprising that the human structures in the landscape (e.g. houses) are often focal points for our aesthetic appreciation in prospect-refuge theory (Appleton 1975; see note 5 above). As we have seen, the spatial world is already inhabitable in various degrees without transformative acts, but building not only improves intelligibility for those who encounter the result, it itself creates further spatial properties that readily afford inhabitation. Transformation makes the inhabitability of the environment we are emplaced in by introducing novel humanly constructed entities with their own differentiating characteristics. In this way, the spatial world becomes entirely invested with human lived experience and affords familiarity. We physically construct the distinctions that previously existed as concepts in our mind, either projected from earlier experiential knowledge or linking-up markings following associated ideas, to form roughly correspondent emergent empirical entities introduced through transforming acts of building.

The built environment consequentially consists of physically constructed boundaries. These distinguish between one space and another by a division of extended markings (e.g. from posts to fences) or transformations (e.g. earthen embankments). We create solids and voids, insides and outsides, by building spatial structures. Van der Laan (1983) and Bollnow (1961) present a more specifically architectonic treatise of this process. Despite the binding and unbinding of the fluxes of the world (Ingold 2008a), these physical boundaries seemingly introduce uniform spatial concepts on both sides of the boundary.[9]

Despite the drastic physical changes incurred, the building of space is a process of the world in formation. Although many physical constructions will endure for long periods of time, many will disappear or transform at later stages through environmental or human processes. Importantly, filled space immediately becomes part of lived experience

9. Intellectually, the understanding of the space on the other side may differ depending on which side of the boundary one is located (see Chapter 5 on formulating an ontology). Experiential and temporal spatial gradients may also occur as the world is in constant formation, and depending on one's location in relation to the boundary. Although the contextual and physical properties of each boundary may vary, the division of one side to the other is necessarily always binary.

and all the characteristics of perception, appreciation, affordance, understanding, modification and transformation apply to it. Therefore all the humanly induced spatial configurations we experience are ephemeral consolidated stages of the built environment.[10] Boundaries, either conceptual (recognised differentiations) or materialised through physical construction (Chapter 2 on 'the material'), are themselves emergent realities, continuously reappropriated upon encounter.

Part of the relative persistence of the composition of filled space may be accounted for by its physical affordances. Furthermore, persistence in the actual world likely also results from filled space's relationship to social formation (e.g. material, energetic, mnemonic, emotional and cultural investments). This resonates with readings of Giddens' (1984) routines for consolidation and again relates to De Certeau's (1988) resistance in everyday practice as catalyst for change. After all, in the present-day world we cling to built heritage and often contest physical changes made to the places we live in, while at the same time we may lobby for desired improvements to our material environment.

In its most elaborate form, filled space, seen as a built environment, accommodates the entire perceptive experience (horizon) and encompasses the full extents of human daily lives as recurring parts of our life-paths (cf. Pred 1977, 1984, 1986 on the micro-geographies of daily life). Such intensity of living in a world filled with humanly constructed spatial subdivisions most likely resembles life in an urban environment. There it is possible that all activities and interactions that are necessary to sustain the requirements of daily life take place within the confines of contiguously filled space (see Chapter 1). However, this consideration already goes beyond human *being* in the spatial world.

A single human being in the spatial world is unlikely to succeed in creating in a world exclusively of his own making and survive,[11] rather than acting upon the furnishings of a concrete inhabitable world of extant physical properties. In such a concrete world we do not inhabit

10. In Vis (2009) I have argued that if stratigraphic layers of archaeological remains contain sufficient detail on the built environment layout, we may study them as consolidated stages of a developing built environment in one location. The processes operating in the previous stage are constitutive of the consolidation of the next stage. The next stage always necessarily includes a reaction to the empirical reality of what was there before. As long as inhabitation of that location is uninterrupted these formative processes are ongoing.
11. The survival and procreation of the human species has been an evolutionary success thanks to social processes and cohabitation. Isolated cases of individual survival, the famous examples of the *enfants sauvages* (feral children), are extremely rare and often questionable.

the spatial world alone, in isolation from others. As advised, this separated perspective has only been installed here as a heuristic device. Instead, we inhabit a world with others, a world that is quintessentially social.

Human being in the social world

Individual human being

A true beginning of human-being-in-the-social-world, which reflects grand theories (cf. Ellen 2010) of the formation of society, begins with accepting the same human conditions and capacities as preceded the discussion of human-being-in-the-spatial-world. In summary, as members of the same species we can intersubjectively understand the position and situation of others to an extent (empathetically self-referential). We know the implications of our physical and temporal being and our sensory abilities to perceive and experience with our bodily functioning. We have emotion to appraise our states of mind, and we have cognition which enables us to think. Through the command of our body we can perform actions, and the space our bodies occupy makes action necessarily spatial too. Being alone in the social world we occupy a unique (exclusive) time-space position on our life-path (cf. time-geography, and see Pred 1984, 1986), and we come to know ourselves and our environment (*sensu* Schütz 1967), assembling a personal experiential biography. As we come to understand ourselves within the world, we become naturally prepared for encounters with others, who we presume to be conditioned like us (cf. humanistic geography, Tuan 1976, 1979).

The social world presupposes the co-presence of human beings, either concerning direct or indirect encounter with their presence. Following the discussion on 'the social' as an entity concept (see Chapter 2), here the discussion will remain on the rudimentary level of any processes of interaction that require more than one person. Sociology, as the study of society, has repeatedly shown that unravelling the social and societal world within which human beings live is a complicated subject (Giddens' (1984) seminal work is but one example). Here I will make no attempt to present a fully detailed grand theory of society or define conceptualisations of specific societal types and phenomena. Instead, this concise presentation of concepts forms part of the framework of conditional statements for inhabiting the world, viewed from a social perspective.

Encounter

If we understand co-presence to mean the existence of more than one person and perceiving and conceiving of the existence of others, encounter necessarily entails interactional engagement. Since time-geography has demonstrated space cannot be occupied twice, encounter necessarily requires two (or more) people to have their own position, and associates any distance between these. Whether it is seeing from afar, e.g. nodding to a stranger in the street, or intimate closeness, e.g. embracing a friend coming to visit, we occupy distinct positions in space, and have arrived there living through necessarily distinct emplaced lived experience.

Beyond immediate sensory perception, our means of communication (acknowledgement, signalling, or informative) are initially limited to our corporal and oral/verbal abilities. In performing acts to engage (interact with) the other, what we truly mean or intend becomes translated, first, into what we are able to send, and, secondly, in how it is received. The latter entails a translation through the receiver's unique biographical position and situation. Therefore, we necessarily relate the encounter and any associated communication to ourselves. This constitutes the self-referential condition of our social or communicative understanding. Even linguistic structures emerging from the development of verbal communication, and deceptively designed to give the impression of neutrality and objectivity, cannot overcome these subjective limitations, causing inaccuracies and misunderstandings (vs. language pragmatics, see Zierhofer 2002).

Self-referential understanding also allows us to understand the presence of others by recognising and interpreting the traces and transformations they left behind (e.g. a camping ground or house). Encounter then relies on indirect co-presence: someone else occupied that space before. In this way, the dynamics of social relations can be extended into situations where it is not necessary to have two people present within the confines of their respective mutually perceptive horizons.[12]

As briefly referred to before, encounters not only necessarily involve the space we occupy, they also imply the distances between those spatial occupations. When we encounter, we set and respect (establish) a certain distance to each other appropriate for our intersubjectively understood

---

12. Incidentally, accepting this possibility is a necessity to conduct archaeology, where being researchers our encounters with our human subjects takes place through material remains only (cf. Fletcher 2004: archaeology assumes the material pattern of behaviour and its recognition outside actual knowledge of the builders).

relation and activity. Differences are already spontaneously expressed in the exemplifying communicative acts of nodding to a stranger and embracing a friend. It was anthropologist Edward Hall (1959, 1968) who, inspired by biological ethology, devised the study of the interpersonal distances that are respected in social interactions through which social relations are established. He aimed to uncover the cultural differences in this 'distance setting' under an approach he called proxemics.[13] The personal territories (i.e. personal space) that emerge from the process of distance setting are the first voluntary spatial differentiations in the social world.

Here it suffices to take into account that people will create interpersonal distances in every interpersonal contact that occurs, and appropriate the distance to each activity (interaction) that occurs. In other words, human beings amongst each other negotiate territories, or comfort zones, for each activity they engage in. This is the first stage in the spatial organisation of the social world, which depends on the relations emerging from encounters.

Projects and institutions

The theoretical framework informing Pred's (1981, 1984, 1986) work on the becoming of place and the micro-geographies of everyday life critically moves along the lines set out by Giddens and Foucault on societal organisation and power. Pred informs us that along their life-paths, people set out to reach goals and perform activities which are conceptually framed as 'projects' (cf. Giddens 1984). Pred's time-geographical adaptation demonstrates how social relations intersect our life-paths, and how projects are formed along the life-path operating in time-space convergences. In projects, arrays of social relationships may converge to achieve a goal that all project participants individually subscribe to (e.g. working in teams or getting behind a protest). As an aside, though, one should acknowledge situations in which individuals become part of projects without intention to subscribe to what is intended by the goal (e.g. a nonunanimous decision reached by a committee, partaking in rituals without sharing the beliefs, or simply following processes of employment pragmatically).

13. Anthropological proxemics is not to be confused with the geographical field of proximics, which was introduced as part of the regional geography of Granö (1997). Proximics is not social, but sensory. 'The proximity is that part of the environment that is perceivable with all the senses and is situated between the observer and the landscape' (Granö 1997: 108). Geographical proximics then studies the types of proximities of the earth's surface and identifies uniform areas and zones.

Projects can either be undertaken individually, as if interacting alone within the spatial world, or institutionally (i.e. in a group). The latter should be described as an individual's participation in projects that involve other people's participation. In everyday practice it is the constant intersection of individual life-paths and institutional projects that dialectically creates social structure (the emergence of open systems). This dialectic both consolidates and negotiates transformations of our relationships with others. Simultaneously, the emergence of social values, biography formation and the transformation of nature occurs (see Pred 1986; Fig. 3.1 below). Transformation of nature concerns the processes that change the physical properties of the world and therefore encompasses at once marked and filled space.

The local, temporal and personal constraints on these occurrences along time-geographical life-paths, and their constant intersections in time-space specific social situations, lay the foundation for the emergence of spatially distinct autopoietic social systems proposed by Koch (2005), e.g. the home. These 'auto self-creating' systems are components

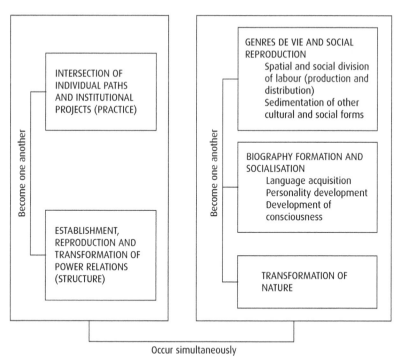

Fig. 3.1 Pred's historically contingent processes of becoming.

These processes form the core of his theory of place formation (reproduced from Pred 1986: 11).

for society in the inhabited social world, but themselves remain emergent entities as their causal power (to achieve goals) is distinct from that of individuals (see Chapter 2). The intensive collision of individual biographies (the accumulation of experience and knowledge), which are closely related in time-space to projects that transform and shape space for inhabitation, creates converging concepts. Since projects depend on emplaced participation, these concepts generate a (communal) sense of place and belonging. All these systemic elements are present in Pred's theory of place as historically contingent process. Together these processes convey the way in which the social world emerges through inhabiting the spatial world. Because the social relations of projects cannot be extracted from their spatiality, the two are intrinsically linked together as the socio-spatial world that is unfolding as a continuous process of becoming.

Autopoietic socio-spatial systems

So far, the conceptual sequences (human *being* in the social and spatial world) have clarified how interaction with spatial and social properties is constitutive of the continuous process of becoming of the socio-spatial world. The constitutive presence of the properties of space in the social world creates the basis for a view on society's spatiality. The constitutive components of society as an emergent entity (see Chapter 2) consist of causal powers of the humanly conditioned generative socio-spatial systems. These systems are themselves in constant formation when performed towards the participatory aims.

Socio-spatial systems have been theorised to be autopoietic (auto self-creative) (see Koch (2005) and Arnoldi (2001) for this view of systemic society). This means they are understood to simultaneously constitute themselves through differentiation from within and from without, i.e. on the inside towards the outside. As Koch (2005) asserts, all elements remain independent (autonomous) and mutually constitutive. That is, the social construction of spatiality and the spatial construction of sociality are mutually dependent. Being part of social systems produces understandings of the spatial properties engaged in the system through a process of differentiating those properties in their systemic environment. That means they make the resultant modified and constructed environment socio-spatially intelligible in terms of social conceptions (e.g. the properties of a building becoming appropriated for use as a home or a business).

In this way, social systems invest the environment within which they occur with meaning, which is likely to be more interpretable depending on the extent of convergence (proximity or closeness) in participation patterns along individuals' life-paths. At the same time, the constitution of meaning through transformations of properties caused by autopoietic systemic differentiation is significant to all human inhabitants of the world. We can imagine that shops and shopping are not completely equal in all cultures, but generally recognisable across several cultures. Meanwhile the physical distinctions, occupation of positions, and assemblages that constitute a shop or shopping hold significance through presence and opportunity for exchange to any human being. Autopoietic systemic differentiation is not just differentiation (phenomenologically simply: something is not something else), i.e. meaning and significance captured in oppositions, but contains its own outside. Whenever through systemic performance a distinction is made or reconfirmed, the nature of the system itself is being constituted.

> Through a structural coupling (a history of recurrent interaction leading to structural congruence) of two or more systems [in the environment], certain features of the environment are constitutive for the autopoietic process [...]. This makes the identification of the boundaries of an autopoietic system problematic, because some parts of the environment are internal to the system, i.e. the system is partially extended into the environment (Vis 2009: 114).[14]

A market place affords a market to take place, but there will not always be a market or indeed other activity distinctly occupying that space. When there is a market, the socio-spatial system of a market stall can be extended far beyond physically visible presence thanks to the voice of the stallholder, while the space of market place embeds the stall in an assemblage. The example of a market suggests that systems are also temporal. They cease to exist when the actions that constitute the system are not performed (cf. Koch 2005) (many systems can be transient and transitional in scale and performance). When a shop is closed, we cannot partake in the socio-spatial system of shopping there. Nonetheless, the opportunity to shop, would it have been enacted, could still be recognisable. It could be said that systems have constitutive (socio-spatial) environments, while actions have constitutive (social and affording) contexts (cf. Bruun & Langlais 2003). This means that existing spatial properties form constitutive environments, while individual participants' biographies of emplaced lived experience form a

14. These specific ideas are predominantly derived from Bruun & Langlais (2003).

social context for the actions that let systems emerge (cf. critical realist causality and emergence, Chapter 2).[15]

Koch (2005) specifically ties the idea of autopoietic social systems (following Arnoldi 2001) to the delimited spaces they occupy or inhabit. In addition, I emphasise that through the transformative interactions constituting them, social systems create those spaces both through and for their performance. Social-systemically occupied spaces (see Chapter 4 on subdivision) thus form socio-spatial systems with a boundary to their outside. How these systems are defined depends on their constitutive environment and their (temporal) existence depends on the (contextual) human actions that operate them. So, it becomes apparent that systems are ongoing and interconnected constitutive processes in constant social and environmental flux that depend on human interaction in space, which shapes the emergence of society. In this regard, the social world as it occurs within the spatial world is just as much a process of binding and unbinding elements, in accordance with the ecological view expressed by Ingold (2008a).

Emergent socio-spatial systems are not confined to any scale. Indeed, society as an emergent entity is probably best conveyed as a causally specific, ultimately complex, version of a project-based institutional system and, likewise, the process of globalisation conveys an emergent global society. This is how the full breadth of 'the social' inhabits the world. The physical properties of the environment that materialised through transformative acts are now structurally coupled to the process of inhabitation. Differentiating autopoietic socio-spatial systems occupy from the inside what is distinct towards the outside in contiguous interrelations. Therefore, the physically and conceptually constructed interfaces (boundaries) are linked to the subdivisions forming filled space, i.e. the built environment.

Inhabited built environment

Based on what has been argued in this sequence of human-being-in-the-social-world, the built environment can now be 'populated'. That is, we can correct our earlier view of filled space in which other people were conspicuously missing.

Let us quickly revisit that view. Without any humans inhabiting it, the spatial properties of systems composing the built environment

---

15. Because individuals are transient system participants, Hillier & Hanson's (1984) often adopted distinction between inhabitants and visitors (strangers) is largely supplanted. The constitutive actions of participation grants all a degree of control over how socio-spatial systemic occupation shapes the built environment.

receive their *congruency* as an architectural system. Koch (2005) distinguishes the spatial system, consisting of geometry, topology and fuzziness, from the associated architectural system, consisting of the materiality (structure) without which it could not be built. This in turn is separated from the social system. Such perspective resembles the pre-emptive elements of territory, place, network scales and network in the topological discussion of socio-spatial relations by Jessop et al. (2008). Here, no such pre-emptive categories are distinguished if they do not directly emerge from these fundamentally human conditional statements. Hence, it is through the physical properties of the material (*sensu* Wallace 2011) of the architectural system that the spatial system is characterised. Accordingly, accepting the material as an emergent entity means that understanding materialised space cannot be separated from the social realm. Nonetheless, the constitutive components at play in any systemic relation will remain distinguishable, and their causality in isolation may differ from the causal power of the system. This reasoning resonates well with a conclusion I reached previously:

> [T]he significance of [built] space is both spatially relational and necessarily material. Relational entails the extension of the borders of spatial entities to the relational constitutive dimension (cf. constitutive environments), while material simply refers to the fact that all [spatial] entities [...] are irreducible to a mental state. [...] Relations are not only social, they are also spatial, because we live and act in a materially heterogeneous world. This enforces that neither objects, nor spaces and communities can be reduced to something one-dimensional (Vis 2009: 116–117).[16]

Although the architectural system includes the characteristics of the internal structure of the residing socio-spatial system, our methodological interest lies more narrowly with the interfaces of differentiation between socio-spatial systems than their internal dynamics. In the light of my earlier example, that is an interest with how the spatial conditions of shopping are shaped, rather than specifying the events of shopping that actually occur. This accords to the coarser provenance that can be expected of enduring remains of the built environment over time. Such physical persistence can be recorded as empirical data. The coarser

---

16. Note that in this quote, 'material' is used in the sense of physical substance, and not 'the material' as an emergent entity used throughout this book (Chapter 2).

nature readily pertains to what Mekking (2009; see Chapter 1) referred to as the walls that divide between an inclusive 'us' and an exclusive 'them'. Through physically transformative acts, these interfaces have become material, which includes their continued occupation by socio-spatial systems (materialisation). They form the empirical reality of built boundaries (Chapter 4) of which the built environment is composed. An understanding of the significance of the built environment to societal inhabitation and development depends on these boundaries.

The socio-spatial complex that *is* the inhabited built environment, composed of built boundaries, is formed in the ongoing differentiating (binding and unbinding) performances of socio-spatial systems. It posits an immediate human and social reality characterised by incorporated physical affordances. As soon as a spatial configuration is introduced, e.g. construction of a fence around a green or a new residential block, it becomes part of the constitutive environment and experiential context of the ongoing systems occupying that contiguous locus. This, in turn, means that the material features that result from the transformative operation of these systems should be understood through that theoretical lens.

Despite the seemingly static wording of 'empirical built boundaries', these differentiations, as dictated by seeing the inhabitation of the socio-spatial world as a process of becoming, are in constant formation. They therefore fluctuate as the system is performed by its participants. Once transformations are introduced, these necessarily occur in relation to physical distinctions created as a part of system emergence. This physical difference tends to be a more persistent and enduring marker than the rationale and intentions of the original interactions that differentiated.

Archaeological 'material remains' confront us with the materialised approximations of human and social differentiation, which appear to us as fixed, but which we can self-referentially infer socio-spatially. The intellectual understanding of transient, transitional and temporal interaction-dependent socio-spatial systems is necessary for interpreting the inhabited built environment, which as a *material* phenomenon (rather than merely physical and empirical) is necessarily linked to the social. This does not withstand the development of geometric and topo-logical (e.g. quantitative) expressions of configurations external to the social perspective, insofar as they associate affording properties to inhab-itation as an ongoing interaction process.

This theoretical framework showing the constitution of the inhabited built environment creates a rigorous elaboration and methodologically viable specification of an approach to interpretive spatial analysis I pre-viously called the 'social positioning of spatialities' (Vis 2009: 133ff.).

The apparent fixity of the built boundaries making up the built environment configurations we observe is not equal to how we understand their constant constitution in the inhabitation process through time. They are merely physical approximations of the outcomes intended by or emergent from transformative interactions, and occur as affording social realities in subsequent encounters.

Following these sequences, it has become determined that to inhabit the world we must recognise differences through emplaced lived experience. When we eventually manipulate the physical properties of our environment, we create entities from the inside towards the outside on a flexible scale. Human-being-in-the-social-world, as such, is constitutively significant on an all-encompassing fluid scale of time and space, which stabilises depending on its action-specific context. Therefore, the inhabited built environment complex we perceive of as an object of study entails composite entities and aggregates,[17] which afford and result from interaction patterns and experiential familiarity. The relative endurance of entities expresses the extent to which the original emergence leading to their occurrence is adhered to in enactments, because it is inevitable that people react to boundaries (differences) once they exist. The entities' internal composition is necessarily part of the intrinsic logic of case-specific socio-spatial significance that belongs to any urban locus. That is, the urban built environment viewed as a functional structure of socio-spatial systems is particular to each city.

Boundaries

Using the framework developed in this chapter we have gained an understanding of the constitution of the inhabited built environment. It reveals that boundaries are of paramount importance because they result from the intellectual and experiential requirements for differentiation that allow the process of inhabitation of the world to take place. We know the built environment as an empirically accessible object of study, and it has become established that, empirically speaking, *built boundaries compose the built environment as outcomes of transformative differentiating interactions*. Therefore, I argue that a study of boundaries conceptualised

17. Note that as the outcome of interactions can never be foreseen, emergent entities and aggregates are increasingly unlikely to be fully intentional on an incremental (socio-spatial) scale, in the sense of realising a single human being's envisioned improvement on position and situation. This applies to both top-down administrative decisions and bottom-up construction, as the capacity of a single human being to transform the world is limited, which is after all why filled space is unlikely to exist in the absence of others.

in accordance with this theoretical framework is indispensable for generating understandings of the socio-spatial significance that material presence poses to the inhabitation of the world (in terms of how boundaries afford and qualify interaction within that world). Moreover, referring to the working definition of the city in Chapter 1, only in urban settings is the transformation of the environment so complete as to fill the perceptive horizon and to envelop the functional necessities of ongoing daily life in a contiguous locus.

Logically, the best understanding of society on the basis of a built environment can be achieved when transformation is most elaborate. It is therefore expected that in urban settings a study of boundaries as an analytical category would be most productive. *Urban form* is then *seen as a configuration of boundaries*. By means of boundaries it is hoped that Griffiths & Quick's (2005) theoretical appeal to study spatial configurations can be further concretised, grounded with the premise that human beings are situated in a holistic physical and social environment.

In a recent discussion on the study of territory as a topological category, Elden (2011: 306) argues that 'there is definitely agreement that the approach to be taken should emerge from the questions asked, rather than being defined in advance'. As a consequence, this theoretical framework sets the agenda for conceptualising our information source (spatial data on the built environment) so as 'to allow the object of analysis [here boundaries] to dictate the way in' (Elden 2011: 306). The following chapter will discuss how a thorough understanding of boundaries steers us along a pathway of engagement with empirical data.

CHAPTER 4
THEORISING MATERIAL BOUNDARIES, UNDERSTANDING SPATIAL DATA

Introduction

According to the theoretical framework of Chapter 3, differentiation is a prerequisite for inhabiting the world. We have seen that in the process of inhabitation, human beings have the capacity to manipulate and introduce differentiations into the world, performing transformative acts. When these transformations construct bounded distinctions, the world becomes subdivided into emergent entities. Progressively, intentional acts that create such boundaries 'fill' the concrete world for the purpose of our inhabitation as a humanly constructed built environment. This spatial subdivision is informed and motivated by conceptions resulting from our experiential understanding of the world. That understanding reacts to and is influenced by environmental and social contexts that cannot be foreseen, because they are always in development. The material nature of the inhabited built environment consists of a configurative complex composed of boundaries affecting and affording our experience, interaction opportunities and appropriation or development for inhabitation. The boundaries introducing material differentiations are inextricably social and spatial as human-made materialised components. Thus, from being material they derive operative causal powers and attain significance in interaction.

The specific merit of boundaries as a 'concept to think' with is the subject of this chapter. Thinking through boundary theory eventually allows us to distil spatial data, demanding a clear understanding of what is truly conveyed by boundaries and how mappings are created from this information. Only from this refined perspective on the translation of empirical reality into spatial data will socio-spatial concepts be formulated in Chapter 5, which marry conceptual or ideational meaning (Chapter 3) to empirical identifiability (Chapter 7).

Theorising boundaries

A closer look at boundaries as a concept in a methodological context is needed in order to better appreciate the information which is unlocked by regarding the inhabited built environment as composed of boundaries that give rise to entities. Differentiation demonstrates that we come to know any entity by its distinctions to its outside, i.e. at the boundary. When we create conceptions of the world around us we start by recognising the binary distinction that something is not something else. This has led to the suggestion that boundaries are the basis for knowledge in general (Jones 2009), and a knowledge based on differentiation sits comfortably with constitutive phenomenology (Schütz 1967). The logical implication of this is that the socio-spatial significance of the material presence of the built environment to inhabitation should not start with the entities that commonsensically jump out to us. These commonplace features are based on our lifetime of acculturation, i.e. immersion in time-space specific socio-cultural contexts. Instead, it should start with the characteristics of the distinctions incorporated in the boundaries that compose it.

In the academic field of boundary studies, mainly spanning across human geography, sociology and philosophy, a focus on the distinctions incorporated in boundaries is exactly what has been suggested in general. One should not study entities, but the boundaries from which they emerge (Abbott 1995; Jones 2009, 2010). Against the background of the discussion of social interaction and relations and the emergence of socio-spatial systems, Abbott's (1995: 860) assessment of entities falls into place: 'social entities come into existence when social actors tie social boundaries together in certain ways. Boundaries come first, then entities.' How entities become physically distinguished by boundaries is the specific constitutive human and social datum of the inhabited built environment.

It could easily be argued that in the context of the built environment, boundaries are merely built distinctions and divisions, whilst 'boundary' as a term is as protean as it is elusive. Yet, it is exactly this flexibility that makes it suitable in the light of how we now understand the constitution of our object of study: the inhabited built environment. When only regarding the 'built distinction' we are unable to capture the full socio-spatial complexity of the differentiation introduced beyond a merely physical empirical outcome of interaction. The term 'boundary' is both accurate and can be invested with the empirical and ideational social reality it specifically represents in the present methodological endeavour.

In speaking about boundaries, however, it should be noted that imagined or ideational boundaries in particular have received much attention in sociological (e.g. Lamont & Molnár 2002) and anthropological research (e.g. Pellow 1996). This discourse concerns what could be called socio-cultural, geo-political or formal and administrative symbolic boundaries as constituents of social categories. In historically and socio-culturally contextualised themes, such as power, religion, economics, etc., boundaries have been the object of research in various guises: from very implicit social boundaries and categories in Van Gennep's and Turner's anthropology of rites of passage and symbolism (see Turner 1969; Bell 2009), to more explicit boundaries of organisation, territory and international borders (e.g. Abbot 1995; Lamont & Molnár 2002; Jessop et al. 2008; Jones 2009). The main strands of scholarly thought from similar socio-cultural, economical and political perspectives that concern built space in particular, are usefully summarised by Archer (2005; for archaeological overviews see Kent 1990 and Steadman 2016).

As argued in Chapter 1, the high-level interpretation resulting from context-specific knowledge, representational analogies or metaphors often required for such perspectives are deemed inappropriate for broad comparative social scientific aims. Furthermore, in Chapter 2 I determined the rudimentary nature in which the social is applied here. On this basis, boundaries will not explicitly refer to differences in class, nation, kin or cultural identity, even though these aspects influence how the differentiation posited by built boundaries is understood in social life.

This is not to deny the existence or importance of such higher-level social specificity. As a case in point, Lawrence (1996: 33) states that: 'It was commonly at the border between private and collective spaces (by the entrance door or at the windows) that residents engaged in expressive behavior with kith and kin.' This quotation illustrates Lawrence's parallel assertion that boundary thinking is capable of converging many disparate social and cultural research interests. So, despite allowing the socio-cultural concepts and categories which often are at the core of boundary research merely a subdued implicit presence, for present purposes I simply acknowledge that they are *inseparable parts* of what the envisioned method studies socio-spatially. Without consistent means and availability of data, our theoretical framework is now delineated so that these aspects of boundaries cannot be *directly* accessed within my comparative research purposes.

The emergent research literature on boundaries is littered with examples of metaphorical representations. These representations seem to accept, as a fundamental empirical and experiential presupposition, that any feature or component of the world is eventually delimited, at which instance it becomes something else. The language and philosophical underpinnings of metaphorical, representational or abstractly analogical and relational approaches to the study of boundaries, borders, barriers, limits and edges often pay homage to Deleuze and Guattari. However, their dense 'geophilosophical' language of space, speaking of deterritorialisations, lines of flight, and smooth vs. striated space, remains overly ideational (especially Deleuze & Guattari 1987).

While Deleuzo-Guattarian ideas are invested with the vigour of politics and power, and are evocative and thought-provoking, within the context of boundaries making up the inhabited built environment a full-blown Deleuzo-Guattarian approach is not deemed appropriate. On the whole, this would remain detached from the physicality of material presence as a vantage point.[1] The foundation of my comparative urban methodological interest is precisely formed by the immediately empirical (experiential) and intelligible nature of physical properties in the social inhabitation of the world. Therefore, since Chapter 1, historical and context-specificity is being avoided. Nonetheless, without pursuing any concrete application or ascribing particular purchase to Deleuzo-Guattarian contributions, their philosophical narratives maintain a background presence for making sense of deconstructing institutionalised and discursive categories. Here, deconstructive notions help to uncover the transformative processes that let spatial entities emerge to constitute a heterogeneous environment in which introduced differentiations evoke a multitude of affective and affording responses.

We take from this that deconstructive discourse in boundary studies merits our attention. Before boundaries as a constitutive datum can effectively be used as an 'analytical unit' in research, its conceptual basis as an information source must be established. How can we access the information that boundaries contain? Jones (2009) argues that the heterogenesis produced by deterritorialisation reveals a socio-spatial complexity that is normally disguised by categorical divisions. Similarly, commonplace built environment terms can disguise socio-spatial complexity with fixity and

---

1. A discussion of bordering and materiality as is featured in the work of Deleuze and Guattari can be found in Woodward & Jones (2005).

apparent 'container units', i.e. entities such as building categories and land use. Even the apparent complexity resulting from seeing urban form as consisting of conjunctions of distinct features with physical dimensions (e.g. shape, size, layout, configuration, etc.) is in fact a simplifying empirical approximation. All these simplifications result from reductions of the intricate negotiation processes (social, spatial and material) which put the built environment there.

Thinking beyond categories

One could readily agree that a lot of research is essentially based on assumed or predetermined categories. Jones (2009) and Abbott (1995) both note that much effort has been invested in establishing categories or entities for research. Jones (2009: 175) argues:

> [T]here is a tendency [...] to analyze the categories rather than the 'process of "bounding" and "bordering"' of which these categories are the result. [...] [T]he problem is not the categories themselves, but, rather, the way the boundaries around the categories are cognitively understood as closed and fixed even when we know intellectually that they are open and fluid. Consequently [...] the key process is the bounding and delimiting of the categories used to understand the world.

According to Jones, this issue emerges from our ingrained mental processes. '[W]e cognitively think of categories as containers, we consequently imagine all categories to be inherently closed, with fixed, stable boundaries between them. Yet, intellectually, we know that these boundaries are almost always fluid and permeable' (Jones 2009: 179). The fluidity, flexibility and transience of any socio-spatial system, as constituting inside coherence and incorporating its own distinction towards its outside (see Chapter 3, also Vis 2009), demonstrates the same insight.

Jones continues his cognitive explanation of categories and the crucial role they play in making sense of the world, claiming that, once installed (imposed and learned), categories limit and control our experience of social life. We could add to that the inhabitation of the world. Consequently, Jones (2009: 179–180) proposes that:

> [G]eography should re-emphasise its connection with these topics through an analysis of the inchoate process of bounding that

delimits the categories that shape daily life and academic work. [...] It is *inchoate* because it occurs over time as the boundary is just beginning to form, is incomplete and is bounding an entity that is lacking structure and organization. [...] [Boundaries are] a *process* because of this ongoing necessity for re-fixing, rewriting and renegotiating the boundaries. [...] Boundaries concomitantly take diversity and organize it and take homogeneity and differentiate it.

Jones takes his cue from Abbott (1995: 857), who notes: 'It is wrong to look for boundaries between preexisting social entities. Rather we should start with boundaries and investigate how people create entities by linking those boundaries into units. We should not look for boundaries of things but things of boundaries.' Abbott (1995: 868) argues further in support for his processual[2] ontology: 'it [does] not really matter what these boundaries were, at first. They began as simple, inchoate differences. They were not boundaries *of* anything.'

In the words of Abbott and Jones we discover a coherence that resonates with the constitutive conditions theorised in Chapter 3. They choose to focus on boundaries as a phenomenon, taken as the distinctions between eventual categories or entities. Yet, we recognise how their arguments for the emergence of entities from boundaries as a continuous process roughly concur with how human beings modify and transform the physical properties of the environment they inhabit. More specifically, Abbott's 'linking' of boundaries conjures up a close mirror image of extending 'marked space' to subdivide or partition the spatial world into 'filled space'. There is also congruency with how project participation through the performance of action internally defines systemic entities to their outside. The similarities shining through are most pronounced in Jones' (2009: 180) comment on Abbott's 'thingness' of entities: '[thingness] is not pre-given but, rather, is only the result of the contingent process of linking up these locations of difference.'

Interestingly, Abbott's (1995) structural resilience of entities resulting from their defensibility in several dimensions of difference can be related to the socio-spatial constitution of autopoietic systems (Chapter 3). Such entities or systems inherently combine the dimensions of the human life-path, social and spatial processes through which the concrete inhabited world becomes invested with differentiations. In the inhabited world, boundaries provide intelligibility, habitability

---

2. Abbott's use of the word processual should not be confused with the archaeological paradigm processualism.

and a sense of (biographical) familiarity[3] through our participation in their continued constitution and development (i.e. interactions with the socio-spatial environment). Their subsequent existence necessarily accommodates the constant processes of binding and unbinding: negotiating the introduced differentiations, while we continue to participate in their constitution. This dimensionally complex combination offers a tentative explanation for why many built (materialised) boundaries are ultimately persistent (or resilient, i.e. emergent stability) over time (a key premise for urban morphology, see Chapter 6).

The togetherness (cf. Hägerstrand 1976) or relations between built boundaries can readily be perceived to connect up the distinctions (subdivisions) by which we come to know and make sense of the inhabited world: i.e. the entities and categories of the inhabited built environment. Even when the performed system that is originally responsible for the introduction of the differentiation of a built boundary ceases to exist and/or is replaced,[4] its material presence continues to occur in our socio-spatial environment. As such, built boundaries remain susceptible to modification and participation as a constitutive contextual component in other interactional relations of inhabitation. Only obliteration is a one-off reconfiguring interaction.

Consolidation and classification

In what I have previously called the consolidated stages of the built environment (Vis 2009; cf. Abbott's (1995) lineage of events), boundaries get physically constructed by human beings, i.e. they are built. At that moment surfaces of matter or substance acquire edges (physical distinctions) that are introduced into the environment. These edges physically persist as a built shape within the continuing processes (fluxes) of the physical environment. This persistence gives rise to a degree of inertia. Persistence disguises the ongoing fluxes (cf. Ingold 2008a) of the environment and the inchoateness of the formative processes as conveyed by Jones (2009). Even though edges are varied according to their conditional nature and their contextual position and situation, the

---

3. Familiarity with (patterned or aggregating) differentiations is intended to be a very broad concept in which belonging, memory and even claimed or emotional ownership (supported administratively or arising through personal investment and participation) can all have a part.
4. Performative existence and replacement should be understood in terms of Sayer's (2000) spatial independence and Mekking's (2009) mismatch between use and intended use of a building type (Chapters 1 and 2).

persistence of built boundaries tends to be strong. That is to say, many past built forms persist into the present and/or have a long lasting effect.

Simultaneously, the inhabited built environment is also ephemeral. During local residence, the processes of inhabitation might not affect or change each built boundary physically with every event of ongoing development. Longer term, however, this material consolidation in the inhabitation process is merely a stage, because the ongoing processes may at any time modify and transform both the constitutive environment of the built boundary (the contextual characteristics) and the material properties of the original boundary. This consolidation process amidst the potential for change in everyday inhabitation practice bears some resemblance to Star's (2010) ideational cycle of standardisation (cf. structuring and imposition), residual categories (cf. De Certeau's everyday resistance) and 'boundary objects'. With any physical change or development, boundaries will often be consolidated again in their new situation or shape. Historical and archaeological data on the built environment should therefore be seen as conveying such an ephemeral stage in ongoing (inchoate) processes.

In contrast to the deconstructive thinking propagated above, thinking on boundaries is commonly articulated by what could be called the 'scientification' of social research conduct. Scientification favours observation used for explanatory law and regularity seeking based on a natural scientific model, instead of social and interpretive approaches pursuing human understanding. Such approaches thrive on the concept of categorisation.

Categorisation sets the expectant norm, for without categorisation observations could not be turned into orderable data. Quantification, determining many kinds of analysis, would not be possible, because it relies on categorisation into discretely separate things. By exception, fuzzy set theory is a quantitative approach that approximates the recognition that distinctions and boundaries are not discrete, but part of continuous processes and complex interrelations (e.g. Fesenmaier et al. 1979; Abed & Kaysi 2003; Tang et al. 2007; Pleho & Avdagic 2008; Yusuf et al. 2010; Kim & Wentz 2011). Conversely, many fuzzy set approaches try to work towards classifications from ambiguous artificially sensed (automatically acquired) data. In other words, observation adheres to static divisions, despite the fact that the natural sciences identify ongoing processes. Likewise, a long-term view in the social sciences will make it appear as if phenomena 'suddenly' appear and disappear, despite understanding that they are part of continuous processes.

Classification in archaeology is conventionally tied to constructing area-specific periodical typologies of artefactual progression. These typologies tend to be based on dimension, shape, and other exclusive characteristics observable in isolated examples, not relationality (Read 1989; though see Hermon & Niccolucci 2002 for an application of fuzzy logic to improve typological interpretation). Read (1989: 184) argues that automatic classification approaches (cf. objective measured approaches) are still some way removed from cohering to the understanding we have of archaeological (cf. human) data for which no solution is yet available.

> If structuring processes are the beginning point of understanding the data in hand, then the initial goal becomes one of relating structuring process to measurable groups in the data and not the reverse. One might devise a sequence going from general process to material realization, but the difficulty arises that the sequence does not predict the particular form the objects should take. Hence it does not predict what will be appropriate measures, with the possible exception of those such as the tip of the point; that is, measures that are clearly constrained by the tasks for which the objects are to be used. If it is not possible to go from measures made over a collection of objects to classes via numerical methods, and if definition of the taxonomic structure does not lead to prediction of form, then it is necessary to devise a means to provide the missing part of the argument.

The preceding argumentation positions the inchoate process of forming boundaries, or bounding, as an operative for inhabitation of the world and the constitution of the inhabited built environment. In concordance with Read's suggestion, one could argue that the built environment is used for inhabitation and therefore possibly the 'measures' of it can be predicted. However, as we have seen (Chapters 1 and 2), there is considerable flexibility and independence of social life from the exactitude of spatial form and physical characteristics. Hence, an ontologically ordered study of boundaries first depends on a 'typology' of the kind of *operation* they facilitate. This operation will not predict boundaries' precise relational situation nor the shapes and sizes in which they occur (cf. Fletcher's (2004) interest in material operations; Chapter 5 features an ontology of types).

In summary, from a utilitarian perspective the built environment serves the purpose of inhabitation. We know, however, that the built environment is necessarily emically salient (see Read 1989) to the inhabitants – incorporating meaning that is only accommodated in a fuzzy way by the socio-spatial significance of material presence. So, inhabitation places the built environment first and foremost as relational and processual, but these relations are in part determined by the contextual influence of shapes and sizes, which permit the measurement of its occurrence.

Studying boundaries

'[T]he problem is not the categories themselves, but, rather, the way the boundaries around the categories are cognitively understood as closed and fixed even when we know intellectually that they are open and fluid. Consequently [...] the key process is the bounding and delimiting of the categories used to understand the world.' To follow Jones' (2009: 175) argument to emphasise the process of boundaries rather than the resulting categories, and to view apparently emergent categories as inchoate, is to let qualification of their study precede or even preclude their quantification. Launching a study of built boundaries then 'allows a move away from [the boundary paradox] and creates space to contest categorization schemes' (Jones 2009: 185) in the sense of moving away from conflating architectural building types or use prescriptions in the built environment (cf. Chapter 1). It entails that in studying the built environment we should be identifying – as inchoate relational social positioning in the whole – those elements of it that materialise (or physically approximate) the meeting of different socio-spatial systems and their participants. So far we have been able to conclude that built boundaries are the components that link up constitutively to form the entities we readily perceive and are inclined to base investigation on.

It becomes apparent that this proposal is in agreement with Schaffter et al.'s (2010: 260) critique of Jones (2009): 'Boundary studies, however broad and theoretical, must [...] remain alert to spatiality and materiality, and not just to processes of construction.' Star (2010) also emphasises the process of construction, though her conceptual cycle arguably leaves some space for versions of her boundary objects to persist. In pursuing a boundary approach towards studying the built environment, social and spatial theoretical constructions are conjoined with a boundary concept that can actually be observed (as data) and mapped, i.e. built boundaries.

This connects to Jones' (2010; vs. Schaffter et al. 2010) argument that non-spatial concepts should not just be left to other (non-geo graphical) disciplines. My interdisciplinary theoretical position clearly articulates that society and (the physical properties of) space cannot be separated. Dialectically constituted by human beings encountering and interacting with and within the concrete inhabited world, the material presence of these built boundaries becomes part of the experiential and intellectual (knowledgeable) biographies of human beings continuing along their life-paths. This principle explicitly integrates boundaries in Chapter 3's constitutive framework.

Jones (2009, 2010) is making strong arguments for geography to be specifically concerned with the categorisation of the world on the basis of boundaries. It is quite interesting to see that in 1929 Granö (1997) defined the geographical discipline on the basis of how we construct geographical regions. In the review of Paasi (2002) it transpires that constructing geographical regions is clearly related more broadly to how we define categories and interpret them, and how they are socially constructed. In this manner, Pred's (1984, 1986) work on the historically contingent process of the becoming of place once more proves pivotal to connect the empirical and physical (predominantly referred to as spatial) to social construction and personal biographies in materialisation.

The foregoing theoretical treatise on the processual cogency of boundaries can thus serve as the 'deterritorialisation' of the entities and categories that habitually determine research perspectives on the built environment. The mechanistic concepts revealing the processes of the constitution of the inhabited built environment introduced in Chapter 3 demonstrate the socio-spatial complexity of differentiation for intelligibility and habitability that constitutive processes represent (which is otherwise at best assumed). This elaborate foundational background now sufficiently informs us to start an analysis of the configuration of the urban built environment on the basis of its constitutive empirical elements: built boundaries.

The task at hand is to convert this conceptual understanding of built boundaries into analytical units (Chapters 5 and 8), which can be placed central to a research practice without the immediate reification of categories emerging from them (cf. Jones 2009). By understanding the socio-spatial complexity of the constituents of the inhabited built environment before devising analytical units, as advocated here, the impoverished understanding which results from subscribing only to the over-simplicity of the static, binary character of categories based on observed or measured presence could be redressed. Dependence on empiricist observed presence stands in contrast to the significance of material presence, which is pivotal for a methodology on social comparison.

Boundaries in the inhabited built environment

My aim now is to turn the general understanding of boundaries into determined analytical units that capture their specific type of operation in the configurative composition of the inhabited built environment. To get to their operation, it makes sense to ask what boundaries *do* beyond initial differentiation. That is, what happens upon a first linking up of boundaries? What are the first aggregate constellations? Chapter 3 actually already provides the answer to this question. The first entities that boundaries form are subdivisions or partitions. Any subdivision is necessarily an inside secluded from an outside by containing an outlined extremity of (or edges to) their extent (cf. Bollnow 1961; Van der Laan 1983; Mekking 2009). All socio-spatial significance of the material presence of boundaries is first and foremost captured in how they seclude an inside (also: me/us) from an outside (also: them).

As part of the inhabited built environment, in reality subdivisions are perceptible from their outlines. Subdivisions are demarcated and characterised by the material properties encountered in the built boundaries of each spatial partition. Through these properties or characteristics each subdivision maintains relations to its outside, its environment, which means that through its composition a discretely bounded space cannot be isolated from that environment. In this way, the seclusion effectuated by a built boundary is always relative to the environmental context in which it occurs. Within this environmental context, emplaced human beings encounter and experience seclusion according to the abilities afforded by physical properties. Importantly, as noted before, this alerts us that built boundaries can never be captured completely by reference to their abstracted spatial-geometrical configuration alone (vs. the basic measures in space syntax (Hillier & Hanson 1984; Hillier 2007); see Chapter 6). Built boundaries require taking into account their physical properties as well as their materially specific context, affected by their dimensions.

The marriage of the socio-spatial and physical significance to the act of seclusion has also been noted in anthropology.

> Humans tend to segment or partition an undifferentiated, continuous environment into bounded space. The environment can be partitioned conceptually through the habitual use of specific activity areas either inside or outside dwellings; environment also can be partitioned physically by means of walls, curtains, mats or other physical barriers (Kent 1991: 438).

Several contributions in Pellow's (1996) anthropological volume dedicated to boundaries actively referred to boundaries' physical aspect, especially devoting attention to their presence in the practices of planning and housing (Lawrence 1996; Rotenberg 1996). Herva et al. (2011) expand such concerns with an example of the perceptive ideas associated with accounts of life in a historical urban setting (cf. Griffiths 2013). There, they argue, materially articulated boundaries furnish the environment. Despite some cases of research sensitivity to the material and physical properties of boundaries within inhabited environments, the boundaries often remain little more than a setting or vehicle for ideational narratives and historical detailing.

Since built boundaries seclude discrete spaces within the inhabited world, it is this operation of their material presence that I argue to be of primary socio-spatial significance. In the inhabited built environment, interaction opportunities are always framed in the way the built space that is occupied during interaction is essentially secluded from its outside. So, having accentuated that historically and socio-culturally contextualised thematic approaches to boundaries are different, studying the material record of secluding built boundaries is precisely restricted.

We revisit the principle that socio-cultural particularities stand in the way of comparative analysis. Instead, my efforts to formalise an ontology of analytical units will only focus on the generally socially affective and affording properties of built boundaries composing a built environment. As analytical units, boundaries will have to focus on the causal effects of encountering, introducing, adjusting and crossing built boundaries in everyday life, specifically in urbanised or urbanising societies. The causal effects of the occupiable material frame they constitute structure interaction opportunities. In other words, as analytical units, boundaries must allow for contextual empirical identification and positioning of the opportunities for interaction afforded by their material presence within the socio-spatial inhabitation of the concrete world.

The differentiations introduced into the world by seclusions (or 'things') are local and interactional. As Abbott (1995: 863) asserts, 'differences are things that emerge from local cultural negotiations. That is, local interaction gradually tosses up stable properties defining two "sides".' Abbott rightfully acknowledges that interaction is fundamental and presupposes actors (inhabiting the world) to perform actions. Interaction is never the *reproduction* of actors themselves or the structures they reside in (i.e. social reproduction), as the social theoretical positions of functionalism and rational choice theory assume, but interactive *production* (in concordance with Chapter 3).

It logically follows that interactive production comprises change, because the outcome of interaction consists of new or modified actors, relations (which are only partially understood between actors) and entities. 'Things emerge not from fixed plans, but from local accidents and structures' (Abbott 1995: 865). One could make this more precise. Things emerge as a result of time-space specific (similar to Abbott's measure of propinquity) conditions for colliding biographies of actors (Pred 1984, 1986), wherein the outcome of interaction and negotiation is the result of intentional acts, but embedded in the outcomes of a multitude of similar ongoing processes. These other ongoing processes were not intended by those acts. So, to specify Abbott's 'accidents', it could be said that outcomes of interactions are 'unintended intentionalities'. In addition, due to the ineluctable individual self-referential understanding of the world and the subjective ordinal purposes of action (*sensu* Von Mises 1998), human beings inherently resist emergent structures (*sensu* De Certeau 1988).

Boundary compositions in built environment configurations

In Abbott's (1995) treatise, entities and structures, presented as plans and scripts, can also be imposed by specific actors. He puts these in a processual context as a phase in the construction of entities, which concurs with Star's (2010) conceptual cycle of boundary objects. Resistance to emergent and imposed entities and structures (such as plans and scripts) implies that formal administrative and socio-cultural schemas of intellectual concepts are themselves inchoate. Even interactions that seemingly conform to entities always bear within the power of interactive production. Impositions have the same effect as the illusory fixity of extant physical transformations to which actors have no choice but to react and engage with upon encounter. Reproduction of the original interactive intention producing them is still necessarily precluded. Planning and building constitute the becoming of protoboundaries (regardless of what these bounded) in the environment. Subsequently these sites of difference are linked up into a single definition for an inside (Abbott 1995) in contrast to an outside, before physically ephemeral consolidation.

Initial emergence of the inhabited built environment is part of the process of settling and cultivating the world, while renegotiating or removing physical consolidation are both intentional and inadvertent effects of continued local inhabitation within such sites of difference. When we see the seclusions – things – of which the built environment consists as resultant from bounding, everything is in constant formation in the mundanely resistant and subjective interactive process of inhabitation.

Temporally all things and entities – including both human beings themselves as actors and the inhabited built environment they produce – are historically contingent (Pred 1984, 1986; Paasi 1991). They continue to exist over a period of time, but continuously change in the *perpetuus* of events. Persistence of impositions and physical transformations embody repetitions of interactional instances that occur in a sufficiently similar way. That is, they are repetitions of socio-spatial systemic negotiations of the entities occupied, from within and without (*sensu* Koch's (2005) constitutive environment and context for interaction; cf. Abbott's (1995) internal reproduction and ecological reproduction). This unties boundary seclusions or divisions from any kind of micro and macro scale (see Abbott 1995), but enables the study of boundaries on a continuous scale in time and space (cf. Vis 2009 on macro scale; whether a house or a country, an instant or a lifetime).

When dealing with systemic detail, it is easy to overlook that aggregation and linking up of boundaries need not stop at the level of initial seclusion. Beyond a singular subdivision from the inside (i.e. a space surrounded by an outside), built environments, and especially urban built environments, are typically regarded as complex multi-tiered aggregate patterns. Rather than a single chaotic whole, the (urban) built environment can be regarded to consist of areas of coherence across multiple subdivided spaces, without prescribing norms about what coherence entails. This coherence results from measures of persistence in the affordances of the inhabited built environment giving rise to entities, which over time become part of the emplaced lived experience of its inhabitants. Abbott (1995) calls the idea that boundaries precede entities by letting entities emerge from their presence 'temporal priority'.

> One could in principle define the neighbourhood system and the potential boundary set and *then* construct the set of which the (potential) boundary set is the actual boundary. [... I]n the logical sequence from neighbourhood system to definition of boundary to definition of set we see a logic of increasing specification that could easily be regarded as temporal, an account of the emergence of entities' (Abbott 1995: 861–862).

This temporal priority of the persistence of affordance of boundaries thus paves the way to an expression of *mereological causality* (see Smith & Varzi 1997, 2000) in which boundaries as constituent elements of the surrounding built environment (cf. Abbott's (1995) neighbourhood system as a constitutive context) let specific aggregates emerge. 'Objects and processes can each be conceived as being put together or assembled out of (respectively: spatial and temporal) proper parts' (Smith 2001: 3). My aim is not to categorise the emergent entities with increasing aggregate specificity and complexity. Instead, my aim is to reveal and understand how assembled entities cohere as affective and affording patterns. Assemblages consist of built boundaries that manifest a pattern of consistency in the relational and fuzzy interactional differentiations structured by their spatial-material properties.

The material presence of built boundaries thus forms a basis for the study of the specific socio-spatial phenomena implied by inhabiting and developing a built environment. Material presence occurs in the assembled constellations of emergent entities on a fluid scale of the experience of time-space specific local inhabitation. Our understanding of the socio-spatial significance of built boundaries depends on their affordances to persist materially, because, being emplaced, perceptive and experiential, we have no choice but to interact upon encounter. Such significance is not exclusive to initially secluded entities, but also applies to the encounter of larger-scale coherent entities aggregating persistent affordance.

Abbott (1995: 873) raises the suggestion that entities have the ability to 'do' social action. Action, then, can be seen 'as any ability to create an effect on the rest of the social process that goes beyond effects that are merely transmitted through the causing entity from elsewhere'. While such definition of action corrupts the more precise one of purposeful action by Von Mises (1998), accepting the effect of any perceived or experienced and conceived entity as *real* is in concordance with the critical realist reading of *causal powers*. Causal power can be of a different order in aggregate or emergent constellations than its separate constituents. The interactive effects of the materialised presence of (aggregate) entities (*sensu* Wallace's (2011) agency without intent) are pivotal for the social study of the full boundary composition of built environment configurations.

Fiat and bona fide boundaries

This chapter emphasises that historically and socio-culturally particular boundaries are not an explicit target of methodological development.

Instead, it maintains a focus on the physical characteristics of boundaries that can be readily perceived and experienced. Ultimately, to translate boundary concepts into analytical units, the protean nature of boundary as a term referring interchangeably to lines, edges, barriers, divisions, etc. needs to be overcome. Such translation must clearly distinguish what boundaries are in terms of observable information (spatial data) on the physical properties of built environments. Although I never concealed my focus on boundaries as an empirical phenomenon, how I explained their constitution will not ward off misunderstandings on an ideational level entirely. In order to definitively disentangle the empirical and ideational boundary concepts in my treatment of boundaries so far, I introduce Smith & Varzi's (1997, 2000; further elaborated by Smith 2001; see also Vis 2014a) distinction between *fiat* and *bona fide* boundaries. Employing this scheme will help achieve an effective operationalisation of boundary concepts in research practice.

Essentially the opposing definition of fiat and bona fide boundaries is remarkably simple. However, this basic idea may get complicated, mostly in the way it affects subsequent concepts for research. Bona fide boundaries are those distinctions that are based on spatial discontinuity (e.g. holes, fissures, slits) or qualitative (physical) heterogeneity (e.g. material constitution, texture, electric charge). Fiat boundaries are those distinctions that are based on differentiation without association with spatial discontinuity or qualitative (physical) heterogeneity. That means conceptual or imagined differentiations, such as national borders and sacred ground. Recognition of this fundamental difference completes the opposition instantaneously. It applies equally to inner and outer boundaries,[5] which in theory does not limit their use to any distinction (Smith & Varzi 1997, 2000; Smith 2001).

Both fiat and bona fide boundaries may form entities, or, in Smith & Varzi's (2000) terms: objects. Adapting their examples, bona fide objects could be a body, ball or cheese, whereas fiat objects could be a property, a hemisphere or the North Sea. For the latter, the North Sea, it is apparent that along the coastal lines fiat and bona fide boundaries coincide. One should add though that the lines delimiting the North Sea on maps are entirely fiat. Although one may argue these lines represent the physical

5. In the present (material) context, it seems counterproductive and inaccurate to introduce a difference between inner and outer boundaries, because how can it *a priori* be defined what can be regarded as entities, which may then contain or allow for inner distinctions to be made? However, once put in a processual perspective it becomes acceptable that when an entity is established (e.g. a hut), inner distinctions of its parts could be made (e.g. eating and sleeping zones). Since the physical properties of the entity's surface continue, distinguishing one zone from the other would introduce an inner (fiat) boundary.

distinction between land and sea, we know that the tides are in constant movement. Therefore, no coastline can ever be truly represented by a static boundary. Instead, as some maps will do, it would gain accuracy by depicting the zone of fluctuating encroachment (cf. fuzziness). It should be noted that most fiat boundaries do not exclusively depend on human fiat, but (as phenomenological experience suggests) involve the underlying material properties of a phenomenon also. Bona fide objects cannot also depend on fiat boundaries. Fig. 4.1 depicts how the basic distinction between bona fide and fiat boundaries works.

Smith & Varzi (2000) further distinguish between individual fiat boundaries and social fiat boundaries. The first kind pertains to the arbitrary choice made on the basis of individual perception and conception, and often results from a single act at a given time. This arbitrary choice can also be determined by e.g. a type of measurement or mathematical calculation (e.g. centre of mass of celestial bodies or the equator). Social fiat boundaries are dependent on the perception of the participating human beings (cf. Chapter 3 on institutional projects and systems) for the arbitrary choice of setting the boundary. In addition, Smith & Varzi recognise the more abstract social fiat boundaries that are imposed, and therefore *appear* relatively detached from causal change (e.g. many policy driven and political borders).

Finally, it can be logically reasoned that bona fide objects are all connected (in the continuum of the physical spatial world), whereas fiat objects may be scattered. Simultaneously, some of the scattered fiat objects may be unified in fiat objects of a higher order, e.g. island groups. It is useful to note these further distinctions as they can readily be connected to the preceding theorising in this chapter and Chapter 3.

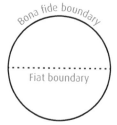

Fig. 4.1   A representation of the difference between bona fide and fiat boundaries.

The difference between the discrete (physical) distinction of bona fide boundaries, represented by the solid line of the circle, and the ideational distinction of fiat boundaries, represented by the dotted line, which indicates what we agree distinguishes the upper from the lower half. Note, however, that fiat boundaries can also occur in dissociation from bona fide boundaries.

Moreover, it should be noted that none of these distinctions changes the first definitions of fiat and bona fide boundaries: a boundary refers to a physical distinction or it does not. As data on urban form and spatial layout contained in the complex composition of the built environment results from documenting and measuring observed physical differences, this philosophical assessment of boundary concepts is highly beneficial for coming to terms with the how and what of the empirical reality our data truly represent.

Next, we delve further into the implications for the concrete empirical world. Because bona fide boundaries are material, i.e. they have divisible bulk or mass, they necessarily occupy space. They must be part of the entities, bona fide objects, which are circumscribed by them. That means that bona fide objects ineluctably comprise their own boundaries, whereas the environment they are embedded in is open (cf. Ingold 2008a). Bona fide objects thus have open complements.

Holes and tunnels, however, are notable examples of where this seems to work the other way around. These are called negative objects (Smith 2001). Where a void occurs in the surrounding material surface, the resulting bona fide object is defined from the outside by the bona fide boundary of its 'host' (Smith & Varzi 2000; Smith 2001). Negative objects cannot be true bona fide objects, as they need fiat boundaries to completely circumscribe them as an entity. That is, the entranceways are not bounded by (observable or experiential) bona fide boundaries but ascribed to them by human fiat (Smith 2001). Here fiat, for example, separates the air filling a hole from the air outside, or an otherwise contiguous ground surface (this idea is taken forward in Chapters 5 and 7 with 'virtual boundaries').

Accepting the open complements of bona fide objects does not imply that when a bona fide object is divided (by fluxes or transformative interaction) it leaves one part open and the other closed (because it comprises the boundary). Instead, the extant outer boundary of the bona fide object is progressively deformed and becomes two surfaces (one for each now separate bona fide object) (Smith & Varzi 2000).

Recapitulating, boundaries as sites of difference are a way of better understanding differentiation: the recognition that something is not something else. The process of differentiation works continuously, through all concepts, perceptions and experiences coming forth from inhabiting the concrete, socio-spatial world. The physical properties of the spatial world lead to differentiation according to bona fide boundaries. In getting to know the world we have the capacity to project divisive fiat boundary conceptions onto and next to those physical differences.

Except for recognising our fellow human beings as physically present entities, most differentiations in the social world are fiat boundaries, i.e. arbitrary, ideational decisions, while in the concrete inhabited world many of the fiat distinctions make use of underlying physical differences.

Following from the time-geographical principles of Hägerstrand (1975, 1976) I already argued that the same spatial location cannot be occupied twice. This logically means that bona fide boundaries cannot coincide, as is indeed acknowledged by Smith & Varzi (2000: 416). However, 'fiat boundaries, because they are not possessed of divisible bulk, do not occupy (fill out) the space where they are located; hence they can be perfectly co-located one with another'. This notion is crucial for understanding how the concepts come about that devise our built environment data.

Conceptual series towards spatial data

Ideational and empirical boundaries

Bona fide boundaries may give rise to and coincide with fiat boundaries, and fiat boundaries may give way to additional (modified or higher level) fiat boundaries. However, the only way a fiat boundary can become a bona fide boundary is through transforming the physical properties of our environment accordingly in the interactive processes of inhabitation. I designated this human construction process 'materialisation' (see Chapter 2 on the material and Chapter 3 on filled space). From that moment onwards the differentiation enters a dialectic relationship in which the fiat boundary and the bona fide boundary continually become one another (cf. Pred 1986). That is, the processes of formation are inchoate (cf. Jones 2009), thus ongoing. Simultaneously, the bona fide boundary and its modifications and/or transformations become an immediate empirical and social reality of material manifestation in space that is reacted to in the same human and social way as otherwise would have been the case. That means the ideational (human or social conception) becomes the empirical (material through physical transformation), and the empirical in turn influences the ideational and so on.

Built boundaries

In the preceding boundary theory and critique I already used the term 'built boundaries'. These are the boundaries resulting from materialisation. Built boundaries express the fact that materialisation comprises constructive human interactions within the environment whereby its pre-existing physical properties are transformed. The making of built boundaries introduces additional physical discontinuities in the environment, i.e. the edges of built features. Built features are intended to be further occupied by inhabitation processes. They are physical things, a surface or textural extent of a mass of substance, comprising their own boundaries to an outside or open complements. These boundaries, perceived of as edges, compose the built environment complex. The built environment thus consists of bona fide boundaries.

Although built boundaries as edges still simply refer to one physical space as distinct to another, and are therefore essentially part of that bona fide object, in constructing occupiable physical subdivisions built boundaries can have mass themselves. That implies the boundaries themselves essentially become a bona fide object, as not only their distinction but their masses too occupy space. The masses of the built boundaries which by their bona fide distinctions circumscribe other (internal) bona fide objects may be important for an ontology of the entire ecological (natural scientific) world, but have no decisive part in this research. Their space is already occupied and therefore they cannot serve simultaneously for human occupation as necessary for social interaction opportunities. Yet, insofar as the characteristics of the mass of boundaries that themselves occupy space influences the relation to the outside or open complements, this physical information can affect our understanding of the precise role their distinction plays in the built environment complex. Regardless, all built boundaries are measured and documented as part of acquiring data on the material and spatial configuration of the built environment.

Boundary lines

When documenting the material-spatial properties of the built environment, the edges of the physical distinctions formed by built boundaries become boundary lines. This means they represent all the measurements and observations that were part of the empirical spatial data acquisition. As representations, boundary lines are fiat boundaries. Boundary lines, as such, do not occupy space, but convey an ideational meaning. They are reductions from the (physical) edges of bona fide objects in the built environment. This reduction needs to be further specified for those bona fide boundaries that themselves comprise mass.

As mentioned above, the space they occupy cannot serve simultaneous human occupation (on the same (ground) level).

Hence, in the representation of the edges formed by built boundaries, edges will refer to the outlines of bona fide objects, which for materially demarcated boundaries include the extent of their mass. The effect for our data is that when a built boundary comprises mass, i.e. is itself a bona fide object and circumscribes a subsequent bona fide object, the documented boundary line will represent the edge that is the outline of the circumscribing built boundary. The spaces that are distinguished by all edges documented so, are generally thought of as, at least in principle, available to accommodate occupation by (a) human being(s) (i.e. a socio-spatial system).[6]

It is thinkable that in particular built environments, built boundaries consist of a mass that is actually occupiable itself (e.g. thick castle walls) and could on that basis be considered as a spatial subdivision. In such cases the researcher should duly declare how this is treated in the data. For the purposes of this study, occupiable built boundaries will be considered to be part of the inside space of subdivision created.[7] In lay terms, the outer limit, or the outside edge, of a wall thus becomes the outline and therefore the boundary line representing the spatial subdivision. It is a pragmatic and purposeful (for comparative reasons, see note 7) arbitrary decision on resolution of detail not to include the mass of boundaries (even when occupiable) in the context of this research.

In addition, in the data in this book, when a materially demarcated built boundary leaves a gap for passage that entails a physical discontinuity on the ground surface, the boundary line representing it will still circumscribe the feature as a closed and discrete subdividing outline. This ensures that a basic visualisation of the spatial data is produced, which consists of equal boundary lines

6. Seeing inhabitation as socio-spatial systemic occupation of bounded spaces brings to mind how Hillier & Hanson (1984: 146) define the inhabitants of single buildings. 'An inhabitant is, if not a permanent [corrig.] occupant of the cell, at least an individual whose social existence is mapped into the category of space within that cell: more an inhabitant of the social knowledge defined by the cell than of the cell itself.' Socio-spatial systemic occupation, however, pertains to all of the urban built environment.
7. The proposed reduction serves the additional purpose of creating data of equal quality for every thinkable case study across cultures, geographical locations and historical periods. This allows data to be derived from various disciplinary conducts, including in cases where a spatial configuration of the past can no longer be fully retrieved and empirically documented. As will be shown in Chapter 7 it is then possible to make use of conjectural datasets of spatial configuration with very incomplete empirically verifiable data available. A careful and critical practice of reduction to boundary lines should secure the comparability of data.

representing outlines:[8] an equal fiat representation of the differentiation between one spatial subdivision and another. As this indicates, there is always a level of detailing involved that is at the discretion of the individual mapper or researcher. Depending on convention, analysis, or research purpose, either per particular built environment or ensuring comparability across datasets, outlined subdivisions could occur on very small scales indeed.

As will be explained below, here a distinction is made between edges of a major occupiable subdivision and those further physical distinctions that logically refer to the precise use and design of that subdivision internally, rather than how it relates to its outside.[9] Depending on the nature of the data and the purpose of analysis, more or less detail could be allowed to appear as outlines of spaces captured in boundary lines. Outlines, then, can be seen as the schematic sketched representations of the boundaries as sites of difference giving shape to an entire built environment complex.

Visualised or presented data

On the basis of documenting separate boundary lines, a fiat outline drawing of the configuration of the built environment can be made. Naturally, such a visualisation or presentation of material-spatial data neither shows mass dependent physical properties nor the ongoing inchoate processes of which the represented bona fide built boundaries are part. So, paradoxically, despite understanding built boundaries to be subject to constant (re)negotiation, their data representation depicts an eventful state in which no transformation whatsoever takes place. They will only ever be an 'accurate' representation of the bona fide boundaries reduced on the basis of human fiat, and an approximation of the fiat boundaries informing the constant formation in time-space specific inhabitation processes.

8. In most contemporary and modern historical plans and maps, the components of the built environment are represented by exactly such indiscriminating outlines, which very often appear as equal lines on the map, though their exact treatment of the mass of built boundaries is unclear (cf. Chapter 7). The convention of OS MasterMap (*OS Mastermap® Topography Layer: User Guide and Technical Specification*, 2007) (in the UK) uses the term 'mereing' to describe the definition of any relationship of mapped boundaries, such as districts and counties, with real life (empirical on the ground) features. Such definitions, however, are not available for each coincidence of a mapped fiat boundary line with a bona fide boundary.
9. Some easily recognisable examples of such distinctions could be the rooms of a building, flower bed designs in and paths through a park, the pedestrian areas (sidewalks) distinguishing the intended method of transport along streets, etc.

We could call the fiat outline drawing a map. The reader should note that through this process we demonstrate that well-prepared ground plans can be used for the social study of built environments based on boundary concepts. However, our traditional view of a map as a static snapshot that appears to refer to a degree of *continuity* needs to be adjusted. The eventful state that is depicted in fiat boundary line maps should instead be regarded as atomic[10] (all occurs at once and is inseparable). Any next atomic stage essentially depends on the occurrence of *any* change (to the physical properties of built boundaries), because all change relationally changes everything that is included in the depicted whole.

If maps are used in a series of 'time-slices' of a continuously inhabited place, they can be linked to analyse its historical development. We know each time-slice is atomic, while we understand the same inhabitation processes (as theorised) are ongoing between them. Therefore one time-slice logically develops into the next. Looking at time this way is akin to approaching historical development as 'transformative', 'revolutionary' or 'eventful' (cf. Smith, A.T. 2001, 2003: 12–21; Vis 2009 on temporal rhythm), though each time-slice's precise historical 'weight' cannot necessarily be discriminated in relation to longer-termed continuity (cf. Bintliff 2010). Yet, its socio-spatial significance in part is interpretable through persistent physical characteristics within the built environment complex, which may feature, thus influence, over long periods of time. Intellectually, though, persistent built boundaries are not identical over time, because with every change the constitutive context of all boundaries within the whole changes.

What is lost in such atomic approach are all the intermediate stages (down to the smallest temporal particle). The better the temporal resolution, the more detailed the analysis can be. While the origin of built features can be expected to be temporally diverse and therefore the map represents a palimpsest, one should be careful not to introduce anachronisms in the data. This implies that special effort should be made to make sure all features mapped did indeed exist contemporaneously at the moment ascribed to the map. Anachronisms could occur if there is a better historical resolution for one building, but not the next. Except for conjectural (Lilley et al. 2007; Lilley 2011a) and historically reconstructive (Keene 1985; Bisschops 2012) mapping, one should aim to come as close as possible to a comprehensive snapshot of the area

10. Atomic here is used in the sense of atomicity. An atomic moment is inseparable: no time passes and everything occurs at once. A map in this sense is a representation of something immediate.

under scrutiny. However, it should be noted that in most cases such level of precision is not achievable. This is why it needs to be clarified which assumptions are made about the source data used.

Towards an ontology of analytical units

In the conceptual series above, we have worked towards a better understanding and appropriate convention for material-spatial built environment configuration (layout) data. The next step is the formulation of analytical units, which need to unite the theoretical understanding of boundaries both on the fiat and bona fide side, as well as the fiat and bona fide understanding involved in conceptualising built environment data. The implications of these oscillations between fiat and bona fide boundaries for preparing our data and devising a research practice based on commensurate analytical units is summarised in Table 4.1. The table comprises four stages, after the ideational and empirical difference of boundaries, in which spatial data becomes converted into appropriate boundary conceptualisations: from the initial acquisition of spatial information, through to processing that information into meaningful ascriptions which lead to analytical units.

A few things should be noted following the data breakdown of Table 4.1. Firstly, the methodology that is emerging here proffers an idealistic presentation of data acquisition. As indicated before, in practice it could logically be expected that researchers will use already extant maps and plans, both commercially and academically produced (from various disciplinary conducts), as well as historical documents, historically reconstructed and conjectured maps. The advantage is that 'legacy data' produced for other purposes could be adapted for applying boundary concepts. However, extant data and plans require treatment with meticulous care. Ambiguities in the reading of mapped material without direct checks of the empirical reality they sprung from are unavoidable. Chapter 7 will present two test case examples of the treatment of divergent data sources for this purpose.

Secondly, the production of, or reduction to, outlines conceals their underlying intricate theoretical provenance. Outlines should logically follow from adherence to a single coherent (the smallest scale) continuous residing socio-spatial system. As the internal arrangements of the functioning and activities of ongoing residing systems cannot be known from the theory, the internal connections or interior design of space(s) within outlines should not be represented. Another way of seeing the argument on built boundaries with an occupiable mass,

Table 4.1 Conceptual breakdown of material-spatial layout data on the built environment.

	Built environment data type	Nature	Acquired as	Format
1	Built boundaries	Bona fide	Measurements and documentation of physical transformations of the environment, i.e. materialised differentiation	Unprocessed empirical observations (data as acquired)
2	Boundary lines	Fiat	A construction and reduction to the outlines of the full, continuous extent of materialised differentiations	Processed and simplified version of empirical observations
3	Boundary visualisation	Fiat	A geographical representation of the outlines	Integral interpretive geographical organisation in an outline plan (full configuration)
4	Boundary line types	Capture a fiat understanding of bona fide	An application of an ontology of analytical units on the outline plan (boundary line type ascription)	Dissected plan of geographically anchored analytical units

This table breaks down how material-spatial layout data on the built environment can be expressed according to the principles of bona fide and fiat boundaries (reproduced from Vis 2014a).

described previously, is to regard this mass as part of the internal arrangement. The definitions of the analytical units (see Chapter 5) will help to make informed decisions at this stage, though a degree of subjectivity in judgment calls and purposeful conventions cannot be avoided in practice (Chapter 7 discusses this for the test cases).

Finally, it should be noted that Table 4.1 does not explicate the temporal congruency that needs to be assumed in spatial data. The ultimate assumption, as explained previously, is that a mapped representation is necessarily atomic, even though it is recognised that the nature of any plan and data acquisition prevents true (immediate) simultaneity. However, in data acquisition of whatever kind, one should critically assess the historical and/or archaeological determination of the temporal span included in the data provided. Only assuming atomicity of spatial data can allow for analysis of material boundary properties across space, as the dataset needs to be complete and to represent features that are known (including critical conjectures filling data gaps in the contiguity of the spatial selection, see Chapter 7). Analytically such 'spatial moments' can be connected through time (Chapters 8 and 9 discuss issues related to diachronic analyses).

Table 4.1 concludes with 'boundary line types'. Chapter 5 is dedicated to how these are defined to form ontological descriptive operatives shaping the inhabited (urban) built environment. As mentioned at the outset, these analytical units will distinguish the types of seclusion operated through the physical properties of built boundaries as they occur in emplaced lived experience. They construct the missing link between a theoretical socio-spatial understanding of the inhabited built environment and an informed empirical study based on spatial data. As such they form the concluding step in formulating what, taken together, could be called an empirical theory as argued by Smith (2011a): the connection between high-level (social) theory and empirical application. The ontological definitions serve the double purpose of empirical identification and interpretive understanding of the constituents of the inhabited built environment, specifically differentiating between the socio-spatial systems that generate and occupy or reside in initial spatial subdivisions and further perceived aggregate entities.

CHAPTER 5
AN ONTOLOGY OF BOUNDARY LINE TYPES

Introduction

In the course of the preceding chapter, abstract theory on the inhabitation of the world came to be connected to built environment data by means of boundary conceptualisations. We moved from a thorough understanding of boundaries and a world of bounding processes to a foundational conceptualisation of what is conveyed by basic material-spatial outline data on the layout of the occupiable subdivisions composing the built environment. This may provide the basis for regarding (urban) built environments as a complex boundary configuration to be visualised as simple lines on a map, but such reduction almost completely conceals any path to further investigate the specific socio-spatial significance of any specific case.

As it has been established in Chapter 4 that the socio-spatial significance of all boundaries is primarily captured in how they come to seclude one space from another, a study of the socio-spatial significance of the material presence of boundaries requires analytical units exclusively defined as distinct operational interfaces of seclusion. The kind of operational interface of seclusion each section of boundary conveys depends on the physical and spatially contextual properties of the built boundaries as they occur in emplaced lived experience, now imagined as lines.

However, the successful application of the 'boundary line types' that Chapter 4 concludes with as analytical units depends on a definition that simultaneously permits their exclusive identification as line sections in the spatial dataset, aided by knowledge of the empirical (material) reality it is derived from. That means that definitions should not only determine the material properties of built boundaries that are intellectually understandable as a kind of seclusion, but should also include a precise reference to the physical and configurationally contextual properties that situate them in particular locations, and their extent within the built environment complex. In this way, these *primary analytical units* will form the hinge between theoretical understanding and enabling comparative empirical operationalisation in mapping practice (see Chapter 7).

Chapter 8 then explains how further analytical units are derived: topological segments, boundary segments, and topological sides. It is only through operationalisation that profound yet broad knowledge on urban life and the developments of urbanisation as parts of the human inhabitation process can be produced. This knowledge can be used to determine the specificity of urban places, and meaningfully explore the consistency of urban traditions or geographical areas as well as contrasts between urban landscapes.

In other words, this chapter supplies a culminating set of concepts, i.e. Boundary Line Types (BLTs), which serve a *purpose* as primary analytical units. However, this set of concepts differs from before, because combined they should provide the elements for a full *ontological redescription* of the built environment conveyed as boundary lines with a view to applied empirical research. This means the definitions of the analytical units contained in this chapter form an empirical theory (*sensu* Smith 2011a) on the basis of which a *method* for their study can be devised.

The BLT definitions rectify the paucity of attention paid to the concrete social relevance of the materiality of differentiation introduced by developing space. First, these definitions counter the indeterminate nature of spatial discontinuity (boundaries) maintained in Hillier & Hanson's (1984) highly influential *The Social Logic of Space*. When we acknowledge that each discrete subdivision of occupiable space is particular to the means by which it is secluded from spatial continuity (outside/open), we must stipulate its discontinuous (differentiating) properties. Second, they completely reverse the notion that 'the very nature of a boundary [...] is to create a disconnection' (Hillier & Hanson 1984: 144). Rather, boundaries are the way in which socio-spatial systems connect into contiguous urban built environments.

Towards the back of this book a supplementary table of abridged BLT definitions can be found, for easy reference throughout the remainder of this work.

Requirements for the ontology

All conceptualisation up to this point was a necessary preparation to enable the use of (urban) built environment data in an accurately defined and informed way. Through this theoretical process it is now known exactly what we are interested in and looking to understand from analysing such data. Yet, in order to acquire analytical units we need to dissect the boundary lines depicting the built environment into secluding sections comprehensively. In other words, we need a boundary line type ontology (see Table 4.1). In the terms of Koch's (2005) architectural systems, the elements of the spatial system need to be defined on the basis of the architectural structure they receive.

This architectural structure comprises the material properties and references to the physical and configurationally contextual properties on the basis of which they can be identified, as mentioned above, but does not prescribe location of occurrence and dimensions. Yet, once empirically identified, both the extent and relative position and the persistent properties will be informative for understanding built boundaries as fixed approximations of inchoate socio-spatial significance, for which their specific seclusion sets the terms of the theoretical part of their definition. Positive identification of line segments as BLTs principally depends on the visual inspection of the spatial contexts in which they appear, and any available information on the empirical reality at the time of mapping their occurrence (this means also the historical period intended to be captured by reconstructive and conjectural mapping efforts[1]).

Kropf (2009) cogently argues that a usable (comparative) ontology should respect certain requirements. These consist of a consistent, coherent and comprehensive set of definitions, which are general enough to be used comparatively in all thinkable contexts, yet specific enough to identify them as analytical units in the empirical reality of datasets. Hermon & Niccolucci (2002) show that when a general typology of flint tools for prehistoric research was devised, similar requirements were met for application to specific time periods. The notion comparative here intends to span the full variety of urban traditions as they evolved worldwide, throughout human history (see Chapter 1). Therefore, the terminology used in the definitions should avoid terms that are suggestive of particular use and socio-cultural contexts, as these depend on additional time-space specific data on each city. Instead, the terminology should always remain on

1. There will be further attention on reconstructive historical mapping and conjectural mapping in Chapters 6 and 7.

a flexible and rudimentary human conditional level. The BLT definitions should fully support an ontological redescription of any urban built environment complex on both disaggregating and mereologically (cf. hierarchy in Kropf's (2009) ontologies: resulting from the causal relation between parts forming entities) generative levels of constellation and aggregation.

What is proposed here could be called an 'ontology of types', which should mark the difference from a full metaphysical ontology which also includes the precise relation between elements. The BLTs must presuppose to represent the whole of that which they are part entirely through relations, but, apart from certain conditional statements, how they are related is contingent on each time-space specific situation. A critical reader might remark that creating types actually means retreating into categories[2] once again (cf. Chapter 4), though this time the categories capture the boundaries themselves as abstracted entities. There is no way to completely avoid this paradox. Empirically BLTs are immediately recognised as 'entities', i.e. analytical units. They do represent the physical demarcation of the socio-spatial specification of 'differences in character', using Abbott's (1995) words. Therefore it is useful to emphasise once more that boundaries are emergent and constitutive contingencies, as in Jones' (2009) inchoate processes, to which in (scientific) observation and day-to-day experience we assume and ascribe a fixed reality.

Actually, the BLTs do not represent a full concrete reality, but merely abstract a situation springing from the material presence of boundaries. This chimes better with Abbott's (1995) assessment of boundaries as 'sites of difference' (on the basis of a property), which should be regarded as atomic[3] units (a point or site) to which differences can be attributed. This same logic can be applied as a description of BLTs, which represent the sites of an elementary operation in terms of the secluding differentiations that are empirically discernible on the basis of the foundational informing theories. As such, it could be argued we are no longer talking about units or categories, but determinant elements.[4] The initial mundane *entities* coming forth from linking up these elements

2. Schaffter et al. (2010) articulate an insightful subdivision of categories in type, class, and concept.
3. It is unclear what Abbott (1995) intends with his use of the word atomic. It could be he means to express the 'smallest part'. However, the fact that he refers to them as 'points' indicates an abstract representation, a reduction of something extant.
4. It should be noted that this depends heavily on the way the theoretical concepts leading up to BLTs are defined and how the reduction (boundary lines) took place. Depending on these definitions and preparatory processes the operational elements referred to could acquire a different definition. By the same measure, someone interested not in configuration and configurative affects but the specificity of all material properties would probably arrive at other definitions.

are not a primary concern in elementary identification. Rather, of concern is their direct and wider contextual placement in association with their configurationally or topologically affective properties, intrinsically positing an empirical social reality (that is, an experiential locale for social interactive processes).

On the basis of an ontology of BLTs, the boundary line visualisation of a built environment complex can now be 'dissected' into segments commensurable with their definitions. This process of remapping itself automatically leads to an analytical or formal redescription with an immediate initial alternative visualisation of the inhabited configuration. Since identification appeals to a flexible human appreciation of a more than abstract empirical reality (as if encountering the situations on site), mapping according to the BLT ontology cannot currently be automated in a computational process. Nonetheless, as a mainly visual process compatible with application on digital data, mapping BLTs opens up an array of hypothetically meaningful quantitative, statistical and analytical operations of ordering and extracting information advancing human interpretation. In turn, more selective or immediately intelligible visualisations could be based on these interpretive measures. Patterns representing entities and aggregates emerging from the boundary relations and processes that are intrinsically part of each time-space or case-specific urban built environment could be explored (Chapter 8 will discuss interpretively promising analytical possibilities). Both disaggregative detail and aggregative patterns may *represent particular occurrences of inherently inferential socio-spatial significance in terms of from-the-inside-towards-the-outside relations within accordingly framed interaction.*

This interpretive potency does justice to Jones' (2010: 266) 'insistence that categories do not have an intrinsic meaning and that their boundaries are always inchoate[, which] is an attempt to disrupt the apparent fixity of the categories ordering the world'. In contrast, the intrinsic logic of BLTs redescribing urban built environments (cf. Löw's (2013) intrinsic logic of cities) lies in their emergent contextual relationships forming *a posteriori* recognised entities, not the potential correlations with *a priori* assumed lay categories. This concurs with how we get to know the world phenomenologically and to Jones' (2009) suggestions of cognitive processes, though it replaces any acculturated arrogation of Schütz's (1967) 'common stock of knowledge' with Sayer's (1985, 2000) emancipating understanding. This does not withstand that questions of interest could be elucidated by correlations uncovered through combining the socio-spatially relative positions of entities with e.g. historical, archaeological, social or anthropological assemblages of information. Ultimately, entities on any scale recognised and understood through a boundary approach emerge from the intrinsic coherence of boundaries in the whole complex as a constitutive context, and do not prescribe their precise forms (see Chapter 4).

Formulating a BLT ontology

The following paragraphs will summarise several specific stipulations to which the ontology of BLTs formulated below must adhere. This ensures, in addition to all else, that the data treatment which the definitions require also maximises comparability.

Since we theoretically depart from a position in which human beings are emplaced in the urban built environment, and therefore by inhabiting it occupy the subdivided spaces that boundaries seclude, the from-the-inside-towards-the-outside notion of the emergence of discrete occupiable entities implies the inevitability of having two sides to each boundary. Although boundaries as an abstract 'site of difference' could be atomic, they have come to incorporate physical properties as built boundaries which will necessarily feature dimensional extents. An emplaced human being encountering a materialised differentiation will always be relationally placed to face or approach one side of it. If the affordance of a boundary to be traversed is realised, i.e. a human being crosses the boundary, this relationship is inverted. Individually we are always on the inside looking out: this situation cannot be inverted even though the relation to the boundary crossed will be. Therefore when on the inside, we understand the potential of a situation of being on the outside (looking in).

To take full account of both positions in relation to the boundary, a BLT definition needs to refer to a boundary from both sides. Extending this argument contextually to the subdivisions that emerge from built boundaries, no boundary line can ever become fully defined by the identification of a *single* BLT. The redescription of a built environment of boundary lines depends on emerging contexts the boundary is part of on both sides. When more than two BLTs are identified along a segment of boundary line, this will be the result of mereological conditional statements in the BLT definition by which some relations become necessary, though not specified.

As the specific way in which seclusion operates depends on how the built boundary is characterised by its material properties, it should be noted that material properties can account for tremendous levels of detail, including architectural textures, style, form, tradition and construction (e.g. Kropf 1996). Because the aim of this ontology is to enable application in comparative research, the *level of detail* needs to be determined on which material properties are deemed relevant. Since many material details can evoke all kinds of sensory and intellectual affects, it should be clear that this comparative aim causes a deliberate limitation. This aim neither purports to be final nor a literally all-encompassing redescription of the built environment. Alternative aims or inclusion of additional or alternative empirical information would logically lead one to a new commensurate conceptualisation. Here the imposed limitations, especially caused by the restrictions of archaeological remains and historical reconstructions by which temporal depth is enabled, initially boil down to major outlines on a close-to-ground level.

Close-to-ground means more than a two-dimensional line, but less than comprehensive three-dimensional information on built volumes, being limited to the ground surface configuration and the influence of obstructions and passages across its subdivisions. The most determinant occupiable spaces and the basic materalisation of their relations should then remain detectable or retrievable through time in a much larger number of well-known or preserved cases. Datasets from prehistory to the present day can be conveyed on the same level of detail. Ideally, it is intended that a trained eye could begin investigation of mapped data with some background information on the empirical reality of encountering the boundaries, but without elaborate background research. However, it cannot be done solely on the basis of unknown line-drawn maps. This is because in order to discern how boundary lines affect opportunities of interaction within the reality of inhabiting a socio-spatial and physical environment, all material properties directly affecting how each seclusion of the contiguously connected subdivisions takes place should be taken into account.

Contrary to the elicitation of 'seclusion', it is determined from here on that in principle all boundaries are crossable and, therefore, open: accessible or permeable. This accounts for the societal necessity to move between spaces in order to function, and the fact that built boundaries change over time. The material properties of 'open' boundaries can be regarded as passive or non-obstructive (e.g. intersected) in the sense that they readily allow traversing. Yet, it is promptly acknowledged that certain built boundaries will literally have to be broken before a crossing and, consequently, direct interaction can take place.[5] Such boundaries, e.g. impermeable walls, form barriers to regular crossings, meaning undisruptive interaction between the sides concerned is not possible. The material property of impermeability is therefore of great importance to the BLT definitions. As the operation of seclusion has *ontological primacy*, the formulation of the BLTs will start with a determination of the ability to close off (make impermeable) a bounded space (subdivision) towards undisruptive interaction from the outside, i.e. a strongly emphasised seclusion from within and necessarily 'intrusive' interactions from without.

The notion of closing off from-the-inside-towards-the-outside results from the understanding of a socio-spatial system occupying or predominantly residing in the spatial subdivision concerned, by which it distinctly extracts itself from the surrounding environment. This also retains the exertion of a mundane spatial power relation, because the same space cannot be occupied twice (Hägerstrand 1975, 1976; Pred 1977) – neither by the mass shaping built form nor by people simultaneously – and thus space is dominated by this seclusion. Closability, then, depends on the physical characteristic of the material properties making a boundary impermeable. As a consequence of the dominant relationship caused by closability (the ability to make impermeable), surrounding BLTs may have a configurative association of dependence. This also implicates that there is an inherent interest in entranceways (Latour's (1992) wall holes), as depending on the material properties these either afford closability (e.g. the temporary manipulations of opening, closing, and locking a door, or Latour's (1992) door hinges rendering a wall hole in a reversible state) or, alternatively, predominantly mitigate impermeability.[6] As a physical characteristic, the dominant designation could be used more flexibly to further specify a BLT or a particular complex of BLTs.

5. It could be suggested that an actual crossing is not a necessity for social interaction, even through a wall. To what extent material properties are permeable is difficult to determine without direct observation of their properties and sensory functioning – e.g. what thickness or which material makes a wall numb sound completely (see also Rodman & Cooper 1996)? Assessing this requires experimental and observational material research. More sensitive and comprehensive sensory approaches in anthropology and archaeology can be found in, e.g., Bull & Back (2003), Howes (2005b), Drobnick (2006) and Boivin et al. (2007).

6. It is worth noting that archaeological evidence may be very fragmentary and, without onsite inspections, even modern maps give little conclusive information on entrances and where they are placed. Their location remains therefore to an extent a matter of informed conjecturing and expert judgments (see also Chapter 7). It would be practical to assume any spatial subdivision in principle is enterable for someone, unless there is evidence for the material property of impermeability along the boundary's course. It is acknowledged here that full onsite surveys of material properties would be commendable, but often unfeasible.

Currently two kinds of dominant BLTs are distinguished: a *dominant* and a *solid dominant*. The latter refers to the single cell configuration (Hillier & Hanson 1984, the simplest configuration of a single space with a relation to its outside) or the single room house (e.g. M.E. Smith 2008). Because the BLTs are based on outlines, and thus disregard internal organisation or interior design, most outlines of structures or buildings would be designated closable boundaries and become solid dominants (i.e. no further differentiation inside).[7] Only through a hierarchical relation, typically an 'enclosure', can dominants create aggregated subsets of boundaries, whilst retaining their closability. Solid dominants could operationally be seen as the mother of all BLTs. However, the primacy of the solid dominants should not be mistaken for a lived experiential primacy for emplaced human beings encountering the world. There is no necessity in any instance of *terra incognita* in the world we encounter that our experience of it starts with spatial distinctions characterised as solid dominants (in any case we have to introduce them first as built boundaries). Nevertheless, it is not coincidental that the human construction of built environments depends first on secluding spaces from each other. The simple construction of a shelter or home bears the physical, architectonic characteristics of a solid dominant. This theoretical understanding of significance is not the same as the primacy of identifying solid dominants in research practice, which follows from the situation of being faced with a pre-existing spatial-material dataset: i.e. the static and holistic selection of an already constructed built environment in which we are not ourselves currently embedded.

It applies to all non-closable boundaries that any demarcation with the material property of impermeability requires the presence of transcendent intersections. It is conceded that validating their existence often requires informed assumptions and critically judged simplification, which is a sacrifice made to the ready applicability of the BLT definitions. However, this does not mean that the ontology presented should be seen as a total prescription to the level of detail permitted by any individual researcher. In principle, acquiring or retrieving the required empirical evidence will allow any boundary to be identified as closable and therefore change its socio-spatial role into a dominant seclusion.

Following the meticulously theorised premise of the inhabited urban built environment, it is inevitable that the physical characteristics of its constituent contiguous spatial subdivisions permit occupation to

---

7. Solids are closely related, though not accordant, to the definition of architectonic space of Van der Laan (1983). Similarly, though the architectonic distinction between solids and voids is inevitably elicited, the term solid dominant is not equivalent to the use of solids in architecture.

such a degree of permanence that a particular socio-spatial system (see Chapter 3) can inhabit (e.g. reside in or structurally utilise) it. In the continuous process of inhabitation, the way a socio-spatial system is established, (re)negotiated, perceived and experienced is responsible for the volatile and flexible intellectual understanding associated with the materialised, ephemerally fixed, approximations that are built boundaries. Defining a BLT that cannot pertain to a partial description of an inhabited spatial subdivision, because it cannot be (predominantly) occupied for example, produces socio-spatially speaking a 'negative space' in the contiguous complex. The effect of this is comparable to Smith & Varzi's (2000; Smith 2001) negative objects: a void bona fide object is defined from the outside by the bona fide boundary of its 'host' material surface surrounding it (see Chapter 4). Because the reasons for a spatial subdivision being defined as negative can differ, it is deemed advantageous to define several BLTs pertaining to negative socio-spatial designations. This allows the contiguous boundary complex of the urban built environment of a locus (such as determined in Chapter 1's definition of the city) to be redescribed entirely, and furthermore enables the imposition of a natural (built environment or city limit) or artificial (data selection) end to the area being studied.

Implicitly repeated in all of the above is the consequence that each BLT is not a concrete object. Although defined and identified separately, BLTs cannot exist in isolation and cannot form the empirical social reality of material presence. Instead, they are still abstract concepts to overlay the reduction to boundary lines visualised as an outline map of the urban built environment. Any built boundary conveyed in this way can only be fully described and understood in socio-spatial terms by considering all BLT identifications it received together. It is a well-known entailment of all maps that they 'lie', or at least never convey an incontestable truth (Monmonier 1996; Wood 1992; MacEachren 2004; Lilley 2011a; for critical historical assessments of how (lying) maps are used, see Clarke 1985; Hutson 2012; Lilley 2012; Beisaw & Gibb 2013). Better said, all maps abstract or select information in a particular way, which is similar to how the theoretical conceptualisations throughout this research abstract and, therefore, fail to contain the entire concrete truth (see Chapter 2; Sayer 1981).

When working on or with mapped representations, it is worth bearing in mind that all abstractions are interpretations conducive to particular understandings themselves. Therefore, in using the BLTs, one should always be alert not to mistake the empirical abstraction for the empirical reality posed by the material presence of built boundaries.[8] For that reason, the BLT definitions will be illustrated with photographs rather than cut-outs of the outline map visualisations that result from analytical mapping practice (see Chapter 7).

The illustrative use of photographs is not to make claims about a greater truthfulness or neutral objectivity in photographs. In fact, here the photographs are enhanced with graphical highlights of the main boundaries occurring in the frame, emulating visual empirical reality. Using photographs is rather motivated by the intuitive understanding of visual perception that can be assumed on the reader's part. Despite being equally selective, photographs offer a window that imitates the familiar situation of someone visiting a new place. The use of maps, and thus reductions informed by one or multiple layers of technical convention, requires at least some prior knowledge of the production of the map. In the case of the outline base plan, one should first understand precisely the critically judged assumptions about, and the analytical use of, the empirical reality it represents. In contrast to such maps, the highlighted photographs direct attention to the boundaries that are being illustrated, which will make it easier to grasp the BLT definitions and how they may be represented on maps. However, photography is a deceptive simulation of the analytical mapping practice. The pictures show potentially confusing 'real world' detail, such as trees and furnishings that are part and parcel of any urban environment. These elements can partially obstruct the view of boundaries, as they would in everyday experience, but in the process of preparing an outline plan such details would normally be omitted, because they do not consistently subdivide occupiable space.

Finally, and importantly, the formulation of BLTs is a direct product of a process of iterative abstraction (Sayer 1981, 2000; Pratt 1995; Yeung 1997), as discussed at length in Chapter 2. This means that what is presented now comprises the most current outcomes of several instances of abstraction, in which initial and subsequent conceptualisations were contrasted to empirical data[9] through attempts to apply them. Here the

---

8. Blaut (1971: 19) insightfully wrote on mapping processes, which would include using BLTs: '[T]he resulting "structural model" [the mapping], although abstract, refers back to processes, if it refers back to the empirical world at all. This is true even if the model depicts, as a map does, *spatial* structure: as we have seen, the map sign-system does not signify pure space, which is unmappable, but rather draws attention to two spatial dimensions and certain other selected properties of selected phenomena, explicitly (if less noticeably) signifies their temporal dimension, and artfully erases away remaining properties along with all the other phenomena which disappear into the "ground", the white spaces on the map (which, of course, have process meaning too).'

9. The data used to test applicability included limited subsections of mapped representations of contemporary cities in the UK, including Winchester, as well as the archaeological maps of Chunchucmil (Classic lowland Maya) and Ostia (Roman) (restricted to pen and paper based

criteria were first and foremost that altogether the ontology adhered to the requirements in the covenant of Kropf (2009): to be a consistent, coherent, and comprehensive set of definitions, which are general enough to be used comparatively in all thinkable contexts, yet specific enough to identify them as analytical units in the empirical reality of datasets. That means that the test applications should demonstrate that all boundary line data is redescribed entirely, and all boundaries could be positively and exclusively identified (though some expert judgment, as discussed in the paragraphs above, is allowed) as BLTs at least twice, accounting for their contexts on both sides.

It is worth noting that as a consequence of the critical realist process of iterative abstraction, this ontological conceptualisation is arguably never truly finished, depending on any further empirical built environment complexes found or created. Each new empirical case may potentially cause revision, or at worst refutation, of the current ontology. There is virtually no explanatory value in presenting this process, due to the idiosyncratic way in which it takes place as a thought experiment. It suffices to say that from an initial ontologising attempt of six BLTs (erroneously pertaining to spaces more than their bounding), reconsiderations in dialogue with the empirical tests increased this number to the current 13. These 13 BLTs are captured below in necessarily formulaic expressions to ensure terminological precision. Chapter 7 will demonstrate that these BLT definitions appear stable in two drastically divergent test cases, systematically leading to a full redescription of their built environment outline plans.

BLT definitions

Accepting the foregoing preamble of requirements, the following paragraphs will define and illustrate the 13 BLTs (see Table 5.1 below for a quick overview, and the supplementary table of abridged definitions towards the back) that have resulted from a careful consideration of built

work). The selection of Winchester and Chunchucmil as test cases in this book will be explained in Chapter 7, but is immediately justified by the strong contrasts required to develop the argument for radical comparative urban studies. To ensure that the BLTs have the widest possible comparative applicability, examples from a range of places (historical and contemporary) were used at this stage of iterative abstraction to formulate appropriate concepts. Not all cases are equally suitable to demonstrate methodological development, while e.g. the publically accessible plan of Roman Ostia contains many archaeological ambiguities impeding accurate application of BLT definitions.

Table 5.1 Presentation of Boundary Line Type definitions (name, number and figures).

Nr.	Name	In figures	Nr.	Name	In figures
1	Closing boundaries	5.1; 5.2; 5.5; 5.6; 5.7; 5.9; 5.11; 5.12	8	Mutual boundaries	5.6; 5.9
2	Facing boundaries	5.1; 5.2; 5.6; 5.7; 5.12	9	Opening boundaries	5.7; 5.10; 5.12
3	Associative boundaries	5.1; 5.5; 5.8; 5.12	10	Neutral boundaries	5.8
4	Extended facing boundaries	5.1; 5.12	11	Man-made boundaries of unoccupiability	5.9; 5.10
5	Directing boundaries	5.1; 5.2; 5.3; 5.4; 5.7; 5.8; 5.10; 5.11; 5.12	12	Not man-made boundaries of unoccupiability	5.11
6	Disclosing boundaries	5.4	13	Not man-made negative boundaries	5.12
7	Enclosing boundaries	5.5	V	Virtual boundaries	5.2; 5.3; 5.7; 5.12

Note that the BLTs have names, where appropriate, deliberately in active voice, so they better convey the processive (secluding) part of their materially present counterparts in the built environment, but for practical convenience also have numerals.

environment outlines. They are presented from the vantage point of the operation of seclusion, starting with its simplest occurrence: the solid dominant.

As mentioned in passing, the definitions are necessarily formulaic, and may therefore come across as repetitive. The complexity and long descriptions of these formulations accomplish the precise internal consistency and comparability needed to move beyond the contextual and conflated (lay) categories in which we tend to see the built environment (e.g. Lynch 1981; Sayer 1985, 2000; Mekking 2009). Yet, mereologically – *sensu* Husserlian metaphysical phenomenology: the parts constituent of the entity (cf. Varzi 2012) – the applied BLTs will still resemble the immediate perception of socio-cultural and (historically) learned or imposed entities and categories. After all, these entities and categories are usually a different order of (context specific) fiat understandings with reference to perceived bona fide objects.

Where critical realism is said to be an 'underlabourer' of a research process (see Pratt 1995), in this context the ontology of BLTs could itself be seen as a socio-spatial underlabourer for investigations into the relations between the built environment and the society inhabiting it, rather than an already all-encompassing, totalising and prescriptive system for studying all its aspects. The BLTs themselves are open to revisions, adaptations, expansions and additions. Moreover, as said above, alternative research aims could result in alternative conceptualisations, which could be used alongside this approach in complementary fashion, and correlations with other extant concepts and methodologies could inform insightful new research directions.

Closing boundaries (1)

This BLT operates on the basis of seclusion from the surrounding configuration with the material property that the boundary is closable towards its outside. As the primary unit of the ontology, it does not contain further differentiation, making it a solid dominant.

Fig. 5.1 BLTs 1, 2, 3 and 4 in context.

Type 1 and 3 both circumscribe the house, because the garden or plot envelops the outline of the house. Types 2 and 4's existence depends on Types 1 and 3 respectively, creating a specification of respective parts of a boundary (entrance to path and entrance to house). Some detail is inevitably obscured by the perspective of the photograph, which depicts the physicality of real three-dimensional objects.

Crossing the closing boundary from the outside secludes one from interactions within the surrounding boundary configuration, and restricts interaction to participation with the socio-spatial system residing within the solid dominant. Crossing the closing boundary from the inside leads either immediately or indirectly towards increasing opportunities for interaction within open boundaries, and opportunities to cross further boundaries.

An example of closing boundaries is best illustrated in Fig. 5.1, which depicts a house in its plot's context. Due to the reduction to outlines, this house is conveyed as a single cell, while the doorway (Type 2) is a specification of its relationship to the outside. In principle each building results as a solid dominant, Type 1. This includes apartment buildings and conjoined houses, where in the former the same entranceway(s) is (are) used to the outside environment, while in the latter the internal divisions result in separate buildings with separate entranceways to the outside environment (see also Fig. 5.2). Although it is not included in the ground level concern here, there is potential to expand the boundary conceptualisations to include affective internal architectural traits and full three-dimensional extents.

Facing boundaries (2)

This BLT operates on the principle of orienting solicitation of interaction with a dominant from the surrounding configuration, and the orientation from within a dominant towards interaction with its outside. Facing boundaries depend on the solid dominant created by Type 1 or the dominant created by Type 7. They consist of any place along a dominant boundary with material properties that are so constructed that, at will, it allows traversing or is stringently closed off. Multiple identifications of facing boundaries along single identifications of dominant types are possible and, therefore, so are multiple orientations. It is a prerequisite for any dominant to receive at least one facing boundary, to avoid a negative socio-spatial positioning in the inhabited built environment (see Type 11). By means of facing boundaries, the residing socio-spatial system can be left to fulfil biological and social sustenance.

Crossing the facing boundary from the outside solicits interaction and participation with the socio-spatial system that constitutes the closing boundary and the extraction from the surrounding boundary configuration. Crossing the facing boundary from the inside leads either immediately or indirectly towards increasing opportunities for interaction within open boundaries and opportunities to cross further boundaries.

A facing boundary in its most usual form is illustrated in Fig. 5.1: a doorway into a house or building. Multiple orientations are possible through e.g. back doors or multiple entrances in larger buildings such as offices. Facing boundaries can also occur on the basis of Type 7, for example as city gates in a city wall. Facing boundaries tend to represent formally constructed doorways and gateways, but not full architectural frontages or façades. It might be possible to discern a typology or hierarchy of facing boundaries in their own right (this could include functional, technical, cultural, symbolic and economic factors). Fig. 5.1, for example, depicts a doorway into a house with a porch, which could be seen as an additional spatial buffer or as semi-inside space. This treatise will refrain from engaging on such level of detail, but recognises the opportunity. Instead it is stressed that at least a single facing boundary is identified as appropriate and within set limits of certainty.

Associative boundaries (3)

This BLT operates on the basis of dependence on a dominant it is directly associated with. Associative boundaries may occur in conjunction with additional associative boundaries with which it forms an adjoining configurative complex. Within such configurative complexes, associative boundaries may occur in successions, which could include Type 8 as well. In the absence of physical evidence for impermeable material properties, associative boundaries are assumed to be open. With physical evidence of impermeability, associative boundaries can become dominants, which consequently extend the dominant they are associated with. Associative boundaries mediate the relationship between dominants and the surrounding boundary configuration.

Crossing associative boundaries from the outside indirectly leads to interaction with a dominant. Crossing associative boundaries from the inside creates opportunities for interaction within the surrounding boundary configuration.

Associative boundaries, as depicted in Fig. 5.1, we usually recognise as gardens (front and back) or plots associated with a building, but the emergent configurative complexes may include a combination of gardens and fields. Without precise and comprehensive knowledge, informed conjectures and expert judgments may be necessary to determine association. It is possible that cultural rules would go against what appears to be topologically dictated (e.g. a single lawn connecting two suburban houses, while there is an invisible legal boundary in the middle). Within the current context, associative boundaries containing outbuildings, which could be seen as subsidiary solid dominants (introducing a hierarchical relation) to the dominant the associative boundary depends on, are simplified as internal organisation. For each study it can be decided whether to add such a level of complexity as appropriate and available data allows.

Extended facing boundaries (4)

This BLT operates on the principle of mutual orientation between any associated BLT identification and the surrounding configuration. It depends for its existence on Type 3 or Type 8 and needs to occur in direct connection (i.e. no further differentiations may interfere, necessitating a preceding crossing) to a Type 2 or several Type 2s. In instances of the latter, the Type 2s belong to a subset of dominants, which each may have their own associated extended facing boundaries in a successive configurative complex involving Types 3 and 8.

Extended facing boundaries may occur at any place along a boundary associated with a dominant that features material properties to accommodate unhindered crossings relative to the remainder of the type it depends on. Importantly, each Type 2 crossing leading into an associative boundary requires indirect connection (i.e. explicit permeable material properties) to the surrounding configuration on at least a single topological side[10] towards the surrounding environment that is not part of the configurative complex of the dominant in question. As with Type 2, identifying multiple extending facing boundaries is possible on the basis of each Type 3 or 8. There is no requirement for the number of extended facing boundaries to concur with the number of Type 2s, as long as direct connection between them is allowed.

Crossing the extended facing boundary from the outside is a step of soliciting interaction and participation with the socio-spatial system that constitutes the mediation of the associated boundary towards a (solid) dominant or subset of solid dominants. Crossing the extended

---

10. A topological side is defined as the occurrence of a continuous extent of a topological distinction of operating BLT identifications determining the socio-spatial description of a circumscribed space from its outside, which allows any form or shape to have distinct sides connecting to the surrounding built environment. That is, the full side of the house connected to the front or back garden is a topological side. Chapter 8 places this in context with further definitions of the BLT data structure.

facing boundary from the inside immediately creates opportunities for interaction within open boundaries, and leads towards opportunities for further boundary crossings within the surrounding boundary configuration.

In Fig. 5.1, we find the expected entranceway into the garden on the street side only very faintly determined by a shallow pathway leading up to the house. This situation suggests that extended facing boundaries can be very informal, or even essentially cover all topological sides of a Type 3 or 8. In contrast, everything is possible, from vegetation, elaborate gated walls and white picket fences. Informed conjecture or expert judgment may be necessary to identify extended facing boundaries. The essentially mutual orientation of the surrounding configuration with the configurative complex of a dominant or subset can be used as circumstantial evidence to designate a topological side as the expected location of an extended facing boundary (e.g. back garden and back alley providing access).

Directing boundaries (5)

This BLT operates on the basis that it directs interaction along opportunities for further boundary crossings, into other socio-spatial systems. The direction of this BLT is enforced by its occurrence in parallels within the configuration. Directing boundaries may connect to a multitude of different BLTs in any number, and form any configurative complex through aggregation.

Crossing this boundary from the outside exposes one to immediate interaction opportunities originating from beyond any other boundary crossing, and creates immediate opportunities for further boundary crossings. Crossing this boundary from the inside solicits interaction with socio-spatial systems constituting other types of boundaries.

As transpires from Fig. 5.2, directing boundaries generally pertain to streets and pathways. While the street network is an essential part of the urban built environment analyses of space syntax (e.g. Hillier 2007) and urban morphology (e.g. Conzen 1960), the definition here refrains from a direct definition of either a network or a formally constructed street. In this way, also more informally and often less geometrically constructed built environments can be better understood and described in terms of structure of the flows through the configuration. For example, Maya cities are usually found to feature few formal streets despite the construction of extensive urban landscapes (e.g. Barnhart 2003).

Fig. 5.2   BLT 5 in context.

A typical urban street scene represents a clearly delimited directing boundary, in sharp contrast to adjoining buildings with doorways directly coming out into a street section, which ends in a virtual boundary with the crossing.

Virtual boundaries (V)

Directing boundaries have a clear correlation to 'virtual boundaries' (in analytical practice and representation (e.g. Chapter 9) a V in front of the BLT number concerned marks the distinction). This is an additional abstract construct to allow directing boundaries, as well as other types when appropriate, to circumscribe continuous surface areas. Where any of the parallel lines determining a directing boundary ceases to exist in a materially constant surface, a virtual boundary on that opposite end is gained. This is a virtual extension of empirical differentiation, without requiring actual material differentiation (e.g. a dead-end street) for both parallels to connect to a configurationally different BLT (e.g. a street becoming a square). Note that this means that directing boundaries can be intermitted by non-directional areas (e.g. the central area of crossings and junctions), which result exclusively from such virtual boundaries.

Non-directional areas are not bounded spaces, but implicit continuations of any of the directing boundaries. Fig. 5.3 demonstrates such a situation. Because virtual boundaries then only connect several directing boundaries, no interactional change occurs so the directing boundaries' operation will be conceived as continuous. In this way, the

Fig. 5.3   Virtual boundaries of BLT 5.

In this T-junction three streets conjoin, meaning three directing boundaries receive a virtual end, while a materially constant triangular central area emerges from the virtual boundaries.

directing boundaries involved maintain their directing operation based on the same principles, but a choice of directions is enabled.

Note that where Types 2 and 4 are openings with a materially continuous surface on either side, their existence is implied by a similar principle of virtuality. This is kindred to the logic applied by Hillier & Hanson (1984) to permit a discrete ideographical definition of inside, or contained, space. Here, the 'stuff' of boundaries (X) acts superordinately to distinguish 'continuous' (open) space (Y).

Disclosing boundaries (6)

This BLT operates on the basis of guiding interaction towards opportunities for further boundary crossings in multiple directions rather than a single particular direction (Type 5). Disclosing boundaries are integrated in the configuration by mutual orientation (guiding inside-out and outside-in crossings), giving it a sense of local centrality. Through the centrality of its connections it discloses various opportunities for further boundary crossings. These can occur in any number and form, but must include immediate or indirect (through Type 3) opportunities to solicit interaction with multiple dominants. In addition, it should be connected in at least one instance to a boundary that is not forming a dominant or the configurative complex associated with a dominant or any negative boundary constituted by unoccupiability (Types 11 and 12). This ensures its boundaries can be reached, and may involve virtual boundaries (see Type 5). The centrality can be recognised from the configurative context

Fig. 5.4 BLT 6 in context.

Despite various aspects of this complex city square being obscured in this view, a number of streets opening up the square are visible, giving it a central local position, while it can just be discerned that multiple solid dominants are associated with it also.

of the connections it discloses. In addition it offers the opportunity to act as a thoroughfare in connection with Types 5 and 9.

Crossing this boundary from the outside exposes one to immediate interaction opportunities originating from beyond any other boundary crossing, and creates immediate opportunities for further boundary crossings, including several leading towards increasing opportunities to solicit interaction with dominants. Crossing this boundary from the inside solicits interaction with socio-spatial systems constituting other types of boundaries, or leads to opportunities for further boundary crossings while exposing one to immediate interaction opportunities originating from beyond any other boundary crossing.

Disclosing boundaries usually pertain to squares and plazas in urban settings (see Fig. 5.4). These can occur in a wide variety of guises. When street space (informally) circumscribes a square, which is even the case to some extent in Fig. 5.4, though largely obscured from view, the designation of the disclosing boundary may incorporate these and it offers itself the opportunity for thoroughfare. When Types 5 completely circumscribe a central area materially, see Type 9.

Enclosing boundaries (7)

This BLT operates on the basis of seclusion from the surrounding configuration with the material property that the boundary can be closed off towards its outside, making it a dominant. However, enclosing boundaries do not form solids as they circumscribe several other boundaries,

forming an enclosed configurative complex or subset. Enclosing boundaries can occur at various scales and seclude a wide variety of BLT combinations. Importantly, an enclosing boundary that only encompasses a
subset of solid dominants and their configurative complexes implies the
existence of a mutual boundary (Type 8) for the interconnectedness of
this subset on the inside. Consequently, if an enclosure of a subset cannot
be closed off, Type 8 is implied.

Crossing the enclosing boundary line from the outside secludes
one from interactions within the surrounding boundary configuration,
but creates interaction opportunities within the configurative complex.
Crossing the enclosing boundary from the inside leads either immediately or indirectly towards increasing opportunities for interaction within
open boundaries, and opportunities to cross further boundaries.

Enclosing boundaries are most readily perceived as city walls (see
Fig. 5.5), which operate on a large scale. In their most stringent and
sometimes intended form, city walls really delimit the entire built environment of a place, leaving only access routes on the outside. More typically though, especially in contemporary settings, cities have grown
beyond their defences. In Fig. 5.5 this can be recognised by the Type 3 on
the right, which belongs to a building (solid dominant) leaning against
the wall on the extramural side. On a smaller scale one can think of gated

Fig. 5.5   BLT 7 in context.

This city wall encloses the old town. The orchard is placed in an associative area, while it is also
noted that two solid dominants (Type 1, which is equally closable) form part of this enclosing
boundary.

communities, which more or less box in a subset of buildings, extracting them from the surrounding environment.

Mutual boundaries (8)

This BLT operates on the principle that it is simultaneously associated with or encompassing a thereby distinct subset of several (solid) dominants (and any associated boundaries), forming a configurative complex with possible successions involving Type 3s. They mediate and interconnect these (solid) dominants contiguously, without further differentiation between them for access and soliciting interaction nor favouring orientation. Mutual boundaries may envelop a subset of (solid) dominants without the material property of impermeability (see Type 7). Alternatively they occur lateral to several (solid) dominants, deceptively akin Type 3 on an amalgamating level. When a laterally positioned mutual boundary creates a dominant through the necessary evidence for the contiguous extension of the impermeability of a subset of solid dominants and any associated boundaries (in the fashion shown in Fig. 5.5), the emerging circumscribing outline becomes a Type 7, while an open interconnecting outline on the inside remains as a mutual boundary.

Fig. 5.6 BLT 8 in context.

This inner courtyard is connected to the surrounding configuration from behind the photograph's view, interconnecting a configuration of several houses.

Crossing mutual boundaries from the outside leads to a position where one is oriented to indirectly interact with a subset of (solid) dominants, and the possibility to solicit interaction with any one (solid) dominant within that subset occurs. Crossing mutual boundaries from the inside constitutes either access to, or soliciting interaction with, any of the (solid) dominants in the subset, or to leave the position of indirect interaction with a subset for a position that exposes one to immediate interaction opportunities originating from beyond any other boundary crossing, and may create opportunities for further boundary crossings.

Mutual boundaries refer to the open arrangements between, and around, the buildings adjacent to secluding courtyards (see Fig. 5.6), cul-de-sacs, galleries and more loosely placed groups of buildings (see Fig. 5.9), similar to farmsteads, etc. This implies that Type 7 is often associated with a Type 8 to describe the arrangement from the inside. Their mutuality means that they are constituted from the inside primarily by a socio-spatial system of interaction originating between the subset of dominants concerned. That is to say, the neighbours necessarily are condemned to closely knit relations, whilst maintaining a mutual extraction towards the outside. Indeed, the sign in the foreground of Fig. 5.6 reads: 'Private area, please do not roam'.

Opening boundaries (9)

This BLT operates on the principle that it creates open, accessible connections towards its outside, while being an integrated, accessible part of the configuration from the outside. This integration in principle, however, does not entail specific orientations towards interaction opportunities with the surrounding configuration. This means that, contrary to Types 6 and 8, opening boundaries do not orientate or guide towards opportunities to solicit interaction with dominants. Opening boundaries do not require any *condicio sine quibus non* (particular boundary connections), although they may connect to multiple different BLTs, including dominants.[11] Opening boundaries with the material property of impermeability, like other open boundaries, should feature

---

11. Opening boundaries may seemingly circumscribe dominants, while maintaining an indifferent (nonspecific) relation. Usually it can be assumed securely that such dominants do not distinguish a socio-spatial system, because they are part of internal design, decoration, or functional specification, and therefore excluded from the current ontology based on outlines (e.g. elaborate seating or storage construction, or follies in parks). If this is not the case, the chances are that we have a substantial building within an estate, that displays some orientation to its outside. Making such distinction may depend on background knowledge, informed assumptions or expert judgment. Expert judgment is part of most 'objective' observation in

Fig. 5.7   BLT 9 in context.

This small urban park or garden shows how the boundaries maintain a very open and integrated relation to the outside, with the streets proffering thoroughfare an effective alternative, though the opening boundary offers a similar opportunity.

predominant mitigation for access. Opening boundaries can never be truly closable. If opening boundaries would be closable, they would become solid dominants (Type 1). Inviting crossings from the outside largely determines its residing socio-spatial system. In addition, opening boundaries may allow thoroughfare, forming through wayfaring in connection with Types 5 and 9.

Crossing this boundary from the outside exposes one to immediate interaction opportunities originating from beyond any other boundary crossing, and may create opportunities for further boundary crossings. Crossing this boundary from the inside would also expose one to immediate interaction opportunities originating from beyond any other boundary crossing, but may include interaction opportunities with socio-spatial systems constituting other types of boundaries.

scientific processes. Because the empirical reality of any case already must have been recorded to have a source map (see Chapter 7 on how to work with variety of legacy data examples), knowledge of this recording process – seldom an isolation or peerless instance of scholarly work – will increase one's casuistic familiarity and expertise. The limitation arising is not one that compromises the applicability of BLTs, but consists of an increased probability that the accuracy of application may diminish due to the ambiguities of imperfect (cultural and experiential) knowledge. Error margins and residual ambiguity are near inevitable in most scientific methods.

Opening boundaries have arguably the most protean of definitions, which confirms the various informal real-world spaces they evoke. Of those spaces, parks, like the one depicted in Fig. 5.7, are arguably the most formalised. Next to this there are areas which are simply used to flow through, multi-purpose areas, and many cases of urban fallow, but also agricultural and horticultural, fields. Fig. 5.12 shows a kind of opening boundary, which has the particular connotation of a cemetery.

Neutral boundaries (10)

This BLT operates on the principle of neutrality, which results from ambiguity and the absence of single association to a residing socio-spatial system. Neutral boundaries remain as partitions that are fully incorporated in the built environment after all preceding (Types 1–9) BLTs have been identified by the researcher, depending on surrounding boundaries for their form. Neutral boundaries are not actively constituted by a single residing socio-spatial system on the inside (*non sequitur*), but result from boundary constitutions on its outside.[12] Its definition from the inside is therefore ambiguous. It may connect to various different boundaries without *condiciones sine quibus non* (particular boundary connections).

Crossing this boundary from either outside or inside does not change the opportunities for interaction when connected to non-dominant boundaries. But, crossing this boundary from the inside traversing into a dominant or associative boundary implicates (in)direct soliciting interaction with the dominant. Vice versa, crossing this boundary from a dominant or associative outside exposes one to immediate interaction opportunities originating from beyond any other boundary crossing, and indirectly creates opportunities for further boundary crossings.

In some cases neutral boundaries may also be associated with urban fallow (cf. Type 9), but more usually one should think of flower beds and areas of no particular social use, but rather functional use (e.g. storage in public space). Fig. 5.8 shows some sort of combination thereof, although in this case it is not possible to enter from the Type 3 behind. Neutral boundaries are retained as integrated parts of the boundary configuration, but are not defined by a claim of any particular residing socio-spatial system. Instead,

12. Here I would like to remind the reader how this is similar to the conceptualisation of (physical) holes in Smith & Varzi's (2000; Smith 2001; see Chapter 4) discussion of fiat and bona fide boundaries, because holes are determined by the boundary lines of the surrounding elements and do not contain their own shape. Such definition from the outside is inevitably part of Type 11 also.

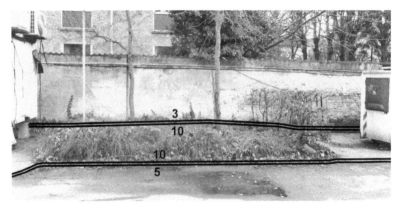

Fig. 5.8 BLT 10 in context.

Alongside the road, this area is distinct and not part of getting one from space to space, but neither does it pertain to a particular single residing socio-spatial system.

they act as neutral, non-associative intermediates between other BLTs, and informally extend the socio-spatial constitution of other non-dominant BLTs. In Fig. 5.8 it is the street space (Type 5) that is informally extended.

Negative definitions

The remaining three types of this ontology are based on the principle of negativity. They restrict the boundary configuration by not being constituted by any residing socio-spatial system, nor having an ambiguous relation to interaction complexes (cf. Type 10). Although they are connected to boundaries constituted by socio-spatial systems, these boundaries do not actively participate themselves in the socio-spatial significance of the built environment. This is either because they have not been built (see Chapter 3 on primordial space), or they represent the edge of space that is unoccupiable; a physical impossibility to inhabit with a degree of permanence. Occurrences of not man-made boundaries eventually determine the maximum extent of the boundary configuration, while unoccupiability does not necessarily affect the continuity of this extent on the ground surface.

Man-made boundaries of unoccupiability (11)

This BLT operates on the basis of negativity (*non sequitur* socio-spatial systems). Unoccupiable ground surfaces mean that no socio-spatial system of interaction can take place.[13] Crossing from either side is only

Fig. 5.9   BLT 11 in context: a railway.

This railway is clearly fenced off from the outside, creating a barrier except for points of arrival and departure. The old mill alongside it creates the loose arrangements of buildings interconnected by a Type 8.

enabled after physical changes are made to the material properties of the surface. For this boundary, this is caused by human building processes.

There are two main examples of this thinkable. Fig. 5.9 shows a railway. Though hypothetically occupiable, and indeed for someone interested in taking a built boundary approach to transport systems (e.g. an intercity approach) arguably of interest, formal and stringent motorways, railways, etc. form barriers on the contiguous local scale within a built environment. Within this realm one can also think of more static, inaccessible structures, such as electrical transformers. The more unequivocal occurrences of man-made unoccupiability, like steep slopes and waterways, canals, moats or ponds, are depicted in Fig. 5.10.

13.   In rare cases, unoccupiability could be caused by atmospheric conditions resulting from human actions, such as nuclear disasters, and even natural disasters, such as volcanic eruptions, and therefore not exclusively relate to the ground surface.

Fig. 5.10 BLT 11 in context: slope and water.

The old defences of the fortifications in this photograph create two distinct areas that are unoccupiable: a steep slope and a moat.

Not man-made boundaries of unoccupiability (12)

This BLT operates on the basis of negativity (*non sequitur* socio-spatial systems). Unoccupiable (ground level) surfaces mean that no socio-spatial system can take place there. Crossing from either side is only enabled after physical changes are made to the material properties of the surface. For this boundary, this is caused by nonhuman processes.[14]

Estuaries and the sea, especially where connected to a settlement such as the example in Fig. 5.11, are clear instances of how this BLT intersects, truncates or delimits the contiguous areal extent of the built

14. Unoccupiability indicates that the surface cannot be inhabited or structurally utilised by a residing socio-spatial system. Note, however, that in certain cases bodies of water are deliberately maintained to function as access ways (e.g. Venice) and steep slopes might be made tractable by gondola lifts, etc. If suggestive physical evidence is found and the surface is rendered occupiable, other Boundary Line Types could apply.

Fig. 5.11   BLT 12 in context.

This quay shows where the city meets the estuary and the built environment is discontinued.

environment. Many alternative (natural) examples can be thought of: big boulders, rugged mountain tops, rivers, marshes and impenetrable dense vegetation.

Not man-made negative boundaries (13)

This BLT operates on the basis of negativity (*non sequitur* socio-spatial systems). The boundary configuration complex outside of this boundary is not primarily oriented towards it, but may be organised to spill into it. Crossing this boundary from the outside leads to occupation within a spatial situation predominantly formed by nonhuman processes. Crossing this boundary from the inside either solicits interaction with socio-spatial systems residing within other types of boundaries, which may expose one to immediate interaction opportunities originating from beyond any other boundary crossing, or are within the confines of configurative complexes resulting from dominant boundaries.

Fig. 5.12   BLT 13 in context.

This view clearly demonstrates how a contiguously built environment is delimited by occupiable hills in the background, which are not constructed by human building activities. It also reveals the cemetery as a particular kind of Type 9.

Not man-made negative boundaries are the natural ends of the built environment, simply referring to any kind of non-cultivated land or wilderness. Even in the example depicted in Fig. 5.12, closer inspection might reveal partitioning of land in grazing areas, etc. In its purest form, however, these boundaries may perhaps contain human traces, but no complete bounded spaces until one reaches another patch of built environment again. True wilderness in much of the heavily settled world is rare, but this construct can also be used to delimited datasets and areas arbitrarily for any case research, or to simply describe smaller regions of limited human developments.

Levels of socio-spatial significance of BLTs

Since an ontology in the critical realist sense consists of abstract causative concepts, imposing an ontology onto the world is necessarily an interpretive act. As explained at the beginning of this chapter, the ontology presented here is not a full metaphysical ontology, as it does not determine the relations of its constituent concepts to each other. Despite (or thanks to) this limitation we have now attained the ability to ontologically redescribe and provide an alternative visualisation of the urban built environment complex by applying or mapping the BLTs. However, gaining a more profound understanding of their socio-spatial significance, as BLTs occur in ontological relations to each other to convey the inhabited urban built environment, requires a thorough appreciation of the contextual relevance of the theory which has informed the formulation of BLT definitions. Since it was also recognised above that as abstract concepts no single BLT actually exists and can fully convey the empirical social reality of the material presence of a boundary in the inhabited built environment, it should be clear that it is only through investigating the interrelational positions in which BLTs occur that genuine interpretation can take place. Taking the entire morphologically and topologically composed BLT complex of an urban built environment, one renders *the ontology intrinsic to a city,*[15] i.e. its *socio-spatial signature of inhabitation*.

From arguments in both Chapter 4 and the current chapter it has been established that the way boundaries seclude contains their socio-spatial significance. Due to the metaphysically partial nature of this ontology, the ontological primacy of the operation of seclusion does not necessarily lead to relations of ontological dependence between BLTs. That is to say, there is no prerequisite of all BLTs that the preceding BLTs exist, starting with closing boundaries, for them to occur. Rather, the generic relation to the strongest secluding boundary, the closing boundary, is lineal or genealogical. The socio-spatial interpretive value of seclusion resulted directly from the way the inhabited built environment has been conceptualised in the theoretical framework presented in Chapter 3, but here this interpretive value can be further specified in terms of contextual relations. This will in turn inform interpretive efforts springing from imposing the BLT ontology onto urban built environments as presented in Chapters 7–9.

The socio-spatial significance of each BLT can be relationally and contextually understood in terms of three levels or incremental spheres, which are not mutually exclusive. That is, all three levels will be relevant and operational indistinctly at all times in all BLTs. These three levels can be formulated concisely and cogently as follows:

A. Dimensional context: boundaries are personally territorial in that they create distances (densities) and spatial extents (size), and are introduced by the interpersonal and project activity process of distance setting.

---

15. In the sense of the process oriented and social practice based working definition of the city provided in Chapter 1.

B. Locational context: boundaries regulate relationally the restricting and enabling conditions affording and affecting our emplaced opportunities and ability to interact, which restricts and enables the accessibility to time-space resources, developmental negotiations and the choices for project participation (activities and services).

C. Aggregative context: boundaries create entities and thus the coherence within entities on an incrementally fluid scale through their relational placement. These incremental entities enter inhabitants into necessary relations of dependence based on their adherence to context within both inhabiting experience and the constitutive development of aggregate patterns, causing knowledge of entities and a sense of familiarity from ideationally conceivingthese.

All these levels are both effectuated and affected by morphological shaping as well as topological relations. While these formulations in themselves contain the core of socio-spatially relational significance between the BLTs as derived from their application, one should note that these relate back directly to the theoretical framework presented in Chapter 3 and should thus be understood in this light. The three scales organise the socio-spatial significance of the material presence of the built environment according to how it accommodates and facilitates the constitutive interactional process of inhabitation.

The dimensional context refers back to the principles of proxemics (Hall 1959, 1968). This ethologically based study on interpersonal distance setting in a great variety of activities and situations searched for cultural differences in human territoriality. As argued in Chapter 3, any (social) interaction is necessarily spatial and therefore involves a location and the distance between the constituent parts of the interaction. Through a personal territory one preserves a distance towards those constituent parts (e.g. people in encounter) which feels and is functionally appropriate or comfortable. The subdivisions composed by boundaries inherently distance one space from another. Their material properties further qualify and mediate the privacy and severity of that distance between neighbouring spaces.

Locational context refers back to the time-geographical and systems theoretical premises (see especially Hägerstrand 1975; Pred 1977, 1981, 1984; Thrift & Pred 1981; Thrift 1983) of the life-path and project participation, which is tied to an ordering and qualification of interaction opportunities afforded by the built environment for movement and accessibility to time-space, natural, social and subsistence resources. It concerns access to interaction opportunities and exchange through boundary crossing, the openness and closability of which are characterised by how their material properties restrict and enable crossing. The interrelational accessibility of any location is a negotiated compromise of the operation of seclusion. As follows from the negatively defined BLTs, relative accessibility is a requirement for all spatial subdivisions to partake in the socio-spatial complex of any inhabited (urban) built environment. Moreover, people require a minimum access to resources (including obtained through social relations) for subsistence.

Aggregative context refers to the very flexible and malleable shapes and scales in which entities and patterns can occur, which are bounded towards their outsides on an aggregating level.[16] This is most readily connected with how we come to know and familiarise ourselves with the world. This applies to experiential knowledge, a sense of place, and biography formation (cf. Pred 1984, 1986), but also to the effects of imposed or formalised learned and acculturated social categories (cf. Sayer's (1985) layman's terms). These aspects of inhabitation mean that all BLTs are always placed in contextual relation to several variably scaled entities which we know about and/or experience (e.g. home, street, neighbourhood, district, city, region, nation, etc.), through which they influence the interaction processes of inhabitation and built environment development. Despite being volatile and flexible, it could be expected that the larger the scale of aggregation, the more people and built boundary investments will partake in any pattern, so the more rigid or persistent it might prove to be (see Jones 2010), even if that is only by incorporating the greatest possible diversity within an area of a dataset. Scales of aggregation express how in inhabitation people always are associated with and adhere to multiple entities and patterns of socio-spatial coherence and thus encounter boundaries against, and as constituents of, those contexts. The material properties qualify the kind of coherence that exists within aggregates.

The levels of socio-spatial significance elucidate how built boundaries continuously let individuals establish a personal position and situation in space, allow them purpose when being in space, and let them be somewhere (a place) in space. If one would rephrase the three levels in

16. As part of an exploratory and experimental research process it is thinkable that a researcher might simply want to predetermine an area over which the pattern of boundary line type occurrence is assessed, or project and impose preconceptualised entities from external definitions to the same end. The levels of socio-spatial significance discussed here guide the interpretation and synthesis of Boundary Line Types on the basis of their endogenous logic.

a pragmatic way the socio-spatial significance referred to contributes to answering the following three basic questions respectively:

A. How do boundaries come about?
B. What do boundaries do?
C. Wherein are boundaries situated?

Note, however, that the 'when' question is not asked. The presence of built boundaries at any point in time is a necessary requirement of their material nature, while it is contingent upon the historical moment selected for spatial-material data collection or mapping whether the boundary appears. That is not to say that the contexts, conditions and properties of the duration or endurance of boundaries are not significant for the interpretation of built environment data. On the contrary, through time the rhythms and patterns of development processes, change, and the weight and characteristics of boundary persistence or perseverance of patterns can be revealed, all of which provide a temporal context respective of the time-slice data available to the levels of socio-spatial significance and nature of seclusion. Comparatively, time then contributes to the creation of time-space specific socio-spatial signatures of cities, and reveals potentially shared characteristics of development. Rather than for redescribed individual boundary line segments, it is expected that a temporal view and analysis provides the best insights for entities and aggregates. In any case, computational analytical measures (see Chapter 8) can help the interpretive process of the highly complex resultant data across space and through time.

Towards practice

On the basis of the BLT definitions and their incorporated levels of socio-spatial significance, research on case studies is now essentially enabled. To better appreciate the position of a research method operationalising these BLTs and to provide a broader support for the applied practices to conduct this, I must declare here that this is not the only potentially comparative method for studying the urban built environment. Providing a concise methodological research context, the next chapter will critically and constructively review the relevance and contributions of most prominent methodologies currently practised. After this, in Chapter 7, the empirical operationalisation of BLTs will be demonstrated as they are applied in mapping practice to two test cases of strongly contrasting urban traditions and diverging data sources. Chapter 8 then turns attention to the analytical opportunities permitted by the spatial data structure thus created, which includes derivative analytical units such as the topological segment. In practice, the 'BLT Mapping' method benefits from various traits previously developed in congenial existing methods, as will be discussed in Chapter 6, and is shown to be adaptable to a variety of built environment research data in support of radical comparisons. Yet, BLT Mapping's epistemological nature and aims are both significantly distinct, as well as diversely complementary, to these preceding approaches to knowledge production.

CHAPTER 6
A CONSTRUCTIVE EVALUATION
OF METHODS ON URBAN FORM

Introduction

Any new method for studying urban form and the built environment in particular cannot stand in isolation. Attention to the topography of cities has been part of academic discourse in Germany since the late nineteenth century (see Rietschel 1897; Whitehand 1981a). Later Geddes (1915), who was influenced by the currency of evolutionary thought in biology (the relationship between biology and urbanism is still being explored, e.g. Marshall 2016) and is credited for introducing the term conurbation, made important contributions to the architectural planning aspects of the development of cities in the UK.

It is difficult to precisely trace the development of the study of urban topography and the morphographic approach to plans of city layouts. Initially, this was mainly practised in Germany, as reviewed with a rich bibliography by Whitehand (1981a). According to Whitehand, 'topographically conscious urban history' gained firmer footing during the interbellum (through the work of e.g. Rörig 1928 and Hamm 1932). After the war, this area of urban history grew swiftly (cf. Keyser 1969) and formed the basis for the morphogenetic approach (see Whitehand 1981a; Whitehand & Larkham 1992a). This has become the predominant kind of urban morphology, also referred to specifically as Conzenian urban morphology (after M.R.G. Conzen, see below).

The aims of this book are not served by reproducing a comprehensive historical overview. Reviews by Whitehand (1981a), Stoob (1985), Slater (1996) and Rutte (2008), including the practice of preparing atlases of historic towns,[1] and for urban history in particular by Denecke

---

1. The research practices discussed in this chapter often use the word 'town' rather than 'city'. Not all languages differentiate between village/town/city (see Clarke & Simms 1985). Town can be

(1988) and Dennis & Prince (1988), all explain the respective disciplinary backdrops against which (historic developmental) interests in the built form of cities could establish research practices (also see e.g. Dyos 1968; Fraser & Sutcliffe 1983, for edited volumes exemplifying various urban historical approaches).

This chapter is at once broader and narrower in scope. Chapter 1 already indicated that my boundary approach to a comparative urban methodology will be reified by using Geographical Information System (GIS) software. Vector-based GIS data offer the appropriate data format and functional flexibility for the geographical representation of line features, such as BLTs (Chapter 5). This chapter will show how a GIS-based research practice applying BLTs (as in Chapter 7) could be developed. I contextualise and demonstrate how its tenets relate to, and result from, preceding methods and techniques.

The pivotal nature of GIS first leads to a consideration of the relation between GIS and urban (social) history as a branch of the rapidly developing field of historical GIS. More specifically, I will evaluate the relevance of GIS for studying historically developed urban form. This includes both historically reconstructed town plans (a promising data source for diachronic applications of BLT mapping), and the analytical potential of GIS data structures to apply the recent OH_FET ontology. As Gregory & Ell (2007) explain, historical GIS (HGIS) demonstrates the well-known ability of GIS software to compile, order and visualise (urban historical) spatial data. This sets the stage for the GIS operationalisation of BLT Mapping.

Going forward, two dominant methods for the comparative study of urban form are reviewed: urban morphology and space syntax. The former is thematically related to the preceding historical GIS approaches in this chapter. Therefore, urban morphology proves especially important to BLT data preparation, description, geometry and diachronic analysis. The latter is a closer match to the social scientific interpretation pursued here, and introduces the continued computational progression of a set of measures. Computationally, space syntax represents the topological mapping and analysis on conceptual grounds to which BLTs are susceptible.

Both urban morphology and space syntax have inspired and strengthened analytical possibilities of BLT Mapping. Various ideas for

more flexible, because it is not tied to administrative city status. In this research the term city is used throughout, but town and city are seen as interchangeable words to refer to urban places, according to the definition laid down in Chapter 1.

measures and techniques will be proposed and explored in Chapters 8 and 9. All approaches share that they are based on mappable and geographically anchored information. This paves the way to integration in GIS, maintaining each method's respective merits. While BLT Mapping is not especially devised to effectuate such multi-method integration, it complements these extant methods and aims, and exploits the technological and data advancements of born-digital GIS approaches. Accumulatively, tenets identified here form the foundation for Chapter 7's empirical operationalisation and Chapter 8's explication of social analytical potential.

Considering methods for studying urban built form

In positioning my methodological development in liaison to other methods, the work pre-emptively transforms from a conceptual treatise into empirical practice and analytical operationalisation. The mapping practice does not inherently require computation, but a digital environment will improve its utility. By preparing BLT data in digital form, the BLT information becomes a versatile dataset for visualisation and advancing its rich formal redescriptive potential (see Chapter 5) – but it also enables additional geocomputational opportunities to unpick and navigate the complexity of urban contexts. A critical review of useful aspects of related methods stimulates our appreciation for the innate abilities of a GIS interface to systematically prepare, generate and structure BLT data.

It will be explained why the grounding and purpose of extant methods renders them unsuitable for understanding and analysing 'boundaries' as defined in Chapter 5. Yet, parsing the processes proper to BLT Mapping is enhanced by elucidating terminology and approaches similar to those that have been developed for historically reconstructive mapping, urban morphology, and space syntax. Extant methods are not necessarily critiqued for how they sustain what they claim to do, but to what extent they could support the comparative urban research commensurate with the aims set in Chapter 1. There I established a common frame of reference to develop long-term comparative urban research – which was previously lacking (Smith 2009b, 2012; Yoffee 2009; Fletcher 2010) – that subsequently was given specific purpose and expression through boundaries.

One gap preventing comprehensive understanding of urban form has been noted specifically through the lack of integration of urban morphology and space syntax (Kropf 2009; Pinho & Oliveira 2009a; Whitehand 2010a, 2010b; Griffiths et al. 2010). Such expressions of dissatisfaction are accompanied by an acknowledgement of the benefits of methodological integration, but this remains an underexploited field. Boundaries are proposed as one way to bridge the conceptual gaps in studying urban form, where disparate research efforts also have been lamented (e.g. Clarke & Simms 1985; Whitehand & Larkham 1992a; Tilly 1996; Conzen 2004). It is paramount to stress that BLT Mapping, whilst a complementary practice, avoids increasing current disparity. Instead, Chapter 7's operationalisation will show that BLT Mapping explicitly maintains the opportunities to combine, analyse and imbue its data with some ideas that reside in extant methods. However, the development of BLT Mapping is not purported to directly serve or advance the integration agenda of other methods.

One could easily argue that quantification and (associated) computation necessarily create comparative and comparable methods. Thus, it must be emphasised that using quantitative measures will not intrinsically lead to (the same) meaningful interpretations. 'A GIS system [...] is a tool, a point of departure for comprehensive analysis rather than a scientific result in itself' (Kalmring 2012: 259). So when, like Kalmring (2012), one is assembling and compiling information into a GIS, this recording and documenting practice still tends to adhere to what the tool prescribes. For analysis and interpretation proper to one's conceptual frame of reference, it is necessary to go beyond the tool and its application as a method. Instead, I find quantitative research must devise methods that incorporate the theoretical concepts which have been formulated in order to comprehend the phenomenon under scrutiny (Chapters 3–5). Tools can be used or designed to operationalise these concepts in analytical measures that are commensurate with the questions asked.

GIS software is not inherently neutral. One should ensure that the way conceptual information is stored and conveyed suits the understanding one has acquired as well as the associated analysis one desires. Putting qualitative data in a GIS does not spontaneously invest the tool with qualitative powers of its own.[2] Hence, I argue that my boundary methodology ensures that the *qualitative use of the tool in aid of interpretation is comparative also, not just its computational underpinnings and its*

---

2. The computational basis of GIS requires empirically measured (quantified) data entries. In recent years concerns have been raised on the positivist and reductionist perception this causes amongst qualitative researchers, and how to advance the qualitative or critical non-empirical use of GIS (e.g. Kwan & Schwanen 2009). It is acknowledged that the quantitative nature of GIS, despite its limitations (see Leszczynski 2009), does not prevent its use for qualitative

quantitative output. Quantification per se often substitutes ordering and objectification for understanding.

Urban historical GIS

Historical GIS (HGIS) for cities

Through Chapters 4 and 5, it transpired that the study of inhabited urban built environments based on boundary concepts relies on surveyed and mapped evidence, whilst leading itself towards a mapping practice. GIS software has become the new standard in draughting maps and plans, storing mapped and spatial data in general. GIS adds a spatial database and statistical analytical powers to digital mapping abilities. While already a popular tool of research and applications in the disciplines of geography, planning and archaeology, recent years saw a distinct rise in the use of GIS for the historical study of cities. This development is part of what could be called a 'spatial turn' in the humanities (see Griffiths 2013), which complements the 'spatial turn' in the social sciences from the 1980s. In history this has led to the rise in popularity of the use of GIS in a variety of research practices (e.g. Gregory & Ell 2007; Lünen & Travis 2013). Increasingly there is also attention for the built environment, seeking integration with archaeological applications of GIS (attested by Paliou et al. 2014).

Chapter 1 discusses the considerable interest in the deep historical origin and definition of cities. Consequently, social and economic generative factors of settlement patterns are emphasised. Much twentieth-century historical work retained that focus on the market as the generator of cities, taking after the influential meta-theoretical ideas of Marx and Weber (Arnade et al. 2002). These ideas attempted to characterise the historiography of the urban in terms of what the city is, what the city is used for and what the city is understood to be. The influential and essentially economic 'central place theory' of Christaller (1933) subsequently guided attention towards city networks and city regions, both in urban geography (Parr 2005, 2007; Meijers 2007) and deeper history

purposes and approaches that are sensitive to societal complexity, diversity, and becoming. In archaeology, McEwan & Millican (2012), Gillings (2012) and Hacıgüzeller (2012) published, within the space of a single year, on the need and opportunities to push GIS approaches further with proper theorising and ontologies, phenomenological sensitivity, understandings of affordance, and non-representational thought. This book takes initial steps towards progress by following such approach in studying the inhabited urban built environment, all the while aiming to avoid the 'black box' effect in employing GIS technology (cf. Griffiths 2013).

(e.g. Verbruggen 2007; Brughmans et al. 2012). As shown earlier, the discipline of history has paid only slight attention to how urban space functions within cities. Griffiths (2013: 154) argues that history's foci on the study of maps as cultural objects and historical space as representation have 'created something of an epistemological blind spot for historians wishing to access and substantively describe "spaces of practice" produced by everyday activity'.

Space in the discipline of history used to be reduced to a meta-narrative (Arnade et al. 2002), but when history shifted its interest to space it did so on grounds provided by critical and cultural human geography. Historical interest in (urban) space became primarily guided by Lefebvrian (1991) metaphorical, representational and socially produced concepts of space draped over geographical locations (Arnade et al. 2002; Griffiths 2013) – i.e. social notions and actions with spatial implications going beyond passive 'container space'. Historians may have been especially susceptible to Lefebvre's theses, because he attends pre-modern cities in his work. Arnade et al. (2002: 522) argue that the multivalence of space in the abstract notions of Lefebvre provides more concrete grounds to investigate historically produced space, because it connects '"the material" and "the discursive", the physical and the ideological, or the experienced and the imagined. Lefebvre insisted that social space is produced and exists at each of these registers.'

Examples of spatial history (e.g. Estabrook 2002; Boone 2002) demonstrate that the empirical specificity of the material presence of space remains largely neglected. An interpretive role for space is claimed based on supposed empirical concreteness and theoretical sophistication for highly particular socio-cultural contexts and meanings. This leads to conflated historical concepts of space (cf. Chapter 1), because it is presupposed that certain spaces are ritual, political, legal, cultural, etc. Research in such predetermined contexts postdicts spaces' existence and only characterises space in its respective social interpretive context.

Readings of produced and represented urban space cannot be reduced to the purely material (Arnade et al. 2002). However, I argue that space's socio-spatially significant role for human inhabitation can only be understood through accepting the material nature of its construction and empirical presence. History's dominant spatial approach is at odds with this view. Their source material might be locational (or contain geographical references), but rarely contains inherent spatial dimensions. Consequently, it is not spatial properties and development that are studied, but the events that happened in space.

This is demonstrated by historical GIS efforts: historians, like human geographers (see Jones et al. 2009), usually map to visualise what happened where and investigate resultant locational relations. Urban applications in the emerging practice of historical GIS are taking advantage of the flexibility in data collation and integration offered by a working environment founded on digital databases, in preference to draughting plans on paper (Lilley n.d.). Despite GIS's geostatistical and geoanalytical underpinnings, historical GIS is aimed foremost at locating historical sources, data and events on a map to visualise them in spatial distributions. This may then help explain historical processes and relations (see Gregory & Ell 2007). Placing historical events and sources in urban space, however, inevitably relates them to locations and situations within a built environment. The physical properties of built environments increase our opportunities to use GIS in an analytically productive way, beyond illustrations and maps.

Urban examples of historical digital mapping practices show a preference for, on the one hand, locating the past on historical plans, and on the other, placing historical city plans in relation to the current city plan by using (semi-transparent) overlays (e.g. Frank 2013; *Locating London's Past* (undated); *Tokyo Cityscape* (Amherst College, 2009); *Paris Cityscape* (Amherst College, 2010); *imagineRio* (Rice Humanities Research Centre 2016); *Istanbul Urban Database* (Tuzcu 2017); Jensen & Keyes 2003). Jensen & Keyes (2003) make an illustrative example of the spatially more intricate practice of locating sources, people and events onto a visualisation of the city plan in a specified historical period (nineteenth century). Their work demonstrates the possibility of applying a GIS approach on an intra-urban level. A city plan[3] of Aarhus, Denmark is derived from historical maps and archives that form the basis for the historical GIS.

We are reminded that no map can represent the only truth (Chapter 5), but that all maps follow an (interpretative/research) agenda (e.g. Lilley 2012; Hutson 2012; Beisaw & Gibb 2013). Historically reconstructed maps, such as for Aarhus, are only one of many possible interpretations of the source material. The plots of which the reconstructed plan consists are invested with information on people (and their occupation) and property (tenure), creating a multi-linked

3. This derivation conveys the most credible cartographic representation of urban space on a specified level of detail. Jensen & Keyes (2003) limited themselves to using the 1870 register map as a basis, which is then cleared from irrelevant features and adjusted with reconstructed features from textual historical sources: the 1801 population census and the 1801 fire register (which contained all buildings). No physical empirical data is used.

database. Despite their intricate spatial compilation of information, most historical GIS applications also reveal limitations to spatial engagement. Eventually, GIS is primarily used to visualise the mapped location and distribution of e.g. the wealth and occupation of urban residents (i.e. social notions with spatial locations). In this sense, GIS produces little more than a progressive scatter plot, albeit directly linked to a transparently grounded representation of actual physical spatial organisation.

This implies that historically specific information is analysed against a map *background*, but the historicity of the physical space itself is not studied (Griffiths 2013). It permits researchers historical interpretation in a spatial dimension, making analogies to ideas on accessibility and centrality, without engaging in the creation of an understanding of such spatial (and material) properties and their development. Projecting social information onto space by geo-locating it is not the same as understanding the constitutive role of space. This is not to say that the researchers are insensitive to the dynamics and change within urban space, 'rather we see it as something dynamic and constantly being contested and renegotiated between the inhabitants' (Jensen & Keyes 2003: 11).

Looking at some other examples, Frank (2013) shows an even richer GIS and a desire to address the intricacies of urban life. However, the implementation does not move beyond the essential limitations of placing history in space. Amherst College's (2009, 2010) *Cityscapes* demonstrate the potential of visual comparisons between time-periods by using the native ability of GIS to overlay city plans (the Amherst Mapping Application (*aMapApp3*) was used to develop these examples). Yet, Rice Humanities Research Centre's (2016) work on Rio de Janeiro shows a sophistication of overlays and mapped data integration. This includes morphological mapping of implemented urban improvement schemes and viewsheds representing the perspective of historical sources.

Such cursory review concludes that urban historical GIS currently mainly utilises the opportunities to compile, collate, store, link and visualise historically sourced or derived information in selective spatial contexts. These examples do not equal a social study of urban space: interpreting the space itself in a social and temporal sense. In social scientific urban historical geography and archaeology, one will want to ask: '*how* was the spatial situation, or structure, of where something happened?', instead of just '*where* did something happen?' Both questions are part of studying the relationships between society and space, which according to Griffiths (2013) is one of the main reasons for historical scholarship to engage with the geographical practice and theory of GIS.

At the convergence of urban geography and urban history, historical scholarship exists that involves the characteristics of urban space in more intricate ways: e.g. *The Study of Urban History* (Dyos 1968); *The Urban Landscape* (Whitehand 1981b); *The Pursuit of Urban History* (Fraser & Sutcliffe 1983); *Urban Historical Geography* (Denecke & Shaw 1988); *The Built Form of Western Cities* (Slater 1990); *Urban Landscapes* (Whitehand & Larkham 1992b).[4] Justifying Jones' (2004) insistence on welcoming an extension to human geography's temporal frame of reference beyond the recent past, (prehistoric and classical) archaeology and ancient history are still virtually absent in this work. Yet, some counterbalance to Lilley's (2011b) warranted alarm over historical geography's neglect of the medieval is offered.

Having established (Chapter 1) that the endurance of the physicality of the built environment (Harris & Smith 2011) provides the evidence for cities throughout human history, the pivotal place of such evidence in the works cited here is explained. The substantial contribution made by archaeology (Clarke & Simms 1985) is clarified. When engaging this evidence, questioning the socio-spatial significance of the material presence of boundaries can prepare historical research for uncovering the entanglement of living in the material-spatial world over the long-term.

GIS-aided historically reconstructed city plans

Notwithstanding current restricted spatial engagement, the inescapable fact that a specific historical situation of a city needs to be mapped is paramount for historical GIS and the boundary approach alike. Regularly historical GIS applications achieve this by simply digitising and/or vectorising historical maps. A complementary tradition of work reconstructs a plan of the city more progressively. This practice predates GIS software's accessibility.

First, there is the so-called 'cross-section method' (see Bisschops 2012) inspired by Keene (1985; Keene & Harding 1987). This approach

---

4. Most volumes cited here are affiliated to urban morphology (discussed below), especially *The Urban Landscape* and *Urban Landscapes*, which are edited by urban morphologists, and more geographical in character than would be expected of history in general. *Urban Historical Geography* offers arguably the most diverse overview of the field. See also Chapter 1 for further thoughts on some of this discourse.

allows series of properties (usually plots of land) to be mapped with reasonable accuracy, while anchoring incidental properties or buildings within each sequence of properties (cf. the notion of plot series, Conzen 1960). Bisschops (2012) points out that his research uses both the 'cross-section method' and historically intensive regressive mapping. Complementarily, then, regressive sequence mapping on the basis of urban plans is derived from urban morphology (discussed below). Lilley (2000, 2011a; Lilley et al. 2007) is the strongest advocate of this approach. In regressive sequence mapping, urban morphology is employed to create a skeletal plan for earlier phases of a city, often departing from the first accurate urban plans from the nineteenth century. Advanced critical historical and archaeological methods are needed to flesh out the process of working backwards in time, producing a comprehensive mapping of the city (Lilley 2011a; Dean 2012a, 2012b). Lilley, Bisschops, and Dean respectively demonstrate that the comparative compilation and matching of information has much to gain from GIS technology.

In addition to historical and archaeological data, comprehensive cartographic reconstruction requires the careful and critical *conjecturing* of missing features (see Lilley 2011a); a data creation practice made more easily accessible by GIS. Only through composite conjecture can the resulting map approximate a complete and reasonably accurate snapshot that represents the town at a specified historical moment. The spatial morphology of a reconstructed plan provides referential shapes that are used to geo-locate and position (social) historical sources. Managing such linked data is greatly advanced by GIS. So far, the methods to reconstruct town plans appear predominantly developed and applied in western (European) historical contexts going back until the (high) medieval period. This implies there is a limitation to the data available – especially where ongoing inhabitation of cities inhibits expansive archaeological exposure – to work on historical situations of urban layouts. Where available, the methods of plan reconstruction become a prerequisite for analytical socio-spatial mapping, such as a boundary approach (see Chapter 7).

Dean (2012a, 2012b) shows that archaeology may uncover significant flaws in urban morphologically reasoned map regression. This renders accurate attempts at comprehensively reconstructing city plans an immensely labour-intensive and complex project. Consequently, the primary concern of many urban historical GIS projects is not with such reconstructions of the urban built environment, but is more usually confined to periods for which reasonably accurate maps exist.

Nonetheless, a growing body of meticulously reconstructed city plans using digital technologies[5] opens up promising directions for future social and spatial research, as propagated here.

Since in the present context reconstructive mapping practice forms a methodological prerequisite, I will make no attempt here to further critique or improve this method. The sixteenth-century part of the Winchester test case (introduced in Chapter 7) is based on Keene's (1985) exclusively historical work (archaeological data was not consistently used in the preparations of these town plans), to contrast with the research practice on the basis of archaeological surface surveys (which here will be exemplified by the material remains of Chunchucmil). Both kinds of source data rely on historically critical reconstructive and conjectural mapping to prepare the basic spatial layout of a specific historical moment in a town's development.

GIS-based approach to studying urban built form

Perhaps unsurprisingly, it is not historians or geographers, but archaeologists and conservationists who are specifically targeting urban built form in GIS. Lefebvre, Rodier, and Saligny (Lefebvre at al. 2008; Lefebvre 2009; Rodier et al. 2009; Lefebvre 2012) have developed a conceptual ordering of the urban fabric that emphasises temporal dynamics and function to store and analyse urban archaeological information. The underlying theoretical model is referred to as OH_FET and derived from the idea of temporal geographical information systems (essentially a simultaneously temporal and spatial database) (Peuquet 1994, 2001). Their practice is based on conceptual modelling: a hierarchy composed of simple and (aggregate) complex objects elucidating the intricate becoming and use of architectural complexes in an urban setting (Lefebvre et al. 2008; Lefebvre 2012). It focuses on eliciting the historical rhythms of built space in development.

Their method embraces the assertion that any understanding of the dynamics of urban fabric over time necessitates the conceptualisation of a constituent object of the urban fabric. In this object, all knowledge about its transformations culminates (*sensu* Galinié et al. 2004), hence the 'historical object'. The historical object is an initial interpretation of analogies

---

5. Excellent examples include: *Mapping Medieval Chester* (Faulkner n.d.); *Mapping Medieval Townscapes* (Lilley et al. 2005); *Pompeii Bibliography and Mapping Project* (Poehler n.d.); *Alpage* (Noizet & Costa n.d.; Noizet & Grosso 2011) and the GIS for medieval Antwerp (Bisschops 2012).

with other information, meeting three fundamental criteria: (1) location and surface area (where is it?); (2) date, duration, and chronology (when did it exist?); (3) function, social use, or an interpretation (what is it?) (Lefebvre et al. 2008; Lefebvre 2009; Rodier et al. 2009).

Lefebvre (2009) explains that any modification of these three criteria causes the disappearance and creation of a new historical object or interpretation. Theoretically this is a logical consequence of the aggregate complexity of historical objects, and not dissimilar to the logic that any change produces a new atomic situation for the entirety of a city (cf. Chapter 4). Note that this methodological endeavour includes more information sets than the material-spatial data used for my boundary approach to emphasise socio-spatial constitution and experience. In contrast, studying the urban fabric with OH_FET ultimately pursues an understanding of the dynamics of the formation of urban space. To that end, detailed *temporal* information is the driving force for generating analytical spatial units, while it remains unclear what the meaning of these features is.

Conservationists might welcome this method, because it separates spatial locations according to how often they changed spatially and/or functionally (a chronographic representation).[6] That on an urban level any change changes the whole social empirical reality of the city receives no particular attention. Prioritising temporal information over a socio-spatial understanding of how things occur to us and play a constitutive role in our inhabitation of the world inevitably leads to poorly conceived and conflated social use types (*sensu* Lynch 1981). In Lefebvre's (2009) and Rodier et al.'s (2009) discussion, established socio-cultural interpretations, which only exist in particular time-space specific cases (cf. Chapter 1), are combined. Such implied specificity naturally precludes broad comparative application.

A further problem is the desire to treat temporal intricacy on the same level as spatial complexity. To achieve this requires equal information across the whole city for each unique moment of (spatial or functional) transformation. In principle, privileging temporal dynamics over the more conventional time-slice or snapshot approach is a laudable pursuit. However, such information is rarely consistently available throughout longer periods of development. No matter how much effort we put into completing information throughout a place's history, we remain data dependent. In reality, retrieving like-for-like detail through time proves virtually impossible.

---

6. This practice bears some resemblance to the more complex hierarchical outcomes of morphogenetic analysis, determining the persistence, or morphogenetic priority, of form complexes (below) (see Conzen 1988, 2004).

Therefore, such GIS mapping conceals necessary extrapolations and may introduce conceptual anachronisms. That said, OH_FET accounts for an insightful critique of time-slices and periodisation (Lefebvre 2009: 1; cf. Mekking 2009) as 'broken down a priori, either in an abstract manner and by century, or on the basis of specific periods in the political history of the town. This breakdown prevents any specific research into the temporality of the town and its own rhythm of functioning.'

In Chapter 4 I declared that taking urban space as a contiguous whole (locus) means that we must accept the atomic[7] assumption of mapped data. As a consequence, the diachronic aspect of the boundary approach relies on time-slices. Temporally speaking, these may necessarily be coarser, but critical application will not allow the obscuring of historical reconstructive and conjecturing efforts when compiling a comprehensive urban plan for a historical moment. Thanks to the atomic assumption, time-slices are inherently better suited for spatial analysis of the whole, and thus the study of the process of inhabiting the urban built environment concerned.

OH_FET disaggregates complex historical objects into temporally specific features. Because of this it is better suited for the intensive study of smaller areas of urban development for which great amounts of historically detailed information are available throughout, which Lefebvre (2012) demonstrates. Working with reconstructed 'time-slice' plans relieves one from integral dependence on consistent and detailed historical information. Time-slicing may imply that, for each diachronic case, best practice is to choose a historical moment for which the best consistent information is available, or for which conjectures are equally justifiable across the entire area (cf. Lilley n.d.; Keene's (1985) 1417 plan). I concur with Lefebvre's (2009) warning that accepting the limitations of available data in this way could lead to a 'source effect' (bias) with regards to understanding temporal rhythms of development. However, not even Lefebvre (2009, 2012) overcomes organisation on a temporal scale (in years and periodic ranges) and, judging from his own chronographic representations, utilises periodic differences in availability of historical information. Alternatively, one might opt to strive for reconstructions of

---

7. Assuming a time-slice is atomic explicates its momentary indivisible nature as a whole. A time-slice is an abstract entirety which is immediate and inseparable: no time passes, everything occurs at once. The assumption that a material presence which is extant in one time-slice appears in a previous or succeeding time-slice constitutes a continuation, is akin to the everyday assumption that the house we live in remains a continuation of the same when we return after absence. This assumption does not withstand that the relative position of the house might have changed because of developments within any wholes (e.g. city) of which it is part.

the same historical moment across cases (time-slices). This second option would naturally make the historical period itself a significant object of research (cf. Chapter 1 on representation and meaning).

Evaluating OH_FET thus reveals that in consolidating the boundary mapping approach some historical and temporal detail on urban development may be lost. While interpretive temporal sensitivity is ensured by its constitutive theory, such understanding is perhaps less historical than it is part of the socio-spatial *processes* of inhabitation. In spite of its inherent risks, OH_FET may be preferred to a boundary approach where understanding temporality on the micro-scale is essential, or archaeological and historical *documentation* of locations through time is required. In this sense, OH_FET returns to the historically invested locations of historical GIS. We are still short of analysing the material record of urban built environments on a socio-spatial and comparative level.

Urban morphology

Background to the method

Urban morphology is often seen as an overarching term for all research on urban built form rather than a single method. As such it may encompass boundary mapping. 'The study of urban morphology is concerned with the description and explanation of the form, development and diversity of urban areas' (Kropf 1993: 212). Explaining the process of formation forms the central tenet. When referring to urban morphology as a method, what is usually meant is the morphogenetic approach of Conzenian urban morphology (specifically town plan analysis) after the German founder of its most influential branch: M.R.G. Conzen. He was influenced by the German morphographic and urban topographic studies of the first half of the twentieth century (Whitehand 1981a, 2001). Since 1994, urban morphological interests have been united in the International Seminar on Urban Form (ISUF), which hosts an annual conference and publishes the journal *Urban Morphology*.

In an attempt to determine their identity, ISUF president Moudon (1997) traced the origins of urban morphology back to three schools of thought: German (Conzenian), French (Versailles) and Italian (Muratori and Caniggia). Nonetheless, the leverage of such ideas was carried wider, which makes the combined origin of the current mix of ideas difficult to pinpoint (see e.g. Larkham (2006) for an overview of the specifically British study of urban form). Whitehand (2007) mentions that Mumford's (1961) seminal work on the historical development of cities also influenced the field. Lilley (2000: 7) posits current urban morphology as a derivative of commonality in the work of the influential scholars Conzen, Hoskins, and Beresford, explaining 'they shared an interest in understanding the physical development of medieval towns and they shared a common belief that the histories of medieval towns could be written using modern maps, coupled with aerial photographs and field work'.

The French school at Versailles was originally influenced by Muratori, but has since lost a coherent presence. Both strands display stronger architectural underpinnings than Conzenian urban morphology. Muratorian urban morphology is still practised, in particular under the guidance of Cataldi and Maffei from Florence (e.g. Cataldi et al. 2002). It can be referred to as a 'process typological' approach in which a hier-archy of 'elements, structures of elements, systems of structures, and organisms of systems' (Kropf 2009: 111) is formed, starting from the materials of architectural construction for buildings and the buildings as elements that establish a hierarchy towards structures of urban tissues (Kropf 1993 offers a full discussion). Process typology enables a study of urban tissue on various levels: the elements always create a whole within a context with increasing complexity, theoretically *ad infinitum* (Kropf 1996; see Fig. 6.1). This, in turn, compares to the structural logic in Conzen's (2004: 123) morphogenesis: 'It is an axiom of urban morph-ology that everywhere in the townscape the systematic form complexes are hierarchically nested in a physical sense.'

One should note how Muratorian ontology results from the consti-tution of form rather than a constitutive process (such as inhabitation). Chapters 4 and 5 establish that the operation of seclusion makes built structure also the ontological starting point for the boundary approach, which itself can be used to uncover a city's intrinsic aggregates. What I have called the 'ontology intrinsic to a city' (Chapter 5) thus partially resembles the organism of a town, which refers to the system of structures altogether (Kropf 2009). Importantly, in Muratorian urban morphology types are forms occurring at all levels of the hierarchy, which is not the way BLTs are formulated. Moreover, as a building is not conveyed by a single BLT (Chapter 5), the ontological starting point is not equal to process typology. While comparing BLTs to process typologies may spur on interesting architectural dialogues, to devise an appropriate meth-odology as a research practice, I deem geographical Conzenian urban morphology more suitable.

Conzen's morphogenetic approach grew out of the German morphographic and urban topographic traditions (Whitehand 1981a).

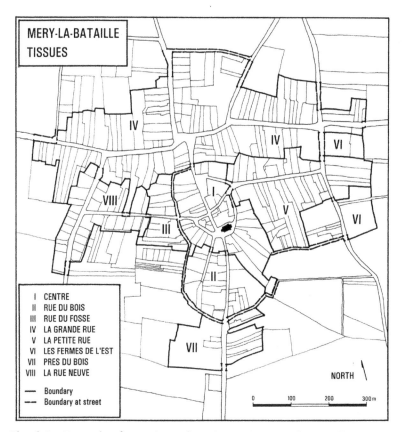

Fig. 6.1 Example of mapping urban tissues (in Mery-la-Bataille).

Physically and historically distinct areas are mapped to identify and describe the character of the town, the units providing a framework for planning and conservation purposes. (Image source: Kropf 1996: 258, reproduced by kind permission of Karl Kropf.)

Conzen's emigration to England initiated wide acceptance of his work in Anglophone discourse (Moudon 1997). Today the morphogenetic approach is therefore mostly a German–British research tradition (Whitehand 2001). Rather than reproducing Moudon's genealogy of urban morphology as practised by ISUF members, the methodological and analytical tenets of Conzenian urban morphology are of relevance here.

It is generally recognised that previously unparallelled maturity and clarity of Conzen's ideas was reached in his 1960 *Alnwick, Northumberland: A Study in Town-Plan Analysis* (Whitehand 1981a). In this work his foundational ideas about the research process known as *town plan analysis* became properly and comprehensively grounded;

its units and terms defined. In the morphogenetic approach, the evolution or development, the origin and history, of the townscape (urban landscape) is traced. The general idea of 'morphology' helped shape the theory of evolution,[8] relating the outside form of organisms to their internal structure and defining its relative constitutive parts (also seen in archaeological typologies and Muratorian urban morphology; cf. Kropf 2009). Urban morphology, then, refers to the study of the historical development of built form and its spatial structure (cf. Gordon 1981; Kropf 1993). Within Conzen's (1960) study, it can be seen that from defining a pre-urban core (see Clarke & Simms 1985, for detail on this specific term) his approach pieces together a *historical explanation* of the origins and the formation of urban form and building fabrics of the town.

The principal premise of the approach holds that a town's built environment is made up of an accumulation of traces of past activities. 'The building or street, as a direct result of the act, can be taken to refer to the time in which it occurred. Buildings and streets are signs referring to particular events. The history of a town is thus written in its fabric' (Kropf 1996: 255). This permits the assertion that the history of cities can be read by means of their physical form (Moudon 1997), which lies at the basis of town plan analysis (Conzen 1960). Acknowledging the tremendously persistent nature of historical built form into current built environments, Lilley (2000: 7) says: 'the form of streets and plots revealed on a large-scale plan of a given settlement provide in themselves clues about their origin and development'. However, as the practice of town plan analysis relies heavily on the use of historical sources rather than urban form alone, the phrase 'in themselves' appears misleading (see Conzen 1960, 1988[9]).[10]

8. Architects Tang & Yang's (2008) *Urban Paleontology* contains an eponymous approach to the evolution of urban forms. Instead of urban morphology, the authors connect their ideas directly to biology, archaeology and geology, ignoring the considerable likeness in the basis of both approaches. Rather than reading town plans in terms of persistence of urban tissue, they excavate plans (reversing urban design) to conceptualise urban form analogously in terms of urban fossils and species. Their aim is to understand the origin of urban forms to improve the planning and prediction of future urban developments. The somewhat forced 'palaeontology' is interesting, but falls short of the methodological rigour of urban morphology.
9. According to M.P. Conzen, M.R.G. Conzen did not give his consent to publish this version of his paper in this 1988 volume. The original was eventually printed in the 2004 volume *Thinking about Urban Form*. References to the 1988 paper have been verified using the original.
10. Similarly archaeological discourse displays a common belief that the built environment reflects the social organisation of its society. However, in reality this type of interpretation relies heavily on the use of analogies on the basis of ethnological sources (e.g. Carmack 1981; Hill & Monaghan 1987).

By constructing a comprehensive building and development history of a town, Conzenian morphology can read and assess the structure of the historical character of a town (e.g. Kropf 1996). Hence, nowadays urban morphology is often applied in planning studies and strategies to do with townscape conservation, growing awareness of the historical grain of cities[11] (see e.g. Whitehand 2007; Kropf 2011). Although Samuels (2010) argues that its adaptation for historical conservation is not yet complete, applications to the management of townscapes have grown over the years, under the influence of Whitehand, as attested by contributions in Whitehand (1981b) and Whitehand & Larkham (1992b). Certainly, urban morphology is a field in motion. Whitehand (2010b: 361) remarks 'the development of further specialities remains an integral part of the expansion of knowledge'.

The practice of town plan analysis

Town plan analysis as a methodological practice merits further attention as foundational aspects dominate research practice on urban form, including the mapping of BLTs (Chapter 7 expands on this adaptation). Town plan analysis explicates and maps the building history of the shape of a town based on historically and spatially coherent plan units (cf. Muratorian urban tissue), which are somewhat subjectively identified within the town (see Conzen 1960, 1968, 1981; Whitehand 1981a; Lilley 2000; Conzen 2004). It thrives on incorporating large bodies of socio-economic historical sources, as well as a degree of intuition, to inform its urban mapping outcomes as a spatial representation of plan units. This entanglement with historical particularities tampers with its comparative applicability. Town plan analysis structurally connects historical context (contrary to what I suggest in Chapter 1) with the processes that

---

11. Whitehand (2007) critiques architecture's and planning policy's limited focus on the historical grain allowing for a piecemeal of external aesthetics. Architectural design philosophies such as Alexander's *The Timeless Way of Building* (1979) and *A Pattern Language* (Alexander et al. 1977) or Krier's *Urban Space* (1979; see Carmona et al. 2003 for further ideas) approach the urban built environment from the pre-existing buildings and arrangements we already know, to arrive at idiosyncratic normative theories championing planning methods that should lead to aesthetically pleasing and well-functioning designs. The seminal works of Kostof (1991, 1992) use similar architectural complexes and socio-cultural divisions to construct readings of urban form through history. These rarely take into account the constitutive elements of the historical grain of the city, but have had much larger public exposure, including architects, planners and policy makers, than more academic urban morphology. Lynch's (1960) popular analytical approach to reading cities or townscapes provides wholly alternative concepts.

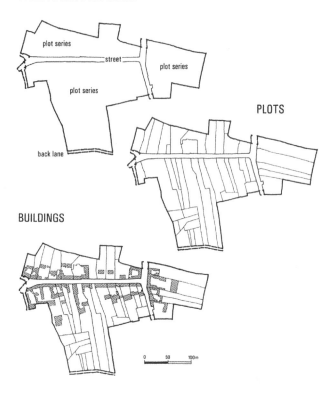

STREETS AND PLOT SERIES

plot series

street

plot series

plot series

PLOTS

back lane

BUILDINGS

0 50 100 m

Fig. 6.2 Hierarchical levels of mapping urban morphological elements (in Mery-la-Bataille).

Most urban morphological methods depart from the three basic elements of street, plot and building, here demonstrated as part of three distinct resolutions of morphological detail. (Image source: Kropf 1996: 253, reproduced by kind permission of Karl Kropf.)

shape urban space to create a townscape consisting of the following form categories: the town's plan, building fabric and land utilisation.

Reading of the town plan in turn depends on an ontology of its composition, envisioned to consist of three elements (see Fig. 6.2): 'streets and their mutual association in a street-system, the individual land parcels or plots and their aggregation in street-blocks with distinct block patterns, and the buildings or more precisely their block plans and the arrangement of these in the town plan as a whole' (Conzen 1968: 117;

for more detail see Conzen 1960). As the morphogenetic practice is based on European historical conduct as much as geographical conduct, it typically does not regress beyond the medieval period. Therefore, for all towns in the western and globalised world, from that period onwards, this ontology holds comparative morphological merit. Indeed, versions of the basic division of elements have become a common influence in urban built environment research. Conzen (2004) had clearly intended his ideas to travel even beyond European historic town, but its casuistic and disciplinary foundation fails to immediately facilitate more radical comparisons.

To conduct town plan analysis, one requires a town plan: a large-scale map 'showing essential detail of layout in recognisable and measurable form' (Conzen 1968: 115), which according to Conzen in practice is nothing greater than 1:5000. This permits one to see the block plans of individual buildings. Town plan can refer to both the cartographic representation (physical layout projected at a predetermined scale) and the physical layout of the town itself. The 'town plan', together with the two form categories 'building fabric' and 'land utilisation', are functionally and genetically connected in the townscape: *as a palimpsest rather than an accumulation*. The duration of persistence (conservation) decreases from townscape to building fabric to land utilisation (Conzen 1968). For the elements of the town plan, the street pattern, the plot and aggregate blocks, and the buildings and their block plans, this usually applies in reverse order.

On the basis of these characteristics, the researcher attempts to define plan units that display a sense of coherence in its historical and spatial development. Lilley (2000) clearly states this process is part subjective and therefore follows a strategy of validation, entailing the verification of drawn plan units with archaeological and historical evidence.[12] Conzen (1968: 120) himself meagrely proffers:

> [T]he recognition of distinct plan units is of great importance and can often illuminate the growth stages of a medieval town [...] when available written records fail to give any information. Such recognition depends on the careful scrutiny of plan detail such as the behaviour of street spaces and their bounding street lines, and

---

12. Although Lilley's (2000) practice is more critical of intuition, it still runs the risk of creating a research fallacy similar to cultural historical and culture area research in archaeology (Lyman et al. 1997; Vis 2009). Here colonial, geographical or linguistic designations introduced biased boundaries around a people or region, the prevalence of which may seemingly be validated by research, because it forms the initial delimitation of analytical outcomes.

the shape, size, orientation, and grouping of plots, all such evidence leading to the identification of the 'seams' along which the genetically significant plan units are knit together.

Those seams are boundaries plotted to establish coherent areas or plan divisions. The behaviour and correlations that would give rigour to the method of identifying units remain unexplained. Continuing Conzenian urban morphological analysis, the genetic plan units act as one form complex, which is the most relevant here, but historical building types and land utilisation can also divide the townscape into coherent areas. Altogether these then combine to produce a map of morphological regions (see Fig. 6.3). The seams or boundaries of units and areas in urban morphology do not concur with BLTs. When identifying and mapping BLTs, rigour is provided by their definitions (Chapter 5) and their establishment through critical realist iterative abstraction (Chapter 2).

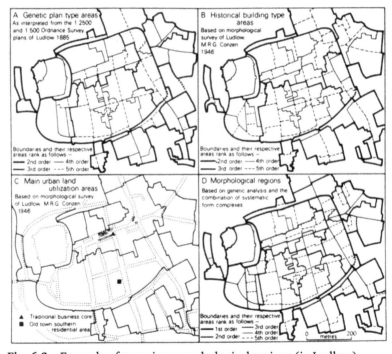

Fig. 6.3 Example of mapping morphological regions (in Ludlow).

Morphogenetic analysis and three mappings of form complexes combine to divide the townscape into morphological regions in Conzenian urban morphology. (Image source: Conzen 2004: 122, reproduced by kind permission of Michael P. Conzen and Peter Lang Publishing.)

It is common practice in urban morphology and historical town plan reconstructions to use the first accurate historical plan of a town, which is usually the nineteenth-century plan. A ground level base plan with relevant features can be produced based on this plan (see Conzen 1960; Keene 1985; Lilley 2000). Producing a base plan has become general practice among associated methods, including space syntax (see below) and indeed BLT Mapping (Chapter 7). Creating a skeletal base plan helps to trace phases of a town's development and grounds historical reconstruction. However, ultimately the analytical unit of town plan analysis itself (the plan unit) is a relatively coarse spatial reference. Plan units cannot reconstruct a town's precursory phases in great detail. The intellectual pursuit of town plan analysis comprises the recognition and comprehension of a town's historical structure in terms of its plan units (Conzen 1960, 1968, 1981).

Emerging terms and processes

Through town plan analyses, an array of urban morphological terms and processes emerged. Conzen (2004: 239–261) provides a relatively comprehensive glossary of these, making repeat of such effort redundant. Together these terms provide a particular vocabulary which can logically describe the spatial processes of the development of urban built form. Some of the main terms convey processes that have the ability to be *comparatively* applied and elucidate urban development processes across the world.

Whitehand & Larkham (1992a), for example, recognise that *development cycles* and *fringe belts* have been successfully applied in divergent case studies. Nonetheless, Whitehand (2012) clearly identifies an under-representation of non-western cases in urban morphology. He argues that the lack of conceptual engagement and the loss of an overarching view are impeding the all-important comparative agenda in urban morphological discourse (cf. Whitehand 2009). It is telling that the development cycle is specifically based on the medieval *burgage*[13] cycle. This is based on a particular historical property arrangement not strictly found in the same way elsewhere or in other periods.

Nonetheless, the process of 'building repletion' on plots of land, involving initial institution of the plot, repletion (development), climax, and recession (disuse and fallow, completed by demolition, clearance,

---

13. A burgage refers to a burgage tenement, which typically comprises the property of the plot of a house with or without associated land that could be rented in medieval boroughs or towns.

obliteration or transformation of plot for redevelopment) (Conzen 1960, 1968, 1981), may have wider bearings. Furthermore, Conzen's (1960) dissection of plots provides a nifty descriptive language for aspects of how its properties affect the built environment, such as: plot head, plot tail, plot dominant, plot accessories, plot series, street-line, building line and building frontage. This allows the precise formulation of logical constructions, e.g. arguing that closed building development is constituted by rows or serried lines that occur when the building line coincides with the plot head on the street line.

On the basis of the (burgage) plot, quantitative measures could further enrich the morphological description and study, as standardised measures[14] of frontages can help to retrieve the original measures of transformed plots (Conzen 1960; see also Lilley n.d.). Building repletion can be measured in density ratios (percentages) that mimic figure-ground diagrams (see Trancik 1986), i.e. built volumes or solids vs. open space or voids (Conzen 1981).[15] Measuring building coverage within the built environment has been developed for urban design purposes.[16] Measuring the dimensions and surface areas of plots and plots per area could help express the effects of plot pattern transformations[17] from intact to meta-morphic, due to processes of truncation, absorption or amalgamation. While BLT Mapping also permits such quantitative measures, purely empirical measures are not intrinsically meaningful in terms of their socio-spatial significance (see Chapters 8 and 9).

Similarly, fringe belts (inner and outer) have been especially associated with modern planning challenges, such as the effects of ring roads (e.g. Whitehand 1977; Whitehand & Morton 2004; Conzen, M.P. 2009; Ünlü 2013). The related process of *fixation lines*, which occur when urban growth (temporarily) comes to a halt, may have comparative relevance. Fixation lines bring about distinctly patterned effects in the further development of the town plan, including circumscribing roads, town

14. Conzen (1960) acknowledges that measures could have a cap for the maximum width of a frontage due to environmental or technical (rather than social, economic or historical) restrictions, and he also mentions the standardised measures could differ between building types.
15. In Chapter 7 it will be demonstrated that the first stage of BLT Mapping visually resembles a figure-ground plan, mapping out the built volumes from the open spaces.
16. If building coverage is used as a measure for the intensity of land-use, the vertical rise of buildings needs to be taken into account. This is demonstrated by the GIS adaptation of this measure by Liu et al. (2010). Conzen (1981) places this issue within the analysis of building fabric and land-use rather than town-plan analysis, which covers building repletion.
17. In cases where there are no previously instituted plots, the piecemeal building repletion of open or unstructured space is called transformative growth (Conzen 1960, 1968), with examples such as a market space being colonised by permanent building of stalls (cf. Rörig 1928; Lefebvre 2012).

walls and irregularly shaped open areas. Fixation lines often mark distinct patterns of morphological development on either side (see Conzen 1960, 1968). In appropriate diachronic cases, persistence patterns of boundary lines, due to their inevitable social empirical presence as well as their aggregation into entities (Chapter 5), may replicate some of the logic of fixation lines and other seams between plan units.

More generically, earlier forms (pre-urban nuclei of either natural or man-made origin) act as *morphological frames* for the formation of subsequent built forms, which in turn can modify the frames. Such process clearly exemplifies the dynamics of transforming the physical properties of the world (Chapter 3). Old field boundaries and country lanes may act as morphological frames for subsequent settling or expansions of towns. These shapes can become incorporated as e.g. streets in the layout of the plan (Conzen 1960; evidenced in the UK and The Netherlands by Hoskins 1977; Taverne 2008; Raue 1982). In transformative instead of additive changes, some traces of earlier phases may be retained. These are *inherited outlines*, which act as morphological frames, while other shapes will be obliterated.[18]

The preceding terminological examples make clear that, although not explicitly its focus, Conzenian urban morphology features an abundance of references to boundaries. Plan units are delimited by seams; plots are delimited by plot boundaries; building lines indicate their extent; growth may stop in fixation lines; morphological frames delimit confines of development or persist as residuals; etc. The important difference with BLTs is purposive. The examples have been defined as spatial occurrences describing shapes which are conceptualised within (historical) processes of formation and transformation. Ultimately, urban morphology uses discrete surface areas as *a priori* spatial convention, although Conzen (1968: 117) recognises that all plan element complexes are interconnected and mutually condition each 'other's origins, physical relations, and functional significance, not just at present but in historical time'. Urban morphological 'boundaries' are likely to be maintained in BLT Mapping as boundary lines (feature outlines) (Chapter 4), but they do not directly concur in any way with the socio-spatial BLT definitions (Chapter 5).

Because Conzenian urban morphology aims to provide a socioeconomic historical explanation of emerging urban forms, it counters the trend that the study of architectural and urban form is usually not

18. Remaining traces from morphological metamorphoses are called residuals (Conzen 1981; cf. Tang & Yang's (2008) urban fossils).

integrated in social and urban history (Tilly 1996). In Conzen's (1960: 5) words: 'plan analysis properly includes the evaluation of physical conditions of site and situation as well as of relevant economic and social development. The latter, indeed, provides the background for the inter-dependence of plan, building fabric, and land use, and the bridge between the morphological and the functional approaches in urban geography.' Within this historicism the interest in 'the social' (cf. Chapter 2), which includes the decision-making processes by agents (*sensu* Sayer 1979; cf. Gordon 1981; Lilley et al. 2007), is subsumed in what can be known through a documentary background (especially Conzen 1988; see also Whitehand 1977). The social empirical reality of its bounded shapes is not regarded in terms of its social significance to inhabitation. Equally, morphological comparability is only ensured for the historically specific framing of the examples on which its practice was based.

Conzen (1988) makes some generic allusions towards the social utility of the town plan. He asserts that the street system as an access pattern is a long-term commitment of a whole urban community, while the social utility of the building fabric is the historically less constant commitment of the respective owners (vs. Mekking's (2009) ideas on representational architecture). Generally it applies that the more people are involved, the more resistant form complexes become to change. So, a building is likely to change more often than the street system. The social utility of the pattern of land utilisation comprises the provision of viable locations for each land-use unit, depending on the access pattern. Conzen (1988) also makes a fleeting remark that suggests that the shape of a town's morphological elements may impede internal communication and the ability to defend.

These social affordances and experiences are not structurally explored on the basis of the town's built layout. However, Lilley et al. (2007) show that urban morphology is a good aid for comparing urban planning designs, and the effects of individuals and authority on their real-isation in roughly *ceteris paribus* situations. *En passant* he also confirms the abolition of the traditional planned versus unplanned dichotomy and their associated organic and geometric patterns[19] (cf. Smith 2007; Vis 2009) – a remark Conzen (1968) already made regarding European medieval towns.

---

19. Following from the openness as asserted by complexity theory (Bentley & Maschner 2003) and the outcomes of interactions leading to 'unintended intentionalities' (Chapter 4, cf. Abbott 1995), the possibility already follows that geometrically regular patterns could also emerge from individual development and settling activities (e.g. aligning houses and/or entrances with respect to their relative location).

In the posthumously published anthology *Thinking about Urban Form*, we find a short essay in which Conzen (2004) acknowledges that urban morphology is in need of a sounder philosophical foundation. This essay enables connections to the phenomenological thought in this book, and spatial cognition in space syntax (see below). Conzen reaches the insight that urban settlements are dynamic complexes in which the causality of the physical, biotic and social collides. This, finally, resonates much better with the social scientific foundations of the boundary approach. Such late realisation does not withstand urban morphology's formative effect on the methodological development of BLT Mapping, as subsequent chapters will show.

Space syntax

Background to the method

An equally social scientific and architectural approach to studying urban form is found in space syntax. Space syntax has its origins in attempts during the 1970s to understand 'the influence of architectural design on the existing social problems in many housing estates that were being built in the UK' (Pinho & Oliveira 2009a: 110). Its theoretical foundation reached cogent completion in Hillier & Hanson's (1984) seminal *The Social Logic of Space*. The general intention was to improve planning practice and normative (or generative) architectural design. Design practice lacked scientific grounding, and produced built form that seemed to harbour the ingredients for detrimental social effects by alienating its residents (Hillier & Hanson 1984; Hillier 2007; Marcus 2010). Hillier & Hanson (1984) propose a conceptual model in which space is a dimension of social life, yet their approach to studying built environment configurations is firmly connected to the quantitative tradition of the 1960s and 1970s (for morphological context, see Larkham 2006). According to Hillier (2005) this places space syntax somewhere between a phenomenological social scientific approach (e.g. Tuan 1977; Lefebvre 1991; Seamon n.d., 2012; and theoretically Griffiths & Quick 2005; this research) and a social physics or modelling approach (e.g. Batty & Longley 1994; Longley & Batty 2003; Bettencourt 2013; Brown & Witschey 2003; Brown et al. 2005; Volchenkov & Blanchard 2008; Wilson & Dearden 2011; Wilson 2012).

According to Hanson (2012), the objective of the research reported on in *The Social Logic of Space* was to develop a new language for space, and each idea was extensively tested on a wide variety of the most challenging built form contexts. While Conzen's (1968) initial comparative ambition was to enable the study of most British towns, justifying his selection of a medieval starting point, space syntax explicitly wants to be comprehensively comparative (e.g. Carvalho & Penn 2004; Omer & Zafrir-Reuven 2010). To this end the terms used for concepts and analyses were kept predominantly abstract (Hanson 2012). Comparability is evidently aided by the quantitative basis of its methods. Consequently the outcomes of space syntactic analyses tend to be quantitative and visualised accordingly, after which they can be compared to real world observations. Against the backdrop of developing its own suite of software, *Depthmap* (by Alasdair Turner), which is freely available and since 2011 also open source, the uptake of space syntax application and development has grown considerably.[20] This not only applies to academic research, but also industry and policy applications through its commercial branch (e.g. Chiaradia & Lemlij 2007; Space Syntax Ltd. n.d.[21]).

Space syntax is now probably the best-known analytical approach to the study of ground-plan built environment configurations and represents a theory and associated family of tools (Hillier & Hanson 1984; Hillier 2007; Bafna 2003; Van Nes in prep.). In its foundation, substantial social scientific claims are made. Space syntax aims to contribute to the man-environment paradigm and the relations between society and space at large (Griffiths & Quick 2005; Griffiths 2013), but does so by initial empirical reference to built form rather than its emergence (cf. urban morphology). Being grounded in social theory, in this book BLT Mapping follows a kindred developmental pathway as space syntax. However, in *The Social Logic of Space* the link between the spatial empiricism of specific architectural analytical units and the human or social empirical purpose is not consistently explicit.

The apparent mismatch this causes between theory and tools is probably best explained by the structuralist antecedents that underlie space syntax's inception. Hillier & Hanson declare that part of their thought exercise was to install a corrective for the over-emphasis on social theory rather than spatial theory, and to consider societies as spatial systems. They argue that 'spatialising our concept of society' works

---

20. See the *Space Syntax Network* (n.d.) website for a download link and full information on the current version: *DepthmapX*.
21. Space Syntax Ltd. is the commercial consulting company founded as a spin-off by the space syntax group at University College London, and showcases example projects on its website.

towards making structure appear 'as a *property of reality itself*' (Hillier & Hanson 1984: 201; original emphasis).

> The primacy of configuration in the 'social logic' of space does not just happen to be the case. It originates in the logic of *space* itself (Hillier et al. 1987: 363, emphasis added).

So, the corrective nested an imbalance in space syntax's development. It ends up being enthralled by capturing and elegantly reducing geometric complexity of spatial configurations into advanced analytical constructions which are only tentatively connected to social theoretical necessity (see Griffiths & Quick 2005; Vis 2009; Van Nes in prep.). This lack of *a priori* causation, in turn, is since incrementally being patched with correlative research outcomes.

Simultaneously, despite temporality forming part of the initial theoretical descriptions, time has been demonstrated to be a structurally neglected aspect in space syntax (Griffiths 2011). Although conducting space syntax can become part of narratives of historical explanations (Griffiths 2009, 2011, 2012a; Thaler 2005), it offers itself no (historically) constitutive logic informing its analysis. As a type of spatial analysis its temporal frame is always synchronous, inhibiting systematic subsequent constitutive theorising or interpretive conduct (Griffiths 2011). Arguably, the generative syntaxes formulated in Hillier & Hanson (1984: 66–81) offer physical boundaries a constitutive role in generating spatial morphologies for human purpose. However, social experience and transformative affordance within space are subsumed by expressing the ways in which the access purpose of design occurs. Particular types of built space configurations are captured in generative formulae that emphasise the connectivity of spatial continuity (accessibility) rather than discontinuity (boundaries).

Finally, but perhaps most frequently, the space syntax theory and analyses are criticised for pursuing cognitive argumentation without having a proper foundation of spatial cognition in place[22] (e.g. Bafna 2003; Penn 2003; Conroy Dalton et al. 2012). Hanson (2012) states that space syntax was built on a hypothesis test approach (contrary to critical realism, Chapter 2). Indeed, its sustained practice correlates space syntactic measures with ethologically derived observations of social

---

22. This is also an issue within the field of architectural communication theory (see Rapoport 1990; Smith 2011a). Applying experimental approaches (cf. Zacharias 1997) could help construct a theory.

behaviour. In contrast, in Chapter 1 I excluded a psychological line of argumentation towards interpretation, while spatial cognition resides in the psychological realm. How we understand and make decisions psychologically may ultimately explain all behaviour, but obtaining complete psychological knowledge on all individual people participating within space is untenable. Because critical realism suggests 'the social' has distinct causal power, even a full-fledged cognitive theory is no replacement for social theory on the outcomes of actions.[23]

With regards to positivist hypothesis testing, space syntax deals its hand when supposing that people have an innate ability to 'read' the arrangement of spatial layout (Hillier & Hanson 1984; Conroy Dalton et al. 2012). On this basis space syntax can start seeking law-like regularities between, e.g., topological geometry and behaviour such as way-finding (pedestrian movement) to uncover the possible rules according to which we understand configurations topologically (cf. Penn 2003; Hillier & Penn 2004). Except for the development of space syntactic viewsheds (isovists) (see Franz & Wiener 2008; Paliou & Knight 2013), there is no direct inclusion of human or social experience. The cornerstones of space syntax methods are formed by spatially distinct convex spaces (conducive of co-presence in space) and axial (visual) lines (conducive to movement), and a somewhat speculative social distinction between visitors or strangers and inhabitants of a place (Hillier & Hanson 1984). Social theory would not deny the importance of co-presence or our senses (here vision) nor movement (cf. Chapters 2 and 3), but these empirical translations did not come forth from a constitutive social framework.

Space syntax applications

Despite theoretical and purposive differences, in continuation my methodological development will reflect various influences of how space syntax strives to connect built space to social life, including its sophisticated method for analysing the topological structure of built environment configurations. To begin with, space syntax analysis distinguishes the interior world (inside a built space, gamma analysis,[24] or now more usually referred to as access analysis) and the exterior world

---

23. One might venture the thought that cognitive theory is more apt to help understand how human beings relate to space, whereas the aim of this book is to enable contributions to understanding space's stake in relating human beings.
24. Incidentally, in archaeology syntactic analyses of interior space are arguably yet more widespread than urban analyses (e.g. Fairclough 1992; Moore 1992; Cutting 2003; Fisher 2009).

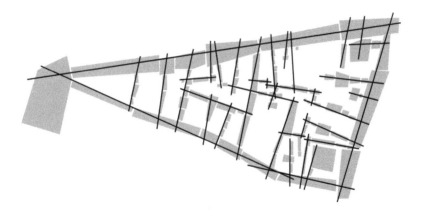

Fig. 6.4 Example of mapping axial lines connecting up convex space.

The grey background shows a configuration of fewest convex spaces. The black lines form the axial map. (Image source: Hillier 2007: 117, copyright Bill Hillier, reproduced by kind permission of Space Syntax Ltd.)

(in a settlement, alpha analysis, or now more usually referred to as axial and segment analysis) (Hillier & Hanson 1984). A roughly similar distinction of 'structurally comparable domains' is maintained in this project as well. The urban scale naturally pertains to the exterior world, whereas the stringent seclusion of a building (Chapter 5), or indeed all major feature outlines, extracts the arbitrary internal *arrangement* of a socio-spatial system from further specifying negotiations with its outside. For me, however, the notion of occupiable 'interior' space remains part of the same domain as all subdivisions (also note that such social formulation acts *contra* Hillier & Hanson's (1984) spatial ideography of generative elements).

Both gamma and alpha analysis depend on breaking up built configurations into constituent parts, i.e. the fewest convex spaces, and the connections between them. In settlements these are conveyed by axial lines, which are the longest lines intersecting convex spaces connecting up the whole system using the fewest lines (see Fig. 6.4).[25] Subsequently, this can be plotted as a graph, which is justified (J-graph) by plotting it from a specified space or node (Hillier & Hanson 1984; see Fig. 6.5).

25. It must be acknowledged that, following sustained critique (e.g. Teklenburg et al. 1993; Ratti 2004a, 2004b; Ostwaldt 2011), geometric and topographical dimensions are being combined in analyses (e.g. Van Nes & López 2007; Mavridou 2012; Van Nes in prep.). For example, in current practice various space syntax measures use segment maps which can be generated from axial lines or road centre lines, which integrate the capacity to measure geometric characteristics (UCL Space Syntax 2017; Hillier et al. 2007; Charalambous & Mavridou 2012).

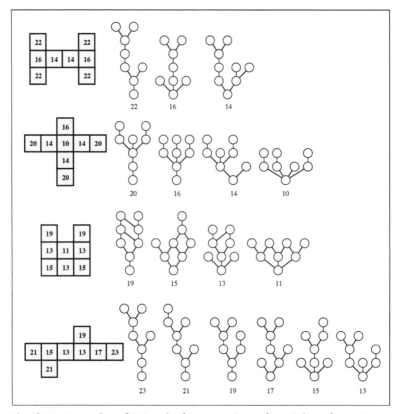

Fig. 6.5 Examples of J-Graphs from a variety of spatial configurations.

The graphs are justified for their relation to one particular space (or node) (in interior analysis that is typically the outside), and showing a hierarchy of step depth from this origin. (Image source: Hillier 2007: 76, copyright Bill Hillier, reproduced by kind permission of Space Syntax Ltd.)

A ground level base plan featuring the built volumes of a town is used as input, which bears similarity to urban morphology and is echoed in applying BLTs (Chapter 5). Software can currently assist in the preparation of these building blocks, although Ostwaldt (2011) argues that the mathematics and theory behind the J-graph is poorly understood, leading to inconsistent interpretations.

While the above analytical building blocks are very abstract and naturally comparative they also clearly do not satisfy qualitative specifications, only quantitative specifications. While the analyses are topological and therefore not primarily interested in metric measurements, it is also clear that the representation of space entirely results from geometric reasoning rather than social causation. Surely, one could argue that a *convex space* is socially significant because it permits *co-presence* (of human beings), but the definition of the convex space is just a spatial derivative.[26]

Similarly, *axial lines* may indeed hypothesise intervisibility, but they dramatically reduce the intricacies of inhabiting built form and topography (e.g. Hohman-Vogrin 2006, on elevation). This reduced spatial representation makes us realise that rather than the physical properties of built form as it occurs to us, space syntax studies the structure of the representation that follows from its own empirical logic (Griffiths 2012b). This space syntactic configuration[27] (an abstract geometrical derivative) is analysed instead of the original empirical (social) reality of built environment morphology to produce an array of relational values, rules and probabilities (Hillier & Hanson 1984; Hillier et al. 1987; Bafna 2003; Batty & Rana 2004; Pinho & Oliveira 2009a; Van Nes in prep. present explanations and overviews).

Because the basic concepts of space syntax do not focus on specifying the properties of discontinuity (see Hillier & Hanson 1984), the actual characteristics of built space are lost. That includes the urban fabric (as in urban morphology), but also, more relevant here, the socially constitutive material differentiations created by built boundaries (Chapter 4).[28] A notable example of mitigating this oversight is the *constitutedness* of streets (i.e. having a building entrance bordering its space) (Hillier & Hanson 1984). This incorporates a building density aspect shaping the sides of occupiable street space into space syntax (e.g. Van Nes & López 2007; and further qualified by Palaiologou & Vaughan 2012). Still, the relation between building and open space is not concrete without including its socio-spatially significant material properties. Nevertheless, space syntax is regularly applied for architectural analyses (see Hillier et al. 1987; Hanson 1989) and for creating typologies and classifications of urban form and land-use patterns (e.g. Jiang 2007; Wagner 2008).

The contemporary planning questions that space syntax is generally applied to produce analytical outcomes which tend to be correlated with social and economic observations of city life. In doing so, the probabilistic

---

26. The theoretical arguments presented in Chapters 3 and 5 prioritise occupiability of space over co-presence, and furthermore support indirect social interaction on the basis of materialisations.

27. Note that Hillier et al. (1987: 363) distinguish spatial relations (between two spaces) from spatial configuration which considers 'at least, the relation of two spaces taking into account a third, and, at most, [...] the relations among spaces in a complex taking into account all other spaces in the complex'.

28. Following Ostwaldt's (2011: 449) discussion, space syntax actually disregards most aspects of (architectural) form, as with its space shaping contours 'a building delineates both the space it contains (its interior) and, to a lesser extent, the space in which it is contained (its site or context)'.

measures become connected to how configurative properties of the built environment (generally permeability, connectivity, accessibility, and movement) (Bafna 2003; Pinho & Oliveira 2009a) afford the occurrence of lively or less lively streets. Liveliness, in turn, indicates economic viability (e.g. Chiaradia et al. 2008; Narvaez et al. 2012; Griffiths et al. 2010; Valente 2012). The probability of liveliness is associated with the cognitive readability or intelligibility of space for way-finding as expressed by global and local integration measures at specified radii of operation (Van Nes in prep.). The otherwise strikingly good fitting correlations, especially pedestrian movement, economic viability, and land-value, again lack a cognitive theory for a true explanation.

Space syntax's predictions for pedestrian movement and navigation are its most successful area (Bafna 2003) and have consequently been adapted for application in historical settings (e.g. Craane 2009; Stöger 2011; Griffiths 2012a). Also when space syntax contributes to social cohesion and segregation, argumentation is almost exclusively tied to movement and rudimentary accessibility (e.g. Conroy Dalton 2007; Hillier & Vaughan 2007). Movement – specifically natural movement as an intrinsic psychologically conducive property of configurations – has been theorised and the correspondent measures adjusted, confirming the suggestion that distance is governed by topology in way-finding (Hillier et al. 1993; Hillier & Iida 2005).

Ultimately, from the outset, the empirical operationalisation of space syntax is incommensurable with how BLTs have come to be theorised here. BLTs foregrounds understanding of *inter alia* social constitution, experience, discontinuity, and materiality, which remain under-explored in space syntax. Furthermore, while inspirational in methodical quantitative sophistication, we do not (yet) know if or how space syntactic measures are socio-spatially significant for the constitutive process of inhabitation.

Comparative applicability of space syntax

How does space syntax's applicability fare in pursuit of radical cross-cultural and diachronic comparisons? As Steadman (2004: 484) puts it, one of its most significant findings is 'that the pattern of movement in a city or urban area is likely to be shaped to an extent by the topology of its route network alone, irrespective of all other factors'. The focus on the connectivity of continuous space in association with lines of sight implies an emphasis on movement and accessibility along streets and grids (e.g. Hillier 2007; Omer & Zafrir-Reuven 2010).

While seemingly pervasive, requiring the presence of formal streets or grids actually limits space syntax's immediate application to 'strange towns' (Hillier 2007: 171ff.). This includes the irregular and dispersed geometry of Maya low-density patterns. Hillier (2007) explains his symbolic characterisation of Maya built form in opposition to the instrumentality of 'normal town'. Such opposition flagrantly brushes over the fact that these cities must be functional everyday living spaces just the same (also Hohman-Vogrin 2005, 2006).[29] Maya cities are known to have few formal streets (Magnoni et al. 2012), while they do contain much differently organised open space (Chapter 7 demonstrates these can be designated with BLTs). Griffiths (2011; Griffiths & Quick 2005) suggests better suited social and historical analyses might become possible through critical reconsideration of space syntax's foundation, and progressive adaptations of its spatial concepts and analytical measures. Indeed, explorative urban space syntax applications are carefully being attempted by Mesoamerican archaeologists (Morton et al. 2012a, 2012b; Parmington 2011 for an elaborate Maya example of architectural access analysis).

In radical comparisons the appropriateness of formal functional space categories such as streets and grids becomes dubious. For such purpose predictive and probabilistic claims seem misplaced, and are therefore best replaced by a more explorative mode of research. For that reason the theoretical framework of BLT Mapping will not contend probability. In other words, spatial dependence does not elicit a direct causal relation between built space and what will actually occur in space, including movement. Yet, social theory would not deny that spatial configuration affords the interconnectivity and permeability which promotes movement and land-use. Instead, movement is present as a presupposition; part of 'acting man'. By mapping BLTs, the socio-spatial conditions in which movement or any other use takes place becomes qualitatively characterised with formal descriptions of each space and positioned within the configuration. Doing so may narrow down likely functions within materialised spatial settings (cf. Sayer's (2000) spatial independence), but does not express the probability of something occurring within a specific space.

29. Interestingly, symbolic (culturally particular) interpretation is no stranger to anthropological and archaeological spatial layout analysis (e.g. Douglas 1972; Schwerdtfeger 1972; Ashmore & Sabloff 2002; Atkin & Rykwert 2005). This approach has not disappeared, but now exists alongside a growing presence of more formal, especially space syntactic studies (Cutting 2003; Thaler 2005; Van Nes 2011; Morton et al. 2012a, 2012b, forthcoming; Fisher 2009; Stöger 2011; Paliou & Knight 2010).

When granting time a substantive role (see Griffiths 2011), the relationship between human action and layout is recursively constitutive (or continuously dialectical). Therefore preferential causal weight can neither be allocated to the configuration nor to land-use locations as fixed attractors in which specific actions dominate (cf. Hillier et al. 1993). Historically speaking, predicting what will occur is particular to present socio-cultural values and processes. It can be agreed that through its common application to road networks and pedestrian flows, space syntax offers persuasive correlations when applied to evaluate economic viability with pedestrian flows, and the ability to generate such correlations can lead us to significant questions. When we detach empirical sophistication from the particularism that underlies space syntactic probabilistic methods, radical comparisons and deep historical cases may be served by a family of ideas and tools with which it is good to think (Griffiths 2012b). In the explorative sense, studying the patterns of boundaries composing the socio-spatial ontology intrinsic to the city (see Chapter 5) could complement Vaughan et al.'s (2010) perspicacious discussion on the spatial signatures of activity centres.

What merits further attention is the apparent value of a topological method for connecting built environment configurations to social life. In the social study of urban built environments, the fundamental conceptualisation of spatial configuration is key for space syntactic innovations (Bafna 2003; Pinho & Oliveira 2009a). In Hillier's (2005: 3) own words: 'Cities are large physical objects animated and driven by human behaviour. By far the most interesting and difficult questions about them are about how the two connect: exactly how is the physical city linked to the human city?' Space syntax chose to address this by applying meticulous topological rigour with great success. Space syntax may not offer the fundamental theory BLT Mapping requires, but paves the way for topological mapping and computation to investigate society–space relations.

How theoretically justifiable spatial analytical measures using BLTs are devised is the subject of Chapter 8. In the potential for topological spatial analysis the similarities go far beyond sharing similar input data. Applying BLT Mapping, boundary concepts come to describe the whole configuration's topology in terms of constitutively significant interaction opportunities, starting with a single boundary merely conveying a spatial relation (*sensu* Hillier et al. 1987). Because BLTs hone in on spatial discontinuity, this contains much more detail on the relations between built volumes and open space, as well as making distinctions within open space itself, without losing comparability.

Efforts to combine and integrate methods

The methodological development of BLT Mapping is indebted to all pre-ceding methods. These methods have been discussed as related but dis-parate (cf. Whitehand 2010a). Some researchers are seeking to exploit the links between them. BLT Mapping contributes a complementary method-ology rather than a resolution. Yet, the nature of a GIS-based boundary method is receptive to this advancement. Following Ley's (2012: 78) characterisation, virtually all of the work drawn on in this chapter is conducted by urban morphologists: those engaged in working on urban form, featuring 'tangible form and intangible processes, present fact and reconstructions of the past, shared usage and individual creation'. This unites practitioners from many disciplines (cited here are pri-marily geographers, historians, architects, planners and archaeologists), although their methods are appropriate for different aims.

Following Lynch (1981), Kropf (2009) argues that the branches of the theory of urban form should interconnect and support each other. Morphological approaches to studying city space should represent a con-fluence of the findings of other disciplines. However, known discrepancies may keep comprehensive unification beyond reach. Kropf (2009: 106) tenders an example: 'There is the disparity between the fact that cities are the result of deliberate and coordinated human effort [design] on the one hand and exhibit characteristics of "self-organization" and emergent behaviour on the other.' These approaches have in common that they work from an existing complex which lacks a clear definition for both its entirety and its composing objects (elements) (cf. Kropf 2009). The *a priori* understanding of the source material (i.e. urban built environ-ments) constructed via Chapters 1–5 seeks to avoid this for BLT enquiries.

For all methods discussed it seems to apply that despite initial empirical compatibility, their respective research purposes keep ready integration at bay. Ley (2012: 79) argues: 'It is necessary to set out clearly the scientific aim of the endeavour and make clear that the categories and criteria involved are inherent in the study rather than the study object.'[30] This could be converted to say that however one's concept of the

---

30. On this basis, space syntax could be argued to confuse its theoretical social aspirations by studying its own derivative spatial or geometrical abstractions rather than social empirical reality.

city is formulated, one's research purpose determines how, with which analytical units, the city should be investigated. I have critiqued some of the analytical units employed by the preceding methods. In return, I have provided a rigorous framework and exacting definitions for my primary analytical units in Chapter 5. Ultimately, all put different demands on data treatment and structure. Considering my theoretical framework postdates these methods it is hardly surprising none offers a ready-made appropriate method to work with boundaries.

So, what has been said on methodological integration so far? Larkham (2006) suggests (British) urban morphology has yet to structurally exploit the possibilities offered by GIS (but see Pinho & Oliveira 2009b; Koster 2009), as well as the complementarity between urban morphology and space syntax specifically (also Sima & Zhang 2009). Soon after, his plea for complementarity and integration found wider support (e.g. Kropf 2009; Pinho & Oliveira 2009a; Sima & Zhang 2009; Whitehand 2010a, 2010b). However, for true integration, degrees of compatibility in the way 'urban form' (or specifically the urban built environment) is treated must be determined. The uptake of this challenge in terms of real attempts to combine methods is scarce (a notable exception is Griffiths et al. 2010), which is testimony to the great conceptual work that still needs doing (Kropf 2009; Whitehand 2012). With regards to space syntax, a degree of methodological solipsism seems at play too (cf. Ratti 2004b).

Jones et al. (2009) demonstrate the potential, arduousness and inflexible limitations of integrating space syntactic results in GIS-based mappings. The particular visualisations that make space syntax results readily intelligible to the untrained eye are difficult to replicate with the same clarity and interpretive adjustability in a GIS environment. Fortunately the open source release of *Depthmap* has led to two software remedies. Initially the plug-in *Confeego* (Gil et al. 2007) brought many space syntax tools to *MapInfo Professional* and enabled the import of *Depthmap* results. Since then Gil et al. (2015) also developed the *Space Syntax Toolkit* as a plugin for *QGIS* (Space Syntax Network n.d.).

Significantly pioneering work comes in the form of the 'place syntax' specification and advancement on space syntax theory. This is an adaptation of space syntax's accessibility measures combined with geographical density and other attraction locations (e.g. transport hubs, businesses), which is technically operationalised in the *Place Syntax Tool* (PST) for *MapInfo* (Ståhle et al. 2005; Ståhle 2012), and also now available for *QGIS* (Spatial Morphology Group n.d.). Their reports show that place syntax can in certain cases improve the predictions of pedestrian flows, and that spatial topology can be successfully combined with spatial topography (or configuration with geographical distribution and density, see Fig. 6.6). As Ståhle et al. argue (2005; Ståhle 2012), the marriage of the description of urban elements in urban morphology and accessibility according to configuration in space syntax is fruitful for analysis, combining descriptive and experiential understanding of urban space. It should be noted that BLT Mapping theoretically also integrates both perspectives.

The development of new and integrative methods using GIS technology is great news for urban GIS applications in general. Strictly speaking, however, there is no established practice for computational mapping according to urban morphological principles (cf. Pinho & Oliveira 2009b). Furthermore, Conzenian urban morphology still lacks appropriate comparative concepts (Kropf 2009; Whitehand 2012). Some initial steps towards urban morphological GIS were reported on by Koster (1998). These efforts resemble customary archaeological GIS mapping, early reconstructive mapping, and include comments on the utility of map overlays (*sensu* Amherst College 2009, 2010).

As discussed, GIS has been aiding the related practice of reconstructing historic town plans (Lilley et al. 2005, 2007; Lilley 2011a, 2012, n.d.; Dean 2012a; Bisschops 2012), while its visualisation abilities

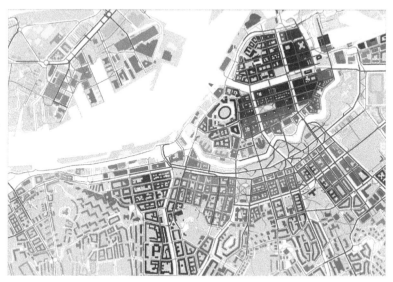

Fig. 6.6 Place Syntax Tool map of Gothenburg.

This PST visualisation shows accessible density (FSI_ Floor Space Index*), which is morphologic-ally relevant, at a 500m radius combined with configurational space syntax integration at 2000m radius. (Image appears courtesy of Gianna Stavroulaki and the Spatial Morphology Group.)

have shown to be of comparative morphological merit (Lilley et al. 2005, 2007). The potential of GIS for developing comparative urban morphological studies is also argued by Koster (2009). Computationally overcoming the laboriousness of converting data representations and technical analyses remains the main obstacle. Because virtually all present-day mapping research takes place in GIS, and thanks to Gil et al.'s (2007, 2015) plugins, effectuating structural computational integration seems right around the corner. Initially, especially space syntactic abstractions seem incommensurable with more realistic topographical representations. Once projected in GIS there is no reason why these data could not be layered in geographical space and associated through geospatial attributes (cf. Koster 2009; Chapter 5).

Chapter 7 will now develop a mapping practice which respects datasets originating from different disciplines. Subsequently, Chapter 8 will discuss the data structure emergent from the mapping practice and provide a rationale for a spectrum of analytical possibilities. An initial sample of these possibilities is examined in Chapter 9. Although BLT Mapping profoundly alters the data structure of conventional topographical maps, BLTs simply trace the outlines of representations of empirical features. Thereby the urban topography is maintained, and integrative efforts are not complicated. Its base plan retains the option to carry out space syntax as well as the option to identify urban morphological elements. By the same token, there is sufficient detail to geo-locate urban historical references to people and events. Naturally, the native ability of GIS for generic quantitative analyses of any geospatial variable remains available. In addition, the database structure of GIS enables all pieces of data (BLTs and analytical derivations) to be invested with additional values and attribute information (e.g. architectural, economic or affective). In this way BLT Mapping merely adds interpretive opportunities.

CHAPTER 7
THE EMPIRICAL PROCESS
OF MAPPING BLTs: TWO
CONTRASTING CASES

Introduction

At this stage all preparations have been put in place to advance a method that is both conceptually commensurate and appropriate for the radical comparative social study of the inhabited urban built environment on the basis of boundaries. This chapter therefore serves to introduce the processes of data acquisition, preparation, and BLT identification. The latter is executed as a mapping practice, BLT Mapping, in a GIS environment. This leads to a specific data structure that can be visualised, questioned and analysed (shown in Chapter 8). To make the operationalisation of boundary conceptualisations easier to understand, the processes will be demonstrated via two test cases. A rationale for their selection will be provided. This chapter adds depth and explanatory detail to the line of argument developed in Vis (2014b).

Legacy data as a starting point

To start, the onsite acquisition of original material-spatial (urban layout) data is not the scope of the processes that will be discussed here. It could be argued that now having exact knowledge about what is needed to apply a boundary approach might inform an effective and original data acquisition process in the field. Instead, I emphasise a contrary argument. The fact that pre-existing or 'legacy' datasets can be used is a particular strength of the workflow presented. Considering that at the basis of BLT Mapping is always an urban survey resulting in a large-scale town plan, legacy data compatibility implies the immediate applicability to a large number of existing town plans of all regions and time periods. This is especially significant with regards to accruing a body of data to support radical comparisons and syntheses across urban examples over time. Moreover, for most projects a new comprehensive urban survey onsite is practically unfeasible. Requiring one to do so would severely limit the potential merits of the method. This applies almost equally to the often arduous tasks of archaeological surface surveys and excavation, the laborious process of historical town plan reconstruction, and the comprehensive walking and mapping of the material specificities of present-day urban built environments. Remote sensing could offer an effective alternative when accepting the restrictions on the material information this makes available.

A research practice capable of working on legacy data, then, creates the greatest immediate versatility and flexibility. It also enables revisiting urban landscapes that were studied previously, thereby promoting scientific progress with debates and multimethod approaches. Nonetheless, the use of any pre-existing map – inevitably produced for different purposes and conventions (see Wood 1992; Monmonier 1996; MacEachren 2004; Lilley 2011a, 2012; Hutson 2012; Beisaw & Gibb 2013) – presents its own challenges. The technical challenge of digitisation (exemplified in this chapter) is integral to the legacy data research process, because many maps only exist as physical documents. Using legacy city plans causes inevitable dependence on the mapping processes and professional skills that produced them. In archaeological cases we rely on surveyors and/or excavators. In historical cases we rely on historians and historical geographers. In contemporary cases we typically rely on the relevant mapping agency (public and crowdsourced mapping forming exceptions).

To demonstrate the comparative capabilities of this methodology, the two test cases have been deliberately selected to represent two very different situations. Therefore, I will first present the rationale for selecting these test cases. Because the overarching aim of this book is the development of a methodology, the test cases are used throughout the following chapters to demonstrate processes and possibilities. Therefore to refer to the case work in this book as test cases is deliberate. They are limited in extent and used to emphasise the explorative and diverse nature of cities, and the associated analytical and interpretive opportunities. In articulating a methodological journey, this book is not the appropriate stage for full-fledged case studies, but my focus is on demonstrating how casuistic social interpretations can be developed and supported.[1]

Selecting test cases

Considering urban traditions to compare

In order to demonstrate the methodological capacity to carry out radical comparisons, the selection of two appropriate test cases needs to ensure that contrast between them is maximised, while striving for potential parity of data throughout. My greatest personal experience of urban contexts (The Netherlands and UK) is part of what can be generalised as the contemporary urban tradition of the western world (e.g. contributions in Slater 1990). This makes it a convenient place to start, because familiarity will result in greater *a priori* understanding of the structure of such urban tradition. Furthermore, there are many examples of cities for which medieval or even earlier origins have been studied in both the UK and The Netherlands. This creates the opportunity for a test case demonstrating historical development. A western urban tradition is thus used to test diachronic comparative ability next to cross-cultural comparisons. So decided, my search became limited to UK or Dutch cities for which data are available and/or could be compiled as appropriate for a test case.

Next to a western historical-to-contemporary example, it is paramount that BLT Mapping is demonstrated on an archaeological case to maximise applicability throughout the variety of patterns produced by urban development in the long-term. In Classical and Near Eastern archaeology, several urban settlements have been mapped to a sufficient extent. Accepting Europe as the heartland of the western urban tradition in both archaeology and geography (respectively, see Storey 2006; Slater 1990), we should consider the relational historical developments that nurtured it. The processes that grew a European urban tradition arguably start with Ancient Greece and the urbanism of conquest that changes the existing tradition in the Hellenic Near East. Here a model is introduced that is continued and perfected by the Roman Empire and

---

1. It must be conceded that applications on cases that comprise more comprehensive data on urban development or, indeed, a fuller extent of the city, will advance the analytical relevance and sophistication of interpretation. Full-fledged casuistic work should also be justified and designed to exert control over possible sampling biases. The preliminary outcomes in Chapter 9 should not be taken as grand claims to understanding each case, but careful statements on early stage evidence that could have impactful future consequences.

exported to their provinces (Butzer 2008: 82–86). Notwithstanding each case's idiosyncrasies, viewed historically, most potential cases could either be considered a close precursor or direct neighbour of the contemporary western example to be selected.

Several contributions in Marcus & Sabloff (2008; also Storey 2006) highlight the meeting of independently developed urban traditions, emphasised by juxtaposing the archaeology of the so-called Old and New World. In ancient encounters between urban traditions, we can nonetheless recognise that there are many aspects of elementary similarity between cities across time and space. Renfrew (2008: 36–49) approaches this similarity as transformations of the same phenomenon, which is explained by a shared morphogenesis. That is, the shape and occurrence of certain traits in cities embodies a similar solution to a similar problem. At the same time, similarity in shape should not be confused with the conclusion that these cities were inhabited in a socially similar way (cf. Fletcher 2010; Chapter 1). In fact, within the similarity of urbanism broadly as well as within cultural regions, there is much internal variation (Butzer 2008). Ultimately, to test BLT Mapping's comparative compatibility it would be most advantageous to select a truly dramatic contrast. Taking an example from both the Old and New World assures long-term developmental and cultural independence. The sharp difference among urban traits is particularly borne out in the lower population densities that are projected for examples of Maya urbanism (Nichols 2006; Rice 2006; Hansen 2008; Hutson 2016: 41–55).

The dispersal of the material settlement pattern that relates to lower population density estimates, especially found in tropical regions of the world, seems quite alien to our western perception of the city. The western urban tradition – not unlike Near Eastern and Islamic cities in this regard (Butzer 2008) – tends to be characterised by a high intensity of built volumes that readily relate to the prevailing urban planning paradigm of densification today. Therefore, the dispersed and often seemingly irregular urban landscapes that belong to what Fletcher (2009, 2010, 2012) labels 'low-density urbanism' would offer a suitable contrast to test the comparative ability of BLT Mapping.

Among these traditions, Maya urbanism fosters the best available variety of archaeological city plans. This is not least aided by the relative preservation of surface remains resulting from a protean developmental history that involves abandonment (rather than collapse, see e.g. Aimers 2007; Turner & Sabloff 2012; McAnany et al. 2016). Fletcher's loose classification contextualises the foregoing debates on the 'urbanness' and 'strangeness' of Maya cities (in Chapters 1 and 6 respectively). This preceding discourse heightens the interest in foregrounding morphogenetic similarity as a lens through which to study how Maya cities function socially. Furthermore, I should acknowledge a personal research history, along with ties to the research community that add background knowledge and convenience to choosing an example of the Maya urban tradition as a test case.

Western urban tradition

The availability of large-scale contemporary city plans was deemed a non-discerning factor. Selecting a test case with historical depth, however, requires the acceptance of some basic facts from cartographic history. The production of city plans in the western world was exceedingly rare till the later sixteenth century. Likely the most notable publication is the *Civitates Orbis Terrarum*, consisting of six volumes published between 1572 and 1617. This work brings together 546 images or prospects of cities from across the world. Not all of these are city plans – there are various orthographic views as well – and those we recognise as a city plan in no way reflect the mapping standards we know today. The *Civitates Orbis Terrarum* was edited by Georg Braun and primarily engraved by Franz Hogenberg, though it combined the work of many different artists and cartographers (Historic Cities Center n.d.). Two pioneer cartographers, Jacob van Deventer (1505–75) and Joris Hoefnagel (1542–1600), produced many of the city plans contained in these volumes.

Jacob van Deventer maintained a meticulous working method. A 'minuutkaart' formed the overview of the entire city plan, based on measurements and sketches combined into a whole. The 'netkaart' displays the city's surroundings, sometimes accompanied by a 'bijkaart' depicting the city's major features in the centre, including defences, streets, and significant buildings (for more detail on Van Deventer, see Vannieuwenhuyze & Lisson 2012). A comprehensive town mapping effort in the UK, after those included in the *Civitates Orbis Terrarum*, was carried out by John Speed (1552–1629), published between 1610 and 1611. Little mapping of cities generally took place between Speed's efforts and the Ordnance Survey maps of the nineteenth century (Carter 1972).

Archived historical plans may be the most direct sources on the historical situation of the built environment when historical or archaeological evidence is lacking, and little of the historic city is preserved in the current urban tissue. However, Lilley (2011a) stresses that historical maps are typically the result of artistic interpretation of the built environment. Furthermore, these maps do not follow contemporary projection systems. Because of their nature, Lilley says, historical maps are almost impossible to geo-rectify. Even if this is done successfully, the results might be futile as mapped features might not correspond to what was actually there. It is not till the nineteenth century that mapmaking reaches the conventional and scientific standards upon which current standards are built. Therefore, urban morphological studies (Chapter 6) usually begin with the earliest appropriate nineteenth-century city plan. For detailed studies of the urban built environment beyond the nineteenth century, critical historical and geographical reconstructive mapping is pertinent.

The Historic Towns Atlas[2] project (HTA), comprising editions in both the UK and The Netherlands among others, forms an initial port of call for finding out about relatively well-studied examples of historical cities (Lobel 1969; Speet 1982, 1983; Doornink-Hoogenraad 1983; Visser et al. 1990).[3] However, because these atlases do not reproduce the historical stages of the built environment beyond the nineteenth century, their usefulness for research purposes has been questioned (e.g. Slater 1996; Rutte 2008). During the preparatory research for this book, it was found that there is potential for historically reconstructed maps to be produced on Dutch cities, but none were available. Notably, the city of 's-Hertogenbosch boasts an appropriate basis were such effort to be made (Rutte *pers. comm.* 2011; Van Drunen *pers. comm.* 2011).[4] Undertaking such integrative and reconstructive work has the making of a separate project in its own right, so therefore it was not feasible to serve as a test case location.

Within the UK the medieval New Towns of Wales have been the subject of historically reconstructive mapping (Lilley et al. 2005, 2007), but Lilley (*pers. comm.* 2011) advised that otherwise knowledge is limited and the cities have probably remained too small over time to have seen major change and development into the present.[5] It transpired that only Chester (Vetch et al. 2011; Lilley 2011a) and Winchester (Keene 1985) had comprehensively been the subject of historically reconstructive

---

2. A list of atlases produced by the European project can be found on the website of the *Irish Historic Towns Atlas* (n.d.). The *British Historic Towns Atlas* (n.d.) is undergoing a revival.
3. The other Dutch atlases of Amersfoort, Venlo and Bergen op Zoom were not readily available to me for consultation at the time of writing, but follow a similar set-up to the ones cited here.
4. Relatively speaking, many urban archaeological projects have been carried out over the years (for an overview, see *Bossche Encyclopedie* n.d.). Van Drunen keeps a GIS with the architectural historical surveys of some 3000 buildings, including 1700 buildings within the old expanded city walls. A space syntax approach on the medieval street pattern's topology incorporating information on the location of professional occupations can be found in Craane (2009). This approach requires less built environment detail (see Chapter 6).
5. Although this book limits itself to testing and demonstrating BLT Mapping principles, the potential to upscale the selected test case to incorporate the whole city as an illustrative and interpretive case study at a later date was deemed important upon selection.

or sequence mapping (Chapter 6). The more recent effort on Chester only produced a time-slice for the situation of around 1500. The inclusion of archaeological evidence and the use of GIS mapping techniques could have created an easier basis for initial testing. Yet, the availability of three medieval time-slices on Winchester (1550s, 1417, 1300s), therewith setting the benchmark for historical work on city environments for long after its appearance (Bisschops *pers. comm.* 2011), proved persuasive. Thanks to this benchmarking potential for greater time-depth[6] in future research, Winchester was selected as a test case.

Winchester (close to the UK's south coast), like Chester, is a typical historical English (and western European) example of a densely settled urban landscape based on a persistent medieval pattern with Iron Age and Roman antecedents (cf. Conzen 1960). Winchester's mappings completely result from a historical research process (see Keene 1985), therefore exemplifying the opportunities offered by digitising historical legacy data – notwithstanding that these could be improved upon by incorporating available, if dispersed, archaeological records (e.g. Scobie et al. 1991). As it stands, Winchester's test case can demonstrate the relevant differences between using results from purely historical and archaeological mapping; the two disciplines that crucially expand the source material for the comparative social study of inhabited urban built environments.

Finally, it should be noted that none of these reconstructive mapping efforts reach the level of individual buildings' fabric. Historic records, and regressive urban morphology in tandem, usually refer to the building plot rather than what occupied it. This means that for the purposes of BLT Mapping, additional 'working conjectures' are necessary to rectify this absence of material evidence. This will be part of the method described later in this chapter.

Maya urban tradition

The selection of the Maya case study has been informed primarily based on the intensity of mapping and thus the availability of archaeological data. Recent technological progress – specifically airborne Light Detection and Ranging's (LiDAR) ability to digitally strip forest canopies

---

6. Keene's (1985) work was preceded by Biddle's (1976) volume on early medieval Winchester. The plans contained in this volume, due to the restrictions of fragmentary historical and archaeological evidence, could not be prepared on the same plot level of detail as Keene's plans and thus would not be suitable for this research method.

to produce ground surface Digital Elevation Models (DEM) – is advancing the availability of increasingly detailed and comprehensive archaeological city plans (see Evans et al. 2007; Marcus & Sabloff 2008; Sinclair et al. 2010; Chase et al. 2011a, 2011b, 2016). Nevertheless, readily accessible (i.e. published) Maya city plans still concern the results of traditional topographical surface surveys of visible remains (Peiró Vitoria 2015). The nature of tropical archaeological remains – usually badly deteriorated by years of overgrowing reforestation and erosion, and therefore difficult to access and measure – implies that a comprehensive plan of the full extent of a city on the level of detail required may not exist, despite some large-scale long-term archaeological mapping projects.[7]

The increased visibility of archaeological remains in the dry northern Maya lowlands on the Yucatán peninsula means better mapping has been possible there. This preselection revealed two likely candidates to provide a test case. The first is Mayapan, originally mapped in the 1950s (Pollock et al. 1962). Since then, the *Economic Foundations of Mayapan Project* (PEMY) (n.d.), directed by Marilyn Masson, has been improving the city plan by integrating several additions, notably including Russell's (2008) extramural areas and estimates (see Hare & Masson 2012). This last project is also adding the results of a complementary LiDAR survey of the area (Hare et al. 2014).

Mayapan happens to be known as a relatively unusual site. It was one of the latest major centres of the Maya culture area to thrive. Furthermore, it is known for featuring a high density of architectural structures in comparison with other Maya sites, and is also uncommon in being walled (for context see Hutson 2016). Few defensive walls are known in the Maya culture area (Ek Balam is a notable well-documented exception), especially after recent doubt was cast on the existence of such defence works in Tikal (Webster et al. 2007; Silverstein et al. 2009).

Due to the quality and availability of the early comprehensive map of the walled city (Pollock et al. 1962), some spatial analysis has already been tried on Mayapan. Pugh (2003) studied specified building type configurations and associated cluster analysis on ritual or ceremonial architectural assemblages. Brown & Witschey (2003) conducted fractal

---

7. No comprehensive overview of the research on, and mapping of, Maya urban sites exists. This tentative conclusion was reached after conducting my own search of Maya site surveys, consulting both literature and several Mayanists for their opinion. Soon after, Peiró Vitoria's (2015) research reproduced and assembled the greatest collection of Classic period urban centre plans in a single volume, in the process basically confirming this assessment.

analysis on Mayapan to support interpretive arguments for the exist-ence of administrative self-organising subunits. Hare & Masson (2012) extend such studies, especially based on a variety of basic metric density analyses, acknowledging that there may be several political or societal models at play. By looking at the density of 'elite building types' (cf. Folan et al. 2009), in relation to other features and specifically wanting to connect polity administrators to local populations, Hare & Masson attempt to understand the neighbourhood structure of Mayapan (see also Adánez Pavón et al. (2009) for a spatial modelling of political catchment areas on the basis of plaza groups). Then, Hare et al. (2014) expand the urban context by placing the city in a wider settled landscape. The exist-ence of a thoroughly evolved and digitised city plan and previous spa-tial analyses would have been an effective foundation for a Mayapan test case. However, as the PEMY project had not made the comprehensive city plan accessible at the time of preparing this book, data provision proved an issue.

The other site featuring a detailed and extensive city plan is Chunchucmil, located in the northwest of the Yucatán peninsula (see Fig. 7.1). Scott R. Hutson kindly agreed for me to use this material (cour-tesy of the Pakbeh Regional Economy Program) even though the full city plan was then still awaiting publication.[8]

Thanks to its Classic period apogee of occupational remains – gen-erally considered ca. 200–900 AD, in Chunchucmil fifth–early seventh century AD (Hutson et al. 2008) – Chunchucmil bears stronger temporal relevance to the prominent Maya urban centres of what is traditionally regarded as the pinnacle of the Maya culture area (e.g. Tikal, Calakmul, Palenque, Caracol, etc.; see e.g. Sharer & Traxler 2005; Andrews 1975; cf. the approach of Peiró Vitoria 2015). Nonetheless, Chunchucmil is also noted for featuring a relatively high density of architectural structures over a relatively large core (cf. Mayapan). This leads it to be designated the most densely occupied Classic Maya city over a sustained area (Magnoni et al. 2012) by current population research principles (cf. Rice & Culbert 1990; Sharer & Traxler 2005), despite its unfavour-able natural environment. At the same time this mapped density of remains could simply reflect the good visibility across the site (Hutson *pers. comm.* 2011–2013), and the scarcity of synthesised results from comparably intensive and comprehensive mapping surveys (though for initial adaptive synthesis see Hutson 2016). Furthermore, its density of

8. Just before finalising the manuscript of this book, Hutson and Magnoni (2017) published a final version of the full Chunchucmil map as part of an edited volume on the city.

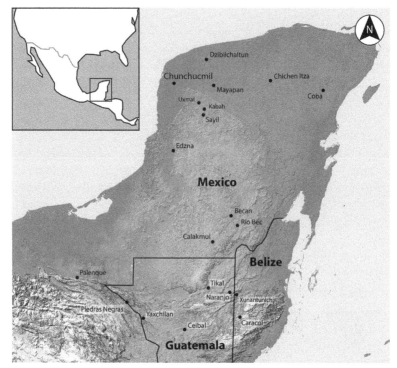

Fig. 7.1 Map of the Maya lowlands situating Chunchucmil among a selection of major sites.

(Adapted from base map, courtesy of the Pakbeh Regional Economy Program with help from Scott Hutson.)

architectural structures is not distantly unparallelled even for the Classic period, and the derived population estimate might only be somewhat lower than Postclassic Mayapan's intramural core (cf. Barnhart 2005; Hutson 2016).

In addition, Classic period Chunchucmil is unique in the extensive occurrence and persistence of structural patterns of *albarradas* (Magnoni et al. 2012). *Albarradas* are often defined as dry stone houselot walls, which are more usual in the Postclassic period (Hutson et al. 2007; Hutson et al. 2008; Hare & Masson 2012). However, their use appears to be much more diverse in Chunchucmil and across the few Classic period sites where they have been found (see Fletcher 1983; Magnoni et al. 2012). Nevertheless, it has been suggested that the divisive principle of *albarradas* might have been much more widespread, but simply not preserved – assuming perishable materials could have been used for their construction instead of stones (Becker 2001). As a consequence of their preservation (stone and rubble construction), Chunchucmil visually offers what seems to be a much more complete picture of the social reality of the built environment. At the same time, one should remain aware of the probable ample use of perishable materials to complement the archaeologically preserved built environment with e.g. internal activity arrangements (cf. e.g. Fletcher & Kintz 1983; Manzanilla & Barba 1990; Becker 2001; Hutson et al. 2007, 2008; Magnoni et al. 2012; Hutson 2016).

Chunchucmil has been subject to some spatial analysis, too. Magnoni et al. (2012) conducted a preliminary analysis on the house group assemblages and houselot areas, within a GIS with limited functionalities (Hutson *pers. comm.* 2013). Hutson & Welch (2016) utilise the superior visibility, detail and extent of the Chunchucmil map to hypothesise a neighbourhood structure based on the large-scale pattern of the pathways left open by the *albarradas*. This results in a hub-and-spoke motif, where routes into the centre 'spoke clusters' are structured in wedges dividing the city. They continue to support this argument, adding in evidence on a more micro-scale, strongly suggesting Chunchucmil's appropriateness for a BLT test case. Considering the general expectation that developing mapping technologies and rapid data acquisition (see Chase et al. 2016) will promote the availability of equally extensive and detailed maps of (Classic) Maya urban centres, makes Chunchucmil an especially significant example.

Final words of caution should be dedicated to the assumption of contemporaneity within Maya city plans. Because Maya cities tend to have been abandoned (yet usually show some extent of continued population or resettlement) (Aimers 2007; Turner & Sabloff 2012; McAnany et al. 2016), the archaeological built environment remains on the surface likely date to various periods. Initially this seems in keeping with the inevitable palimpsest of the urban landscape (Chapter 6), but the archaeological argument for approximately simultaneous occupation across an entire built environment complex is less straightforward to make than the premise of accumulated historical development.

Fortunately, at Chunchucmil, the artefact assemblages roughly indicate consistency for Classic period occupation across the whole settlement, including finger extensions (Hutson et al. 2008; Hutson *pers. comm.* 2011). Only few of the architectural groups may not have been occupied during the sixth century (Magnoni 2007; Hutson 2016). While there is a central barricaded portion that indicates Terminal Classic and even later reuse of the monumental core (Dahlin 2000; Hutson et al. 2008), Hutson assured me that the assumption that the entire mapped layout was once roughly in synchronous use is relatively safe to make. In preparing the data, however, some decisions on poorly preserved or apparently truncated structures may need to be made to maintain one contiguous configuration for which occupation can be assumed.

Preparing the datasets of Winchester and Chunchucmil (1)

From here on, this chapter mainly follows the workflow of mapping practice that creates BLT data. Progress is tracked by the bracketed numbering in the headings. This workflow can be summarised heuristically in the following steps:

1. Preparation of datasets: acquiring, assembling, digitising and converting the source materials to the same format (usually concerns pre-existing or legacy spatial data and/or maps);
2. Mapping (tracing) the outlines of major occupiable subdivisions of the built environment as represented in the source material to create equivalent spatial information as the foundation of the outline base plan;
3. Case-specific conjecturing to resolve any remaining data gaps and ambiguities (data needs to be spatially contiguous), and subsequently revising the resultant outline base plan to ensure equivalent spatial data with topological integrity;
4. Identifying the BLTs by remapping (tracing) the outline base plan with conceptually validated individual data entries (polylines), while also revising and correcting the resultant spatial data structure to assure topological integrity.

In practice it can be expected that these steps, while presented discretely, bleed into each other reflexively (especially steps 2–3 and 3–4). This will be referred to in my report below on how these general steps play out in case work.

The initial stage of preparation means converting the mapped data to an equal and appropriate digital *format* across all datasets. This technical format needs to be achieved before the further steps are taken, in order to ensure that the datasets will basically represent the same level of conceptual detail and ultimately follow the same conventions to convey *information*. Chapter 6 highlighted the methodological and integrative potential of GIS software. Here ESRI's *ArcGIS*, version 10, was used as the primary GIS environment to conduct all methodologically specific mapping. *ArcGIS* was selected because of its widespread use in academic contexts, both in geography and archaeology, as well as its versatility in handling topological information in vector data (i.e. lines, points, and polygons. Lines and their connections are of paramount importance here). Nonetheless, for digitisation and data conversion other software packages were used and will be named when relevant.

The following account is provided with the aim of enabling those pursuing a similar workflow. The four steps are somewhat simplified. When working with increasing familiarity on each particular case and each individual data source, rules of thumb pragmatically emerge in the data creation processes that resolve ambiguities, uncertainty, and confusing data situations with certain degrees of subjective judgment. For our two cases and their data sources, the rules of thumb that emerged in this research are submitted at the end of this chapter. Besides such case-specific particularities, the general steps of the workflow can be pursued as stated. In this account the technical details are kept concise, and generic information on digital work is omitted. I will focus on the sequence of work and decisions for data preparation that produced usable results in the variety of situations that my test cases comprise. It can be expected that various software-based work sequences will be superseded by software updates. That means that the principles are more important than my precise actions within the software. Where instrumental for the results, the processes will be described.

Winchester maps

The Winchester city plans used consist of both the present-day situation and historical situations. The contemporary situation is based on the current large-scale mapping standard of the British Ordnance Survey, called MasterMap (from here on: MM). MM is a digital product of the Ordnance Survey (from here on: OS), updated up to every six months. The version for Winchester used was downloaded at the end of October 2011 (University of Leeds academic license for EDINA services) with the OS providing the complementary *OS Imagery Layer* (OS official aerial photography) and *OS Address Layer* (version 2) on disc in April 2012. The first historical time-slice is based fully on the first edition of the large-scale (1:500) OS city plan published between 1871 and 1872 (from here on: OS1872) (University of Leeds academic license for EDINA's Historic

Digimap). This is in keeping with common practice established by urban morphology (Chapter 6). The additional time-slices are sourced from the reconstructed plans for the later medieval period by Derek Keene (1985), respectively for around 1300, 1417 and 1550. Within the confines of testing the methodology the Winchester case does not revert further than the period around 1550 (from here on: 1550s), which demonstrates the same principles as would apply for the processes required to use the two further possible time-slices. Future research could also consider making the temporal resolution between time-slices more fine grained.[9]

To emphasise, the three city plans thus used are each of a different nature. MM is a born-digital plan, fully enabled to convert into GIS formats and visualisations, and represents the best British national mapping standards of accuracy. OS1872 is, while produced to be accurate, essentially a historical document. It is acquired in geoTIFF format (i.e. TIFF image files with a basic level of georeferencing: projecting, locating, and scaling it), containing the digital scans of original sheets. Finally, 1550s is a historically reconstructed map, dependent on the academic cartographic and historical research practice producing it.[10] Interestingly, the mapping standards of OS1872 feature more detail than MM. In contrast, the burgage plot based historical research of Keene (1985) to produce 1550s provides only a basic level of detail, especially omitting the architectural morphology that would give us building outlines. Regardless, before any data standardisation can take place, OS1872 needs vectorisation and georeferencing to MM, while 1550s needs digitisation and vectorisation to be geospatially linked to the other two.

Starting with 1550s: the Keene plans of medieval Winchester needed digitisation. Keene (1985) reproduces them at a 1:2500 scale, separated out in numerous small sections. While these could be scanned from the books and digitally stitched together, the match errors of so many seams would compromise the quality of the resulting plan.

9. Between the OS1872 and 1550s, Winchester's 1750 Godson survey was also considered as the basis for an additional time-slice. A digitisation was commissioned, compiled from the two four-sheet copies held by the Bodleian Library and trialled for georeferencing in GIS. The effort was abandoned as the combination of geographical discrepancies caused by the historical survey technique, style of depiction and imprecise edge matching of the printed sheets would not yield the required detail and generate a host of topographical ambiguities. For effective interpretations of the spatial properties of individual representations of topographic features, substantive original historical research would be required. Furthermore, throughout the twentieth century various detailed city plans have been published which could serve as additional time-slices.

10. Keene (1985) prepared his plans in reference to the then current OS city plans of the 1970s, which used planimetric technology closer to present standards (Keene *pers. comm.* 2012). In addition the 1872 OS plan and the 1750 Godson survey were used as points of reference for shaping features in the built environment.

Therefore the originals were tracked down at the Winchester Research Unit (curated by Martin Biddle and Katherine Barclay), which stores them in the depot of the Winchester City Museum. These originals consist of large sheets of film on which the line drawing of the map was draughted. These sheets display the medieval city in only five parts: the walled area; and the north, east, south, and west suburbs. Their large-scale as well as their less fragmented and unannotated nature would likely increase the quality and direct usability of the digital end product tremendously.[11]

To avoid photographic lens distortions, digitisation was carried out using roller scanners. These scanning machines scan large physical documents in flatbed fashion. The large high quality 400–600 dpi resolution raster images needed cleaning and filtering to remove digital noise and original blemishes on the films, enhancement for contrast and definition, and stitching together to compose one entire city plan.[12]

Accepting MM as the standard of accuracy, georeferencing and georectification of the historical time-slices are carried out in direct relation to MM. This is alternative to a practice where a proper set of control points are set up onsite with dGPS (differential GPS, cf. Lilley 2011a). GPS error margins could cause unwanted discrepancies between the points taken and MM, which would require superfluous rectifications of MM in addition to the historical layers. Instead, assisted by Keene (*pers. comm.* 2011), historically persistent points in the current built environment were identified and photographed onsite for future reference. These historically persistent locations and photo directions were then documented as a GIS layer on top of MM as point data (the photographs themselves show little context). According to expectations of urban development, fewer points persisted from the 1300s than each more recent time-slice. The historically

11. The film sheets were all in relatively good condition, but there is no accounting for any errors resulting from 40 years of ageing of the carrying material (Biddle *pers. comm.* 2011).
12. Proprietary functions in *Adobe Photoshop* were used for these processes. *Photoshop* puts a cap on the maximum pixel count (30,000) in either of the two dimensions of raster files. This may inhibit the use of very large files, requiring one to reduce resolution before processing. The first roller scans were produced at 400 and 600 dpi, courtesy of Geoff Denford, Winchester City Council. Additional scans of oversized documents were made at the University of Portsmouth by Katherine Barclay at 500 dpi on a larger roller scanner. The quality of definition on the 500 dpi scans was intrinsically superior, possibly due to other technology in the machine, but their lower resolution determined the quality of the final stitched scans. Sharp, full plans were finally produced at a manageable 400 dpi. All scans were visually improved by image processing in *Photoshop*, thus ensuring readable solid lines, suitable for semi-automated vectorisation (see below). The precision of the plans is inevitably somewhat compromised by the stitching process, which relies on an intuitive visual weighting of matching errors between the seams of each sheet using proprietary graphical processing tools in *Photoshop*. *ArcGIS* offers an alternative to match edges of vector files, which would be possible if the separate scans were vectorised first.

Table 7.1 Results of georectification for the OS1872
time-slice.

Plan	No. of Points Used	Warp	RMS error
OS1872	74	Adjust	0.03241

The low RMS error is not a reflection of visual precision,
but could be explained by the combination of local and
global correctives that the operation 'Adjust' uses, which
corresponds with the much higher density of control points
within the walled city as opposed to the suburbs.

persistent points served as an initial set of control points for georeferencing
and georectifying the historical layers.[13] Although OS1872 is delivered with
a basic level of georeferencing, to achieve a closer geographical match with
MM these control points were used on that time-slice also.

Initial georeferencing of OS1872 using these control points
enabled me to pick out a series of additional points across the time-
slices that clearly related to specific corner and intersection locations in
MM. Employing *ArcGIS* proprietary higher order georectification warps,
through an iterative and visual process of selecting appropriate points
and warps, such additional points improved the relative accuracy of
each time-slice. In the georeferencing process errors cannot be avoided
(see the result in Table 7.1). An additional error is introduced as an
effect of OS1872 consisting of multiple sheets. The sheets of OS1872
were published separately over two years, while the city was developing
at a rapid rate, causing imperfect matches (see Fig. 7.2). The rectifica-
tion can be fixed by transforming the raster file[14] (most effective is saving
to TIF with LZW compression), which creates a new raster dataset

13. In addition, the GIS record of listed buildings and monument sites was obtained from the
Winchester City Council (courtesy of Ian Scrivener-Lindley and Tracy Matthews). These
polygon and points were prepared on the basis of MM and so would relate exactly to the contemporary source. Because heritage listings serve a policy purpose (protecting and managing
current sites), their shapes could not be trusted to convey any historical reality. In Winchester
these heritage records followed unclear dated standards, which had not been fully integrated
across the recording systems in operation over the years, and exclude archaeological excavation plans. Aided by online resources such as *Heritage Gateway* (n.d.) and *National Heritage
List for England* (n.d.), only limited and very cautious use could be made of these records.
Where possible, then, Keene's (1985) accounts on the plots concerned were prioritised, but
the records did indicate plausible historically persistent features for the 1300s through to the
nineteenth century.
14. For unclear reasons, the less permanent command 'Update Georeferencing' did not function
on the OS1872 files, requiring a definitive transformation directly. A backup of the original
raster image in combination with saved link tables makes sure the process can be repeated and
corrected if necessary.

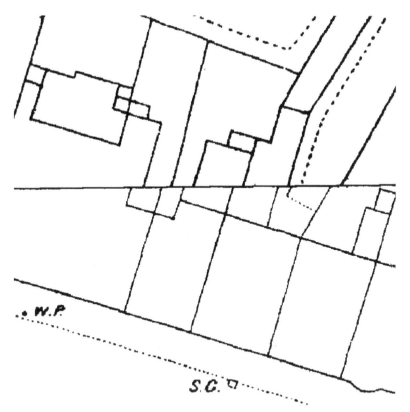

Fig. 7.2 Mismatch at a plan seam in OS1872.

The intrinsic mismatches at the seam (horizontal line in the middle) between two sheets in OS1872 cause inevitable errors in georeferencing. (Image extracted from originals: © Crown Copyright and Landmark Information Group Limited 2013. All rights reserved. 1872.)

incorporating the warp. On this basis vectorisation takes place. Since for OS1872 this immediately entails extracting the base plan, this is described later.

Taking into consideration the intensity of the mapping processes to carry out initial methodological tests for diachronic comparisons, a small test area (approx. 175x200m, Fig. 7.3) was selected to proceed work on Winchester. This area was deliberately chosen to include an intramural and extramural part of the city where the city wall has been removed, so it would show clear contrasts between persistence and change. The eastern part of the city centre, around the former East Gate and bridge, offers good diversity of spaces within a historically well-developed suburb of the city. Nonetheless, note that a small section could never incorporate the full variety of spatial morphology within the urban built environment concerned.

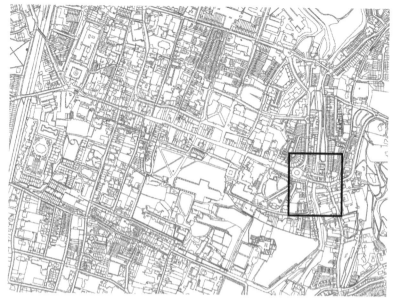

Fig. 7.3 The approximate location and extent of the test case area
indicated within MM of the historical core of Winchester.

For the next historical time-slice, 1550s, the approach differs from
OS1872. As original scans, after image processing (cleaning, enhancing
and stitching) the file is as yet completely ungeoreferenced. Since the
image file contains an unannotated line drawing (similar in nature to
Fig. 7.2, without text), classification in two value classes only (i.e. a bi-
tonal image) would make it susceptible to automated vectorisation. Thus
prioritising vectorisation, I established separate feature classes (geodata
files) to distinguish Keene's (1985) own original historical conjectures
from urban features he deemed certain at the time. On this basis, 1550s
was vectorised before georeferencing and georectification, thereby significantly improving the manageability of the file size in the *ArcMap*
environment.

Gregory & Ell (2007) warn that although in principle the historical researcher's best friend, automated vectorisation is not sufficiently
effective in practice to take over vectorisation. The extent of manual
editing afterwards would be equal to the manual vectorisation process. In
spite of several years of development, even on the very clear line-drawn
1550s map I had to decide that fully automated vectorisation could not be
trusted. Issues occurring include: undue cessations along thinner lines,

directional confusion along thick lines and unintended disorder along dashed lines (the software does not recognise drawing conventions). However, *ArcGIS*'s ArcScan tools provide a semi-automated form of vectorisation, which significantly speeds up the manual tracing of the original image with polylines. This process still requires human intervention to avoid improper ruggedness in the shape of polylines derived from thicker originally scanned lines. The upside is, however, that one has direct control over the data produced, significantly reducing the aforementioned errors from automation.

Confusingly, the geoprocess akin to georeferencing raster image files is called 'spatial adjustment' in *ArcGIS* when it concerns geographically relating vector data to another dataset (here the vectorised 1550s layer to MM). Fortunately, spatial adjustment operates on very similar principles and thus ends up being quite intuitive for those familiar with raster georeferencing. Because in spatial adjustment snapping exactly onto vector data nodes is enabled, much more accurate placement can be achieved (directly connecting the node within 1550s with the respective node in MM). When the internal scale between the vector datasets is equal, the remaining error should come out nought between co-located nodes (i.e. in the exact same geographical location across layers). Where one is certain a selected node is identical between the two vector layers, these can be fixed as a geolocated connection (hammering in a virtual nail to join both layers) called an 'identity point'. Now, in subsequent geoprocessing to warp the dataset, this point cannot move from its position (contrary to control points in georeferencing). This warp process is called 'rubbersheeting', which entails the stretching of vector data between the identity points based on additional control points added locally to achieve a more precise match. Determining 42 identity points in total over an area of approx. 600x600m, encompassing the test case area, proved sufficient for the successful processing of the data assisted with locally added control points. No residual error is produced in this process.

Chunchucmil map

In contrast to the Winchester plans, the Chunchucmil map results from an original archaeological topographical surface survey. This intensive process entailed pacing from the corners of a 20x20m grid system with a compass to map archaeological remains. This grid system was based on a pre-existing grid left by henequen cultivation expanded with additional grids using theodolite measurements, and connecting them up using high precision GPS (Hutson *pers. comm.* 2012). The archaeological plan was acquired directly from Scott Hutson (courtesy of the Pakbeh Regional Economy Program) in digital format. Hutson directed and completed the mapping project on Chunchucmil, taking over from Bruce Dahlin. Frequent contact with Hutson was invaluable to preparing the GIS, and using and interpreting the plan. Being the product of an archaeological survey, it contains the interpretations and professional judgments of the mappers. In mapping archaeological remains the result comprises a representation of an empirical material situation as encountered onsite. At the same time, the exact condition of the onsite empirical situation cannot be conveyed just by the lines composing the map. In order to better understand why the mapped lines appear as they do, i.e. their characteristics as lines rather than what the legend tells us they convey, contact with Hutson was indispensable.

As said, for Chunchucmil's archaeological plan I will assume the synchronicity of ca. sixth-century occupation. The map cannot serve for diachronic comparisons. The abandonment of the city left traces of a maximum phase of occupation covering a large area contiguously. No large Maya site has ever been excavated in its entirety, and investigations into earlier phases of development is typically confined to monumental architecture in the centre and individual buildings (Fash 1998). Such research indicates that monumental architectural successions often consist of superposing a new phase onto the preceding one. Andrews (1975) shows the hypothetical evolution of a 'quadrangle group' of buildings, in which the group increasingly clots together with elaborate architectural volumes from several related but separate buildings. Ultimately, we know precious little about the development of cities on a settlement scale. In the case of Chunchucmil work done on the chronology of the settlement, based on limited excavations, suggests a 'filling in pattern' that maximised the system of *albarradas* (Stanton & Hutson 2012). The finger or corridor extensions leading to outlying satellite centres of settlement appear to have been actively occupied during roughly the same period as the rest of the city (Hutson et al. 2008). Only additional archaeological research could enable efforts towards reconstructing earlier phases of the urban built environment.

The main purpose of the Chunchucmil test case is to demonstrate the compatibility and effectiveness of applying BLT Mapping to archaeological data, revealing radically different urban traditions. To account for the relative unfamiliarity with this urban tradition and the lower density of built features, a considerably larger area was selected to conduct the test case at Chunchucmil. On Hutson's (*pers. comm.* 2012) advice, a test case area was selected on the northwest side of the monumental core

Fig. 7.4 The approximate location and extent of the test case area indicated within the archaeological map of Chunchucmil.

Please note that in this overview map the detail of the archaeological survey has been simplified. (Base map courtesy of the Pakbeh Regional Economy Program with help from Scott Hutson.)

(see Fig. 7.4), where consistent observations during mapping raised the expectation that preservation is slightly better than for other parts of the site. The test case area covers approximately a square kilometre north-west from the site's mapping centre, overlapping a small section of the monumental core. This represents almost a tenth of the total contiguously mapped area of the city and is intended to contain a reasonable proportion of the spatial morphological variety of the built environment.[15] With

15. This area does not stretch far enough to also include the more dispersed settlement mapped farther away from the monumental core.

an eye to up-scaling the test case to a full-blown case study in the future, the whole map was subjected to the initial data preparation.

The mapping of Chunchucmil took place over a period of 12 years, during which many team members were involved in the work. Contrary to more recent archaeological practice, it was early on decided that the city's plan would be drawn up in *Adobe Illustrator* (.ai extension). This is not software with GIS capabilities, but visually oriented graphic software, albeit functioning in vector format. This means that although the Chunchucmil plan concerns born-digital data, none of that data is geospatially stored. Therefore the data had to be converted to an *ArcGIS* proprietary format, and geospatially located and projected before further work could commence. Unfortunately the .ai format could not directly be imported in *ArcGIS*.

This inability necessitated a laborious conversion process for legacy *Adobe Illustrator* data, which was originally set out by Wunderlich & Hatcher (2009). This process could roughly be followed, but software updates make the processes here slightly different. Most of the process takes place in *Adobe Illustrator* itself, which serves to prepare the data for conversion to other formats and to avoid conflicts or corruption at that stage. Since software is constantly changing, this process is not reproduced in full. The generally important steps include the separation of all image layers, especially to separate out different kinds of digital information (e.g. lines, text, fills). To preserve the shape of automatic visual renders (e.g. curves) of drawn features, the distribution of the anchor points (vertices) needs to be densified. This way the locations of points giving a polyline its more precise shape can be maintained in other formats. *Adobe Illustrator* can then export the separate layers to *AutoCAD* formats.

Following Wunderlich & Hatcher (2009), a hereditary *AutoCAD* exchange format was used (the 2000/LT2000 version for .dxf), which is assumed to store information in a simpler and more stable way than newer versions. Interestingly, no stage of the process requires the operation of a version of *AutoCAD* software itself (although one might want to check the condition of the data). *ArcGIS* is then able to import .dxf files, but for unclear reasons the *ArcGIS* proprietary conversion tools produced grossly compromised results, beyond easy repairs. Through trial and error it was found that *MapInfo Professional*'s Universal Translator tools produce reliable results. Here the file converts first from .dxf into *Mapinfo*'s proprietary .tab, and subsequently from .tab the same tool can convert to .shp (i.e. shape file) developed for *ArcGIS* and other GIS packages. These shape files, finally, can be loaded in *ArcGIS* without issue (text annotations still remained unsuccessful throughout this conversion).

In addition to converting the .ai data to sufficiently reliable .shp format, the .ai map was converted to PDF, and in turn in *Adobe Photoshop* converted to TIFF. Since the originally shared map only showed a partial grid around the site's centre, the same was done for the PDFs (provided at a later date) containing the 10 gridded blocks with labelling in which the site plan was organised. These blocks provide coded references for mapped features to improve navigation and referencing across the city plan.[16] Adding a raster image layer of the whole city plan as a dataset in *ArcMap* enables essential visual checks for the integrity of the converted vector data, and shows the annotations (labels) that did not convert well in the earlier process, aiding interpretive work. After assigning the correct projection to the imported raster data, using the coordinates for the site's centre point, the TIFF containing the entire plan could be georeferenced.[17] Knowing the partial grid across the centre consists of 250x250m blocks, the georeferencing could be scaled (using five points on the grid in quincunx fashion). This can subsequently be extended to include the grids of the 10 label blocks by using the four extreme corners of each grid. The results of this georeferencing process can be found in Table 7.2.

Next, the generated shape files containing the vector data of the original plan were imported as layers in the GIS. Using the spatial adjustment tools as described for Winchester, referring to the four extreme corners of the partial centre grid (this grid was included as part of each separate .ai vector layer before), each layer could be displaced and scaled exactly (i.e. literally without processing error) onto the corresponding coordinates. With the vector layers overlaying the raster images, the quality and integrity of the vector data conversions could be checked for each detail as well as for overall completeness. On inspection, only few minute details seemed to be missing (likely due to visual rendering techniques). As relatively easy manual edits could resolve any issues in subsequent processes preparing data parity (below), the data were deemed fit for use.

---

16. Now, fully integrated versions of the map can be downloaded at Hutson & Magnoni (2017) in .jpg format.
17. (Projection system (in metres): UTM>WGS 1984>Northern Hemisphere>UTM zone 15n). Although several GPS points were recorded across the whole of Chunchucmil, the inherent errors of GPS geolocation technology would add unnecessary uncontrollable errors in contrast to using the regularity of the calculable coordinates across the grid system.

Table 7.2 The residual errors of
georeferencing the TIFFs from the
Chunchucmil plan data.

Raster file (coverage)	RMS error
Chunchucmil's entire plan	0.01945
Block 0	0.00543
Block 1	0.00952
Block 2	0.00339
Block 3	0.00887
Block 4	0.00030
Block 5	0.00072
Block 6	0.00274
Block 7	0.00574
Block 8	0.00605
Block 9	0.00329

The errors have been kept low by closely
zooming in on the relevant intersections
of the grid in each raster image, then
entering the calculated (thus accurate)
coordinates manually into the link table.

Making outline base plans and resolving data gaps (2, 3)

The next stage for both test cases is to prepare an outline base plan, which as an end product upholds the standard of spatial equivalent information decided on for the study. Making an outline base plan actually involves two separate steps: mapping major occupiable subdivisions (2), and complementary conjecturing (3) to resolve data gaps. While two distinct processes, it is pragmatically more convenient and efficient to consider both steps when scrutinising each section of urban space. The principle of the outlines of major occupiable subdivisions composing the built environment and what they convey is explained in Chapters 4 and 5. The comparative information standard depends on the resolution and purposes of the research, and the researcher's judgment on separating the interior and exterior domains (cf. Hillier & Hanson 1984; Chapter 6). This standard determines the level of detail on which features of the built environment are designated a proper outline. Prior knowledge of the

BLT definitions, which will eventually be applied, can sometimes guide particular decisions on which lines to include or exclude as outlines. It is important that for comparative purposes the same standard can be achieved across all datasets intended for comparison. The ultimate aim is to lay a basis for equivalent spatial data with the same internal consistency and detail.

Winchester base plan

Preparing an outline base plan on the basis of MM is less straightforward than its contemporary pedigree suggests. MM as a mapping product aims to satisfy policy and legal use requirements, as well as depicting the physical layout of the built environment. MM omits entrances to buildings, while many separate single buildings are represented by several polygons. How these polygons construct a comprehensive building remains unspecified. This contrasts sharply with the way material information is conveyed by archaeological mapping. Here the *OS Address Layer* (version 2) will give an indication of the location and number of addresses at an approximate location, which helps the interpretation of the physical and social reality. Nonetheless, it cannot securely serve to generate the aggregates of polygons that represent each building completely. Furthermore, MM keeps a record on the development of features (extensions, adjustments, etc.), which adds further polygon confusion, preventing one from grasping empirical reality. MM also offers very basic and generalising land use classifications, and will often (but not always) indicate the provenance of a feature as either 'natural' or 'man-made'. Yet, most man-made open spaces are merely described as 'multi surface' or 'general surface', which does not reveal much of the empirical reality that is actually mapped.

This demonstrates that even when working on contemporary maps, pragmatism (rules of thumb) is an absolute necessity to map a base plan. Given that MM records the contemporary situation, further information sources can be used to interpret the empirical situation represented. These sources are *Google Street View*, *Google Maps*, *Bing Maps*,[18] and the *OS Imagery Layer* (vertical aerial photography). Although this can clarify much of what is represented in MM, including revealing minor discrepancies with on-the-ground reality, still various aspects of the built environment are largely inaccessible to us. This restriction mostly concerns the backs of buildings and their gardens, small alleyways, or legally and

18. Online mapping and imaging resources can be updated without prior notice. The work on Winchester took place between May 2012 and April 2013.

functionally censored areas. When absolute certainty is required, only a dedicated urban survey might be able to fill in the gaps left after cross-referencing various sources.

So, creating outlines based on MM involved intensive cross-referencing of various sources – photographic sources being the most intuitive – to select those lines which, firstly, convey physically existing outlines only and, secondly, are not part of internal design or composite functions within an occupiable subdivision. In exceptional instances, original MM lines received minor amendments to more precisely convey the actual physical difference on the ground and represent the topological connections accordingly. The greatest ambiguity is associated with separating buildings by internal divisions (e.g. adjoining or terraced housing) and, likewise, with complex plots, and open areas around the back. *Ceteris paribus* the general assumption across the whole was that in inaccessible areas all lines of MM would be physically recognisable onsite. Therefore, in principle, all features could potentially be used as outlines. Although MM itself is topologically integrally developed by the OS in GIS format, the tracing of lines is a manual process, using *ArcGIS* editing tools to produce original data. The result of determining outlines in MM is shown in Fig. 7.5.

Likewise, OS1872 introduced its own interpretive difficulties and ambiguities. Some ambiguities are created by its two-year publication period, showing the city in development (see Fig. 7.2). Because the preparation of the base plan is a manual editing process, any mismatches were intuitively weighted to retain more or less continuous regular shapes (see Fig. 7.6). The image resolution and definition, as well as some detailed use of symbology, made OS1872 unsuitable for using the semi-automated raster tracing with ArcScan. Therefore, the vectorisation entailed a manual redrawing of the lines intended for the base plan.

Digitally delivered historical OS plans do not come with a legend explaining the symbology and abbreviations used. Although Oliver (1993) mentions the existence of coloured versions of OS1872, these were not available via EDINA's Historical Digimap services – hence, the simple black-and-white line drawing shown in Figs. 7.2 and 7.6. This often makes it ambiguous as to what kind of (physical) distinction is represented by each single solid line. Coloured plans normally convey differences between built-up areas and open areas, as well as to a degree the materials used (Oliver 1993). Nonetheless, relatively accurate reading of OS1872 can be achieved through intensive study alongside consultation of other maps of the same era at the same scale (see

Fig. 7.5 Example of the outline base plan overlaying MM.

An example of the outline base plan (thick black lines) prepared on top of MM. The remaining grey lines (from MM) are not considered to be outlines in this methodology. (Based on OS MasterMap. © Crown Copyright 2013. All rights reserved. An Ordnance Survey (EDINA) supplied service.)

National Library of Scotland: Town plans n.d.), and an extensive list of abbreviations used in various OS mapping projects over the years (see *National Library of Scotland: OS abbreviations* n.d.).

OS1872 clearly attempts the comprehensive representation of the physically present features of the city. The general resolution for detailing was 15cm on large-scale city plans (Oliver 1993), which displays greater architectural details than MM. In addition, functional furnishings of the city were often included. Strangely, contrary to Oliver's supposition, gates and doorways are not consistently featured on OS1872, while archways (in walls) do appear.

Vectorising towards an outline base plan thus involves selections and interpretations (e.g. excluding the furnishings and some architectural details, see Fig. 7.6). Similar to MM, accuracy cannot be guaranteed for areas around the back of buildings or within larger building

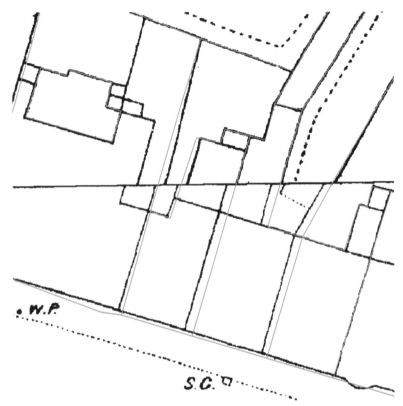

Fig. 7.6 Weighting the plan seam mismatch in vectorisation.

The mismatch along the seam between map sheets, with the weighted shapes of the outlines shown in red. (Image prepared on originals: © Crown Copyright and Landmark Information Group Limited 2013. All rights reserved. 1872.)

complexes. These are too compositely mapped to make secure inferences on what each line conveys. Likewise, separately mapped extensions were interpretively incorporated or divided into discrete buildings with internal divisions. Outbuildings are particularly complex as a great variety was used in the Victorian city. Instead of including each feature separately, clusters of outbuildings were given a single outline. Already having the outlines of MM to refer to, in manually vectorising OS1872, features that are tantalisingly close to MM lines were traced directly, so these become consistent data through time. When the shape and direction changes in OS1872, the MM lines were deviated from.[19]

19. The Winchester City Council records mentioned earlier could only rarely (at the frontage) be trusted to convey a feature that could be historically projected into the past for OS1872 or 1550s.

1550s was vectorised at the previous stage of the process. This vectorisation comprises the merged data of the adjusted plot-based and conjectural mappings of Keene (1985). Due to the historically *self-selective* reconstructive mapping process responsible for the creation of this data and its coarse plot level of detail, 1550s includes no unnecessary or confusing detail.[20] The challenge for producing a base plan here is rather the reverse. The limitations of topographical reconstruction on the basis of the historical records (see Keene 1985; cf. Bisschops 2012) may cause unaffordable gaps preventing it from serving as an outline base plan. As mentioned, most conspicuously, buildings are not included (except for those with public and administrative functions). Importantly, as the plans are based on property records, little certainty exists on the physical empirical reality of the lines. Moreover, beyond the surface of a single property, no physical subdivisions are mapped. Keene's (1985) abstracts of compiled historical records on each property in his gazetteer are used to detect clues about the possibility of multiple buildings, plots or gardens forming part of a single property. Oftentimes evidence for what was on a property is scant or even entirely absent (which also causes some of Keene's own conjectures). This implies a rather crude level of conjectural mapping to add the missing built environment features as the following step, which then merge into a comprehensive outline base plan.

Keene's (1985: Fig. 155) smaller-scale plans, indicating the built-up and probable built-up frontages along the streets, provide an additional source in aid of building conjectures onto property plots. This information is used to decide that a building needs to be conjectured. However, there is no pretention that the shape of a building reflects reality. Lewis et al.'s (1988) book *Medieval Hall Houses of the Winchester Area* depicts three examples of shops surveyed in the city of Winchester, which were between approx. 10 and 15m in length. These dimensions are taken as a rough maximum for typical buildings in the test area, alongside the more detailed knowledge of smaller separate properties along the High Street area. Without readily usable direct sources to ground morphological intervention, ensuring the base plan includes topological distinctions is deemed more important than the appearance of buildings and garden plots.

---

20. As opposed to archaeology (mapping all material remains) or remote sensing technology (detecting all physical features of the actual situation), historical reconstructions are self-selective due to being restricted to a preconceived level of detail that is available in, and taken from, the sources.

To illustrate the coarse effect this practice has, Fig. 7.7 shows the clear difference between the west and east sides of the northern end of current Chesil Street. The west features large subdivisions on sizeable plots, because no evidence was available beyond the suggestion that this area could have hosted a few substantial medieval buildings. The east, however, has been subdivided into smaller built environment features according to plot sizes. The one historical building still in existence (The Old Chesil Rectory) was indicated to feature two tenements with a probable communal arched entrance (Keene 1985). The neighbouring plots in that sequence feature frontages (probably built-up, according to Keene) with comparably dividable dimensions (4 or 5m each). On the

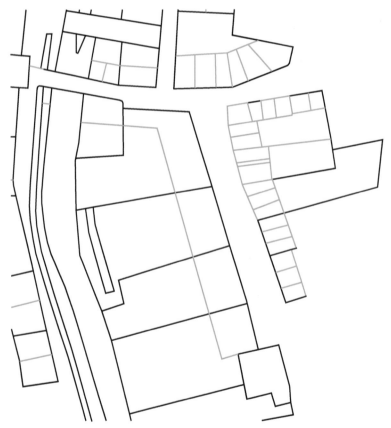

Fig. 7.7 Crude conjectural effects in the 1550s outline base plan.

The effect of crude conjectures based on scarce information on the material situation within the test case area. Dark grey depicts the lines based on Keene's original plan, pink the building and plot conjectures added. (Image prepared on originals, reproduced courtesy of the Winchester Research Unit.)

opposite corner, towards the north, there is an indication that at some point during the late medieval period there could have been six shops occupying this site. In these cases, the open areas behind the buildings are not subdivided as they could well have been shared.[21] Open areas are only subdivided if prompted by Keene's (1985) discussion of the records.

Although these conjecturing efforts ensure the same level of detail on a conceptual level – restricted by the self-selectiveness of historical reconstructions, fragmented archaeological records or even the different nature of geographically representative city plans (e.g. MM vs. OS1872) – true equality in actual detail cannot be guaranteed. It would be a gross over-interpretation to start conjecturing absent outbuildings or architectural details. As a consequence, comparative analysis wishing to include more detailed sources should justify the simplified composition of other sources accordingly.

Chunchucmil base plan

Since the Chunchucmil plan originated as vector data, the process of creating a base plan is predominantly limited to tracing the appropriate lines with *ArcGIS* editing tools, as was the case for MM. Because by their very nature archaeological remains are fragmentary, straight away regular editing tools were used for conjecturing any apparent gaps in information. First, however, tracing those lines determined to be outlines revealed structural issues with the digital data and the topological integrity of composed features. The compromised data structure most probably results from the initial *Adobe Illustrator* drawing technique.

Visually presentable figures revealed line constructions that were unsnapped or simply did not match the features' geometry in minute detail (Fig. 7.8). Effective tracing requires continuous (non-intermittent) lines. Despite measuring no more than a few centimetres or millimetres in geographical space, copying these errors by tracing would compromise the topological usability of the outline base plan. Therefore the tracing process required additional editing to clean up and sometimes completely redraw features, ensuring a proper topological structure for the outlines, which are always conveyed by a single polyline. Similarly, mapped features within and across different classification

21. Little is known about the actual (physical) subdivisions of open areas associated with buildings in the medieval period. Archaeologically there could have been fences, paths and hedges (cf. Becker's (2001) perishable *albarradas*), all used to section off small bits of space. In any case, it seems likely the medieval city saw a variety of plot divisions and shared open areas (Dean *pers. comm.* 2013), which is also suggested throughout the properties in Keene's (1985) gazetteer.

Fig. 7.8 Compromising native data quality in *Illustrator* and *ArcGIS*.

Illustrator data (left) and converted ArcGIS shape files on top of raster image (right). (Image appears courtesy of the Pakbeh Regional Economy Program with help from S. Hutson.)

layers (e.g. architecture and *albarrada*) can come conspicuously close to connecting – yet virtually never do these features truly connect. As a rule of thumb, detached mapped features of equal or different classifications would be connected (as snapped polylines) immediately within the outline base plan GIS layer if approximately under 50cm of width. Any larger yet analogous or conspicuously positioned gaps would be connected in a separate conjectural layer.

After having traced all originally mapped features that designate outlines, conjectures were also used more progressively. These more progressive conjectures are intended to fill in the inevitable data gaps due to fragmentary archaeological preservation. Both to respect the theoretical foundation (Chapters 3 and 4) and to enable topological spatial analyses, it is required that all the integral subdivisions composing the built environment are included as a base layer of information, avoiding any data gaps. To date, no other Classic Maya city is known to manifest such a constellation of elaborate house groupings, pathways and boundary walls in the areas outside of the monumental centre (Hutson et al. 2008;

Magnoni et al. 2012), so conjecturing analogically is largely unfeasible. Therefore I decided to follow a bold but distinctive approach to conjecturing.

First, fragmented buildings would be finished continuing the shapes suggested in the observed remains. Second, fragmented boundary walls are completed exclusively with straight lines (without crossing any others), directly connecting two ends of mapped lines of the same class or onto another feature, using parallel and perpendicular alignments (see Fig. 7.9). In the highly irregular and curving urban form of Chunchucmil, straight lines will emphasise that these conjectures are not intended to represent informed *reconstructions* of the actual features' shapes. Instead, they complete the spatial data by restoring a close approximation of the expected topological

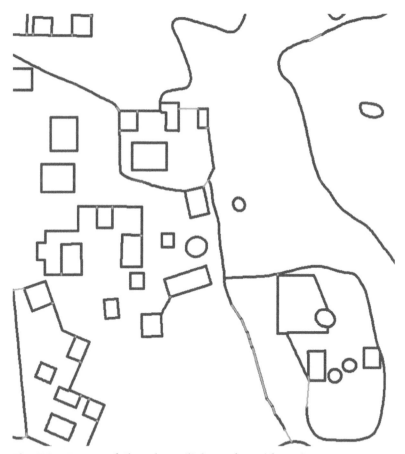

Fig. 7.9 Extract of Chunchucmil's base plan with conjectures.

This extract consists of traced outline features (in grey) and minor and coarse conjectures (pink). (Image prepared upon original data, courtesy of the Pakbeh Regional Economy Program with help from S. Hutson.)

relations that would have existed between subdivisions. While this unavoidably affects the morphological integrity of the data, suggesting actual morphological knowledge of the features amounts to over-interpretation. Conjectured information can always be retrieved as this is kept as a separate data layer (see Fig. 7.9). Naturally, if no suggestive archaeological remains at all were mapped, no additional conjectures are invented.

These crude conjectures are a requirement of the conceptualisations behind this boundary approach (as based on outlines of discrete subdivisions, Chapters 4 and 5). It is *not* suggested here as general archaeological practice, and is not a necessity for each form of analysis and interpretation on the basis of the plan (as demonstrated in Magnoni et al. 2012; Hutson & Welch 2016).

To ensure critical evaluation, the complementary conjectures went through three iterations. The initial phase concerned the coarse connecting up of features on screen. Then these were revised based on the principle that directly or indirectly all spaces within an urban environment must be accessible to partake in the socio-spatial inhabitation of the city. This comes down to: how is one able to traverse the site respecting the actual physical barriers mapped? As a shorthand to revealing possible accessibility patterns, open surfaces and alleyways affording movement, flow, and access to building complexes were drawn on a semi-transparent sheet over a high-resolution printout of the test case area. The conjectures were then adjusted accordingly to better facilitate or enable traversing where necessary. The final revision is a side-effect of the actual process of BLT identification (see below). This process highlights any subdivision where a specific discrete outline was intuitively expected, but absent.[22] The particular relationship between virtual boundaries (Chapter 5) and conjectures is discussed later in this chapter.

In keeping with outline logic, furnishings and internal arrangements as indicated by archaeological artefacts, stelae and quarries are excluded in the base plan. A quarry could only be (partially) included when its shape suggests incorporation as part of a built boundary. Querns or *metates* (grinding stones) within gaps breaking up the course of walls are taken as an indication of a probable passage way, because the arduous task of grinding in all probability had a social element to it (Hutson *pers.*

---

22. All conjectures can be retrieved by directly comparing the traced data with the original plan. It is likely that more means and information will become available to improve and correct the conjecturing (or even a comprehensive reconstruction) when additional archaeological research is carried out. This would not just lead to revisions, but also requires adjusting any subsequent analysis accordingly.

comm. 2012). Bedrock, however, is included as these outcrops of the natural substratum would have impeded thoroughfare and are often incorporated in boundary walls and even minor architecture.

It is a common expectation that various structures within groups of buildings could have been perishable (Becker 2001; Magnoni et al. 2012; Hutson 2016). The *chich mounds* (low piles of rubble) mapped on the original Chunchucmil plan have been suggested as having formed the foundations of (perishable) buildings (Magnoni et al. 2012). Indeed, regular placement in association with building groups of (circular) chich mounds conspicuously resembles the round architecture mapped onsite. Ancient Maya buildings do not typically straddle *albarradas* (Magnoni et al. 2012) and therefore, in revised iterations of the base plan, chich mounds with dimensions similar to round architecture and placed detached from *albarradas* are included in the base plan assuming they carried a structure. Chich mound outlines are excluded in the rare instances where they are located along (*albarrada*) margins or their shape seemed illogically irregular for an occupiable structure, though a partial edge may coincide with another outline.

Magnoni et al. (2012) offer a population estimate which is partly based on the count of *residential* structures (the method of Rice & Culbert 1990). The boundary approach is based on only material-spatial information and cannot consider functional links between structures partaking in a building group. Becker (2001) gives a good overview of possible structures' functions, but also how few of them are systematically identifiable.

There are also ambiguities such as the 'screen walls' connecting structures in building groups in various Classic sites, mentioned by Becker (2001; Tourtellot III 1988). These could easily be confused with remnants of communal platforms and do not often form a discrete subdivision. In such cases, the mapmakers' expertise is a cautious guide for where they indicate a group (or platform) on the plan (with block annotations). In addition, various fragments of *albarradas* can also be found 'dangling' inside house-group-lots. Rather than creating actual subdivisions, these dangling lines may form part of internal arrangements in concordance with the activity areas and perishable boundaries mentioned above.

To enable a critically reflexive research practice, all ambiguous features are initially traced as part of the base plan (see Fig. 7.10). Where a feature is clearly truncated by another feature, in the sense of being subject to later modification of any type or having become obsolete, only

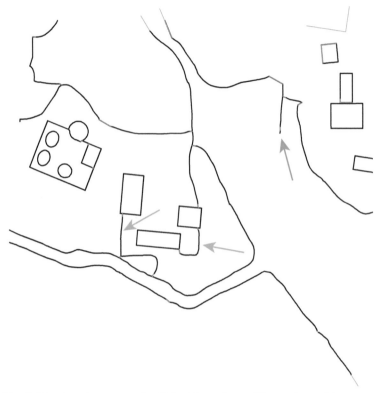

Fig. 7.10 Another example of the Chunchucmil base plan with conjectures (in pink).

The green arrows indicate incomplete subdivisions (possible screen walls), while the red arrow indicates what currently looks like a real dangle. How both situations are treated will need to be settled during BLT identification. (Image prepared from original data, courtesy of the Pakbeh Regional Economy Program with help from S. Hutson.)

the feature that appears responsible for the truncation (supersedes) is taken into account. There is too little knowledge about these architectural palimpsests on the basis of the survey alone to know the correct order or composition.

The stage of identifying BLTs is an interpretive process on top of the base plan. The BLT identification process may indicate where or how conjectures would be expected in order to complete a discrete subdivision. With this in mind, all dangles or incomplete subdividing features that remain after BLT identifications can be removed from what then would become the actual 'final base plan'. The researcher should always be mindful of the possibility that, consciously or subconsciously, readily perceived or concealed, subjective patterns could emerge from the anterior decisions and rules of thumb regarding outlines and conjecturing. The 'final base plan' could be said to be an exact copy of all BLT identifications taken together at once.

Topology checks for outline base plan and BLT identifications (3, 4)

After creation of the outline base plan, we must consider checking the quality of this new standardised spatial data. Despite using GIS tools throughout, making the base plan is a manual and interpretive process and thus prone to imprecision and human error. Problems similar to the ones depicted in Fig. 7.8 would inhibit the usability of the base plan data. BLT identifications in turn are based on manual tracings of the base plan, and thus require continuous lines in contiguous connections. This means that for the base plan to support this work effectively, one must ensure topological integrity throughout the dataset. Similarly, the BLT data after identification must maintain topological integrity. To this end *ArcGIS* has developed the 'topology toolbar', which can carry out several data checks based on a predetermined topology rule set. Carrying out topology checks are therefore a necessary technical step in both step 3 and 4 of BLT data creation.

To apply the tools in the topology toolbar, all separate layers (if any) making up the base plan are best merged into one comprehensive dataset. Then, within ArcCatalog, any feature class (layer), stored as a so-called geodatabase, can be subjected to a topological rule set. When the rules are validated, any found errors can be inspected and corrected within *ArcMap*. The first step of constructing topology rules is to set a cluster tolerance to simplify the data structure (i.e. any features below a measured threshold are regarded the same).[23] Then the rules themselves are selected from pre-given options. Options include rules that help to make sure the data does not contain: unintended dangles; unsnapped vertices or nodes; intersections; unwanted duplication or coverages; unconnected polylines, etc. Table 7.3 shows the four relevant topology rules selected to check the base plan and, later, to subject BLT data to (step 4, described below).

---

23. Of course automated simplification is not 'intelligent'. Though the accuracy is maintained to the resolution specified, at very large scales, some shapes will manifest counterintuitive alterations: e.g. right angles might have become slightly flattened and curves less smooth. Unwanted changes can be manually edited. Simplification will have a small mitigating effect on the earlier densification of anchor points in *Adobe Illustrator* (for Chunchucmil).

Table 7.3   The selection of topology rules and how they have been applied.

Topology rule	Outline base plan	All BLTs (except Type 2, Type 4, and V)	Type 2, Type 4, and V
Must not have dangles	X	X	
Must not self-overlap	X	X	X
Must not self-intersect	X	X	X
Must not overlap			X

Despite technical limitations,[24] this semi-automated process will speed up subsequent work and immediately improves the quality of any derivative data. When checking the errors found upon validation, any unfinished but ambiguous subdivisions intentionally kept in the base plan to inform the BLT identification stage, as well as all 'edge effects' (incomplete subdivisions truncated by the maximum extent of the test area), can be marked as exceptions in the correcting process. Genuine errors are resolved by manual editing or automated fixes.

The cluster tolerance should be a measure commensurate with the precision achieved in the mapping resolution. For Chunchucmil, 10cm was specified, which might be smaller than the actual mapping resolution achieved onsite, but would retain most of the interpreted shapes (e.g. curves) as originally mapped. For Winchester, the cluster tolerance was specified as 5cm, which reflects the higher level of detail and precision in MM, as well as the features generated in the vectorisation processes of the other time-slices directly in GIS.

Since all boundary mapping is based on outlines, its GIS layers will always consist of polyline feature classes. The essential difference with the data structure of the outline base plan and each separate layer conveying a BLT (see below) is that *each polyline feature in the BLT*

24. Topology rules appear unable to handle composite rules regarding more than one feature class (layer) at once. However, they can run multiple questions simultaneously, each treating a single layer. Complementary coverages can be checked by using tools for selecting on location. It is also possible to set topology rules before mapping and check up on data created in a (semi) live way, during data editing. This could be more efficient if most eventualities are known upfront. Likewise topological rule sets can be adjusted if it is found that the rules do not adhere to the intended logic.

layers must convey a BLT identification in its entirety. In contrast, for the base plan it is only truly important that all lines that shape outlines are included, always maintaining topological integrity. If the data resulting from the BLT identifications are intended to undergo further computation for visualisation, spatial analysis or conversion into other formats, then it is paramount that not only the outline base plan, but also the BLT feature classes are checked against an appropriate topology rule set (see Table 7.3). Types 2, 4, and V are distinct from other BLTs in that they do not circumscribe a space in isolation.

The flexible polyline format enables a further visual data check. *ArcGIS* offers a tool to generate polygons from polylines by closing them. These then visualise as filled areas in *ArcMap*, which cannot happen if the lines are not continuous or the ends not snapped. (Vice versa, the interpretive intricacies of the BLT data structure cannot automatically be generated from polygons.) One should remain mindful, however, that in complex data errors are easy to overlook. Besides, generating polygons automatically lacks human understanding, so inner and outer BLT designations lead to separate polygons. So, despite offering an additional visual check, to serve alternative (analytical) purposes (cf. Magnoni et al. 2012), the generated polygons require a degree of manual editing to remove intellectually unwarranted polygons.

Identifying BLTs (4)

Identifying BLTs is the final and most analytical stage in the data creation or mapping process. For each instance a BLT is successfully recognised within the outline base plan, according to Chapter 5's definitions, an individual segment of line is traced entirely. This is a manual editing process in *ArcMap*, using the tracer in the editing tools. Each data entry (i.e. each polyline) created at this stage is a complete and meaningful empirical identification of the material socio-spatial reality of a boundary operation occurring at the (historical) moment represented by the city plan. For each BLT (Table 7.4 lists the BLTs with name and number), a separate layer (feature class) is created. This improves clarity whilst conducting the accumulatively complex identifications, but it also enables immediate visualisation of each BLT separately and can visually approximate combinations of them. In addition, if the boundary method would at any stage be combined with other methods or data, each separate meaning carrying data entry can be retrieved and further information can be attributed in the spatial database.

Table 7.4   List of all BLTs with name and number.

Boundary Line Types			
1	Closing boundaries	8	Mutual boundaries
2	Facing boundaries	9	Opening boundaries
3	Associative boundaries	10	Neutral boundaries
4	Extended facing boundaries	11	Man-made boundaries of unoccupiability
5	Directing boundaries	12	Not man-made boundaries of unoccupiability
6	Disclosing boundaries	13	Not man-made negative boundaries
7	Enclosing boundaries	V	Virtual boundaries

For abridged definitions of all BLTs, please consult the supplementary BLT table towards the back.

Although the exact order in which BLT identifications are carried out is not prescribed, there is a logical starting point following the onto-logical primacy of seclusion. Chapter 5's formulation of the ontology of types commences from the ability to close off (make impermeable) a bounded space (subdivision) towards undisruptive interaction from the outside, i.e. a strong seclusion emphasised from within and shielding 'intrusive' interactions from without. In its simplest form this creates a 'cell' with a relation to its outside (cf. Hillier & Hanson 1984): here represented by buildings' impermeable material properties. Initial BLT identification thus reads the outline base plan to find these materially *closable* outlines of an occupiable surface (not negative). In identifying Type 1s, such socio-spatial systems are, as it were, extracted from the goings-on in their environment. This is not to say that Type 1s are a pre-requisite for other BLTs to occur (see Chapter 5) (even though an urban built environment without Type 1s would be extraordinary) as the BLT ontology of types does not fully define relations between types.

There is, however, the ontological necessity for Type 1s to require at least one Type 2 in order for the Type 1 to partake in the socio-spatial configuration and not become a negative void. A Type 1 without a Type 2 would become a Type 11 (negative), as its inside is not accessible for occupation. Because BLT Mapping is intended for built environments, especially urban settlements, the identification of any BLT implies the existence of others specifying its socio-spatial context. Hypothetically speaking, a configuration of only one Type 1 plus 2 would also be designated a Type 13 for the undeveloped surface area surrounding it (or the limits of the selected area of data coverage).

The singular seclusion of Type 1s (dominants) thus becomes the first identifiable point of reference in an outline base plan, from where increasingly their environment is inspected to identify further BLTs (see

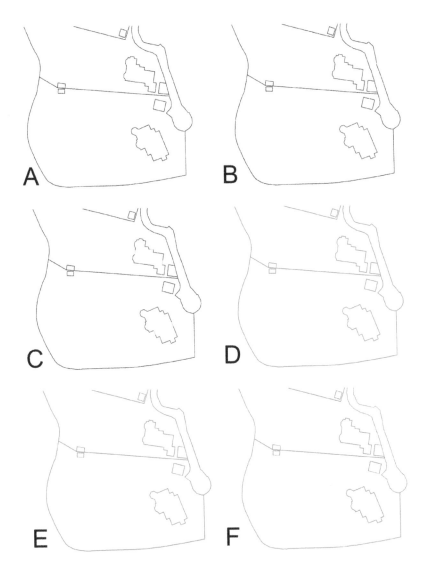

Fig. 7.11 A sequential representation of stages in BLT mapping.

A composition of six consecutive images (left to right, top-down) of the same configuration showing BLT identification starting with (A) outline base plan, then (B) Type 1 (brown), (C) Type 2 (light green), (D) Type 3 (red), (E) Type 4 (dark green), (F) Type 5 (blue) and Type 9 (pink). (Derived from OS MasterMap. © Crown Copyright 2013. All rights reserved. An Ordnance Survey (EDINA) supplied service.)

Fig. 7.12   Example of diachronic figure-ground diagrams of Cincinnati.

(Image source: Scheer & Ferdelman 2001: 22, reproduced by kind permission of Jeremy Whitehand, editor of *Urban Morphology*.)

Fig. 7.11). It is clear that, beyond the rugged line morphology of the outline base plan, a degree of (material) knowledge is required to identify the properties of a building (in Winchester's MM supported by aerial photography and online mapping products). This initial stage resembles mapping a figure-ground diagram (see Trancik 1986; Fig. 7.12), as one essentially separates the built volumes from the open spaces (see Fig. 7.13). Such a figure-ground plan approximation can aid readability of the boundary visualisations.

From here on, there is an augmentative quality to the overall order of identifying BLTs that initially roughly pertains to the order of presentation in Chapter 5. In Fig. 7.11, Type 2 first qualifies the Type 1s. Then associative boundaries (Type 3) naturally encompass Type 1s, which in

Fig. 7.13   A figure-ground approximation of part of the Chunchucmil
test case.

By generating polygons from the Type 1 identifications an approximation of a figure-ground
is achieved, which can aid readability. (Image prepared based on original data, courtesy of the
Pakbeh Regional Economy Program with help from S. Hutson.)

turn are made accessible by Type 4s. Then on a larger scale a Type 5 and
Type 9 tie this configuration together.

Fig. 7.11 reveals several things worthy of note, which apply to BLT
Mapping in general:

- First, the consequence that no single BLT identification can fully
  define the material reality that a boundary line represents means
  that all BLT identifications overlay each other. Situation F thus
  contains six BLT layers (once the BLT identification process is
  completed the outline base plan is no longer necessary);
- Second, the entrances (Type 2 and 4) are partly conjectured, based
  on (aerial) photographic sources and the shape and size of the

outlines. With such large buildings one expects more than a single entrance and entrances connecting the building with the shape of its immediate environment. Only onsite surveying can confirm how correct these conjectures are;

- Third, Type 3s encompassing Type 1s (or indeed any BLT encompassing another BLT) bound a space with an inner and an outer boundary that do not meet. That means that the two polyline features are part of (caused by) a single Type 3 identification. However, they do not concern the same boundary line. Once applied, the abstract character of BLT definitions reconfirms that in isolation they cannot capture empirical reality. The inner Type 3 coincides with the Type 1, while the outer Type 3 coincides with other Type 3s, Type 5, and Type 9 respectively (disregarding the Type 2s and 4s). The combinations alone fully describe each unique boundary;

- Fourth, this composition shows a situation in which more architectural structures are outlined than only the main building. These associated auxiliary structures (outbuildings, follies, garages, sheds, garden houses, and further functional varieties in other cultures or different historical periods, etc.) add a layer of subjectivity which commands the expert judgment of the researcher, who must decide on the auxiliary nature of such structures and apply the appropriate BLT consistently thereafter. The more pronounced and unambiguous a 'material recording' (as in archaeology) and one's knowledge of the recording process in the field, the more work can be done without any socio-cultural background knowledge. Though accuracy in the decision can increase with additional knowledge or prior familiarity with an urban tradition, the interpretive decision which outline(s) is (are) 'dominant(s)' (Type 1s) is precarious.

There would have been several ways to approach the conundrum that building groups pose (see Figs. 7.14 and 7.15). So why decide to identify the auxiliary buildings as Type 3s? I used the descriptive term 'auxiliary', already suggesting a relation of dependence. Indeed what this alludes to is the idea that a building is predominantly occupied by a socio-spatial system that may extend into several associative boundaries. Some additional Type 3s are strongly marked thanks to their architectural construction. When preserving these structures' outlines as a successive Type 3 arrangement, future research wishing to distinguish architectural building types and/or functions could still be done. The current

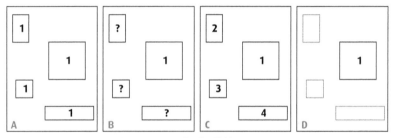

Fig. 7.14 BLT mapping options for building groups.

A: all buildings are a Type 1, thus the open area a Type 8. B: one building is designated Type 1, the rest remains unknown. This causes impossible data gaps. C: all buildings within a group function distinctively. This requires hierarchical and/or functional information beyond (comparative) reach in spatial-material data. D: one building is designated Type 1, the rest discarded. This would mean losing a lot of architectural information.

absence of evidence (within standardised comparative boundary data) is not evidence of the eternal absence of properties allowing such further distinctions.

Nonetheless, in many cases the relation of dependence is not so clear, e.g. agricultural and industrial complexes or special design clusters of equally large or elaborate volumes. In such cases, the seclusions are validly deemed equivalent: all are identified as Type 1s. This changes the relation between BLTs. Instead of a successive Type 3 arrangement, this would become a Type 8 (Fig. 7.14: A). Without additional knowledge this distinction will always remain somewhat arbitrary, often evolving as a practice-based rule of thumb as one accustoms oneself with the patterns occurring in an urban tradition or within a case. For example, the internal comparison of material

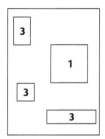

Fig. 7.15 Chosen solution to mapping building groups as shown in Fig. 7.11.

This solution for mapping building groups retains architectural detail, while restricting specialist judgment to a more comparative binary distinction between structures (e.g. large and smaller; central and peripheral).

properties could lead to the conclusion that a farm *house* still bears closer resemblance to a town house than a farm *shed*.

The basic consideration described here makes an important contribution to comparative work. The alternatives – such as introducing a full hierarchy or functional distinctions between structures to create distinct interrelated 'dominant complexes' – sound attractive, but introduce false certainty (over-interpretation) about how structures are related. This could only result from the availability of equivalent additional information across datasets. Notwithstanding its interpretive nature, the chosen solution (Fig. 7.15) retains morphological detail, while only making one main binary judgment on building groups without the pitfalls of Fig. 7.14: B–D.

Maya settlements are characterised by a high frequency of grouped architectural structures. Although some might actually serve several specific functions that are associated with e.g. a house separately, extensive research also suggests that building groups would have been occupied by multiple nuclear families (Johnston & Gonlin 1998; Magnoni 2007). In Chunchucmil, for example, virtually all groups contain more than two buildings, meaning that with greater confidence these likely contain more than one Type 1. The associated open areas in either case comparably end up as a Type 3 or a Type 8 constellation, resulting from one-to-one or one-to-many building(s) relationships.

Allowing the existence of successive Type 3s (or Type 8s elsewhere) creates sequences of the same adjacent BLT identifications. Such distinctions could otherwise have been discarded as internal arrangements. Retaining this empirical reality at identification gives the researcher greater flexibility later. One could choose to disregard configurative complexes of interconnected Type 3s (or Type 8s), or one could focus part of the analysis or interpretation on specific differences they convey.

This brings me to a final point. From a purely intellectual perspective, the BLTs that do not circumscribe a subdivision but qualify the relation between two subdivisions, i.e. Type 2 and Type 4, should be traced twice, creating two polylines. Ultimately, each entrance of a boundary is a qualifying part of each co-located BLT (e.g. the reciprocity of any passage or doorway). This would therefore duplicate identifications in such instances. However, for both visual and analytical purposes this would introduce unnecessary complexity in the data structure. The length, construction and location of any such boundary is immediately recognised and utilised from the single identification. The same applies to virtual boundaries.

Virtual boundaries

Virtual boundaries (V) were introduced in Chapter 5, following from junctions where Type 5s meet (i.e. usually street crossings). Vs are an intellectual construct that chimes with everyday understanding and interaction within the built environment, but which cannot be empirically observed directly. Contrary to all BLTs, a V denotes an implied presence. This presence is implied contextually at certain positions in the empirical material reality of built boundaries: a 'virtual extension' is required to connect up boundaries to create discrete subdivisions. That means that in the sense of Smith & Varzi (1997, 2000; Smith 2001), Vs are a fiat presence in a bona fide material world. They are restricted by the empirical configurative context and thus less volatile than completely imagined boundaries. In Chapter 4 it was already indicated that the gaps in built boundaries serving as (closable) passage ways (usually Types 2 and 4) would be closed as feature outlines to create discrete subdivisions. When any open boundaries meet, they might be traversable via gaps where the surface material simply continues (no differentiation). The circumscribing built boundaries that leave the gap(s) morphologically suggest an experiential distinction (e.g. grass fields with intermitted fencing). This resembles the way marked space gives way to subdivisions of space (see Chapter 3).

In contemporary maps it cannot always be determined whether lines convey gaps instead of materially articulated or demarcated boundaries. In archaeology the number of Vs can be much greater, as gaps are mapped (perishable materials used for fences or doors etc.). Archaeologically, then, Vs likely become overrepresented. This starts a dialogue between conjectures and virtual boundaries. Basically a conjecture should fill in a missing material built boundary, but at BLT identification it sometimes becomes apparent that a V is more sensible, or even necessary, to traverse the configuration effectively. Vs can resolve numerous dangles remaining within the outline base plan. Especially within archaeological situations they reflect some interpretive contention also.

In Chunchumil's case, it would be a logical expectation that there were (possibly closable) openings in *albarradas* which allowed people to access the areas they circumscribe. When conjecturing, boundary lines could have been created where such openings did originally exist. There is no way to distinguish on the basis of the mapped material remains whether any opening was intended, destroyed, deteriorated, caused by decayed perishables (e.g. incorporated cacti or trees), removed (by

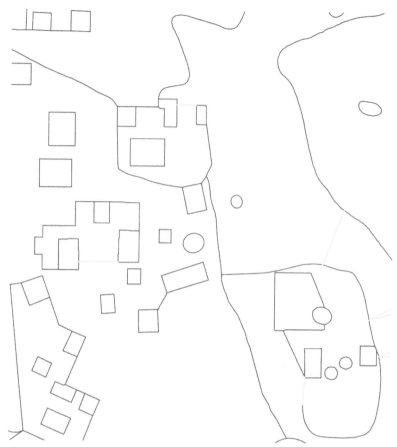

Fig. 7.16 An example of virtual boundaries in Chunchucmil.

Chunchucmil's outline base plan (grey) with several virtual boundaries (light blue). The virtuals on the right hand side follow from Type 5s (see Chapter 5) and would not have originally been included in the base plan. (Image prepared from original data courtesy of the Pakbeh Regional Economy Program with help from S. Hutson.)

animals or humans) after abandonment, etc. (Hutson *pers. comm.* 2012; concurring Becker 2001; Demarest 1997). At the same time, no wall or material distinction must complete a circumscription contiguously. Indeed, in Chunchucmil several platforms tying building groups together gradually descend into the ground, creating a slight ramp facilitating unimpeded access (Hutson *pers. comm.* 2012). Vs are used to mark-up situations in which missing physical differentiation would not have detracted people from experiencing the spatial distinction in the context of that location. This enables further discrete subdivisions to be mapped (Fig. 7.16). Note, however, that Vs denote places of unimpeded access, but entrances (Types 2 and 4) do not require virtuality, nor do Vs only occur based on previous conjectures.

The dialogue between boundary line conjectures and Vs is a clear example of how BLT identification can cause changes to the original outline base plan. The Vs connecting up actual gaps in boundary lines, or marking where Type 5 circumscriptions meet, would not have been included in the outline base plan. Therefore, it is a mistake to assume that the outline base plan must already contain all the lines on top of which all BLT identifications occur. Only merging all BLT identification layers together (including Vs) will give a 'final base plan' copy of the BLT morphology.

Mapping practice and the research process

It should now be beyond dispute that BLT Mapping is also a highly interpretive process, looking beyond the formal BLT definition. The nature of each case and data source requires specific preparation, selection, and creation processes. The four-step data creation process maintains a level of iterative reciprocity (e.g. the outline base plan anticipates BLT identification and is revised by it). As I referred to previously, in mapping practice and with increasing case familiarity, rules of thumb emerge to resolve ambiguities, uncertainty and confusing data situations when preparing data in anticipation of BLT identification, and while identifying BLTs itself. A good reflexive subjective research practice must carefully document and report the (arbitrary) rules of thumb that were consciously applied in data creation. How are the rules of thumb positioned in this research process?

Let us briefly reconsider the research process so far. The BLT ontology of types serves the specific purpose of the study of the sociospatial significance of material presence to the inhabitation of urban built environments. Therefore disparate ontologies of the built environment might be necessary when one intends to study other aspects of its existence. BLT Mapping declares and articulates its own analytical and interpretive limits through its critical realist research design, theoretical framework and resultant conceptualisations. One could immanently critique the theoretical premise of BLT definitions or the reasoning that subsequently forms its research concepts. Once applied, one could contest and demonstrate fault with instances of the identification of BLT definitions. Progressing empirical research on any city could in time also lead to commensurate revisions of both the outline base plan and resultant BLT identifications.

Furthermore, in keeping with critical realism (Sayer 1981, 2000; Yeung 1997), the BLT ontology of types itself could be improved and expanded through iterative abstraction. The iterative abstraction process then ensures that unexpected empirical situations encountered during the process of identification (i.e. flawed practical adequacy, Chapter 2) will be accounted for by revising the BLTs. In addition, correlative research might gain from retaining the specific data structure produced in this process (see Chapter 8) by combining it with other information directly using spatial database attributes. Such correlations alone could enable the asking of disparate or more detailed (socio-culturally specific) questions than the current radically comparative remit allows.

The rules of thumb in mapping practice, then, give rigour to the subjective remit of interpretive leeway that the researcher permits to account for imperfect knowledge of the source material, and the socio-spatial empirical situation that is documented by the source material. Such rules could be critiqued for inconsistent application, being overly ambiguous, or simply confront differences in professional opinion. The following explanatory lists omit comprehensive illustration of the issues described. Such illustrations would duplicate the preliminary analytical and interpretive explorations in Chapter 9.

Rules of thumb

Mapping practice at Winchester

(1) The first aspect demanding attention is particular to Winchester as a diachronic test case. In instances where the boundary *line* remains in exactly the same location through time (e.g. differentiations spatially close enough to justify copying back in time from later phases), any *concurring* BLT identification on that location must be identical to the more recent phase(s). So doing helps to keep the data clean by eliminating confusing insignificant differences in spatial morphology. Most instances where this applies concern historical building frontages, retaining the same doorway(s). Unsurprisingly, due to data preparation processes such as scaling and georeferencing (see above), outline base plans rarely end up in the exact same position. The upscaling of 1550s to MM alone causes a scanned line thickness of 50–60cm in geographical space (see Fig. 7.17).

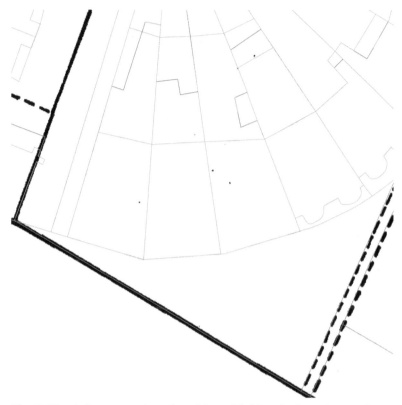

Fig. 7.17 A demonstration of working with historical persistence in spatial data.

The thick black lines show the upscaled 1550s scan. The grey lines represent the vectorisation process for the 1550s base plan. The blue lines are the base plan of OS1872 and the red the MM base plan (building modifications at the back). The front entrances (green) in the middle of buildings existed there in both MM and OS1872. (Partly derived from OS MasterMap (© Crown Copyright 2013. All rights reserved. An Ordnance Survey (EDINA) supplied service); original scans: © Crown Copyright and Landmark Information Group Limited 2013. All rights reserved. 1872; and original plans, reproduced courtesy of the Winchester Research Unit).

(2) Due to the same line style dominating OS1872, it is not until BLT identification forces the researcher to disentangle what these lines convey that the appropriateness of outline base plan selections is revealed. Similar to the iterative revisions of conjectures in Chunchucmil, the OS1872 outline base plan revisions are more impactful during the BLT identification process than is the case for either MM or 1550s. At the same time, only OS1872 offers extra certainty for conjecturing entrances thanks to additional details on architecture, furnishings and park or garden design.

(3) Because the back of buildings cannot be satisfactorily assessed, there is little secure information on back entrances in each time-slice. The general assumption is made that back entrances are necessary for structures which have a plot around the back. Unless the shape and mutual orientation of the outlines and further identified BLTs suggests differently, the back entrance is conjectured broadly opposite to the front entrance. Only for elaborate architecture, complex contexts, or on the basis of additional factual information could more entrances be designated. It should be noted that because many entrances are conjectured (cf. Chunchucmil below) their dimension is less relevant than their topological existence. The width of entrances is at best indicative.

(4) Working on an urban tradition that is familiar to the researcher means that there is a greater immediate understanding of what built elements could be expected. This applies especially to outbuildings, garages, sheds, follies, etc. as mentioned before. In contrast to Maya settlements, where groups of buildings are justifiably identified as Type 1s, outbuildings are typically understood as auxiliary to, and under the intended influence of, the 'main structure' of the constellation (i.e. the extension of a single socio-spatial system). It seems detrimental to go against that *a priori* understanding. This would have the consequence that most gardens become the socio-spatially distinct Type 8, despite experiential knowledge that there is a single Type 1 determining the configurative complex. Outbuildings in MM and OS1872 are thus treated as sequential occurrences of Type 3s or 8s, disregarding instances where their material properties are impermeable akin to closable solid dominants. This leaves the choice of how to treat configurative complexes thus defined for later, as deemed appropriate for the comparative analysis at hand (e.g. matching coarse and fragmented historically or archaeologically derived maps). Indeed, this may be necessary for certain diachronic analyses comparing with 1550s, which lacks outbuildings altogether. Moreover, it removes the need to repeat the interpretation process entirely if specific outbuilding information is later desired.

(5) On MM, boundaries of unoccupiability (Type 11 or 12) are primarily based on MM's own 'natural' or 'man-made' classifications. On OS1872 they are based on the symbology appearing on the original scans, and on 1550s they are limited to bodies of water only, because reconstructive self-selection means no additional physical information is included in the test area (see note 20 above).

(6) Garden plots situated like housing plots, without maintaining a direct association with a building, are quite particular to the medieval period. Though justifiably identified as opening boundaries (Type 9s), they are something of an oddity. Their open character logically makes these gardens a Type 9, but the known function is quite distinct from parks or other open areas. This difference is similar to distinguishing an agricultural field from a park, which resonates well considering that garden plots could have been used to grow crops rather than to serve modern leisure functions. Besides built-up frontages, Keene (1985: Fig. 155) identifies likely 'open ground', which seems to indicate land without any particular identified use. Occurrences roughly follow the general plot pattern. The current BLT ontology prevents such functional differentiation. Functionally, Type 9s thus have a protean referral record, somewhat reflecting the elaborate differentiations in urban studies (Stanley et al. 2012; M.L. Smith 2008). Although from a social perspective (outside the realm of spatial-material evidence), ambiguity due to the lack of a predominant socio-spatial occupation could justifiably render any unused space a Type 10 (e.g. fallow).

Mapping practice at Chunchucmil

(1) The first rule of thumb concerns building entrances (Type 2). Because the archaeologists mapping Chunchucmil estimated the extent and rough shape of structures from piles of rubble and debris, it is typically not possible to define entrances based on archaeological evidence. This leads to conjecturing entrances firstly based on the analogical assumption that buildings face each other (directly and indirectly). This pattern preference is found throughout the Classic period in the Maya area in plaza, patio and platform groups, as well as civic and ceremonial quadrangle groups (e.g. Becker 2001, 2004). Conjecturing additional entrances may depend on boundaries in their direct configurative complex (e.g. facing outward to open space) or to allow access to monumental or palatial architectural types (e.g. Andrews 1975; Parmington 2011; Jones 2015). Alternative locations for entrances are identified when the spatial morphological context displays a persuasive measure of orientation elsewhere rather than building groups facing each other. Hutson (*pers. comm.*

2012) suggested that small structures in the middle of plaza groups could have been entered from any side as they could have served as elevations to address audiences.

(2) As previously mentioned, all mapped architectural structures (usually located in groups) have been identified as Type 1s (see also Fig. 7.13). This might include a proportion of what in western and globalised cities would be considered (functional) outbuildings associated with a residence (although many actual outbuildings could have perished also). This leads to an abundance of associated Type 8s and relatively few Type 3s, which is believed to reflect Chunchucmil's particular Classic Maya socio-cultural nature.

(3) Regarding extended facing boundaries (Type 4), it could generally be assumed that platforms are accessible from all angles as they are low enough to mount without too much trouble. Similar to encountering a low front garden fence, however, it would be logical that there are preferred places to access a platform. In many cases the platforms have been mapped to gradually descend into the ground on one or more sides. Such access design was confirmed by a detailed excavation of a platform group (Hutson *pers. comm.* 2012). Caution is indispensable, as a discontinuous platform outline could have a number of other causes besides intentional architectural construction. When subsiding platform sides have conspicuous locations this is regarded as an indication for places to ascend onto and access the platform. In instances where a full outline is mapped (possibly including a conjunction with *albarradas*), a wider opening between buildings or orientation towards the surrounding configuration is accepted as an indicator for an access way.

(4) Architecturally, *albarradas* are regarded to be materially impermeable (although Hutson (2016) claims they tend to be lower than the human field of vision). Yet, they are usually open boundaries due to the conspicuously fragmented and often virtual nature over their course, which occurs even in well-preserved areas. Impermeability is then permanently mitigated by probably wide and/or multiple passages. Only *albarradas* mapped over a complete circumscription could become identified as (closable) Type 7s (i.e. enclosing boundaries). The same is considered for rarely occurring high platforms with an outer outline formed in conjunction with structures, circumstantially leading to a probable formal entrance.

(5) The parallel definition of Type 5 is applied in a flexible sense, sometimes including mirroring line directions and contextually derived directionality. This means that two boundary lines

forming a relatively narrow (in context) but irregularly shaped corridor in a mutual linear orientation (broad parallelism) are likely to be identified as a Type 5. Type 5s running long contiguous courses are rare in Chunchucmil (few formal streets exist). Deciding between a Type 5 or a Type 9 is subjective to the degree that one needs to judge when the observed general parallel structure is sufficiently lost.

(6) Though Type 6 depends on opening out onto several Type 1s, it is set apart from Type 8 because of its integration and sense of local centrality. It would seem that plaza and some platform groups make good candidates for Type 6s, but usually their bounded area is spatially removed from the 'open' flows of traversing the site from anywhere within the spatial system. Generally identifying a Type 6 is closely associated with nearby or connected Type 5s and Type 9s, along which Type 8s, in contrast, would often be placed laterally.

Taking BLT mapping forward

By conducting the processes this chapter discusses, the result is an intricately layered GIS of immediately visualisable BLT data. Within the confines of this developmental project this has only been done for the small test case areas as defined. This BLT Mapping could be seen as a formal redescription of the urban built environment in socio-spatial terms. On top of already complex morphology and topology, however, their profound complexity is only revealed when focusing on small areas at once to find out which BLT combinations each space is composed of, and connect and embed it in the built environment. In order to create better visualisations and greater insight, appropriate tools are needed to rework and (re)order the data thus created. To devise functional tools, the data structure that emerges through BLT Mapping needs to be better understood. Moreover, we must reflect on which analytical measures and selections could provide meaningful results. So, before I turn to a closer inspection of the specificities of the test case areas and what we may learn from such redescription directly, Chapter 8 will explain the data structure and the opportunities for spatial analytical measures this enables.

CHAPTER 8
IDENTIFYING SPATIAL ANALYTICAL MEASURES THAT EXPLOIT BLT DATA

Introduction

By demonstrating that BLTs can be applied as a mapping practice, in essence an original data creation process is established. BLTs are a vehicle for making the socio-spatial information contained in the material differentiations of the built environment explicitly accessible for analysis and interpretation. While the other methods for analysing the urban built environment considered in Chapter 6 are influential precursors, none of these maintain a commensurate perspective and research agenda. The next step is to consider how this new data can help to enable and equip the radical comparative study of the inhabited urban built environment. For this, the meticulous BLT definitions are not enough. We must know how BLT data is significant. In order to devise a rationale that connects BLT data to the interpretive levels of socio-spatial significance determined in Chapter 5, first a thorough understanding of the intricate spatial data structure is necessary. Failing to understand the data structure emerging from BLT identification will prevent the interpretive reading of BLT visualisations and the development of appropriate analytical measures.

Therefore, this chapter will first clarify the data structure produced by BLT Mapping. It then introduces a way to visualise this data beyond current capabilities within *ArcGIS*, and discusses the computational difficulties of working diachronically. Next it will harness BLT Mapping's future potential by proposing analytical and quantitative measures, providing a rationale for the use and questioning of the primary analytical units (i.e. BLTs) and their derivatives.

For social scientists and humanities scholars, GIS software evokes something of a 'black box' effect (cf. Griffiths 2013; Lilley 2012), causing people to steer clear of its computing powers, which are deemed impenetrable. This chapter, too, is inevitably dense and abstract. However, by providing structural links between the data created in the mapping process and interpretive purpose, it is intended to mitigate such effects and facilitate immediate appreciation of the analytical opportunities. It must be stressed that this is a chapter of ideas. Many of the proposed analytical measures are hypothetical and require future geocomputational development to become operational. A number of already accessible possibilities raised in this chapter will be explored with and without geocomputational aids in Chapter 9. In other words, this chapter lays the foundation for a much more extensive analytical GIS toolset to optimise utilisation of BLT data.

Understanding the BLT data structure

Revealing the data structure is best started by recalling Fig. 7.11. The consecutive coloured lines build up an increasingly complex picture, yet also conceal much of the layered structure in the BLT data. There, I posited that *each polyline feature in each respective BLT layer must convey a BLT identification in its entirety*. As an implication of the BLT definitions, each instance of a BLT identification should shape (circumscribe) a space, even though a single BLT identification cannot comprehensively redescribe the emergent socio-spatial structure of that space.[1] However, looking at Fig. 7.11 the vast majority of eventually *visible* lines do not shape spaces in a polygonal fashion. This is a logical effect of exactly co-located features presented in the layered fashion of a vector GIS. In fact, this aspect of vector GIS can actually complicate an effective, comprehensive and secure identification process due to the lack of immediate overview. The practice of BLT Mapping will alert one to the visual problem, making it especially worthwhile to reveal the layered data structure resulting from a completed identification process.

Fig. 8.1 provides a schematic (exploded view diagram) representation of the BLT data in GIS of a familiar example. A 3D representation of a terraced house on a street with a back yard sits at the centre (for clarity the neighbouring houses are not drawn). Although we only consider ground level (Chapter 1), having the roof complement the image merely aids to

---

1. In mapping practice, the only exception could result from the edge effects of a delimited sample area cutting off features and therefore any associated BLT identifications.

conjure up a sense of material empirical familiarity with encountering a house. After all, this material empirical reality BLT Mapping redescribes on top of the outline base plan (here in black). Fig. 8.1 uses the same colour scheme as Fig. 7.11: Type 1 is brown, Type 2 is green, Type 3 is red, and Type 5 is blue. At the top, the BLTs are represented in an exploded view of GIS layers. The light grey guidelines show how the BLT features would be co-located in the GIS to make up the house and plot outlines. This reveals that, as necessary and expected, the original and discrete Type 1 identification of the built volume of the house remains intact when further identifications follow. The same applies for all BLTs.

The lower section of Fig. 8.1 makes this more technical. It collates the GIS layers (symbolised by the horizontal black hairlines) on top of each other, following the line of the street that meets the front of the house. The

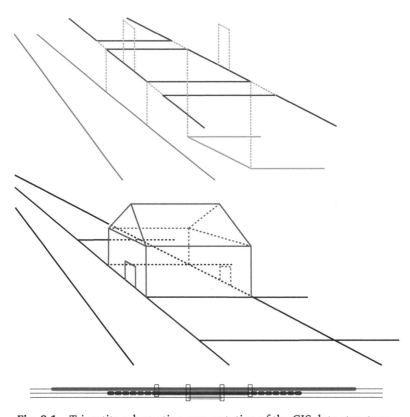

Fig. 8.1 Tripartite schematic representation of the GIS data structure.

This is a tripartite schematic representation of the GIS data structure resulting from conducting BLT mapping. From top to bottom: an exploded view of BLT identifications; a 3D representation of a mapped terraced house; a schema of the data structure in GIS of the front of the house (see in-text discussion).

black rectangles represent the nodes (not shape-giving vertices) of the BLT data representing the front of the house. These nodes comprise the start and end points of the polylines used to identify BLTs, and the points where separate BLT identifications first meet and eventually depart. (Two or more BLTs following the course of a line do not turn any vertices covered along the way into BLT nodes.) Because the BLT identification is conducted with *ArcMap's* tracing tool, it is ensured that each polyline is exactly co-located with the outline base plan and other BLTs. As an effect of the BLT nodes, the front of the house becomes divided into three complete socio-spatial descriptions of sections of boundary line: the doorway itself, and the wall left and right of the doorway up to the corners. These three emergent elements are all topologically distinct and thus uniquely determined socio-spatially structured boundary line segments.

I derive three kinds of socio-spatially structured boundary line segments from the co-location of BLT identifications as primary analytical units:

1. *Topological segments*: a topological segment refers to each unique instance of a combination of BLT identifications persisting for any length along a boundary line in the outline base plan;
2. *Boundary segments*: a boundary segment refers to any continuous part of boundary line contained in the outline base plan;
3. *Topological sides*: a topological side distinguishes the occurrence when a continuous length of (a)BLT identification(s) determine(s) the socio-spatial description of a circumscribed space from its outside (e.g. where the (outside) park meets the (inside) garden wall). This allows any shape, including rounded shapes, to have distinct 'sides'.

The topological side differs from the topological segment mainly by excluding the topological distinctions emerging from Types 2 and 4. This highlights that, to identify a Type 4 along a boundary associated with a dominant, this dominant is required to have a Type 2 along the topological side establishing that association.[2] Scrutinising Fig. 8.1 once more with these definitions in mind, the following can be noted: the

---

2. Built environment morphologies are thinkable where it is not an absolute necessity that a boundary associated with a dominant is disclosed directly by a Type 2 (entrance) to the dominant. For example, houses built on a slope could potentially have gardens which would be geospatially adjacent, but topologically detached, only to be accessible via a detour crossing unassociated boundaries. Simply put, however, this only means that such topologically undisclosed associated boundaries cannot have a Type 4 (extended facing boundary). This impossibility formally describes that entering the area circumscribed by the associated boundaries does not lead to an opportunity to cross into the dominant also. Only rules of thumb could cause

topological segment, redescribing the front door of the house as a Type 1-2-5 combination, occurs along the topological side of the Type 1-5 combination.

Having exposed the BLT data structure, the definitions of these derivative segments allow the division of BLT data in sections according to differing logics. The resultant analytical units can each inform and structure further investigation and interpretation of BLT data in their own ways. Moreover, depending on future purpose, these units could be invested with additional appropriate information (e.g. GIS attributes) for a fuller description of each concrete element. Only the topological segment, however, conveys the *full* socio-spatial redescription of any part of the built environment. That does not take away the analytical use of each BLT in isolation. While BLTs may not refer to the full social empirical reality of each boundary, BLTs still circumscribe each separate subdivision (space) of the built environment (*nota bene*, the data structure of the outline base plan has not been set up to do this). Therefore BLTs can become a heuristic vehicle for investigating the socio-spatial composition of subdivisions.

The topological segments, as unique instances of BLT combinations, form the *smallest meaningful elements* out of which the ontology intrinsic to each city (Chapter 5) is composed. Topological segments are now considered as materially present elements of socio-spatial significance for the (developmental) process of inhabitation. Their shapes and connections form the topological and morphological built environment configuration. The urban built environment composition consists of the total count and variety of the unique BLT combinations that occur. This count and variety thus supply an immediate (statistical) characterisation of any study area as a whole. While examining the BLT data structure emphasises mostly topological properties, note that the topological structure still concurs with the preserved topographical morphology that the boundaries on the outline base plan represent. This keeps the material and spatial formation of shapes and their dimensional properties within direct analytical reach. Conducting BLT Mapping thus demonstrably supports both topological and morphological analysis of socio-spatial significance.

erroneous identifications of Type 2s (false positives due to flawed or restricted information). Overall it would be a logical assumption that adjacent associated boundaries are disclosed by a Type 2. Additional sources (functional, architectural and topographic) may support identifications of associated boundaries without Type 4s. Apropos, there is no contradiction with sequences of associated boundaries featuring sequences of Type 4s.

Visualising BLT data

The trouble with the usual layered visualisation within GIS (Fig. 7.11) is that co-located features are obscured. Often there is the option of semitransparency, but this cannot offer a solution here. The colours would immediately confuse and any lines where the same BLT occurs twice (inside and outside identification) would be indistinguishable. This urges for a better way of visualising BLT data holistically at the synchronic time-slice level. An effective visualisation would enable the interpretive reading of the map showing the BLT combinations of all topological segments. This would at least provide a basis for intricately contextualised redescriptions of (aspects of) an urban built environment complex.

To this end a geocomputational Java plugin for *ArcGIS* was commissioned.[3] The hypothesised visual operation would function on the basis of proportionate scaling and displacing the polyline features of each BLT feature class (GIS layer), in respect of the particular polyline features with which it is co-located (across layers) by the thickness of the line symbology in the *ArcMap*'s data frame. The tool would enable a visualisation of each BLT identification laterally adjacent to each other (horizontally stacked). This implies each shape is uniformly expanded or shrunk slightly, to present each BLT nested inside each other consistently (non-circumscriptive BLTs placed along the outside of the subdivision they specify). This specification requires detailed and complex rules-sets to effectuate the polyline hierarchy that would scale and displace features respecting geographical locations and spatial morphology. After all, scaling (up or down) and displacing (left or right) must avoid that the areas of subdivisions cross, and must ensure that all polylines remain in their respective stacks. What good is a BLT map if confusing detachments and jumbles of lines make it unreadable? In other words, the line visualisation must maintain the topographically intelligible essence of the original topological and morphological relations.

The complexity of developing a resolve for such geospatial visualisation rule-set proved to attract a greater resource than I had available. Therefore, for the purpose of methodological demonstrations, a more accessible first-sweep geocomputational approach to producing BLT maps was attempted. This retains only the principle of displacement,

3. All programming and software development is executed by Dr Andrew Evans, University of Leeds, creating software specifications that support working with theoretical and conceptual stipulations in this book.

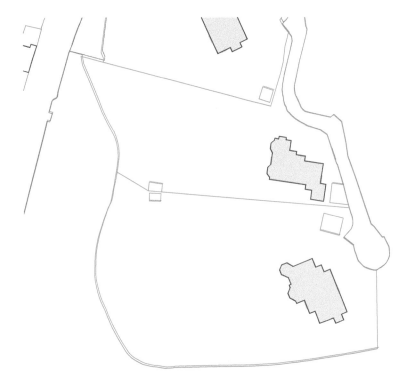

Fig. 8.2   Section of the BLT map for Winchester MM based on Fig. 7.11.

Note how the lines show multiple colours following roughly the same (displaced) course. (Based
on original OS MasterMap data © Crown Copyright 2013. All rights reserved. An Ordnance Survey
(EDINA) supplied service.)

but on layer-by-layer rather than feature-by-feature level. Consequently,
line intersections and disjunctions cannot be avoided, but will at best be
minimised. Nonetheless, when shifting each entire layer (feature class)
in respect of the others, it would be possible to see all BLT data as individual identifications on a single time-slice at once. Fig. 8.2 exemplifies
this preliminary usable solution on the basis of Fig. 7.11's data selection.
Chapter 9 will elaborate on the use and merits of such BLT maps.

Diachronic data structure and comparisons

Conventional representations of the (urban) built environment would
convey an image where socio-cultural or functional categories can be
readily recognised through their topographical expression. Making
explicit the socio-spatial significance of the material presence of

boundary differentiations with BLT Mapping has the initial downside of complicating this conventional built environment image. Where a synchronic situation might still allow for an intelligible visualisation of a colourful constellation of lines (Fig. 8.1), diachronic multiplication of all BLTs across time-slices muddles one's vision with jumbles of lines in 28, 42, or more distinct shades.

Fig. 8.3 demonstrates that despite the advantages of vector data in promoting clarity and rigour for work on spatial morphology, the diachronic image of three outline base plans simultaneously is already very complex. On close inspection, it is much easier to see quite

Fig. 8.3 The Winchester historical layers of outline base plans simultaneously displayed.

These are the Winchester outline base plans overlaid for the test area: MM (red); OS1872 (blue); and 1550s (green). The major changes from 1550 to 1872 are formed by the removal of the city wall, widening of the bridge and the intensification of built-up space, e.g. along the river. The major changes from 1872 to the present concern infrastructural adjustments to street lines, some major new buildings and clearing up the mishmash of development along the west bank of the river. Some of the plot boundaries along Chesil Street are amongst the most persistent features. (Partly derived from OS MasterMap (© Crown Copyright 2013. All rights reserved. An Ordnance Survey (EDINA) supplied service); original scans: © Crown Copyright and Landmark Information Group Limited 2013. All rights reserved. 1872 and original plans, reproduced courtesy of the Winchester Research Unit).

specific relations between the time-slices than would be possible with the usual semi-transparent raster overlays of historical GIS (described in Chapter 6). Vector data offer enhanced flexibility to pinpoint and distribute data of events or inhabitants from social history by connecting these directly to spatial data features. Linking socio-historical information to spatial features in BLT Mapping means they are immediately contextualised by association with the interrelated socio-spatial position of the material boundaries. Nevertheless, beyond focusing on small areas to untangle such specific relations, it is still very difficult to get an overall impression of the development processes from this vector data. If this applies to the relative simplicity of a sequence of three outline base plans, it is wishful thinking that human perception alone could achieve much when all BLTs are engaged on each time-slice.

This means that for effective diachronic analyses we require the aid of geocomputational tools. When Chapter 7 addressed the preparation of outline base plans and the identification of BLTs across different time-slices, I argued that, to some extent, the coincidence of built features through time is a matter of interpretation. The most recent period (MM for Winchester) is used as the most accurate mapping available. However, uncritical projection of mapped features into the GIS layers representing the past is exceedingly contentious on the basis of limited and disparate documentation. As a consequence, I adopted a practice in which only features that end up tantalisingly closely resembling each other through time would be copied from the more recent period. Consequentially, for BLT identification purposes, all boundary segments retaining the same identification should remain identical data features in each time-slice to avoid confusing and unwarranted discrepancies introduced by manual work (Fig. 7.17). In practice, multitudes of small changes on top of error margins resulting from geospatial processing still imply that the spatial data contains many near matches that do not coincide.

As a consequence, in diachronic analysis and comparison, any spatial analytical tool would need to incorporate a buffer zone. The smallest difference matters in computational terms, whereas the human mind would regard various features as sufficiently similar to be a continuation or partial match of the same line. Similarity and closeness are computationally usually a much greater challenge to detect than intersections and exact matches. Moreover, similarity requires that just *how* things are similar is determined. In the case of diachronic analysis there will usually be a mismatch between the topographical compositions of two time-slices, even though part could be regarded as the same boundary lines persisting. A (deliberate) change to the physical urban environment can only be decided by considering chosen similarity variables (such as line location or shape) incrementally. At some point any difference is then no longer down to interpretation or geospatial error, but treated as 'true' change.

Not all data created in the preparation processes is suitable for meaningful change detection. Although the outline base plan may convey the comprehensive shape of all the subdivisions within the urban built environment (Fig. 8.3), the data structure of the outline base plan is fully contingent on the editing practices that produced it. That is to say, the outline base plan's separate GIS data features do not impart any specific meaning. Also, the outline base plan may still contain super-fluous data that eventually were not taken forward in BLT identifications. The BLT identifications themselves would only enable comparisons on a polyline feature-by-feature basis, which may only flag up similarities and differences from entire identification to entire identification across time-slices.

The first consideration of change detection, however, is to compare the boundary line topography between time-slices. Are the boundary lines either co-located or in the (very) close vicinity of a boundary line in another time-slice? This refers to the existence of change in materialised sites of differentiation across time, rather than change in meaningful analytical units. In data terms, we establish incremental buffers to look for similarity and difference in any part of boundary polyline topography between time-slices (cf. Pierce & Weiss 2010), not changes in the topo-logical composition of any polyline features created for the purpose of BLT Mapping.

The best way to start such change detection is to merge all BLTs into the 'final base plan' (Chapter 7) and to explode those polylines into the straight-line segments (i.e. the smallest possible boundary segments) between vertices (the points shaping the polyline). Then, set a buffer zone along the path of each straight-line segment and layer multiple final base plans (see Fig. 8.4). In this way, the existence of any other line segment falling (for a percentage) within the buffer zone (including intersecting the source line segment) could be detected as similar. Any line segment outside or cutting the buffer would be detected as diffe-rence, since this indicates the boundary line is moving farther away. Subsequently, one may compare 'similar' line segments for orientation (degrees from cardinal north), i.e. the direction of their path. Those that fall within a margin of tolerance for deviating from the source can be selected as similar.

A further complication is then that the buffer might be signifi-cantly larger than each line segment (especially in intricately shaped

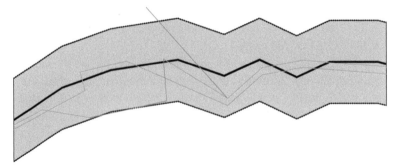

Fig. 8.4 Computational hypothesis for historical polyline data change detection.

A fictional source polyline (thick black) with a buffer zone (grey), with potentially similar polylines: the green line segments fulfil the similarity requirements; the three red ones do not.

morphologies). Especially in (semi-automated) vectorisation processes, such as tracing processed *Adobe Illustrator* data, some tiny elements of ruggedness could become incorporated in a polyline. Therefore, change detection must observe a minimum length per line segment, below which a dramatic difference in orientation should be disregarded (Fig. 8.4: green line, left side).

Once this approach of detecting similarities has been carried out, the line segments that are sufficiently similar between any two time-slices should be selected for the next step. Now the selection constitutes a historically persisting boundary line composition that can serve as the basis to inventory the BLT identifications that intersect or coincide, and the topological segments that co-locate. Comparing results across pairings of time-slices allows the tracking of change in BLT identifications and combinations that the same boundary lines partook in, and what topographical and BLT change they connected to. To further assist analysis and interpretation, such change detection software could enable visualisations that express kinds of persistence and volatility found through time. BLT change detection analysis can start revealing deeper socio-spatially significant patterns of urban developmental rhythms, transformations, constructions, removals and recurrences, both as an interpretive counterpart to urban morphological processes and to aid their further specification.

Unfortunately there seems to be no definitive solution to the problem of comparing the composition and geometric shape of vector topologies in a GIS environment. The most promising direction for measuring the differences between two datasets of polylines may in part be based on a geocomputational implementation of the Hausdorff distance.

Hausdorff distance basically measures how similar two geometries are (which in practice usually means how close all nodes and vertices of one dataset are located to all nodes and vertices in another). This is being developed to include extended buffers (Min et al. 2007) and topological connections (Li & Goodchild 2010, 2011). Software solutions have been developed to measure Hausdorff distances,[4] but these are not readily available as *ArcGIS* tools.

The current purposes for this technique focus mainly on conflating divergent datasets on the same phenomenon. Except that diachronic outline base plans cover the same area of geographical space, it is not a necessity that boundary datasets convey different versions of essentially the same information.[5] For BLT Mapping it would merely be a first step towards analytical change detection. One would need to assure that geocomputational Hausdorff distance development will support the interpretive urban morphological questions that combinations of topographical and BLT change detection may address. Ultimately, setting the buffer and tolerances that guide automatic change detection is an interpretive decision. Still the researcher decides when changes are deemed large enough to be treated as urban development instead of georectification and vectorisation error margins.

While change detection puts stringent demands on geocomputation, without it we are not left completely empty handed. The results of any analysis conducted on a separate synchronic spatial dataset can be systematically compared across time-slices (see below). Visualisations such as Fig. 8.3 still support the selection of areas of interesting change to manually investigate the specific combinations, layout and connections between e.g. BLTs and topological segments (Chapter 9 exemplifies such a manual approach).

Although more laborious to execute and limited in complexity, manual practice could still serve as a basis to ascribe and locate (attribute) case-specific socio-historical information onto intricate BLT data. This advances socio-historical opportunities for visualisation and analysis based on modern maps (see Bisschops 2012) and historical raster overlays. The BLT data structure thus offers various first steps in questioning and elucidating very specific society–space relationships in the past, and socio-spatial processes through time (cf. Griffiths 2013).

4. Examples of such solutions can be found online at *ST_HausdorffDistance* (n.d.), and *JTS Topology Suite* (n.d.).
5. *ArcGIS* itself does offer a tool to detect changes made to the editing of features and symbols in different versions of a map with Layer Snapshot tools (*ArcGIS Resources: Identify feature changes between map editions* 2012).

Developing more appropriate geocomputational tools can further advance the rigorous comparison of the socio-spatial structure of the built environment through time. This is important because only dia-chronically can the exact role (significance) of materialisation in the mutual constitution of settlements and inhabitants (Chapters 2 and 3), as well as effects of urban planning and development, be revealed in the long-term. Synchronically analysis is restricted to how spatial-material frames co-constitute speculative social opportunities (affordance and experience), and formally describe how actual events or activities are accommodated in-the-world (Chapters 3 and 6).

Understanding proposed analytical measures

In the following sections I will hypothesise an array of potential analyt-ical measures which could form the basis for devising geospatial tools. Before this review of opportunities identified on the basis of the BLT data structure, I consider why and how working with (experimenting and exploring) quantitative measures can be meaningful. What can quantitative analysis add above and beyond the intrinsic interpretive value already contained in the BLT identifications and BLT maps (formal redescriptions) themselves?

BLT Mapping shows how the affordance and experience of encounters, interactions, and development is socio-spatially conditioned and contextualised by the specific structure of a materially emergent place (e.g. city). The formal socio-spatial redescriptions of each sub-division qualitatively characterise the potential for any use, movement or development for each occupiable location, and contextualise that location's interrelated socio-spatial position within the configuration. The socio-spatial condition and location may narrow down likely functions of materialised spaces (Sayer's (2000) spatial (in)dependence), but BLT Mapping will not reveal the probability of a particular activity occurring within any particular space (see Chapter 6). BLT Mapping *makes explicit the (affording and affecting) conduciveness of the materially present characteristics of the differentiations that make and shape the built environment.* The GIS data structure that contains the intricacies of the characteristics and properties of a BLT-mapped built environment can only readily be exposed on larger scales (the whole dataset at once) with the aid of computational spatial analysis.

Moudon (1997: 8) said that 'all morphological analysis is carried out for the purpose of theory building'. Insofar as theory building means hypothesising, the analyses I will propose serve the same purpose. Descriptions and explanations (the how and why) of the socio-spatial signature of inhabiting a particular built environment, and its influence on urban life and development, could be hypothesised by assessing the outcomes of spatial analyses. Through evaluation of the functioning aspects of urban built environments that are deemed desirable, it could also serve to hypothesise an informing or aspirational (guiding or prescriptive) theory of city design. Utilising diachronic urban development, including knowledge of implemented urban development plans, hypotheses could be formed about the impact of urban planning interventions and/or structuring power relations, as well as comparing normative designs to their emplaced lived effects.

Whatever the hypothesis-building purpose of the analysis, each analytical measure should be meaningful in the light of the theoretical framework and the associated interpretive realm of the levels of socio-spatial significance: the dimensional, locational, and aggregative context (Chapter 5). A focus on redescription will reveal simple relations and compositions on a local micro-scale, while operationalising the levels of socio-spatial significance through spatial analysis can progress a deeper constitutive understanding of the ontology intrinsic to cities and across multiple scales. Spatial analysis does not produce deterministic insights. Instead, appropriately designed computational tools aid *interpretive explorations*. Computational tools extract patterns, rhythms, and compositions of interconnectivity, position, and variety, coherent and heterogeneous aggregates, persistent similarities and marked changes, etc. that are inherently present in any urban built environment. They equip these outcomes for comparison across urban built environments.

So, geocomputational spatial analyses help the careful exploration of the characteristics of the large and complex BLT datasets created. These explorations can ground interpretations and hypotheses. While there might be an enormous variety of spatial analyses that could operate on empirical properties alone, within the comparative study of the inhabited urban built environment as I propose, any analytical measure must be justified by being theoretically, thus interpretively, comprehensible. The empirical BLT data structure itself has morphological, topological and geometrical properties, as can be expected from geographical representations. All aspects of these empirical properties can in principle be used for spatial analysis. However, only a *theoretical grounding* for isolating empirical properties within the BLT data structure ensures that an analytical measure can produce interpretable results.

Resources for developing analytical tools will always be limited. Therefore, the consideration of theoretical grounding should guide developmental efforts, not the fact that empirical properties could be analysed. The question of whether the selected property of the spatial data structure is quantifiable to the appropriate benefit of interpretive analyses always needs answering. Only then can interpretive exploration be argued to serve comparative and constitutive socio-spatial understanding of the material presence of boundaries in the process of inhabitation.

Simply put, we can only get understanding out of data that is already invested in those data. Indeed, the intensive study enforced by BLT Mapping practice already leads to a different and better understanding of certain socio-spatial patterns particular to the case study. Some of the rules of thumb in Chapter 7 express a crude initial understanding of the built environment, resulting from working with case-specific data constraints. While the levels of socio-spatial significance put down constraints that create interpretive potential for each spatial analytical measure, their application is not predestined to produce useful or intelligible results. Analytical outcomes could prove indeterminate or insignificant. Experimenting alone can determine the true value of spatial analysis. In that sense, this chapter is an invitation for the continued development of analytical measures and toolkits to exploit BLT data. Only some preliminary geocomputational functionality could be tested in this book to demonstrate the merits of this methodology (Chapter 9). The approach to selecting analytical proposals in this chapter aims to prevent the arbitrariness of a fully experimental approach exploiting empirical data properties alone. Nonetheless, it is not an exhaustive predetermination of analytical and interpretive potential. The risk of ineffectual techniques or meaningless outcomes cannot be precluded, and is only concluded from a lack of inferential value.

To put this in context, space syntax (Chapter 6) recognises and faces similar problems of spatial data complexity. The topological possibilities of constructing a configuration in a limited grid can already be beyond intellectual grasp (Hillier 2007). The situation at hand is mirrored by Franz & Wiener (2008: 577), who limit their efforts to the spatial properties of the isovist as devised in space syntax:

> [T]he mathematical combination of a few basic isovists and visibility graph measurands results in a multitude of further description variables. The meaning and relevance of such descriptors are difficult to estimate a priori. A brute-force analytical approach is

practically unfeasible, and, moreover, it severely increases the risk of producing statistical artifacts. On the other hand, cautious conservative correction methods based on the number of comparisons might completely mask effectively existing effects.

This effectively means that research faced with such a problem, though having the luxury of experimental freedom, will have to decide on a rationale to restrict and direct research efforts.

The agenda of *applied* space syntax techniques has obscured the original potential for analytical theory, and therefore development has concentrated on very particular configurational aspects (an 'access topology') of its theoretical ideas. Recently Marcus (2007, 2010) has developed an approach to measure what he calls 'spatial capital'. This goes some way to further qualify space syntactic analyses to open an ideas exchange and integration with urban geographical and urban morphological analytical measures, e.g. plots and buildings. Here the space syntax concern with *accessibility* is connected with *density* and *diversity*, e.g. access to density and access to diversity, which leads to improvements in the evaluation of the economic exchange-value and use-value of areas in urban complexes. 'Although not all needs require high spatial capital, on the most fundamental level this seems to be what cities offer: the support of the generic need for people and societies to access differences as a means for social, cultural, and economical development' (Marcus 2010: 39).

Marcus suggests space syntax should expand from its narrow definitions of experiential space (notably convex space and axial lines) to incorporate legal spatial notions of plots and properties, which when captured in those terms would serve assessment of economic resilience afforded by urban space. Marcus' ideas connect to the analytical measures that I will propose. Yet, my 'non-economic' emphasis remains on how the material presence of e.g. plots, properties, buildings and public spaces affords and experientially structures socio-spatial interaction. Nonetheless, as shall be shown, accessibility (restricted and enabled by boundaries), density of features (differentiating spatial opportunities at various scales), and the diversity of built differentiations (across the entire urban built environment and any subsets) make important analytical bases that unify along affordance and affect in urban form.

Franz & Wiener's (2008) solution – to direct and restrict analytical effort – is exactly the kind of 'intermediate' theory-driven approach to exploration that is being proposed here. In continuation, this chapter will employ Chapter 5's levels of socio-spatial significance to select and inform quantifiable spatial measures to exploit BLT data.[6] Analyses then marry the empirical identification and the interactional operation captured in the BLT definitions to their presence in the contextual interplay of the 'territorial', 'regulative', and 'entity adherent' aspects of these interpretive levels. The final implication of this interplay is that the levels of socio-spatial significance simultaneously confine the interpretations of analytical outcomes. Each particular analytical measure might give more prominence to any single level of socio-spatial significance, but this does not contradict the continued relevance to the others. The rudimentary understandings analyses bring about are afforded by the complete theoretical framework, but do not reproduce it as the BLT data is intrinsically particular to each time-space specific case. The value or significance of each measure to each specific case cannot be foreseen.

Analytical information in the ontology intrinsic to the city

Any tool at least originates from its compatibility with the BLT data structure (Fig. 8.1). As a first step, therefore, is a tool to acquire basic knowledge of what the BLT dataset contains. This entails geospatial recognition of the co-locations and connections, the count and combination, of BLTs relative to one another.[7] Such inventory would yield an overview of how many, and which, BLTs co-locate with any other, as well as how many and which BLTs are connected to another. While the basic statistics for the dataset are of interest, in itself the overview might not be particularly intelligible. However, broken down heuristically, per BLT or predetermined BLT combination, the visualisation of these selections on the BLT map could support global interpretations of patterned

6. A keen reader would find several concurrences between the 'measurands' used by Franz & Wiener (2008) and the measures presented here. It is stressed that, while to a large extent coincidental, this is part explained by the similar empirical properties of the data used. Franz & Wiener's aim is, however, to improve the theorisation and congruent definition of measurands for space syntactic isovist analysis. This is disparate from analysing how the material presence of spatial layout structures affordance and experience here, in which human visual perception plays an *indistinguishable* role.
7. Accessing the same inventorying information for arbitrary selections of boundary segments or geographical areas within which BLTs are located would be desirable to increase flexibility. Currently, this would require the manual creation of a selective area of mapped boundaries, because such spatial selections are not inherent to the data. The same limitation applies to other analytical measures.

occurrence utilising the formal redescriptors of the built environment (Chapter 9 exemplifies global dataset statistics).

The topological segment (as above: the smallest meaningful element in the dataset) can make important improvements to knowing the BLT dataset. To work with the full collection of emergent topological segments, a geospatial tool must detect or 'section' the BLT data into individual topological segments. Sectioned topological segments would essentially produce a new classification of full socio-spatial boundary descriptors and their relations to each other. Although a hypothetically incomprehensible total number of unique topological segments could result from the BLT combinations occurring,[8] the constraints within the BLT definitions are expected to keep the variety at a relatively manageable level in each real-world case.

This variety of topological segments, together with the number of occurrences of each unique one and the variety and number of their connections, would make a quantitative expression of the socio-spatial signature of a city (or the ontology intrinsic to a city) (see Chapter 5). When the variety of topological segments and connections is expressed proportionately (i.e. in percentages), the resultant values may be used comparatively, e.g. as an ordinal ranking, taking into account the magnitude of difference between proportional stakes. An initial geocomputational tool was developed in-house, to produce these global statistics to index some key information contained in any entire BLT dataset (i.e. as if the data selection comprises an entire city or intentional section). Chapter 9 will briefly discuss the initial results of this.

The next, still hypothetical, step would be to literally dissect the original BLT data according to the topological segments, and to make each kind of topological connection selectable. Dissection would enable compound selections and geographical visualisations of the spatial distribution (occurrence) and variety of topological segments and their topological connections. From this point onwards, topological segments can be used as *derivative analytical units* supporting further specified and selective spatial analyses as the smallest meaningful elements. Without such data dissection all analytical measures based on topological segments below remain hypothetical.

---

8. A tentative approximation of the *minimum* number of possible combinations is given based on combinations of two BLTs. Taking combinations of two out of the 13 available types (excluding V as specifier), stipulating that the order in which the two occur is not double counted (13*12 over 2 = 78), but double occurrences of a single type are possible (+13 = 91), with two types (entrances) only occurring with either one of two possible others (-11-11= 69). This could multiply when including combinations of more than two BLTs.

Indexing of topological segments can include Vs, even though these should not influence the statistics in which unique BLT combinations express the ontology intrinsic to each city. Instead, Vs can be used to better appreciate the extent of the effect of visibility and preservation issues within the original onsite (or (remote) sensing technologies) data acquisition, as well as distinguishing between data structures of equally well-preserved built environments. That is, distinguishing a relatively informally shaped urban built environment from a strict physically enforcing urban built environment (notwithstanding that socio-cultural rules concerning actual use and function could be equally strong in both instances). Calculating the percentage over the total length of topological segments, and/or their proportional presence in density counts (see section on distances and density below), will indicate something about the extent and the kind of role virtual boundaries play.

Proposing analytical measures: dimensional context

From the dimensional context it is immediately clear that size and extent across geographical space matters. Interpersonal distance setting, and territoriality as well as appropriate sizes for certain activities and their interactional negotiation, will influence at which distance to each other boundaries will occur and thus how large the subdivisions are that they form. The first quantifiable measures therefore consider the distance between topological segments, their length and position.

Distances and densities

The distance between all topological segments is best approached by measuring and visualising densities over Euclidian space using algorithms, which include a method of inverse distance weighting, to produce a 'heat map' of how many or how few topological segments occur. Inverse distance weighting does not only count points across a radius, but takes into account how close a point is to the starting cell. For this, the centroid (midpoint) on the polyline of the topological segment could be used, which implies that usually (assuming most built environments are composed of series of relatively convex spaces) fewer points can be expected when the length of the topological segments is larger. In principle, the way to interpret such heat maps would be to regard higher values as more intensely differentiated built-up space, implying more intense encounters between socio-spatial systems. It allows making the distinction between (areas of) settlement with propinquity to let socio-spatial systems reside spaciously or restrictively.

A logical starting point would be to try calculating such densities per arbitrary unit, such as a hectare (i.e. differentiations in approximately a 56.42m radius). However, it would be more telling to select a surface value that has a meaning relative to the data. This could be the largest subdivision available in the case study area, or an average surface area of Type 1 (closing boundaries being the strongest inward-looking extraction from the surrounding environment). Using such values gives a view of the differentiation across the entire case area in direct relation to the largest occupiable area without further differentiation or related to an average of the strongest seclusions. Such relative measures are preferable for comparative studies, as *ceteris paribus* a built environment with larger shapes will necessarily avoid high density of boundary differentiations.

This distance measure could subsequently incorporate the diversity of the topological segments occurring in the heat map. The diversity of topological segments leads to an insight into the heterogeneity (complexity) of socio-spatial differentiation across space. The less diversity in the topological segments, the more monotonous and evenly conducive an area can be expected to be. Similarly, densities could be calculated for any particular BLT combination. An easy example would be the density of entrances. At the same time difference in the density of the same topological segment indicates probable socio-spatial diversification of the kind of interaction that is structured locally. Ideally, the computational tool used not only visualises the density pattern, but makes it possible to select and thus inspect the individual features in ordinal classes of density. In this way, the characteristics of the occurrence of absolutely measured density patterns themselves can be studied in their place-specific context.

Essentially, all analyses on boundary diversity and characteristics here link the dimensional to the locational context (first and second level of socio-spatial significance). The gradual plot of a heat map is fundamentally a display of clusters of higher and lower density across specified surface resolutions. This therefore directly relates to the aggregative context (third level of socio-spatial significance), creating a specific persistence and coherence in how differentiation occurs, which would be part of emplaced lived experience. Exploration in the aggregative context can lead to further discoveries by conducting density analyses to identify emergent heterogeneous or homogeneous areas within an urban built environment, or to describe the pattern for the entire complex. The first allows internal comparisons across space, and the second comparison between cases. It is through comparison internally or across cases (or time periods) that interpretive rigour moves beyond redescription towards (constitutive) insight.

Lengths and sizes

Density is not the only way to let the dimensional context inform analytical measures. While possibly the most abstract type of distance, a geometrically more complex analysis could consider the measured minimum distance one would travel from a specified topological segment to another, while remaining within a single subdivision (i.e. respecting the shape of bounded space). In this way, for example, an indication of the distances from the entrance to a building to the access to any of its associated boundaries would be revealed. More complex questions could address how soon one would reach an entrance to a dominant configurative complex from an open boundary that partakes in the circulation system. These are ways into discussing the absolute distances between relatively public and private (more and less secluding) areas.

Simply inventorying the lengths of all topological segments (the continuity of a particular relationship between two spaces) can assess the strength with which that relationship determines the occupation of those spaces. Relating topological segment length to the lengths of separate BLTs could help uncover socially determinant particularities. How often does a BLT identification become differentiated with different BLT combinations relative to its length? This could indicate which BLT operations are most prone to socio-spatial volatility and constancy, and of what kind, thus placing the occurrence of particular BLT operations in internally and externally comparative perspective. Further, cases where the longest lengths often include materially impermeable properties could indicate segregating qualities to how spaces can be occupied. If the longest lengths often involve continuous Type 5s, this indicates a relatively strong enforcement of certain directional interconnections within a built environment. Combining the density counts of occurrence across space with the relative density of topological segments along a BLT identification's length will indicate which BLT operations might, due to their especially protean or volatile nature, play a causal role in high densities.

Chapter 9 introduces a geocomputational density tool (sourced in-house) to measure the average length of a BLT that can be *expected* per square metre calculated over the rectangular area of the total data selection. The example given relates Type 6 density to the density of all occurrences of any single BLT within that rectangular area. Ordinal ranks based on percentages of such a measure make heuristic use of the BLT as a primary analytical unit. We obtain an indication of the relative importance of each BLT operation in constituting the subdivisions of the built environment.

The polygonal surface areas of subdivisions resulting from a specified BLT could also be used as a heuristic vehicle. Comparing subdivision to subdivision, how a specified BLT serves to structure interaction opportunities in areas partly determined by its own particular operation produces a sense of the relative influence that is exerted by such socio-spatial differentiations within the system. By only looking at pre-selected topological segments that co-locate with each specified subdividing BLT, a more local and contextually relative influence of that BLT operation can be revealed. Note that classifying merely the absolute measures of surface areas resulting from subdivisions would substitute an analysis of space[9] for an analysis of boundaries. Such a measure could become interpretable within the framework of boundary concepts when combining differences in size with the topological segments involved in composing them. As topological segments qualify and constrain the interaction opportunities that occur in space, it can be of interest if particularly structured space can be related to relative sizes of their persisting influence. While not based on geocomputation, Chapter 9 will provide an example of making this last possibility explicit on the basis of a Type 6 operation in Chunchucmil.

Constitutively speaking, the distances, densities, lengths and sizes are the result of distance setting (creating territories) associated with societal negotiations, activities, personal and cultural 'territorial' patterns (see Hall 1959, 1968). Such negotiations include exerting power and control over space, but are distinct from how power and control are exerted, which is not always about dimensions. Because territoriality can be expressed by how particular differentiations are related

---

9. There are many opportunities for combining this with additional information sources on e.g. architectural volumes and activity areas, as well as alternative conceptualisations accounting further for the social significance of size.

across space (e.g. how impermeability is mitigated by other partaking boundary operations), it supports initial understandings of relations between topological segments. The absolute values produced by the calculations related to density and size proposed here only start making sense when respecting that the occurrence of BLTs and topological segments is the result of intentional placement (construction) in space. So, BLT Mapping's approach to size is structurally but indirectly related in theory to Hall's proxemic principles. Therefore, it cannot substitute for the exactitude of the regularities in absolute radii of Hall's interpersonal distances.

The measures suggested through the dimensional context are open to additional analysis through time. Diachronic analysis would seek to compare and determine the processes in which the scales of boundaries develop, change or consolidate, and whether certain BLT operations increase or diminish their claim on space, or how distance could be used to increase or diminish socio-spatial relations as part of urban development.

Proposing analytical measures: locational context

The locational context shifts focus from the occurrence of boundaries in space (constitutively, how they came about) to the specific inter-actional interfaces connecting space, thus the characterisations of the differentiations (what boundaries do). The dimensional section already demonstrates that the interpretive value of analytical outcomes is not tied to any single level of socio-spatial significance. Similarly, the locational context suggests additional analytical measures, which when applied could be of relevance to all levels. The focus below lies in particular on the restricting and enabling qualities of boundaries following from their general (material and contextual) characteristics, collated as topological segments as well as in localised contexts. The analytical measures presented in this section are all hypothetical. Yet, Chapter 9 will engage and demonstrate the tenets of the interpretive merits of stripped down versions of some of these measures (excluding orientation) on the basis of extracting and explicating patterns visually by reading BLT maps.

Topological segments in context

Dimensional contexts can become particularly empowered by the interplay with the material property of *impermeability*, physically enforcing the secluding performance of boundaries by being closable. Closing off from the outside at will, even if this is not (fully) enforced at all times, is an important social marker that frames interaction opportunities and how interaction comes about. When closability forms a dominant boundary, the presence of boundaries associated with the dominant boundary nevertheless increases mutual interaction opportunities in relation to the socio-spatial system occupying the closable space. This works in a mutual way: the dominant boundary extending its (dominating or claiming) influence, and the boundaries associated with it ameliorating the severity of the seclusion. Boundaries in direct association with a dominant operate as intermediaries, part warding off and part inviting interaction.

This observation regarding dominants indicates a wider concern with analysing the diversity of topological segments in the locational context. Here the analytical measures address more specifically the context rather than the space (dimension) within which different topological segments occur. Where and in which (surrounding and connected) contexts are topological segments located? Here we are looking to reveal the role and prominence of topological segments through their contextual distribution across built-up space. When this is expressed in distribution patterns, any areal persistence and coherence of patterns extends this analysis into the realm of the aggregative context. The interpretation can be supported by proportional stakes in the overall diversity of topological segments, and in relation to particular others. This can be tied to density measures also. By uncovering how specified topological segments are relationally positioned, the socially dynamic composition of occupiable subdivisions and areal aggregations becomes intelligible.

Concentrating on dominant BLTs on a local level as an example – in Hillier & Hanson's (1984) terms, increasing a configuration beyond a single spatial relation – we can address the socio-spatial characteristics of dominant configurative complexes. Where (geographically) and in which situations are non-dominant boundaries directly associated with dominant boundaries? What is the socio-spatial composition of thereupon emergent configurative complexes? This can initially include indexing the number and diversity of associated BLTs and topological segments, which can be presented on an ordinal scale, and subsequently the distribution patterns of particular complexity in diversity or number. A further specification may consist of the sequence of associated boundaries and how they are connected to the outside.

Linking configurative complexes up with the dimensional context, the distance from (relevant) topological segments involved with a dominant BLT to the maximum and/or average extent of the associated boundaries becomes an appropriate analytical measure. This gives a quantitative expression on the extent of mutual interactional influence of configurative complexes, which if placed on an ordinal scale can be used comparatively. Emphasising the characterising focus of the locational context once more, this can extend into a circumscription of relative dominant influence. How many topological sides does a dominant configurative complex have, and what boundary operations form these? That is, when and what kind of boundary operations restrict which dominant configurative complexes from the outside?

Orientation

The qualifying aspects of the locational context can also be expressed in a specific morphological way. This is the principle of *orientation* brought about by the shape of boundaries. Orientations reveal preferences to how inhabitants are led towards interaction opportunities within the morphology of the urban built environment. Of particular interest is whether and how these are *restricted and enabled* by the characteristics of the boundary concerned. The principles set out below would permit the manual measuring of degrees of orientation, but recurrent and reciprocal patterns in orientations would carry the greatest significance. (Examples include: temples all symbolically facing the same way; avoiding certain directions for environmental reasons; neighbours facing each other; open space and built volume facing each other; concealing entrances from the street; etc.) With appropriate geocomputational development, orientations could receive full consideration. Meanwhile, simply reading BLT plans may give one an immediate general impression.

Orientation is again anticipated to be especially relevant in relation to dominants and configurative complexes, particularly the mutual orientation between closing boundaries (Type 1) and the directly surrounding composition of the environment. Such relations are primarily characterised by entrances (facing and extended facing boundaries, Types 2 and 4). The orientation of boundaries is perpendicular to the overall direction of a boundary's length (between start and end point) (Fig. 8.5) and could be expressed as an axis in degrees from the map's north. When relevant, the measurement should

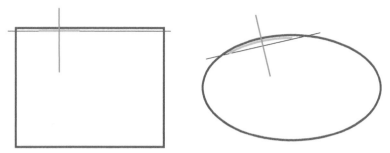

Fig. 8.5   Diagram of the main principle of measuring orientation.

This diagram hypothesises the measuring of orientation of two Type 2s as part of Type 1s. The hairline indicates the direction of the boundary, with the red arrows indicating the orientation.

include detecting on which side the dominant BLT lies to differentiate the axis' inside-out or outside-in facing orientation (i.e. from the dominant, e.g. a walled residential compound, towards its outside or vice versa).[10] The distribution (potentially combined with density) pattern of (clustered classes of) orientations could be visualised by locating them in the dataset.

Because multiple facing and extended facing boundaries can be identified per topological side, multiple orientations are a logical consequence. Therefore the analysis of orientation should include the differences in degrees that may occur within a single dominant boundary and configurative complex. Then the distinction between either single or multiple orientations in dominants only, or in dominant configurative complexes, can be made. In turn this can be connected to the context of topological segments (and configurative complex composition) in which they occur.

Building on the qualitative distinction in BLTs between facing (Type 2) and extended facing (Type 4) boundaries, the orientational relationship between them can be analysed. Indiscriminately relating all Type 4s in a configurative complex to one or all Type 2s in a dominant may prove indeterminate. Instead, the causal relation between any Type 2 and either a directly linked Type 4, or any Type 4s on a topological side, can be used. Analysis in this way distinguishes between mutual interactional orientations from the inside and from the outside respectively.

10. Taking into account the unusual situation of two adjacent dominant BLTs, the size of each subdivision might be considered for a hierarchical mutual orientation. Normally internally accessible dominants become one as a single outline.

Comparing such interrelated orientations[11] may indicate several things of interest.

First, the orientation between dominant and surroundings is stronger from the inside if Type 2(s) and Type 4(s) roughly share their orientation. Second, the mutual orientation is unambiguously diversified by a Type 2 related to multiple Type 4s on a single topological side, and ambiguously diverse with orientations on multiple topological sides. Third, mutual orientation is weakened or obstructed by strong mismatches between the orientations of causally related Type 2(s) and Type 4(s) (e.g. a house entrance not aligned with the street line).[12] This last possibility could be further examined by measuring if the other topological segments on the topological sides of the involved associated boundary do share the Type 2's orientation (e.g. a plot to the side). When such orientations are predominantly not shared, but materially emphasised associated boundaries are mitigated by Type 4s that are not aligned (e.g. gates in unaligned garden walls), the break in mutual orientation is stressed. The orientation(s) of a configurative complex is/are decided by Type 4s, which could be ambiguous if different on one topological side. In all cases the frequency of particular orientations within the same complex could be used to qualify the connectedness to a particular inside or outside relationship.

To improve the analysis of orientation from the outside, the orientation of the shape of the entire subdivision should be related to the orientation of the entrances involved. A separate piece of software (*Morphal*) has been developed in recent years to measure plot-based morphology (in roughly rectangular geometries), including compositeness and orientation (Grosso 2011). Additional development would be necessary to enable such urban morphological measures in more irregular morphologies. Note, however, there is no theoretical interpretive support for the socio-spatial significance of the exactitude of measuring orientation in degrees,[13] but orientation is theoretically supported in the interrelated way that it qualifies and articulates connections between subdivisions and aggregates.

---

11. There is obvious potential to apply orientations to conceptualisations of greater architectural detail, e.g. the front or façade of buildings and plots.
12. Note that these ways of looking at orientation bear some resemblance to the space syntactic idea of constitutedness (see Chapter 6; Van Nes & López 2007; Palaiologou & Vaughan 2012; Van Nes in prep.).
13. See Chapter 1 for a discussion on the disparate *high-level* meanings where orientation is tied to socio-culturally particular (religious, cosmological, ideological, etc.) ideas and symbolism. This analysis, however, could still be used in support of those conceptually different approaches and aims.

Paths and crossings

The locational context also manifests itself in the way that any location within a system is connected to other locations. Therefore, this involves the socio-spatial means to reach (and use) natural and social resources residing in the urban built environment (i.e. access routes to any activity, service or facility). While the metric distance of any path traversing the built environment complex could be measured and, together with e.g. the local relief topography, can assess relative closeness through mobility cost analyses and speed of travel (see e.g. Richards-Rissetto 2012; Richards-Rissetto & Landau 2014), BLT Mapping emphasises the qualitative socio-spatial differentiation of movement.[14] In boundary terms (geographically associated with metric distance), each path or route is characterised by boundary crossings. After each boundary crossing one finds oneself in a location (subdivision) that is composed of new socio-spatially restricted and enabled interaction opportunities. This essentially constitutes a relative distance between origins and destinations within a built environment. Preliminary examples of traversability and an origin-destination path (the socio-spatial effects of going from A to B) are presented in Chapter 9, while more generic analysis of path/crossing characteristics would become feasible with computational tools.

The hypothetical analytical function to index for each occupiable subdivision or location (the result of one entire single BLT identification) which topological segments and connections that occupiable subdivision is composed of, was already suggested for the dimensional context. Such effort can be repeated for the locational context, and in particular the way interaction opportunities anywhere are restricted and enabled. This could result from an overview of the number, diversity and order (connections) of topological segments (here seen as boundary crossings) per location. With such overviews, hypotheses could be addressed, such as the expectation that streets (collectively) direct one to the greatest diversity of interaction opportunities (as qualified by topological segments).

The diversity of boundary crossings for each location can be presented relative to the total unique topological segments occurring in each dataset or case. This proportional correction reveals how diverse the conglomeration of topological segments forming any subdivision is,

---

14. There are commonalities with space syntactic accessibility analysis, though disparate theory and analytical units eventually lead to markedly different measures and interpretations. I remind the reader that BLT Mapping cannot provide a probability of movement. Chapter 6 contains a discussion of such space syntax applications.

as a divisor of the diversity in the whole urban built environment. This measure would make selections of relative locational diversity insightful either in internal comparisons to all subdivisions taken together, or per BLT. The analysis of the order of topological connections of a subdivision indicates the homogeneous and heterogeneous construction of how each location is connected to other locations, and how many changes in interaction opportunities that represents. When the results of analysing the socio-spatial composition of subdivisions are plotted geographically, the morphological situation in which they occur can also be engaged.

Envisioning a path through the occupiable spaces of a built environment is like traversing beads on a string. It is clear that between any origin and destination, a number of boundary crossings is expected. Furthermore, with each crossing a particularly characterised socio-spatial situation with associated opportunities is encountered. Taken together, the amalgamation of all these socio-spatial qualifications provides the full socio-spatial redescription (or ontology) of an origin-destination path.

In principle, each topological segment could be seen as the site for a boundary crossing, even if it involves the material property of impermeability. As defined in Chapter 5, the axiom of BLTs is that they can be traversed except for the ones that are materially impermeable, and therefore closable or (negative) boundaries of unoccupiability. So, analytical explorations to socio-spatially characterise routes could easily be instructed to disregard the possibility of crossing boundaries that are materially impermeable in general, and/or avoid dominants and boundaries of unoccupiability. Designing such constraints is justified following the logic that crossings are inhibited if transformative, and/or unsolicited acts would be necessary to cross (see Chapter 5). That is, disruption of the material properties and secluding (closed-off) social properties of the configuration should prevent passing. In addition, it is not predestined that when a boundary is crossed there always is *direct* social interaction at play. That will only happen when the residing socio-spatial system is being performed at the moment of crossing into it. Yet, the self-referential understanding of the crossing as a materialised socio-spatial interface itself is not lost when this is not the case (cf. Chapter 3).

Furthermore, Chapter 7 stipulated as guiding premise for interpretive work on built environment data that all occupiable spaces must be reachable from eventually openly accessible locations. This is a bare necessity for fulfilling the requirements for the functioning and coherence of the residing society and the survival of its individual members, who require access to resources either directly or through social contacts, exchange and services. Within an inhabited urban built environment, the accessibility of resources for subsistence and maintenance has become intertwined with the arbitrariness of social structuring, mutually constituted by (encounters with) the material presence of the built spatial configuration. It logically follows that the number of potential routes accommodated in an urban built environment is almost infinite. As a consequence, the analysis of routes or paths and boundary crossings would be largely unintelligible when comprising an entire dataset at once.

Instead, paths and crossings should probably be directed by *a priori* human selection. Path analysis could always be used to assess hypothetical individual routes (cf. Chapter 3; time-geographical life-paths, time-space resources and the micro-geographies of everyday life, especially Pred 1977, 1984, 1986; example in Chapter 9). On a larger scale, it may support existing hypotheses in achieving more profound understanding, or build new hypotheses on urban functioning.

Using topological segments offers the opportunity to generalise path analysis computationally, assuming the relative distance between specified topological segments is of interest. An analytical tool could enable one to find, with or without particular crossing constraints, metrically ordered paths (respecting the polygonal borders of subdivisions) between two points, and return the number[15] and kinds of boundary crossings for these paths. Paths could entail starting from a specified topological segment to reach a particular kind of topological segment, or paths between any pairing of predetermined topological segments. In the scenario of a specified topological segment (i.e. the starting point[16]), this could help hypothesis building on particular functional intent and the efficacy of connectivity in the city. The alternative generic scenario seems complicated beyond inhabitants' comprehension. The outcomes of such generic analyses of boundary crossings would comment on the relative socio-spatial coherence between all locations in space. This readily pertains to the aggregative context.

To make path and crossing analyses less abstract, there are a multitude of possibilities to combine with additional sources on actually navigated paths,[17] land-use, activity areas, production sites and other

15. Another comparison with space syntax is possible, this time with global integration values and topological depth (see Hillier & Hanson 1984; Van Nes in prep.). The number of boundary crossings along a path is also a form of topological depth.
16. In analysis, the starting point is a particular boundary crossing. This is an analytical construct as boundaries are actually fiat sites of difference (Chapter 4) which cannot be occupied themselves.
17. Integration with space syntax's probability of viable routes could result in better understanding as well as more elaborate hypotheses. Especially in more contemporary settings, one might want to differentiate modes of transport also, making the state of technology of importance diachronically.

(economic, social, political and cultural) functions. No doubt, this will form an interesting future direction of research. For example, path analysis could tie subsistence and economical strategies to socio-spatial patterns. Furthermore, all measures suggested by the locational context are open to additional analysis through time. This would seek to compare and determine the processes in which e.g. impermeable material properties, mediation of dominants, configurative complexes, socio-spatial paths, subdivisional composition and other qualifying properties, such as orientation, persist or change within urban development. Diachronically speaking, adding data on the labour investment in creating and maintaining built subdivisions (cf. Maya construction labour: Hutson et al. 2006; Guderjan 2007) and the obliteration of materially impermeable boundaries (i.e. enabling the actual crossing or transformation by penetration of such sites, e.g. the Berlin wall) forms another way to investigate the connection to resource use and access that boundaries make explicit.

Proposing analytical measures: aggregative context

As Chapter 5 describes, the aggregative context captures the way that coherent (whether consistently homogeneous or heterogeneous) patterns emerge or become imposed from ideas and emplaced lived experience that inhabitants adhere to. The aggregative context at once holds the most simplifying power of all analyses, as it can address incremental amalgamations at all-encompassing scales within a case study in a way that the dimensional context and the locational context cannot. Simultaneously, it concerns the most intangible of ideas and interpretations, as the emergence of entities can occur in almost every way and shape, depending on each individual inhabitant. Aggregative boundary complexes are understood as contingent outcomes of the full breadth of interaction processes of inhabitation, and can attain any scale (cf. Marston 2000). The aggregative context as a level of socio-spatial significance was necessarily preceded by an understanding of constitutive processes. Because this constitutive understanding has been structurally invested in BLT data, analysis with regards to the aggregative context can contribute to the goal Marston (2000: 221) sets geographers: 'to understand how particular scales become constituted and transformed in response to social-spatial dynamics'.

Where aggregates emerge, it could be said that there is some relevance to the dimensional context again, as the size of aggregates relates to overarching socio-spatial systems appropriating and manifesting a materially constructed signature within the urban built environment. In the sense that boundaries form entities, the entity of the subdivision is already an aggregate. Similarly, the (dominant) configurative complex represents an aggregate. These are both aggregates in a restrictive sense and therefore part of the analytical measures discussed above. With the aggregative context we move into considerations of neighbourhood effects, districts and (social, functional, morphological, etc.) zones.

In practice, many opportunities for aggregative analytical measures depend entirely on the aforementioned measures, as has been indicated at various points. In the more radical freedom of overlooking the entire composite complex of the built environment, aggregative analytical measures may differ slightly. At various scales then, experimentally detecting emergent entities can diminish the complexity of how a BLT map formally redescribes all of the urban built environment at once.[18] Furthermore, aggregate entities can have their own temporal dynamics and development patterns, the complexity of which may cause blurry edges. When trying to identify aggregates it is paramount to keep in mind whether the structure of an aggregate as a whole makes sense interpretively. If there is no sensible interpretation for the pattern, chances are they are a statistical artefact (cf. Franz & Wiener 2008). All entities, including aggregates, form internally coherent and contextually dependent seclusions.

The variable scales, unfamiliar diversity and associated complexity of aggregates imply that besides experimenting with computational aids, the researcher's analytical intuition and awareness are key (cf. urban morphology, Chapter 6). The sheer complexity of all socio-spatial differentiations contained in an aggregate might regularly prove beyond unambiguous comprehension. Chapter 9's diachronic example shows how a minor preliminary approach to small-scale predetermined aggregates can be used on the basis of extracting information from reading BLT maps and a(n) (encultured) understanding of the represented topography.

Adherence to patterns

The patterns emerging or imposed from inhabitants' ideas and emplaced lived experience usually refer to larger-scale processes inhabitants feel they are part of. This could include the overarching ideas about

18. Here a connection to urban morphological plan units and regions can be made (Chapter 6).

participation, belonging and connectedness to something, which would have been consciously conceptualised and/or learned (Chapter 3). Functioning in an urban built environment complex also implies the often unconscious participation in socio-spatial systems on a grander scale. These mediate between and connect the socio-spatial systems of which we are aware we participate in. For example, we unconsciously co-constitute macro-scale transport routes to connect from home to the market. Both home and market are examples of participants' adherence to a specific kind of socio-spatial system, the coherence of which is accommodated by the inhabited built environment configuration that includes transport systems. Aggregates can be both thematically defined as socio-spatial patterns occurring on one particular scale, or, alternatively, an incremental hierarchy in which, by and large, minor emergent entities absorb into larger ones.

The ideas and experiences of coherence we adhere to are volatile and protean.[19] Ideas are not fixed. Experiences change and nurture their development, and their translation into actions does not lead to perfect intentional outcomes. This means that although it is advantageous for simplified, deeper understandings to look for aggregate entities formed by coherent patterns, such structures may occur in virtually infinite versions of order and shape. In many cases it should not even be expected that their edges are defined clearly; edges could be extremely amorphous. All detected patterns might feature partial overlaps, which would be best visualised in gradually changing zonal distributions in plans (cf. the heat map), and (partial) coincidences from forming part of multiple aggregates. Therefore, there is pertinence to combining outputs of different aggregating analyses. Their edges could either reinforce each other or show significant deviations that indicate flexible and fuzzy interplays of constitutive socio-spatial factors. There is no *a priori* way of knowing all the different forms of coherence.

Uncovering consistency within an area can result from any of the topological and morphological measures discussed before. While quantitative analysis can help identify consistent patterns, the final judgment about coherence and where lack of consistency constitutes a significant break in pattern is down to the human mind. Making such a decision is

---

19. On an everyday emergent scale it combines what I do and the frequency of that (role) with how far (socio-spatially relative distance) the socio-spatial systems I participate in are removed from areas familiar to me, whilst always being exposed to ideas outside my own experience, which I could learn and that could be imposed on me. I live in a neighbourhood that is connected by a traffic artery that gets me to work, only part of which is in my neighbourhood. My neighbourhood is part of a district, which is part of a city. The city has limits but is also part of a conurbation, so what I know and what I experience are not the same, etc.

inherently subjective, even though it is guided by and confined to the current theoretical framework.

The boundary crossings discussed for the locational context provide the most radically free and potentially different aggregative analytical measure. When analysis of boundary crossings is not route dependent, it can reveal the versatility or homogeneity of the interaction opportunities accommodated throughout the spatial configuration. Analysis can assess the order in which the crossings occur, regardless of the likelihood of the route chosen. The aim is then to uncover patterned clusters within the sequential distribution of boundary crossings. When applied to the whole dataset it is not about how many boundaries are crossed, but in which order they appear. However, the larger the number of boundary crossings concerned, the more complex the rhythms in the string of steps that could be revealed. Nonetheless, this step-based approach seems interpretively shorthanded from the outset due to the randomness of hypothetical rhythmic paths. A more fruitful technique could be to focus on choice.

Focusing on choice of boundary crossings across the entire complex, the number and the diversity of choices is analysed after each boundary crossing. All paths are tried (somewhat like a dendritic maze), with possible restrictions for impermeability, dominants, negatives, or the mitigating informality of virtuality, and logically terminating at solid dominants (crossing into Type 1s). Any pattern in the options one encounters (possibly incorporating a weighting for the metric distance to the next crossing) amounts to potential interpretable consistency. At this time, to me it is unclear what the best technology to implement such 'all-to-all' analysis is. Developing a *tree hierarchy* clustering tool might be an effective way forward. Tree hierarchies could help recognise inherent limits to consistent patterns in choice options. Another way to inform such cluster analysis is by incorporating the order of the topological connections comprising how a location (occupiable subdivision) is connected to other locations. Accounting for how a location is linked into boundary crossing sequences and/or its geographical position, recurrent or persistent patterns in this topological composition could be identified. Whatever option is selected to carry out this large-scale analysis, it can be expected that limiting the variety of BLTs or topological segments that are deemed significant will improve the clarity of results as the experimental combinatorics are reduced.

Since looking for aggregate entities necessarily covers the entirety of the data selection, in aggregative analyses the relation to the world outside the data selection can be of importance. This is especially true for analysing patterns of boundary crossings as steps along routes. In a generic analysis of paths to all locations (with or without selections and constraints), an informed starting point can still be chosen. Within the confines of the dataset, an informed starting point could be formed by topological segments involving a Type 1–2 (closing and facing boundary) combination, as places where one departs from the most secluded locations towards the rest of the system. Starting outside the delimited area covered by the dataset could be informed by topological segments involving open boundaries, especially Types 5, 6 and 9 (directing, disclosing and opening boundaries). Around the geographical limits of the dataset these BLTs are particularly conducive to movement. When originating from the outside, incoming movement is necessary.

Using informed starting points, one approach would be to simply assess the number of steps (cf. space syntactic topological depth). How many steps are needed simultaneously departing from all specified starting points to cover the entire complex? In comparative perspective this could form a basic indicator for the socio-spatial differentiation one is likely to encounter traversing the urban built environment. Going further, pre-set arbitrary numbers of steps could be used to reveal which parts of the built environment can be reached in that number of steps (and how local vicinities or border areas are structured). One could also investigate if few or many steps are involved in reaching a particular location. Again employing any number of possible constraints, both the order and depth of the sequences could help position and cluster locations socio-spatially with respect to the starting point and within the entire built environment.

When clusters are identified and seem interpretable, the edges and fuzziness of the cluster in geographical space and in relation to the BLT data need to be determined. Because the boundaries are merely sites of difference which do not occupy space, any pattern 'ceases' somewhere within a subdivision. This interpretive practice bears resemblance to morphological seams (Chapter 6). The edges of zones can interpretively be associated with a contiguous line of topological segments. Through time this boundary line could persist with or without constancy in the topological segments, reinforcing the socio-spatial significance in different ways. The characteristics of zonal edges of any detected aggregates have elevated constitutive significance as they comprise aggregate sites of difference.

Although BLT data maintain morphology, the BLT data structure is not sensitive to, and expressive of, shapes. This naturally improves comparative applicability, but means that the theoretical framework lacks conceptual support for analysing particular geometrical shapes as a unit. Additional conceptualisation on this point would enrich the current approach, possibly in conjunction with architectural concepts enriching the basic material distinctions considered in this research. For example, one may hypothesise the socio-spatial significance of rectangularity and whether rectangles involve windows or decorations. As it stands, consistency and change in the BLT data structure need not affect or be replicated by architectural properties. Instead, I contend that the rudimentary socio-spatial significance captured by BLT Mapping retains the performative essence of inhabiting spatial morphology, regardless of specific shape and architecture. Vice versa, it applies that any (aggregative) pattern detected within the current data structure that remains unintelligible could become intelligible when integrating supplementary (architectural or shaping) aspects of the urban fabric. When analysing, one should always be aware of the interpretive limitations imposed by what has been theorised.

If there is information available on the zonal divisions (including land-use) of a city, it seems advantageous to work with these in conjunction (cf. Stanley et al. 2015), comparing the socio-cultural, political, administrative, economic, etc. knowledge with the entities emerging from pattern analyses. There is no need for any of such known zones to be reproduced in BLT data, but differences and concurrences make possible vantage points for research questions and hypotheses. At the same time, the socio-spatially emergent zonations, if interpretable, are always significant as they are likely to indicate practice-based and possibly subconscious structuring within an urban landscape. Inadvertently, this could still have had some causal effect on the concepts that are instated.

Again, all measures suggested by the aggregative context are open to additional analysis through time. This would seek to compare and determine the processes in which aggregates form, consolidate, change, and disappear or hierarchically dissolve within urban development.

Final remarks on BLT analyses

Two final remarks concern the general understanding of, first, diachronic analysis and, second, accounting for interpretive flexibility in BLT Mapping. First, I discussed the data issues and opportunities for developing diachronic analyses on the basis of the proposed analytical measures. The premise of diachronic analysis is to reveal the patterns or rhythms of development through time. That is, determining the processes of urban development particular to each case and, across cases, identifying similarities and differences in those processes comparatively. The persistence and recurrence of socio-spatial characteristics indicate particular socio-spatial significance of that site of difference.

One major distinction of diachronic analysis is that the morphology of the boundary lines is expressly part of the analysis. While a different BLT data structure through time constitutes change, the actual site of difference itself could have persisted, either along a continuous length or intermittently. This means that both developments that reconstitute a thus *persistent* boundary line, and developments in the BLT data structure that occur very close to a *preceding* boundary line, are relevant. The latter will help differentiate between modifying shifts (e.g. widening, straightening roads for cars) and substantial transformations of the configuration.[20] This reconfirms the importance of enabling the aforementioned computational detection of morphological or geometrical change between time-slices. While the interpretive confines of this research will not permit explanations of why a built environment develops through certain processes, the processes themselves can be understood in terms of the constitutive interaction opportunities each stage offers to its inhabitants.[21]

Second, in many cases there will have been a degree of ambiguity or flexibility in the interpretive practice of BLT Mapping. Running any analytical tool therefore never produces an absolutely final outcome or insight. To account for known ambiguity in interpretations (e.g. knowing that covered markets would often be open like street spaces in daytime), it could be of interest to run analyses more than once, on different thinkable scenarios.[22] Naturally, several of the most frequent uncertainties will have been resolved by rules of thumb (Chapter 7).

20. While minor and even major scale enlargement may not affect topological relations, the increase in surface volumes will decrease density, which is a qualifying variable to distance setting and encountering (changes in) interaction. Typically scale enlargement will not be able to fully maintain existing shapes, as in confined space not everything can grow equally, also leading to potential changes in (mutual) orientation.

21. Weber (1979: 385) might have had something else in mind when he wrote: 'A genuinely analytic study comparing the stages of development of the ancient polis with those of the medieval city would be welcome and productive. [... The aim should be] to identify and define the individuality of each development, the characteristics which made the one conclude in a manner so different from that of the other. This done, one can then determine the causes which led to these differences.' Nevertheless, his reasoning is both astute and appropriate, as determining the causes of what occurred in terms of built form depends on supplementary lines of evidence and enquiry.

22. In space syntax studies the benefits of running analyses on several data scenarios is also acknowledged (Hillier & Hanson 1984; Van Nes in prep.).

Critical research practice should include the marking up of substantive varieties of flexibility and ambiguity, so respective data entries can be retrieved later. Similarly, the conjectures in historically reconstructed and archaeologically derived outline base plans could be critically reassessed when warranted.

On the basis of the proposals for analytical developments in this chapter, Chapter 9 will be dedicated to carrying out some preliminary explorations, utilising redescriptive and analytical opportunities currently available. Resource limitations mean that in this book, the full scope and breadth of computational developments and experiments that I have suggested, and that offer hypothetical technical opportunities, cannot be addressed. The BLT Mapping methodology can therefore only be demonstrated with initial and promising indications of interpretive potential. What is realised here and in Chapter 9 can act as a guide to future geocomputational development. Demonstrating the output from preliminary software advancements, and the extraction and compilation of formally redescriptive information from readable (visually intelligible) BLT maps, establishes that interpretive potential. The BLT data of the test cases merely evaluate the basis for full-fledged casuistic and radically comparative future work. By deploying GIS as an exploratory, visually redescriptive, and inferentially invested tool and work environment, I hope that the social scientific and humanities 'black box' effect (cf. Griffiths 2013; Lilley 2012) abates.

CHAPTER 9
EXPLORING SOCIO-SPATIAL SIGNIFICANCE WITH BLT MAPPING: TWO TEST CASES

Introduction

The BLT data structure and the analytical measures devised in Chapter 8, guided and informed by the interpretive levels of socio-spatial significance, have opened up a wide array of experimental investigative opportunities. The methodological development this book set out to realise now culminates with an exploration and evaluation of the functioning of a preliminary range of achievable analytical possibilities. By enabling not only an empirical mapping practice, but now achieving visualisations, analyses and interpretations, this chapter concludes that the theoretical grounding and methodological development of BLT Mapping has been successful. It also illuminates the casuistic and comparative potential this imparts. In other words, this chapter confirms that my principal theoretical premise can be translated into practice, how this unfolds in actual analyses and visualisations, and what we might learn from applying BLT Mapping.

The explorations offered here are facilitated by the test case BLT data created through the empirical mapping processes described in Chapter 7. At this fledgling stage of BLT Mapping, the complications involved in achieving a successful implementation of full-fledged casuistic research would put unnecessary strain on the salient demonstration of interpretive and radical comparative potential. Recapitulation of, and engagement with, holistic case-specific challenges here risk muddling the clarity that the explanation of the principles, processes and opportunities of BLT Mapping applications demands. Because this methodological development forms a reply to a plea for radical comparative urban studies (Chapter 1), the primary concern of the test case analyses is to offer a sound foundation for future applications and adaptations.

Next-stage casuistic research could seek profound understanding of the particular socio-spatial functioning of inhabiting a city or urban tradition, as well as the differences and regularities between examples thereof. It may also seek to use BLT Mapping for the purpose of evaluating the effects of past and future urban development on inhabitants. Furthermore, there is a plethora of correlative approaches thinkable, from complementary multi-method integration to adding in socio-cultural information sources to examine degrees of spatial (in)dependence (Chapter 2). The current experimental nature of early-stage BLT Mapping means the final developments in this chapter are necessarily bound by what data parsing and visualisation could be made technologically (geocomputationally) possible with limited resources (cf. Chapter 8). The interpretive explorations in this chapter therefore serve the purpose of showing a preliminary selection of possibilities for using the BLT data structure and the information they contain. I envisage these experiments to act as signposts for further efforts of refinement, development, and innovation of measuring and visualisation tools and techniques.

The chapter opens by presenting the basic global statistics that are geocomputationally derived from Winchester's MM and Chunchucmil's BLT data to mine their 'socio-spatial signature'. Then, Chunchucmil will be used to exemplify more detailed descriptive explorations and interpretations based on various visualisations and quantifications, including native GIS abilities, the BLT map, and diagrammatic innovations. This is illustrated using examples of spatial relations affording 'open circulation' and spaces associated with architectural groups. Since the built environment patterns of Maya urban landscapes serve the purpose of including urban development that is considered to be radically different, I provide a brief research context for my BLT explorations. This reiterates that extant and progressive geospatial approaches have only seen limited applications that exploit the increasingly available configurational spatial-material evidence. The historical Winchester data will primarily be used to perform an initial demonstration of opportunities offered by diachronic analysis (urban developmental trajectories), using similar techniques. Taking both test cases together, some incidental and explanatory contrasts will be sketched out. These comparisons give concrete expression to what is implied by inhabiting a 'high-density' versus a 'low-density' city. BLT Mapping thus enables a step change in providing a rigorous comparative context for tropical dispersed and low-density urbanism.

Geocomputational statistics on the ontology intrinsic to the city

Chapter 8 introduced the idea that topological segments, as the smallest meaningful elements, compose the ontology intrinsic to each city, or its socio-spatial signature (an interpretive notion proposed in Chapter 5). The BLT ontology is a conceptual ontology of types and therefore constitutes a partial ontology. Only the interrelated way in which the BLTs occur in a city unveils the full ontology particular to each city. An originally developed geocomputational GIS plugin enables the automatic detection of topological segments to reveal or mine the global characteristics of a BLT dataset. Current BLT datasets are restricted to test case areas, which were selected following a pragmatic and methodological rationale (Chapter 7). This may limit their interpretive potential, because as a unit they do not represent a section of spatial data we know to be socially significant. Global statistical output, however, will treat the test case data holistically, as if it would present an entire city or a meaningful part.

The present statistics consider the test case area of Chunchucmil and an area of Winchester's MM time-slice (extended from Fig. 7.3 to cover where the eastern extramural suburb meets the city centre to improve representation and comparability of the spatial morphology). The two areas are topographically comparable in the sense that they both take a section of each city bordering the monumental or administrative core (indicative rather than accurate terms) stretching outwards. For Winchester this means the eastern side of the city centre (formerly intramural) stretching east across the river. For Chunchucmil it comprises the north-western edge of the centre, containing the largest monuments, continued in a north-western direction. Any comparison between the two should be seen in terms of making a first contrast between inhabiting an example of a high-density urban tradition and an example of a low-density urban tradition, of which the historical period is an arbitrary aspect.

First, the tool[1] allows us to inspect how many different topological segments occur in the composition of each city's ontology (cf. Chapter 8, note 8). Not counting the additional specification of virtuality (i.e.

---

1. The readings of the geocomputational tool developed for this project show certain discrepancies with the topological segments that would intellectually be expected, which causes minor differences in the statistical values. Although every attempt has been made to minimise data errors, these cannot be excluded (see Chapter 7 on topology checks, while some interpretive ambiguity was intentionally allowed during the BLT identification process). The software interacts with native *ArcGIS* binaries, and debugging the native algorithms is beyond the remit of this book. In the following statistics I have filtered out erroneous results manually,

Vs involved in combinations creating topological segments), though isolating the virtual Type 5s that allow for direction choices in traversing (i.e. the number of options at intersections), Chunchucmil contains 70 and Winchester 43 unique kinds of topological segment. At first glance this is suggestive of considerably less complexity in Winchester than in Chunchucmil. However, the tool also shows that the Winchester test case does not contain examples of Types 6 and 7 identifications, which could have increased the complexity in Chunchucmil far beyond the 70 topological segments currently detected. The test cases have 38 topological segments in common, meaning that Winchester features only five combinations unique to its situation, while Chunchucmil features 32.

The tool also provides us the absolute measurements of the test case data. These dimensions allow us to derive further statistics on the topological segments. Table 9.1 contains the total count of topological segments, the total length of the combined boundary topology (i.e. the final outline base plan selection resulting from successful BLT identifications), and the total rectangular area[2] of each test case, after corrections for errors as identified in note 1, above. The proportion of virtual boundaries in Chunchucmil accounts for 11.4% of the count and 7.34% of the length. This is 2.84% and 4.92% in Winchester. It is likely that archaeological preservation in Chunchucmil is partly responsible for the higher virtual boundary stakes, but it can further be expected that in Winchester there is a social need to materially mark all distinctions completely, rather than circumstantially.

Table 9.1   Absolute measures of the topological segment ontology for the test cases.

Test case	Total count (n)	Total topology (m)	Total area (m²)
Chunchucmil	5202	62370.62	886817.12
Winchester	5178	34229.23	324875.24

which is possible because the combination of BLTs in the topological segment should not contradict itself and fulfil the ontological requirements stipulated in Chapter 5. Nevertheless, the errors are within acceptable limits, accounting for 1.3% of the total count and 1.0% of the total topology length in Winchester, and 1.5% and 1.3% respectively in Chunchucmil. The interpretive ambiguity accounted for 0.3% (count) and 0.2% (length) in Winchester, and in Chunchucmil respectively 0.2% and 2.4%.

2. The native binaries of *ArcGIS* responded inconsistently to attempts at applying the slightly more precise (i.e. more tight circumscription) convex hull as a measure for the area. A convex hull virtually creates a minimal convex polygon which includes all data.

The measures used in Table 9.1 allow the calculation of the proportion in which each topological segment occurs (its relative count), and the proportion of the length of the boundary topology it partakes in. In addition, the number of centimetres of topological segment that can be expected to occur per metre squared (a measure of density, see Chapter 8) is calculated.

Figs. 9.1 and 9.2 present the pie charts of the relative counts of topological segments for Chunchucmil and Winchester. Due to the large number of socio-spatial differences found, these have been simplified at the bottom end. This means that the lowest values have been lumped together. When a topological segment occurs up to 19 times within the subset, it is included in the small values class. When implementing this simplification it transpires that the most infrequent socio-spatial differences are responsible for the greater diversity within Chunchucmil's topology. Without these infrequently occurring topological segments,

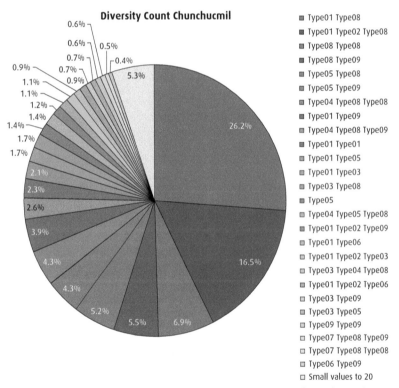

Fig. 9.1 Chunchucmil's proportional diversity count of topological segments.

The legend of topological segments is arranged from large to small quantities of occurrence.

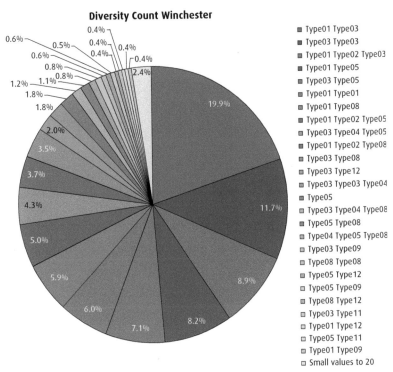

Diversity Count Winchester

Legend (large to small):
- Type01 Type03
- Type03 Type03
- Type01 Type02 Type03
- Type01 Type05
- Type03 Type05
- Type01 Type01
- Type01 Type08
- Type01 Type02 Type05
- Type03 Type04 Type05
- Type01 Type02 Type08
- Type03 Type08
- Type03 Type12
- Type03 Type03 Type04
- Type05
- Type03 Type04 Type08
- Type05 Type08
- Type04 Type05 Type08
- Type03 Type09
- Type08 Type08
- Type05 Type12
- Type05 Type09
- Type08 Type12
- Type03 Type11
- Type01 Type12
- Type05 Type11
- Type01 Type09
- Small values to 20

Fig. 9.2 Winchester's (MM) proportional diversity count of topological segments.

The legend of topological segments is arranged from large to small quantities of occurrence.

both cities retain 26 more frequent socio-spatial distinctions. This may be an inadvertent figment (bias) of test case area selection. However, if these areas would be roughly representative (of the entire city), these global statistics suggest that in Chunchucmil a larger number of specific socio-spatial activities or situations are connected by material markers to regular materialised socio-spatial differences. This could be indicative of society requiring a variety of specialised material patterns to form distinct architectural compositions that accommodate a very specific activity or status. Such argumentation could be further developed with a larger coverage, e.g. including the monumental core where specialised and unique patterns would logically be expected. Another argument could posit that Winchester accommodates a more equal and constant pattern, suggestive of higher demand for developing similar social functioning across space (e.g. residences, commerce or mobility).

Focusing on the proportional length, perhaps unsurprisingly we see a very similar division: the same topological segments play important

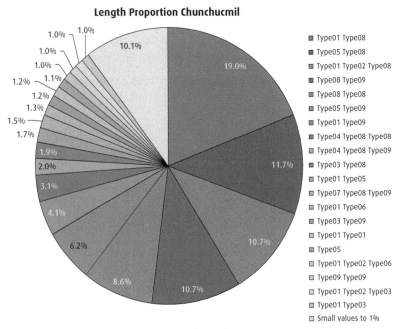

Length Proportion Chunchucmil

- Type01 Type08
- Type05 Type08
- Type01 Type02 Type08
- Type08 Type09
- Type08 Type08
- Type05 Type09
- Type01 Type09
- Type04 Type08 Type08
- Type04 Type08 Type09
- Type03 Type08
- Type01 Type05
- Type07 Type08 Type09
- Type01 Type06
- Type03 Type09
- Type01 Type01
- Type05
- Type01 Type02 Type06
- Type09 Type09
- Type01 Type02 Type03
- Type01 Type03
- Small values to 1%

Fig. 9.3 Chunchucmil's lengths of topological segments as proportion of total.

constitutive roles (Figs. 9.3 and 9.4). Two things stand out relating count and length. First, in Chunchucmil there is a strong drop after the stake of the top two topological segments (Type 1-8 and Type 1-2-8, Fig. 9.1). Their consistent top position basically means that a large number of smaller sections of boundary involving impermeable architecture (buildings) form a greater socio-spatial constant in everyday life than the relatively longer, but less frequent, Types 8 and 9 operations. Second, in Winchester there are four top determinant topological segments that display a contrast in proportional stake between count and length. These are firmly placed amongst the 10 most frequent topological segments, while they take a sharp drop in proportional stake in the length. These all involve Type 2 or 4 operations and are thus revealed as entranceways. As explained in Chapter 7, precise empirical evidence on entrances is scarce for Chunchucmil's archaeology, and therefore longer indicative boundaries have been identified in conjectural practice. Nonetheless, the irregular and often large architectural shapes and built environment features could equally cause such difference.

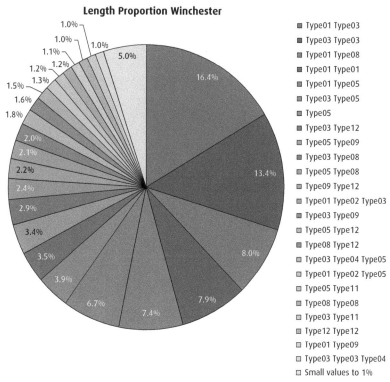

Length Proportion Winchester

Legend:
- Type01 Type03
- Type03 Type03
- Type01 Type08
- Type01 Type01
- Type01 Type05
- Type03 Type05
- Type05
- Type03 Type12
- Type05 Type09
- Type03 Type08
- Type05 Type08
- Type09 Type12
- Type01 Type02 Type03
- Type03 Type09
- Type05 Type12
- Type08 Type12
- Type03 Type04 Type05
- Type01 Type02 Type05
- Type05 Type11
- Type08 Type08
- Type03 Type11
- Type12 Type12
- Type01 Type09
- Type03 Type03 Type04
- Small values to 1%

Pie chart values: 16.4%, 13.4%, 8.0%, 7.9%, 7.4%, 6.7%, 3.9%, 3.5%, 3.4%, 2.9%, 2.4%, 2.2%, 2.1%, 2.0%, 1.8%, 1.6%, 1.5%, 1.3%, 1.2%, 1.2%, 1.1%, 1.0%, 1.0%, 1.0%, 1.0%, 5.0%

Fig. 9.4 Winchester's lengths of topological segments as proportion of total.

Ending my clearly non-exhaustive whistle-stop tour of the global statistics, there is an opportunity to address the terminological contrast of high- and low-density urbanism (e.g. Fletcher 2009, 2012) with a concrete empirical comparison. Fig. 9.5 presents a graph of the length density (a geographically absolute measure of cm per m²) of the topological segments that Chunchucmil and Winchester share. With an average density of socio-spatial boundary distinctions that is 2.5 times higher in Winchester (0.25cm) than in Chunchucmil (0.1cm), it is hardly surprising that the strongest contrasts show higher values for Winchester. Yet, several topological segments involving a Type 8 operation form an exception to such expectation. Generalising from this crude quantification, however, it appears that in high-density urbanism there are 2.5 times more opportunities to change one's socio-spatial position across geographical space. In one way this offsets the greater diversity in Chunchucmil, because one is likely to have to travel considerably longer

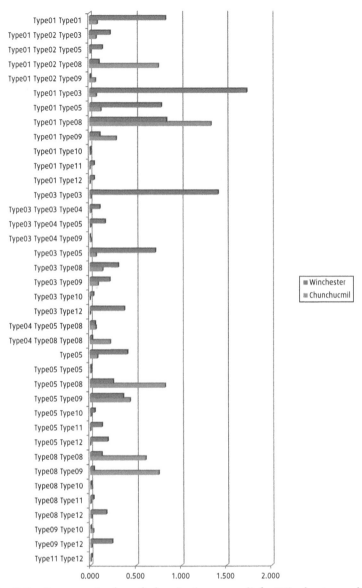

Fig. 9.5 Comparative length density (cm per m²) for Winchester and Chunchucmil.

in order to encounter the opportunities this diversity offers. In other words, in daily practice Chunchucmil's inhabitants may need to purposefully seek out the diversity that was statistically found to be greater in Chunchucmil than in Winchester.

It is clear that these global statistics guide questions for further, more detailed investigation. While an attempt was made to develop the detection of topological segment nodes (how BLT combinations connect), this functionality proved unstable in GIS operation. This causes a lack of insight in the contextual composition within which the found topological segments occur. Furthermore, the statistical tool is currently unable to visualise the distribution pattern of occurrence and make geographical selections. This puts limits on the interpretive argumentation that the statistical overviews can support. In the proceeding paragraphs I take a non-automated manual way forward. First, the visualisation technique permitting the reading of BLT patterns as a map is presented. Then, an especially devised diagram is introduced to aid the extraction of detailed contextual descriptions and smaller-scale quantification.

Exploring Chunchucmil's BLT data

Spatial analysis is not new to Maya intra-settlement or intra-urban research.[3] Nevertheless, few urban surveys yet exist as GIS data (notable exceptions besides Chunchucmil are Mayapan (Russell 2008; Hare & Masson 2012), Palenque (Barnhart 2003, 2005), Coba (Folan et al. 2009) and Copán (Richards-Rissetto 2012; *MayaArch3D* n.d.)), so the body of generic spatial analytical GIS applications is growing slowly. Following on from an established practice of calculating the overall density of archaeological remains over a surveyed area, and basing population estimates on this (see Rice & Culbert 1990; Hutson 2016), GIS is used to measure density. This use typically focuses on a nearest neighbour density clustering approach (e.g. Folan et al. 2009; Hare & Masson 2012), and helps generate a general feel for the dispersion pattern of administrative hubs and occurrences of the elite classes throughout a site. It tentatively helps to identify possible residential zones and neighbourhoods (Hare & Masson 2012). Recently, a nearest neighbour clustering approach was used in conjunction with dispersion to explore patterns in grid alignment and orientations amongst architectural groups. The approach was point (polygon centroid) based, so did not conform to the extensive data preparation conducted for BLT Mapping (Bevan et al. 2013). An early GIS, not including conversions of all data and full functionality (Hutson *pers. comm.* 2013), was used on Chunchucmil to support interpretation of

3. Spatial technology is more often used for site distribution patterns, e.g. *The Electronic Atlas of Ancient Maya Sites* (Witschey & Brown 2010).

urban life, especially by using surface area calculations of residential groups' plots (Magnoni et al. 2012).

Other research focuses on assessing the spatial patterns of Maya cities in terms of political or administrative zones or catchments (Adánez Pavón et al. 2009; Bazy 2011). Adánez Pavón et al. (2009) hierarchically tie their interpretation of political units in Tikal to different types of plaza plans (Becker 2004). This generates a more formal architectural version of the ethnohistorical approach of linking settlement layout to socio-political organisation seen in Carmack (1981) and Hill & Monaghan (1987). Bazy (2011) uses generalising observations on the private space of buildings and public space of plazas for schematic socio-political interpretations of the layout of Piedras Negras (cf. Parmington 2011). Bazy takes into account the material properties of architecture affecting privacy and intervisibility to distinguish public from private spaces. The operationalisation is mainly geared towards examining the dynamics of the development of connected architectural complexes through time.

In these examples, often the urban level material-spatial characteristics of social functioning stay out of reach. Some advances in this direction are being made, too. Lemonnier (2012), also using a schematic interpretive rather than formal spatial approach, demonstrates a more intricate consideration of spatial relations between architectural group types. She takes into account topographical and geographical feature details to argue for probable socially connected units. Richards-Rissetto (2012; Richards-Rissetto & Landau 2014) develop a sophisticated Least-Cost Path (LCP) analysis of topographical and Digital Elevation Model (DEM) data in GIS. Built and natural features together shape the urban landscape, conditioning the relative cost of traversing the city. Measuring the likelihood of *through* and *to* movements, arguments are made for social integration and inequality patterns.

The current development of spatial research on Maya cities reflects the availability of better mapping data and GIS implementations. Together with more meticulous conceptual consideration of the shape and materiality of (urban) architectural features, this will lead to the development of a greater diversity of analytical methods. At the same time, many of the cited examples still depend predominantly on arte-factual, stylistic and ethnohistorical information to guide interpretation. The intricacies of the role of built space in constitutive social functioning on an urban scale require a more comprehensive treatment of the fragmentary spatial archaeological record. Rigorously conceived morphological and topological GIS data structures can help progress the eventual integral analysis of urban space. While the degree of automation and the number of fully operational measures based on BLT Mapping at this stage is limited, the following discussion of Chunchucmil's BLT data will demonstrate key stepping stones. In anticipation of greater accessibility of extensive tropical Maya city plans thanks to the advance of LiDAR surveys (see Chapter 7), BLT Mapping opens new avenues for interpretation on the basis of appropriately theorised, prepared and formally redescribed material-spatial data.

Reading the BLT map

The hypothetical opportunities for advanced spatial analysis beyond general statistics (as described in Chapter 8) largely remain a future prospect due to the additional software development this requires. Nonetheless, simple visual data inspection allows the exploration of some principles exploiting the data structure and properties BLT Mapping produces. The inevitable limitations of manual visual work on GIS data will restrict the representative validity of analysis and interpretation. Still, early findings can reveal a number of promising directions for continued research. In order to extract, represent and study the BLT data, the BLT map needs to be readable.

The unavoidable problem of BLT identification is that co-located polylines are obscured (see Fig. 7.11). Both an ideal and pragmatic preliminary map visualisation solution have been discussed in Chapter 8. The pragmatic solution to produce BLT maps is implemented in another purpose-built tool that manipulates feature layer display in *ArcGIS* according to a predetermined offset along the X and Y axes. This tool shifts each BLT layer a number of (geographically scaled) centimetres with respect to the one overlaying it. The top layer is retained in its original position, acting as the geographical reference location for the displacement of layers. To attain a readable map – i.e. the shape of the mapped features and their originally co-located relation must still be recognisable – displacement should be kept at a minimum. It was found that usually 10cm suffices. Since across all BLT layers (when all occur) this still amounts to a maximum displacement of 120cm (130cm incl. Vs), considerable visual distortion is caused. It is therefore advisable to combine several standard *ArcGIS* symbology options alongside this layer displacement tool.

An effective set-up is to remove Vs, Type 2s, and all layers not containing any data from the selection to be displaced, so shifts are not made unnecessarily. Following Chapter 5's ontological primacy of seclusion, Type 1 is best kept in the top position (when excluding Type

2 from displacement this keeps Type 1-2 combinations visually unques-
tionable). Otherwise the following order was used, mainly based on the
expected frequency of direct relations between BLTs: 1; 3; 5; 4; 8; 9; 7;
11; 12; 10; 13. Type 10s are near the bottom because their 'neutral' or
ambiguous definition usually extends pre-existing relations between
other BLT identifications. Type 13 is at the bottom (though not present in
the test cases), because it would most usually form the border of the data
selection. Type 7 is placed below Types 8 and 9, because it can contain
complexes of all BLTs and its enveloping relation is expected to remain
recognisable even with a larger displacement.

After geoprocessing the displacement, the Type 1 based figure-
ground polygons (Fig. 7.13) can be added for clarity. Underlaying the
displaced (in the GIS tool's terminology: exploded) layers, the Type 2 and
V layers can be reintroduced. Vs would logically not concur with Type 1s
appraising the material evidence needed to identify Type 1s. Therefore,
after displacement, being in their original geographical location Vs fill
unpopulated 'voids' in the data frame. The Type 2s would either co-locate
Type 1s, or appear next to related Type 7s, if present. Maintaining Type 1 as
the top layer, while increasing the line thickness of the Type 2 polylines in
their underlying position, makes them bleed out from underneath the Type
1s. An example of the end result of this visualisation is shown in Fig. 9.4.[4]

On the basis of this kind of visualisation, one can work to extract
further information contained in the BLT data. Extraction of data structure details can clarify relations and characteristics that a cursory reading
of the map may not immediately relinquish. The BLT map in Fig. 9.6 initially reveals that the centrally placed large opening boundary (Type
9) does not directly relate to many closing boundaries (Type 1) or any
boundaries directly associated with dominants. It further shows that this
Type 9 permits transition between several directing boundaries (Type 5),
and that relations to Type 1s are mainly effectuated through crossing over
disclosing boundaries (Type 6) first. To help one's understanding of the
jargon that BLT maps give rise to, we can put this formal redescription
in more mundane terms. This Type 9 circumscribes a large open area
that is bordered by many boundaries that prevent one from accessing
further distinctly restricted interaction opportunities (the unrestricted

4. This technique has two main disadvantages. First, co-located lines of the same type remain
invisible (appear as a single line). Second, depending on the built environment morphology,
displacement in one direction along X and Y axes can follow the actually existing geometry,
which can virtually prevent underlaying lines from revealing themselves. In general, a lot of
panning and zooming actions are needed to properly see *all* the detail, while the jumble of
intersections (originally absent) caused by the displacement can be confusing. Prior knowledge
of the conceptual principles and mapping practice is therefore required to read these maps.

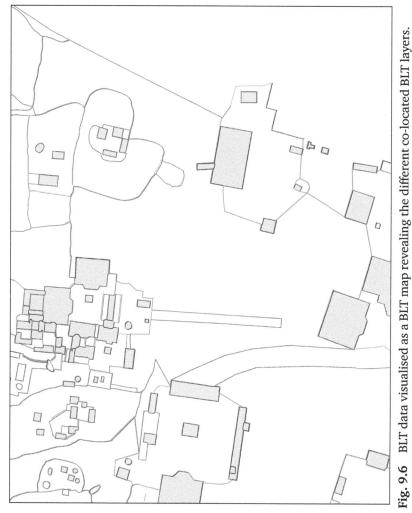

Fig. 9.6 BLT data visualised as a BLT map revealing the different co-located BLT layers.

The centrally placed opening boundary (Type 9) will elsewhere be referred to as 9A.

circulation of Type 9s themselves exposes one to all inhabitants). At the same time, the area acts as a flexible mobility zone, giving people the choice next to either engage in an interactional subsystem in which several buildings partake, or move on in other directions.

Strung beads on a string

The preceding socio-spatial description of the Type 9 in Fig. 9.6 leaves many of the intricacies of the constitution of this space unmentioned. It is difficult to systematically extract the patterns and relations from an irregularly formed and unfamiliar geometry. The initial subdivisions of occupiable surfaces (Chapter 4), socio-spatially reconceptualised by the BLT identifications, can be seen as a string of beads, assuming that one can traverse from one into the other. At the same time, the way these spaces are bounded is as a string of BLT combinations (linked-up topological segments). On this basis each BLT subdivision can be represented equally as an ideogram removing their topographical morphology (irregularities, shape, scale, etc.), allowing us to concentrate on the BLT information instead. To this end I have developed the polygonal 'clock diagram', in which each vertex represents a topological segment. Fig. 9.7 shows the clock diagram for the Type 9 in Fig. 9.6. (Please note that in this chapter each BLT circumscription of the same type will be distinguished by adding a capital letter and, if spatially connected, a lower case letter

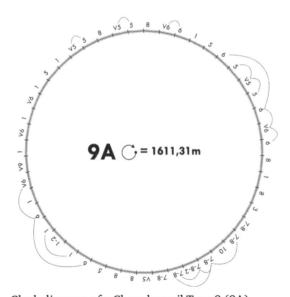

Fig. 9.7 Clock diagram of a Chunchucmil Type 9 (9A).

This diagram represents the same subdivision as the central open space in Fig. 9.6.

can be added. Thus, from here on, our first Type 9 will be known as 9A.) Importantly, clock diagrams use their internal BLT, the primary analytical unit, as a heuristic device. Reading the BLT map the topological segments emerge, as analytically derived 'smallest meaningful elements' (see Chapter 8), from the internally binding BLT circumscription.

The clock diagram in Fig. 9.7 consists of 47 sides, which represent the string of boundary differentiations constituting the space. These sides also partition topological segments that are distinct by virtue of virtuality. Excluding Vs, 9A partakes in 42 separate BLT combinations. The curves along the outside linking two or more topological segments indicate that, although these topological segments are separate in this string of boundary differentiations, crossing them one would enter into the same subdivision on the other side. That is, these topological segments are part of binding the same outlying space. Excluding these repetitions linking the same opportunity for interactional change, 9A borders onto 34 discrete spaces. Note that the curves linking some occurrences of Type 7 partaking in BLT combinations refer to the hierarchically superseding space that such enclosure creates. The larger and smaller curves together divide two discrete spaces, enclosed at once, but with separate subdivisions bordering 9A. Dismantling this hierarchical amalgamation means 35 discrete spaces border 9A. The total length of the string of boundaries bounding 9A is 1611.31m.

With this information now extracted from the BLT map, it is possible to calculate some of the socio-spatial characteristics this conveys. Referring primarily to the section on the dimensional context in Chapter 8, this diagrammatic representation of the data allows calculations on differentiation over length. To make the results of such exercise more worthwhile, however, first a number of clocks are produced for additional spaces. These spaces are selected on the basis of their expected roles in 'open circulation' or traversability of the site: Types 9, 6, and 5, the definitions of which in Chapter 5 stipulate that the subdivisions formed by these can serve as thoroughfare. My aim here is to demonstrate the potential and value of calculations based on careful readings of the BLT map. Such methodological illustration will not purport to stand in for representativeness. In total, three Type 9s, one Type 6 and five Type 5s (relative locations become pertinent later, and can be inspected in Figs. 9.17 and 9.19) have been selected to approximate the proportion of the numbers of these BLT identifications in the Chunchucmil test case area (Figs. 9.8–9.11).

Based on the clock diagrams, Table 9.2 calculates the average rhythm of topological segments occurring over the length of the involved boundary topology (circumscriptions). In order to better appreciate these

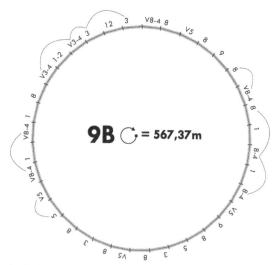

Fig. 9.8 Clock diagram of a Chunchucmil Type 9 (9B).

calculations over length, Fig. 9.12 displays the sizes of the BLTs under scrutiny here relative to each other. This gives an immediate impression as to how the average distances between boundary differentiations

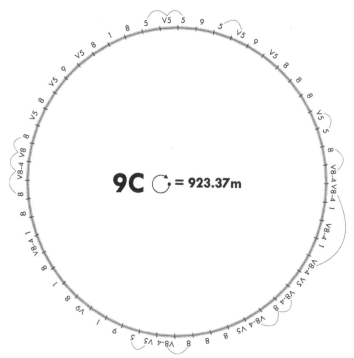

Fig. 9.9 Clock diagram of a Chunchucmil Type 9 (9C).

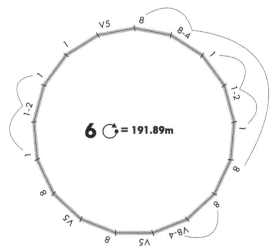

Fig. 9.10 Clock diagram of a Chunchucmil Type 6.

should be regarded. Boundary differentiations express the possibility to change interactional opportunities by crossing the topological segment. This change could either be contextual (if the boundary engages two BLT identifications of the same type), or an actual change when the opportunities on the other side are socio-spatially differently structured.

Examining the numbers in Table 9.2 in the light of Fig. 9.12 becomes more revealing. Unsurprisingly the largest example, 9A, also

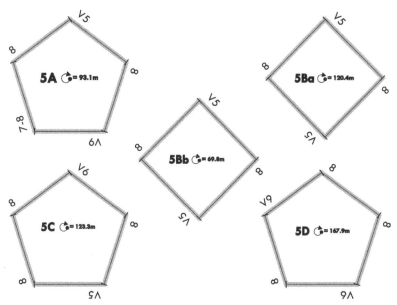

Fig. 9.11 Clock diagrams of Chunchucmil Type 5s (5A–5D).

Table 9.2   Boundary differentiations along the length of BLTs in Chunchucmil.

Frequency of boundary differentiation over length in metres								
Clock number	9A	9B	9C	6	5A	5Ba	5Bb	5C	5D
All segments	34.3	16.2	17.8	11.3	18.6	30.1	17.5	24.66	33.58
Corrected for virtual partitions	38.4	17.7	23.1	12.0					
Corrected for spaces	47.4	21.0	23.7	19.2					
Aggregated sequence length					33.68			Idem	33.58

This table shows the average distances between boundary differentiations along the length of the selected BLT circumscriptions in Chunchucmil.

has the largest distance between boundary differentiations, but at the same time the much smaller 5Ba and 5D are not far behind. Larger again than any Type 5, 6 is clearly the most intensely differentiated boundary. Relatively speaking, 9B, 9C and 5Bb are all closely similar in their intensity of differentiation, despite considerable differences in size. When the calculations on topological segments are corrected for discrete bordering spaces, logically the distances grow as the frequencies diminish. 9A still retains the markedly largest average distance between differentiations that connect two distinct spaces, while the averages of 9B, 9C and 6 grow closer together.

It is also revealed that instances of virtual partitions play the greatest roles in 9A and 9C. This possibly expresses the transitional character of the two largest spaces in this selection, but at the same time could indicate how building a materially emphasised boundary along the border of such large spaces is deemed less important. Be aware, however, that these averages may not be particularly meaningful when referring back to the irregular shapes of the topological segments in the actual topography of the city. The clock diagrams cannot express the relative lengths of each topological segment, which would be more accurate but would introduce a visual complication akin to the original BLT map. A recently developed software suite to visualise the human genome, *Circos* (Krzywinski et al. 2009), may have graphical abilities that could advance the adaptability of circular abstractions from BLT data. Furthermore,

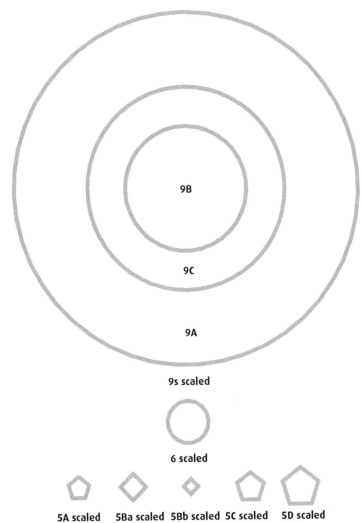

Fig. 9.12 The relative scale of the BLT lengths selected from the Chunchucmil test case.

It is the size of the figure representing each BLT that is scaled rather than the length of their lines.

future computational solutions are thinkable to automate the drawing process of clock diagrams, generating them directly from GIS.

The final row in Table 9.2 refers to the aggregative dimension discussed in Chapter 8. 5A, 5Ba and 5C appear as a sequence in the layout of the city, only separated by virtual boundaries. When calculating the average differentiation over length across these three Type 5s, it turns out the differentiation density is 33.68m. This is remarkably close to 5D, which is a stretch of road continuing the sequence after having passed 6. 5Bb splits off from 5A and is part of another sequence. Despite the inclination to tentatively conclude from this observation that how distance travelled along these paths may determine the differentiation measure, it should first be stressed that the width of these *callejuelas* (alleys or 'corridors') forms an additional quantitative determinant. Not only would a proper study require checking a representative selection of Type 5s and their sequences, overall it will be important to combine this BLT characteristic with actual metric distances of centre-lines and possibly LCP analysis.

Traversability and routes

Clock diagrams are more versatile than just as indicators for a density of differentiations over length. Since we are dealing with BLTs that were preselected on their possibility to serve as thoroughfare, extracting information about the diversity of choice to traverse subdivisions as structured by topological segments is a next step. Figs. 9.13–9.16 show the same clock diagrams now displaying the pattern of route choices to traverse 9A, 9B, 9C and 6. The Type 5s are excluded as their directing nature necessarily results in a linear pattern across.

The BLTs previously identified for their likelihood to be involved in traversability have been put in bold font and lines. The pattern in white expresses the pattern of choices to traverse across each respective BLT circumscribed space, while the sides of the polygons still express the topological segments involved in such crossings. The virtual partitions and virtual versions of topological segments are always places affording easy traversability, but one should bear in mind that doing so could be a social faux pas. Likewise, boundaries for which material evidence exists that obstructs crossing, even though they involve a combination of types likely to be involved with traversability, are excluded from the choice opportunities (grey areas).

It is immediately clear that in contrast to Type 6 in Fig. 9.16, the Type 9s redeem their suggested position within the circulation system. Even when excluding the virtually bounded options, choice in each instance is greater than for the Type 6. The choices across the Type 9s are also more widely dispersed along the boundary's length, emphasising multi-directionality as their probable function in the urban circulation system. However, these multiple directions do not necessarily represent differences in topographical orientations, but rather socio-spatially distinct directions. 9C (Fig. 9.15) demonstrates that most of its boundary differentiations afford ready crossings and through movement, while the boundary differentiations of 6 (Fig. 9.16) afford the least.

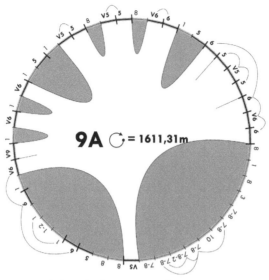

Fig. 9.13 Traversability clock diagram of Chunchucmil's 9A.

Considering Type 6 is a disclosing boundary, thus emphasising its transition towards the impermeable socio-spatial seclusion of buildings, this is not surprising (even though there are only two buildings oriented towards the Type 6 in this instance). Nonetheless, its distinct character as a place of inclination toward buildings is supported by the limited multi-directionality of traversability, which is more conducive to gathering in front of buildings.

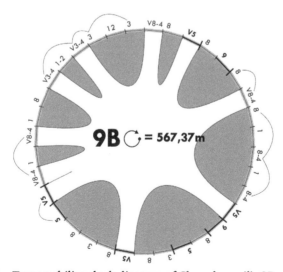

Fig. 9.14 Traversability clock diagram of Chunchucmil's 9B.

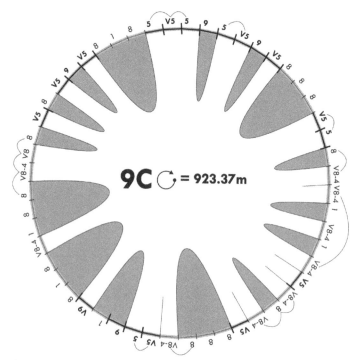

Fig. 9.15 Traversability clock diagram of Chunchucmil's 9C.

Table 9.3 Crossable boundary differentiations along the length of BLTs in Chunchucmil.

Frequency of boundary differentiation over length in metres									
Clock number	9A	9B	9C	6	5A	5Ba	5Bb	5C	5D
Per traversable opportunity	146.5	56.7	46.2	48.0					
Per traversable space	161.1	70.9	51.3	48.0					
Per entrance	805.7	63.0	102.5	48.0					
Entrance corrected per space	805.7	94.6	131.9	48.0					
Entrance corrected per configurative complex	805.7	113.5	131.9	48.0					

This table shows the average distances between boundary differentiations along the length of the selected BLT circumscriptions in Chunchucmil specified for traversability.

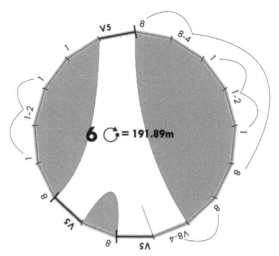

Fig. 9.16 Traversability clock diagram of Chunchucmil's 6.

Table 9.3 applies the density of differentiation over boundary length to the selection of topological segments creating traversable opportunities and entrances (topological segments involving Types 2 and 4). The latter is included because, in real life, people could always solicit access to the socio-spatial system occupying the space constituted behind an entrance. Between them, these topological segments reflect the opportunities for interactional change from the originating space, crossing boundaries with respect to the material integrity of each differentiation. Although the distances calculated refer to different kinds of topological segment, in the case of Type 6 the number of opportunities is equal in each case (see Fig. 9.16), hence the repetition of the same metric value. Again 9A is constituted by the greatest stretches without relevant differentiation. The very high values for 9A when looking at entrances indicate that 9A clearly does not accommodate a variety of direct relations to other more secluded socio-spatial systems: only two entrances appear along its boundary. When looking at entrances, the greater density of differentiation of 9B in contrast to 9C, as first manifested in Table 9.2, is maintained, but this is reversed when considering traversable options and spaces. This expresses the multi-directional choice clearly visualised in Fig. 9.15.

Logically, traversing space in a chain of boundary crossings forms a route constituted by specific socio-spatial characterisations. This refers back to Chapter 8's locational context analyses. The selection of the BLTs under scrutiny here allows us to construct an origin-destination path from the sequence they are in: 9A-5A-5Ba-5C-6-5D-9B. Fig. 9.17

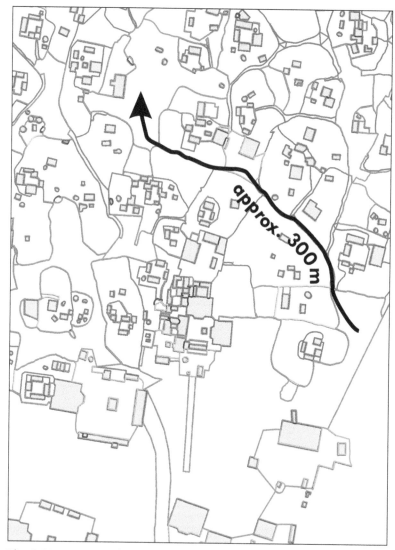

Fig. 9.17 Section of the Chunchucmil BLT map displaying the 300m route from 9A to 9B.

(Image prepared upon original data, courtesy of the Pakbeh Regional Economy Program with help from S. Hutson.)

shows the approximately 300m route on the BLT map, whereas Fig. 9.18 reorders and rotates the clock diagrams of Figs. 9.7, 9.8, 9.10 and 9.11 so they diagrammatically symbolise the same route, crossing the topological segments where the BLTs meet as socio-spatial interfaces.

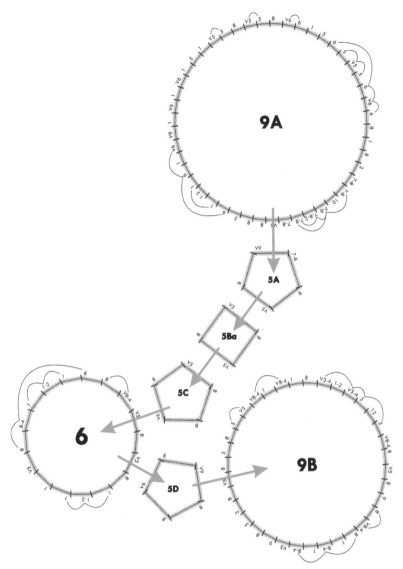

Fig. 9.18 Origin-destination path as a sequence of clock diagrams.

The route across Chunchucmil from 9A to 9B represented by the sequence of relevant clock diagrams. Potential splits of directions in *callejuelas* take place in the virtual spaces between 5A and 5Ba, and 5Ba and 5C.

So at the basis our origin-destination path consists of the following boundary crossings (cf. Chapter 8): V9-5; V5-5; V5-5; V5-6; V6-5; V5-9. While the order of type notation in the BLT combinations may analytically not matter – after all, the nature of the combination is the same regardless of that order – it does make somewhat of a difference when

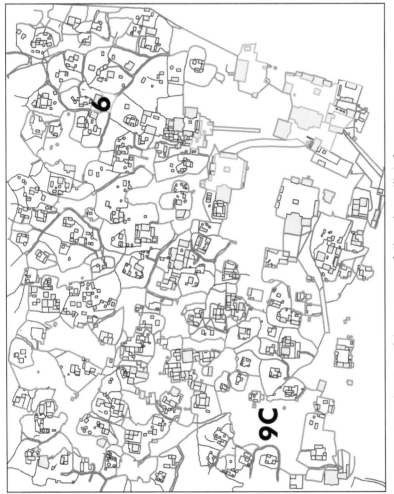

Fig. 9.19 Visualisation of the structure of Chunchucmil's infrastructure.

This shows Chunchucmil's 'infrastructure' of connectivity by Types 5 (blue) and 9 (pink), with Type 6 (orange) also highlighted to contrast the position of the indicated Type 6 to the others. Note that the monumental core is located towards the lower right (southeast) of this area. 9C is indicated to position it in contrast to the route of Fig. 9.17. (Image prepared upon original data, courtesy of the Pakbeh Regional Economy Program with help from S. Hutson.)

a position is known towards a boundary, as in origin-destination paths. That is, here the first crossing is from an inner 9 and outer 5 to an inner 5 with the prospect to an outer 5 and reflecting a now outer 9 if one were to revert. The order thus expresses the difference in socio-spatial situation the person following the origin-destination path will go through. That brings us to consider the broader nature of assessing possible origin-destination paths, which is the progressive and accumulative experiential change in afforded and affective interaction opportunities.

Placing the current origin-destination path into context, simple panning around the Chunchucmil test case area with the circulation-prone Types 5, 6, and 9 switched on lets transpire that Type 5s (predominantly *callejuelas*) are often used to connect up two Type 9s, or alternatively lead to a specific configurative complex based on one or multiple dominants. Taking Type 5 and Type 9 together, it seems at first glance that the entire test case area is connected up (Fig. 9.19). Although the Type 6 selected for illustration purpose here is conspicuously located to suggest it plays a greater role in circulation than other Type 6s in the test case area, this space could be avoided using the infrastructure of Types 5 and 9.

As a contextual aside to the origin-destination path, it can be noted that all Type 6s in Fig. 9.19 are located at close range from each other. Using the general statistics tool (as described above) on the basis of this single BLT reveals that Type 6s only occur in a rectangular area that covers 26% of the total rectangular area of the test case. Calculating the length density of the topological segments involving a Type 6 operation over the total rectangular area, in contrast to the rectangular area in which only these topological segments occur, makes clear that within the test case area these are among the ones that show the strongest localising effects (i.e. highest ranking topological segments). Especially when this density calculation is combined with a (clustered) geographical distribution (see Fig. 9.19), such a quantitative indicator could be used to specify the socio-spatial patterns which may reflect neighbourhood effects. Our path, roughly speaking, leads out of this potential neighbourhood.

Allowing some speculation on the basis of how the preceding observations structure socio-spatial experience, the movement along this origin-destination path could be imagined as follows. Entering the *callejuela*, the inhabitant's opportunities to do something other than moving through are very limited. One might wave at people occupying bordering Type 8s where the *albarradas* allow. At the next two crossings, one might expect other pedestrian traffic, although the effect of the second crossing is more limited due to its proximate destination complex.

Passing through the next crossing, one might get distracted by or even partake in some activities proper to the Type 6 socio-spatial system. Thoroughfare may become centralising and activities may develop a relation to the disclosed dominants (buildings) and their specific functions. After that, crossing into the *callejuela*, opportunities dwindle again. Passing pedestrian traffic could already alert one to the possibilities that lie ahead. Finally, the destination, 9B, is reached.

Origin-destination paths demonstrate how BLT evidence can anchor interpretive hypotheses and narratives. This offers an enticing option that would benefit archaeological and urban planning purposes, as well as enrich other formal and quantitative urban analyses. Logically, assuming this is an actual origin-destination path that relates to various activities undertaken by an actor, at this point one would want to know how, from A to B, the actor's socio-spatial situation of afforded opportunities has changed. For this we need to move beyond the realms of density and accessibility glossed so far (cf. Marcus 2007, 2010; Chapter 8) and introduce a context of relative frequency and diversity.

Frequencies and diversity

Because the origin-destination path defined before (Fig. 9.17) leads from one Type 9 to another, the example of relative frequency and diversity of BLT combinations presented here focuses on the selected Type 9s. First, however, the frequency and diversity for which the Type 9s are responsible in comparison to all selected BLTs (Tables 9.2 and 9.3) should be put in context. Fig. 9.20 presents an adapted clock diagram representing this subset of BLT data. The sides represent all unique topological segments which taken together constitute the selected Types 5, 6, and 9, and the columns represent the frequency count of their occurrence.

The original clock diagrams (Figs. 9.7–9.11) clearly show that a greater number of topological segments partake in the constitution of the Type 9s than any of the others. Fig. 9.20 demonstrates that it also applies that the Type 9s are responsible for most of the topological segment diversity in this selection (13 out of 21 possibilities). This makes Types 9 on the basis of this subset socio-spatially more diversely constituted, which especially in combination with their size (cf. Fig. 9.19) suggests they could have served multiple functions associated with their boundary diversity, and within the city as a whole. This information is indicative of patterns that might be revealed as general trends and consistency markers in the aggregative context as approached in Chapter 8.

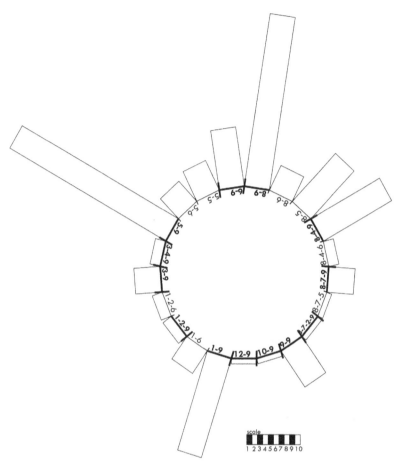

Fig. 9.20 Scaled frequency clock diagram of topological segments in Chunchucmil.

This scaled frequency clock diagram displays all topological segments in Chunchucmil's selected BLTs. The centre represents an aggregate of all selected Type 5, 6, and 9 circumscriptions.

If we further specify our selection to the socio-spatially constitutive pattern of Type 9s, we can create a frequency clock diagram that displays the average topological segment diversity per Type 9 identification (Fig. 9.21), which may form a base for expectations about further Type 9s in Chunchucmil.

From Fig. 9.21 we can see that the majority of Type 9 boundary differentiations are co-constituted by operations involving Types 8 and 5. It is also clear that although a relatively large number of Type 1s (thus buildings) are part of the selected Type 9 operations, it is fairly rare to find

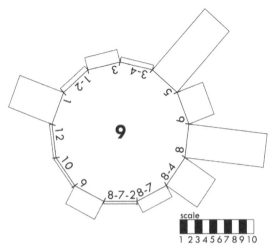

Fig. 9.21 Frequency clock diagram displaying the average diversity taken across 9A, 9B and 9C.

an entrance to them from this side. While in the discussion of 9A earlier it was remarked that its constitution showed little direct engagement with boundaries related to complexes involving dominants, Fig. 9.21 demonstrates this may be out of the ordinary in comparison to 9B and 9C. A possible explanation is 9B's and 9C's position relatively further away from the monumental core (see Figs. 9.17 and 9.19). This finding can be illustrated using the frequency clock diagram in a relative manner.

In Fig. 9.22, 9A's diagram shows that contrasted to the average of this Type 9 selection, there is not only a conspicuous absence of topological segments involving Type 8-4 combinations, but also an under-representation of combinations involving Type 8. This indicates that 9A is socio-spatially speaking more distant from dominant complexes with shared plots, which are known to be a common residential pattern (Magnoni et al. 2012). Instead, 9A is very well connected to dis-closing boundaries (Type 6s), which consolidates its transitional pos-ition between the more building-specific functions likely to take place beyond those boundaries. When referring back to its original clock diagram (Fig. 9.7), looking at the order or rhythm of how topological segments link up, it is revealed only one Type 6 circumscribed subdiv-ision (occupiable space) is not also directly neighbouring one or more buildings. This further clarifies why, despite numerous connections to buildings, inhabitants would be expected to cross over designated dis-closing boundaries first. The underrepresentation of Type 8 involve-ment is also assessed more clearly by looking at the topological segment order. This reveals that most Type 8s along 9A's boundary are

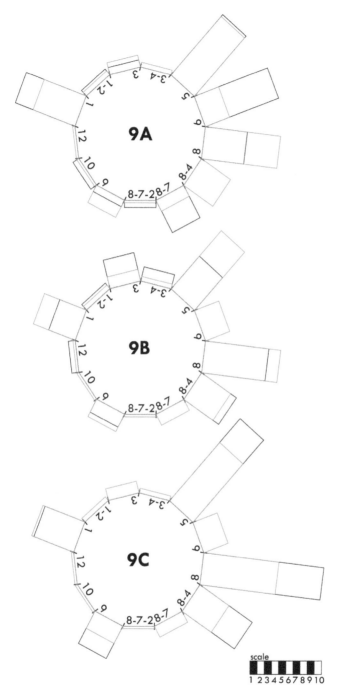

scale
1 2 3 4 5 6 7 8 9 10

Fig. 9.22 Scaled frequency clock diagrams of Chunchucmil's 9A, 9B and 9C.

These scaled frequency clock diagrams of 9A, 9B and 9C display the relation between their individual topological segment diversity counts (black) and their combined average (pink).

concentrated along a relatively small stretch of boundary line, thus located in socio-spatial proximity to each other, which is suggestive of an orientation to the social functional organisation of the space.

In contrast, 9C dramatically over-performs in connecting to such Type 8 combinations. It is also better connected for through movement in various directions (Type 5s), reinforcing the redistributive functioning that Fig. 9.15 already indicates. While 9B may be worse connected with regards to movement, this seems to result primarily from an overall better connection to direct entrances (Type 3-4, 8-4, and 1-2 combinations), which further specifies the quantitative pattern of entrances that Table 9.3 indicates.

Finally, the above glossary of Type 9 diversity tells us a little more about the possible purposes of our hypothetical origin-destination path. Originating from a clearly transitional 9A, the inhabitant moves along a few traffic corridors and passes an area accommodating more specific functions (Type 6) to arrive at a location which would likely have formed the final boundary before solicitation for access (requests and visits) to more secluded socio-spatial systems. As discussed in Chapter 6, what actually would occur cannot be concluded from BLT analyses, and it therefore cannot be precluded that e.g. the inhabitant had further to travel along one of the bordering Type 5s. 9B itself is more conducive as a location for activities on which some of the bordering more secluded individual dominants or configurative complexes had stronger purchase, and which could have formed a destination for inhabitants located elsewhere. In other words, 9B could serve as a focal node for a neighbourhood.

This brief discussion on the diversity of Type 9s taken together for internal comparison suggests the following: that adding and combining an increasing number of observations implicates rather precisely (thanks to systematic application of formal concepts) the socially functioning roles accommodated by the constitution and composition of each of these boundaries. Nonetheless, within this particular and limited subset, perhaps the strongest conclusion is the large variety in the nature of Type 9 operations that has been revealed. Characterising the nature of their diversity in more precisely defined possible socio-spatial roles could form a direction for further research.

Accessing size

As a final example based on the Chunchucmil test case, the BLT analysis will be combined with a much more morphological consideration of size. Rather than replicating the study of Magnoni et al. (2012), this example will briefly look at size related to access. The observation made above on 9A's under-involvement with Type 8s becomes particularly striking in

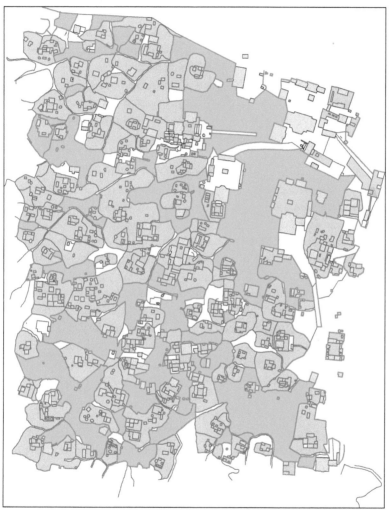

Fig. 9.23 Visualisation of the general coverage of Chunchucmil's Types 8 and 9.

These are the surfaces of the subdivisions created with Types 8 (purple) and 9 (pink) inner circumscriptions in Chunchucmil's test case area, virtually covering the entire area. (Image prepared upon original data, courtesy of the Pakbeh Regional Economy Program with help from S. Hutson.)

the light of size. Subdivisions resulting from Type 8 identifications can be as big as those resulting from Type 9s (even though the maximum surface area for Type 9s is much larger still). Fig. 9.23 makes it immediately clear that, in fact, subdivisions with an inner Type 9 or 8 circumscription represent the vast majority of the occupiable surface area in Chunchucmil's test case. Supported by the general statistics, Types 9 and 8 accumulatively partake in an impressive 89% of the boundary topology's length, 86% of the count, and over half the socio-spatial diversity. In other words, these operations play a strongly determinant constitutive role in the social functioning of Chunchucmil.[5] Fig. 9.23 confirms that the Type 8s involved with 9A are all located in the north, and are located fairly close together in both the geographical and socio-spatial sense. Furthermore, it can be seen how 9A's situation within the whole is distinct from the other Type 9s, the boundaries of which are all very tightly knit with Type 8s.

Let us entertain a moment of speculation about the presumably more static occupation of buildings and shared plots (i.e. at these more secluded complexes is where one would expect activities with longer duration, such as dwelling and production) by Chunchucmil's population. Chunchucmil's population is estimated to be notably large amongst its Maya urban peers (Magnoni 2007; Hutson et al. 2008; Hutson 2016). This highlights the possibility of relatively significant pressure on space for movement and centralising activities tied to soliciting engagement with buildings (Type 6s). While presumably there would have been plenty of space that is in part determined by Type 8 or 9 boundary operations, thus accommodating socially very open interaction towards and in addition to interaction concentrated on designated social subsets, secluded (private) and movement space could have been crowded.

By combining the preceding BLT visualisation techniques with the morphological variable of size, it is possible to clarify the relation between the opportunities to access discretely subdivided spaces and the size over which the anticipated (on the other side of the boundary) socio-spatial interactions persist. Fig. 9.24 (for size references see Hutson et al. 2006; Magnoni et al. 2012) applies this logic to the Type 6 selected earlier.

The huge contrast in size between the shared plots constituted from within by a Type 8 and the other accessible spaces jumps out. Furthermore,

---

5. In contrast, Types 8 and 9 partake in 28% of the topology's length, 20% of the count and less than half the socio-spatial diversity in Winchester's MM. Despite Winchester's 2.5 times higher density of socio-spatial differences, Types 8 and 9 operations combined feature a denser occurrence in Chunchucmil than Winchester's overall boundary density.

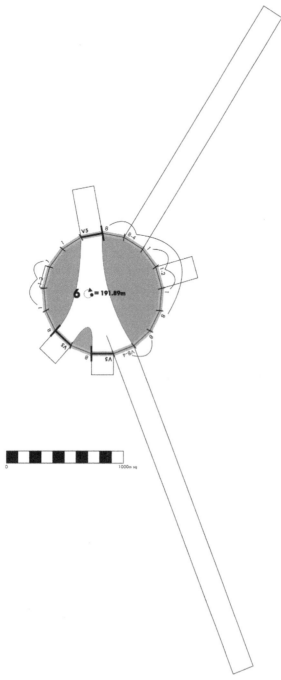

Fig. 9.24 Traversability clock diagram for Chunchucmil's Type 6 with accessible space sizes.

This traversability clock diagram for Chunchucmil's Type 6 is combined with the readily accessible discrete spaces connected to it. The length of the columns represents the number of square metres.

one of the directly accessible buildings rivals the *callejuelas* for surface area, but the other building is the smallest space by a major margin in comparison to all other accessible spaces. From the perspective of the socio-spatial system occupying the Type 6, this means that it is closely related to a wide variety in interactionally distinct continuous surfaces. The fleeting open interactions of the directing boundaries (Type 5s) are consistently represented and, overall, materially least restricted. Both buildings display a similar order of topological segments and materially emphasised seclusion, but will most likely have represented different social functions as associated with their strongly contrasting size. Both Type 8-4 entrances lead to shared plots of considerable size (although as Fig. 9.23 shows, definitely not excessively large in comparison to other examples), and would likely have been functionally arranged in sections respective of the buildings amongst which the open space acted as a common (see Killion et al. 1989; Fedick & Morrison 2004; Hutson et al. 2004, 2006, 2007).

Upon closer inspection these two mutually bounded areas share a reciprocal entrance, but are otherwise externally separated by an *albarrada*. Such internal connections suggest that neighbourhoods could potentially be made up out of sequences of these large shared plots, creating hierarchical aggregating complexes. BLT analysis can only indirectly support arguments on the social stratification of such areas. For this purpose, BLT Mapping could thus help to complement the social organisational interpretation of the size of residential complexes at Chunchucmil (Hutson et al. 2006; Magnoni et al. 2012), by informing how they could be grouped. Using material-spatial evidence to determine the configurative complex of plot groupings characterises the nature of their internal connections and how their outer borders are externally defined (topological sides). As suggested in Chapter 8, here, morphological interests in building lines, plot series, blocks, etc. smoothly integrate with socio-spatial BLT interpretation. Similarly, the plausible crowdedness of the occupation of directing boundaries could potentially be further specified and hypothesised by making correlations with space syntactic movement probability measures.

Exploring Winchester through time

Chapter 6 has discussed at length the prevalent families of methods for studying the (western) urban design tradition that is, broadly speaking, exemplified by Winchester. Having positioned BLT Mapping in relation to what these extant methods do, it is unnecessary to review examples of how studies have applied these techniques to western urban form. It is evident that the analytical possibilities and tendencies demonstrated for Chunchucmil could also be applied to the Winchester test case. However, instead of repeating my demonstrations of techniques and analytical arguments based on BLT Mapping, this section will carry out an initial exploration of how such techniques could be used to support diachronic studies of the inhabited urban built environment. After all, time depth is a unique investigative dimension facilitated by selecting Winchester as a radical comparative case (Chapter 7).

While some further general comments on the comparative insights between Chunchucmil and Winchester will be made, in the following the diachronic merits (application to intra-urban developmental trajectories) of BLT Mapping are emphasised. The interpretive argumentation will also reflect that general contemporary and historical knowledge on British urbanism is much greater than for Maya urbanism. For various locations and situations in Winchester, BLT-based interpretation can be directly verified by how current inhabitants inhabit persistent (materialised) spaces in everyday life. Permitting a similar kind of interpretative control, British urban history is described and presented in comprehensive historical overviews (e.g. Palliser 2000; Clark 2000; Daunton 2001), whereas the functioning of the Maya urban tradition is still mostly unknown. Therefore, the exploration of the Winchester data can offer important proof of concept when BLT analyses broadly reproduce the general expectations and knowledge we derive from direct observation and historical accounts. By and large, building an archaeological interpretation relies on stacking or scaffolding evidence (cf. Llobera 2012, 2015), since the deep past of archaeology rarely allows for cross-checks between sources. If cross-checks pan out with contemporary observation and historical documentation, such verification lends analogical validity and credibility to BLT Mapping results in archaeology.

Using BLT maps diachronically

BLT identifications are unique for each moment in the development of a city for which an atomic outline base plan representation is made. That is, every time-slice undergoes its own unique (customised) process of identification. It logically follows that it is impossible to trace 'the same' BLT identification through time: the BLT itself does not exist as such. Even when locally a situation remains the same to such extent that the BLT identifications would be predominantly replicated, these identifications are still a fruit of the particular material-spatial situation of that time-slice in its time-space specific context. Nonetheless, because we know from urban morphological principles that much of urban space in fact is quite resilient to change, using geographic approximation the change of space through time could still be made the subject of research. As Chapter 8 discusses, unfortunately geocomputation has yet to develop effective geometrical principles into readily usable software applications to aid informative change detection. Therefore, a more intuitive approach was followed here to demonstrate the principle of working through time.

Chapter 7 (Fig. 7.3) already explained that, for the purposes of this research, taking the Winchester test case back through time was only applied in a limited area of approximately 175x200m. This area is located right over the bridge that in medieval times would have led to the east gate to the city. Because BLT identifications cannot be used regressively, the geographical location of the bridge was used as the basis for selecting the diachronic example area. The river crossing remains roughly constant despite its change and development through time. The contiguous stretch of boundary lines that incorporate the southern edge of the bridge (see Fig. 9.25) was used to select circulation-prone

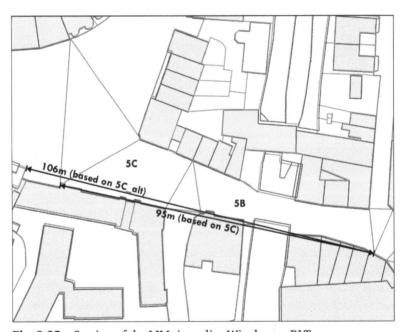

Fig. 9.25 Section of the MM time-slice Winchester BLT map.

This section of the MM time-slice Winchester BLT map indicates the selection of the contiguous stretch of boundary lines incorporating the bridge. (Based on OS MasterMap. © Crown Copyright 2013. All rights reserved. An Ordnance Survey (EDINA) supplied service.)

BLT identifications. This selection could then also be crudely compared to the earlier assessment of the selected BLTs of Chunchucmil's circulation space. The idea is to keep both the location and the length of the combined contiguous boundary lines (as the crow flies, rather than tracing the exact morphology) relatively equal in all three time-slices.

Going from MM to OS1872 is relatively simple to relate, as major architectural features and infrastructural development had already taken place in the nineteenth century. However, it was immediately clear that a change in boundary outlines of subdivisions has logically affected the identification of BLTs on the OS1872 time-slice. The outline change supported my subjective decision in the twenty-first century situation to slightly 'lengthen' the High Street that comes in from the west in Fig. 9.25, by using the architecture of the building towards the south that still follows the direction of the High Street. Fig. 9.26 shows the situation for the OS1872 time-slice, which demonstrates how the slight change in subdividing outlines (loss of a small strip to the front of the building which itself remains the same) causes such discrepancies in identification.

For the benefit of diachronic analysis that respects the relative constancy in the architectural binding of street space, I suggest a pragmatic 'fix' for this discrepancy that essentially creates the topological sides (see Chapter 8) of the contiguous boundary line I proposed to follow. An alternative course for the virtual boundary cutting off the parallel direction of the Type 5 representing the High Street could be imagined when constructing the clock diagrams for the two Type 5s concerned. When doing so, the length as the crow flies only differs one metre from the OS1872 situation (Fig. 9.26), and this can undoubtedly be ascribed to the slight changes to the morphology of the road crossing the bridge towards the east, as shown on the MM BLT map (Fig. 9.25).

In contrast, the much more dramatic morphological changes from 1550s to OS1872 are immediately visible. The contiguous boundary line selected 'grows' a bit. Changes in the course and frontages of the street are likely responsible for this minor change as the crow flies. Moreover, the area to the west of the bridge has clearly been completely redeveloped between the sixteenth and the nineteenth century, resulting in a markedly different (unrelatable) endpoint there.

Quickly assessing the situation sketched in the BLT maps of Figs. 9.25–9.27 reveals that opening boundaries (Type 9s, pink) virtually disappear from this small area from the sixteenth to the nineteenth century. The nineteenth century sees an increased number of Type 8s (purple), which may not be very large, but significantly create small subsets of buildings in the same way Type 3s (red) do across all time-slices.

Fig. 9.26 Section of the OS1872 time-slice Winchester BLT map.

This section of the OS1872 time-slice Winchester BLT map indicates the selection of the contiguous stretch of boundary lines incorporating the bridge. (Vector data derived from original scans: © Crown Copyright and Landmark Information Group Limited 2013. All rights reserved. 1872.)

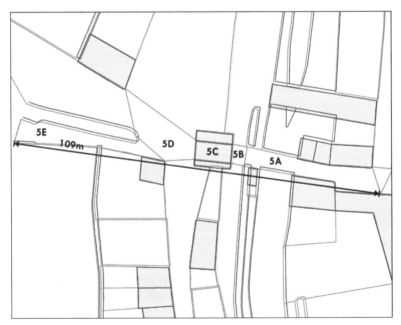

Fig. 9.27 Section of the 1550s time-slice Winchester BLT map.

This section of the 1550s time-slice Winchester BLT map indicates the selection of the contiguous stretch of boundary lines incorporating the bridge. (Vector data based on original scans, reproduced courtesy of the Winchester Research Unit.)

This BLT-specific finding is fortuitous. Historical discourse reveals that the rapid development of the Victorian city comprised, amongst other things, a process of transition in which an emphasis on shared open areas shifted to increasingly individual open areas associated with residences (contextually expected to be identified as Type 3s) (Daunton 1983). This process even reached the point where planning policy was put in place for the construction of urban residences including such individual open areas. According to Daunton, these changes were introduced earlier in the large cities, after which they found their way into provincial towns. Winchester was such a regional town, and the OS1872 time-slice seems to capture the city in the middle of this transition. A good representation of both situations (i.e. specific spatial morphologies) is still experienced by its inhabitants. The BLT Mapping of the OS1872 time-slice in fact makes this experiential division immediately explicit.

A main difference with Chunchucmil's urban built environment, on the other hand, is how the Type 5s do not only direct to situations leading to further unrestricted interaction opportunities. Along the directions of these Type 5s, numerous strongly secluded boundary operations (especially Type 1s, buildings) are, connected up. While after the sixteenth century the settlement in the city seems to intensify in terms of Type 1s (buildings), this nature of Type 5s in Winchester applies throughout history. Furthermore, looking at the 1550s time-slice, various Type 9s occur, but clearly differ in the position and socio-spatial situation to those identified in Chunchucmil. These Type 9s concur with the Chunchucmil ones in that any necessary material evidence that would truly prevent access is largely absent. Therefore these Type 9s could also partake in the circulation of traversing Winchester. Yet, the fact that they tend to be placed in lateral relation to Type 5s, instead of head-on as is usual in Chunchucmil, suggest their open transitional character might refer to other social functions, or a different contextual emplacement of similar functions occupying the resultant spaces.

Before moving on to the clock diagrams produced for each time-slice's situation respectively, it is worth noting the obvious increase in the number of topological sides resulting from separate subdivisions on the northern side of the selected contiguous boundary line in 1550s, as opposed to the other time-slices (road sections numbered 5A–5E in Fig. 9.27). The three 'additional' Type 5 identifications result from the presence of the gate house in association with pathways running along the city walls, which were removed some time before OS1872.[6] While the Type 5 that directs people through, underneath the gate house, is

6. Actually the gate house was removed before 1750, as the Godson survey shows. However, at that time the removal of the entire wall had not progressed to the same extent.

itself clearly bounded, 5B and 5D on either side are mainly virtually bounded due to the confluence of parallel directing boundaries ending onto these. The fascinating thing about these virtual bindings is the clear difference in shape and size in seemingly similar positions. The presence of the virtual boundaries assumes particular significance by emphasising the liminality of the city wall and the spaces directly outside the gate house.

The presence of these additional emergent Type 5 subdivisions with such a porous socio-spatial definition suggests a particular use of these areas. It is easily imagined how, after passing the city gate, one would be greeted by an abundance of activity: services being offered, requests made, potentially duties paid, etc. The relatively oversized tendential space emerging from the confluence of Type 5s seems to accommodate this appropriately. At the same time, the much smaller but similar subdivision on the outside may suggest the more transitory use of this area, either for passing through or bidding the relatively quick request to enter, with probably limited time spent waiting there. Alternatively, in a much more controlled environment, the process of permitting access could have been strictly organised or effectively run through such a small area. Moreover, 5B neighbours two Type 12s, which are by definition inaccessible and therefore would literally have restricted movement. Whether still current in the sixteenth century or not, this conjures up an image of a remnant of a socio-spatially defensive situation, which is naturally supported by our supplementary historical knowledge of city walls. Additionally, a bridge is an expensive construction, which means the creation of further occupiable surface space could only be achieved at considerable investment of labour and resources.

Exemplifying diachronic BLT development

According to my explanation, each time-slice demands comprehensively unique BLT identifications. Figs. 9.25–9.27 show the consequence through time, with different shapes and numbers of Type 5s constituting part of the contiguous boundary line selected for diachronic exemplification here. This implies that it is impossible to trace the same clock diagram through time. Therefore individual diagrams for each of these time-slices need to be produced. Figs. 9.28–9.31 contain the clock diagrams for each respective material-spatial situation depicted in the time-slice sections in Figs. 9.25–9.27.

We can take from the contrast between these clock diagrams that purely in terms of topological segments each individual Type

5 operation in 1550s is constituted by less differentiation, except for MM's 5C/5C_alt. By the same measure, MM's 5B is historically speaking the most differentiated subdivision along this contiguous boundary line. Unfortunately, this presentation of clock diagrams is not the most immediately intelligible way of investigating the developmental differences in socio-spatial constitution through time. To improve diachronic comparison, the topological sides caused by the currently separated subdivisions partly constituted by Type 5s should be aggregated into a diagrammatic representation of a single occupiable space (subdivision).

Carrying out diagrammatic aggregation also demonstrates how studies into readily comprehensible amalgamations or subsections from a given data selection can be undertaken. Automatically, such approach moves the interpretive value of this diachronic comparison to an *arbitrary* level in the aggregative dimension. That means that by making my boundary selection on the basis of a measured diachronic observation, it cannot be claimed that this aggregate as a unit necessarily has socio-spatial significance to the emplaced lived experience of the inhabitants. Vice versa, the contrary is uncertain too. Instead, it can be suggested here that the extended street space along the bridge is considered as far as MM and OS1872 are concerned. This selection may well have made sense to many inhabitants. The experiential coherence of this entirety is superficially less convincing for 1550s, although the arguably 'added' area designated

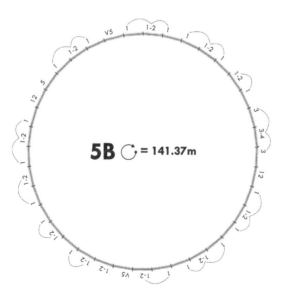

Fig. 9.28 Clock diagram for 5B in the MM time-slice (see Fig. 9.25).

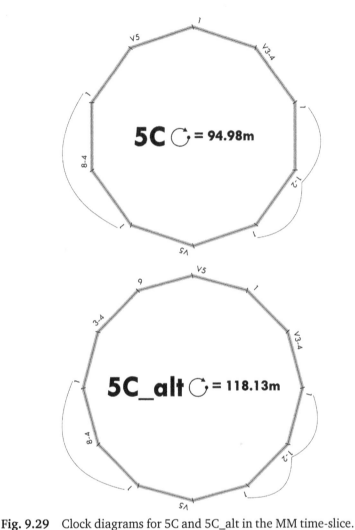

Fig. 9.29 Clock diagrams for 5C and 5C_alt in the MM time-slice.

These clock diagrams comprise 5C and the imagined geographical diachronic equivalent 5C_alt in the MM time-slice (see Fig. 9.25).

by 5E still forms a logical continuation with regards to the precinct of St. Mary's Abbey, accessible by the V5-3 boundary in the western extremity of Fig. 9.27.

Heuristically aggregating the subdivisions in each time-slice into a single occupiable space means that the respective clock diagrams can be aggregated into a single one for each time-slice. For the reasons stipulated above, in the case of MM 5C_alt shall be used for this purpose to increase historical continuity of the boundary line, topographically speaking. In addition, to not over-represent the street direction

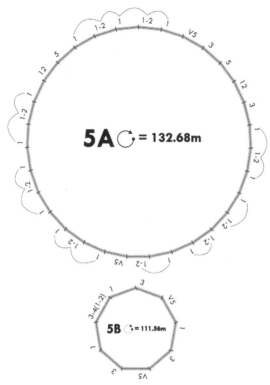

Fig. 9.30 Clock diagrams for 5A and 5B in the OS1872 time-slice (see Fig. 9.26).

choice in 1550s in comparison to MM and OS1872, the geometry of the latter aggregations include the 'virtual extensions' (road crossing areas) of the Type 5s to the west. Finally, as detail on distinctions in natural features is limited for OS1872 and 1550s, the two Type 12 subdivisions under the bridge (river flow and riverbank) in MM are amalgamated.

To aggregate clock diagrams, one should meticulously subtract the virtual boundaries currently separating the discrete Type 5 subdivisions, taking into account any duplication. In addition, one should also add virtuals to continue to include the heads of Type 5s meeting the new aggregate subdivision when removing the crossroads, to appropriately recalculate the total circumscription length.[7] Furthermore, care should

7. The length of the circumscription symbolised by the clock diagrams' polygons can normally be retrieved in the GIS environment, as the BLT identification exists as a single data feature. When aggregating this is no longer the case, as these larger circumscriptions have never been mapped as separate features.

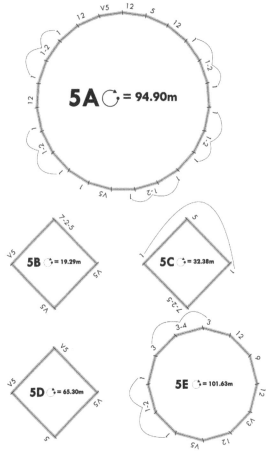

Fig. 9.31 Clock diagrams for 5A–5E in the 1550s time-slice (see Fig. 9.27).

be taken that the final order of the topological segments reflects the situation on the BLT map. The results of these aggregations can be seen in Figs. 9.32–9.34.

The effect of the aggregated clock diagrams is that we have an immediate overview of the boundary differentiation for the entirety of a geographically close continuous occupiable surface in each historical situation. The respective number of topological segments (1550s: 40; OS1872: 39; MM: 49) shows less difference between the sixteenth and nineteenth century than the dramatic morphological changes perhaps suggest. Simultaneously, and historically expected, from the nineteenth to the twenty-first century we recognise an intensification of

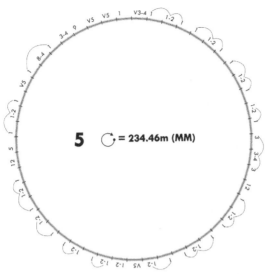

Fig. 9.32 Aggregate clock diagram for the MM time-slice.

differentiation. More importantly, the aggregate clock diagrams assist us in producing relative counts of overall topological segment diversity and the diversity regarded per discrete connected space. Furthermore, we can integrate whether these discrete spaces are readily accessible (i.e. does the space feature a virtual boundary or have an entrance

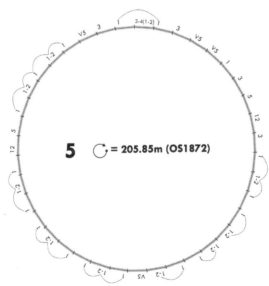

Fig. 9.33 Aggregate clock diagram for the OS1872 time-slice.

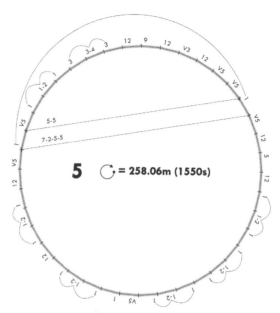

Fig. 9.34 Aggregate clock diagram for the 1550s time-slice.

The two diagonals that 'slice' the polygon (Types 5-5 and 7-2-5-5) represent the gate house, which must be crossed in order to reach the areas beyond, but the boundaries associated with that crossing do not form part of the circumscription of the aggregate subdivision.

as (part of) the boundary interface with the aggregate subdivision?). The diagrammatic representation of these statistics is shown in Figs. 9.35 and 9.36.

From Fig. 9.35, it transpires that the 1550s urban built environment, by a small margin, materially presents the socio-spatially most diverse situation, while OS1872 features the least diversity. As originally suspected from Fig. 9.27, the situation surrounding the city gate in 1550s results in a greater choice of directions for continued thoroughfare (Type 5s). The distinct rise in frequency of Types 1 and 1-2 in MM clearly captures the role played by buildings in intensifying differentiation, while at the same time the number of roads sees a small decline. Both these observations are reconfirmed when corrected for the number of connected discrete spaces in Fig. 9.36. Another important insight that becomes clear is that not-man-made boundaries (Type 12) still play a dominant role in 1550s, even though manipulation of these natural features was possible, as testified by the encroachment onto the river of buildings constructed along the bridge (see also Keene 1985). This may indicate that integrating 'natural' boundaries within the built environment might have enabled a greater contribution to resources or the facilities needed for everyday inhabitation (e.g.

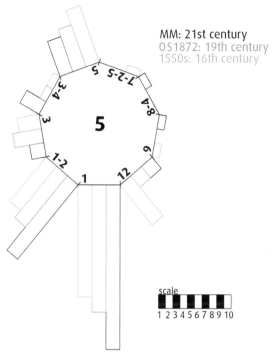

Fig. 9.35 Frequency clock diagram for the diachronic diversity of topological segments.

This frequency clock diagram displays the diversity of topological segments of the aggregated Type 5s across all three time-slices. The unique 1550s 7-2-5 segment originates from the city gate, while following Fig. 9.34's diagonal slice, 1550s also features an additional 5.

access to streaming water). Furthermore, it suggests that the pressure to develop additional occupiable surfaces to maximise interactive opportunities must have been low enough to retain these boundaries affording interaction with the natural environment. Considering that Winchester as a city had been in decline (Keene 1985), this is a reification of the social developmental effects.

Although taking in the overview of the whole section of the MM BLT Map in Fig. 9.25 the historically upward trend of Type 3s as a determinant operation is unmistakable; in my small boundary line selection this trend also shows up. While Fig. 9.36 shows that the number of discrete spaces resulting from associative boundaries shows a decline from OS1872 to MM, the number of times inhabitants gain ready access towards dominants through Type 3s rises strongly. This demonstrates their increasing socio-spatial importance in structuring daily life. Similarly, there is a sharper rise in the proportion of

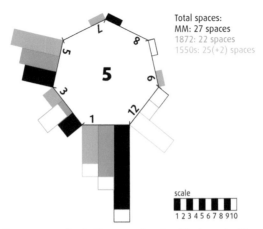

Fig. 9.36 Frequency clock diagram for the diachronic diversity of connected discrete spaces

This frequency clock diagram displays the number of connected discrete spaces, with the solid coloured columns representing the proportion of readily accessible spaces. The two additional spaces in 1550s result from the hierarchically distinct space of the walled city (Type 7) and the consequential street space under the gate itself.

buildings accessible directly from the street between OS1872 and MM than between 1550s and OS1872. While the hierarchically enclosing effect of Type 7 disappears after 1550s, not to return, by having used 5C_alt (see Figs. 9.25 and 9.29) we can recognise the disappearance of a Type 9 operation in the nineteenth century, which reappears in that geographical vicinity in the twenty-first century. Whether this is suggestive of a rhythmic developmental regularity (hypothesised in Chapter 8) could only be revealed by studying a large number of similar situations across time.

Lastly, it is easily overlooked that actually the bridge, river, and street spaces, as well as their general pattern of relating to buildings, across all time-slices are cogent examples of stability in development over time. Within their modifications these boundaries have shown more resilience than transformation. Both change and stability are afforded by the material and socio-spatial properties of boundaries in the process of inhabitation.

Taking a radical comparative perspective

After some initial remarks of the radical comparative potential already afforded between these test cases, I dedicate some final thought to comparing the historical progression of Winchester to sixth-century

Chunchucmil. While I can offer no rationale for the particular comparison of these two cities, British urbanism is considered part of the globalised high-density urban tradition, and Maya urbanism shows characteristics of tropical low-density urban traditions that have now disappeared. The analytical techniques demonstrated in this chapter offer a preliminary yet rigorous capacity for visualising and quantifying concretely what such opposition means socio-spatially. Thereby BLT Mapping has opened a route towards radical comparisons that can acquire an evidence-base and diversify interpretive understanding of the full range of morphological and configurative possibilities for urban development. In addition to the general statistical approach opening this chapter, Table 9.4 repeats the three

Table 9.4 Boundary differentiations along the length of Type 5s in Winchester diachronically put against relevant values in Chunchucmil.

	Aggregate clock	All segments	Corrected for spaces	Entrance corrected per space
	1550s	6.45	10.32 (9.56)	32.26 (28.67)
	OS1872	5.28	9.36	22.87
	MM	4.79	8.68	13.79
	Clock number	**All segments**	**Corrected for spaces**	**Entrance corrected per space**
	9A	34.3	47.4	805.7
	9B	16.2	21	94.6
	9C	17.8	23.7	131.9
	6	11.3	19.2	48
	5A	18.6		
	5Ba	30.1		
	5Bb	17.5		
	5C	24.66		
	5D	33.58		

Frequency of boundary differentiation over length in metres (vertical axis label)

This table contains the average distances between boundary differentiations along the length of the selected BLT circumscriptions in Winchester diachronically, while adding the corresponding values from Tables 9.2 and 9.3 on Chunchucmil. The values in brackets include the walled enclosure (Type 7) and the gate's street space in the first instance, and only the gate as an entrance in the second. (Although the same phrase as in Table 9.3 is used, there are no multiple entrances for any single discrete space in Winchester's data selection.)

most relevant quantified formal descriptive measures of Tables 9.2 and 9.3 on Chunchucmil to now include the diachronic test case on Winchester.

One should bear in mind that no entrances edge onto the sides of Type 5 operations in Chunchucmil, nor are there instances of materially facilitated traversability (these pathways have materially continuously demarcated sides), thus the last rows in Table 9.4 have no valid counterparts in Tables 9.3 and 9.2. Discounting Type 5s for 'entrances corrected per space' on the lower end of Chunchucmil (48) compared to the higher end of Winchester (32.26 or 28.67) produces a minimal contrast in differentiation density, which is proportionally fairly similar to the results of 'all segments' and 'corrected for spaces' over the boundary length (11.3 against 6.45; and 19.2 against 10.32 or 9.56 respectively).[8] These contrasts only increase as Winchester develops over time and are gigantic when taking Chunchucmil's maxima instead (34.3; 47.4; 805.7 respective to the measures in Table 9.4). Diachronically Table 9.4 also shows that while connected discrete spaces take a slight fall between the sixteenth and nineteenth century (see Fig. 9.36), the intensity with which connections to these spaces occur remains virtually the same. During the same period the intensity in terms of soliciting access or coming out onto the Type 5s rises ('entrances corrected per space'). This last observation was not that apparent from Fig. 9.36 earlier.

In addition, it can be noted that the constitution of inner Type 5 operated subdivisions in Winchester is socio-spatially more diverse (as well as more intense). In Chunchucmil, Type 5s involve a variety of five different topological segments (Figs. 9.11 and 9.20 taken together) versus a maximum of nine (in 1550s aggregate) in Winchester. However, if we compare Type 5s in Winchester as circulation spaces to Type 9s in Chunchucmil as an essential component of circulation space, the socio-spatial diversity is greater in Chunchucmil, with thirteen against nine different topological segments. To further advance such a comparison it would be necessary to compile all circulation spaces and/or those directing for access to specific destinations (i.e. Type 5s leading to a dominant (complex)). In a representative study, not only the number of differences but also the (recurrent) kinds of differences are significant to find out about socio-functional characteristics. In this way, trends in the nature of interactive opportunities seen from a city's most readily (and plausibly most often) traversed spaces in

8. The differentiation density difference in this BLT selection fluctuates between max. 1.5 and 1.9 or 1.7 and 2 times denser (= averagely more frequent change along a boundary) in Winchester.

inhabitation could be uncovered, which also would make a good proxy for what a casual stranger to the city would most likely encounter.

It is promptly acknowledged that the analytical examples visualised and discussed in the preceding are interpretively limited and most definitely not exhaustive. In contrast to many of the analytical measures discussed in Chapter 8, which would require some form of geocomputation, this chapter shows that stripped down and visually more intuitive versions of various analytical variables are immediately within our grasp once BLT Mapping has been applied. While one should appreciate the strong restriction on data selection in these tests, a few insights have been completely new or beyond expectation, and comparisons without representative validity are highly speculative. The interpretive register of unequivocal interest is that all of these hypothesising insights can immediately be brought into (radically) *comparative* perspectives, on both intra-city and inter-city level. Doing so will increase our understanding of the *nature* of the social opportunities urban built environments offer their inhabitants, conveyed on the low interpretive level (Chapter 1) of emplaced lived experience (Chapter 3).

Chapter 2 argues that explorative research outcomes do not necessarily conclude, but merely hypothesise. The validity of the insights reached is determined by their practical adequacy in terms of empirical tenacity and whether they are causally sound in constitutive processes. In extension, it is reassuring to see several instances in which analysing Winchester's material-spatial composition reproduces, confirms, or suggests things we know from historical research or would familiarly expect to be the case, e.g. in terms of diachronic development processes. Such reproduction of knowledge in a familiar case means that arguments formulated about the social life in the radically different urban landscape of Chunchucmil can assume greater credence.

The sheer variety of analytical and interpretive opportunities created in the preliminary explorations above show great promise for more extensive future research. Especially when building a body of case studies, BLT Mapping may push the boundaries of knowledge, lend existing hypotheses socio-spatial support, produce insights by integrating other data sources, or discover patterns in correlation with other methods. Particularly exciting is the prospect of fully unlocking more of the analytical measures suggested in Chapter 8, especially through geocomputational development. Such developments could strongly increase how many aspects of the BLT data can be scrutinised and improve both the representative validity and fundamental relevance of analytical outcomes. GIS-based spatial analyses make an effective basis to achieve powerful insights simply by being more flexible and more efficient for (comparative) data parsing and visualisation.

In this book, BLT Mapping has become my methodological reply to a plea for more inclusive and rigorous comparative urban studies. The demonstrations given here invest me with confidence to assert that a new field of interpretive knowledge has been made feasible. Future innovation on tools and analytical measures, alongside growing a wide field of applied examples, will contribute to our critical understanding and appreciation of patterns of urban life and development. Other researchers may choose instead to engage with the theoretical and philosophical premises, metaconcepts, and underlabouring social science of BLT Mapping, or embrace a boundary approach more broadly. BLT Mapping provides formal concepts to conjure up a fuller image of the afforded processes and affective experience caused within the material-spatial frames that accommodate the continuous events of urban inhabitation. With that, we shift interpretive perspective from inferring what happens in space to considering how it matters what space is like to inhabit.

CONTEMPLATING THE FUTURE OF BLT MAPPING

Current results

Before glancing into the future, let me first reflect on what is achieved in this book. I set out to enable the radical comparison of cities as a socially interpretive study of the material and spatial characteristics of the urban built environment. When we consider that the world is still urbanising at a rapid rate, and this is the continuation of a deeply historical process humanity has been living through for millennia, we need to acquire emancipating knowledge on our relationship with the spaces we build to inhabit. From a comparative perspective, the deep past and present provide a wealth of examples of developmental trajectories and socio-cultural responses to transforming landscapes in a variety of environments that meet the demand for space that effectively accommodates social life. The natural and environmental scientific work on cities notwithstanding, the essentially human and social scientific concern here appreciates that any engineering, design or planning implementations have social effects for how urban inhabitation functions. To make a substantive and rigorous contribution to improving our knowledge of the greatest diversity of urbanisation patterns and urban life as a fundamentally human process of inhabitation, we require appropriate theoretical and methodological frames of reference. In developing a dedicated research process that addresses just such a frame of reference, this book has produced a series of major conceptual research outcomes, before devising a generally applicable method for analysing and interpreting urban built environments.

Much space in this book has been devoted to theoretical and conceptual argumentation and definitions. The progression through these stages of development stand in testament to the fact that the empirical BLT Mapping method simply cannot be divorced from the theoretical framework and concepts that directly inform and set up its practice. It is in the precursory parts that my arguments resonate even beyond the variety of disciplinary fields that unite in urban studies. From its initial inception, this book is overtly interdisciplinary, liberally blending broadly conceived historical humanities, existential, philosophical, social theoretical and spatial scientific interests. As a physical-material adaptation of critical realist research design, a treatise on society-space relations, an empirical mapping translation of boundary theory, and an interpretive application of spatial data structures in GIS, its relevance is not strictly confined to the built environment and urban theme.

The opening arguments in Chapter 1 led to formulating an original working definition of the city as urban life taking place in spatial transformations. By foregrounding process and social practice in designed landscapes, this definition aims to overcome the comparative limitations resulting from framing urban studies with socio-culturally predetermined categorisations. Consequentially, a case was made for a low-level social interpretive approach to ensure comparative validity. Adopting a rudimentary interpretive goal steers clear of the pitfall of acquiring insights according to the particular cultural and historical contexts of time-space specific cases. This inevitably restricts and abstracts what interpretations can mean specifically. Yet, I subsequently demonstrated the comparative rigour and advancement enabled by retaining exclusive reference to material-spatial data sources, which are subjected to strictly constitutive and experiential low-level analysis and interpretation of urban built environment morphology. As a result BLT Mapping claims a deserving spot in the spectrum of empirical urban theories (Smith 2011a).

In Chapter 2 it was found that such an appropriate research process could take inspiration from critical realism. Picking up Wallace's (2011) challenge to unlock the theoretical cogency critical realism could bring to archaeology, I adapted the empirical research processes previously embraced in human geography to specify a research practice suitable for social studies of materialisation. Fully utilising critical realist's strength to place conceptual and empirical research in a dialectical relation, I positioned the built environment as an ontological category within the emergent entity of 'the material' to open a differently informed research path. Revolving around distinguishing spatial dependence from independence, the inhabited built environment can be studied from the perspective of the causal powers conveyed by material properties. The ensuing chapters of this book demonstrate the effects of a critical realist organisation of interpretive research on physical (material) evidence, roughly pertaining to the philosophical pillars of immanent critique, conditional statements, ontological causal powers, iterative abstraction and triangulation (Chapters 3–7). The book's endgame consolidates my pursuit of practically adequate knowledge, welcoming multiple methods and quantitative exploration accepting of the hypothetical nature of interpretations bound by necessary conditions and causal contingencies. As an example of adapting critical realist research processes, this book may influence and progress the material turn currently ongoing in the social sciences.

Chapter 3's theoretical framework establishes that the encounter and understanding of material differentiations co-constitutes human being in the world. When we make our world for the purpose of inhabitation we shape it by introducing material transformations that subdivide the world. Put differently, we construct boundaries around the spaces we occupy to organise and structure how our environment functions. The experience of interactional opportunities this affords and affects, in turn, bears a constitutive relation to the continuous societal development of that landscape. Approaching cities in this way implies appreciating the significance of the material presence of boundaries to inhabiting urban built environments. Chapter 4 therefore focuses just on how boundaries bind and link up to form entities. It explains how the crucial philosophical ideas of Smith & Varzi (1997, 2000), on fiat and bona fide boundaries, help to make a structural connection between boundaries conceptualised as sites of difference and empirical evidence on built boundaries. Fiat and bona fide boundaries eventually impart a profound understanding on exactly what boundaries, captured as spatial data (lines) and visual representations thereof, convey.

In this way the road is paved to face the empirical reality of urban built environments. In the empirical world, each spatial subdivision operates on the principle of secluding itself from its outside. Chapter 5 is the pivot where the specific secluding differentiations that built boundaries effectuate (causal mechanisms) are distinguished. Equally interpretive and empirically identifiable definitions are created to capture these distinct operations. Ultimately, all spaces of the urban built environment can be formally redescribed in such boundary types and mapped as lines, which therefore results in an ontology intrinsic to the city. In crossing a boundary in the built environment, an inhabitant experiences how interactional opportunities are spatially dependent on that boundary. This means that the interpretive contribution of each distinct boundary is restricted to how it constitutes the affording and affecting qualities of the material frame of a spatial subdivision. The interpretation of the ontology intrinsic to the city mapped in Boundary Line Types (BLT) is supported on three levels of socio-spatial significance, which refer to the dimensional, locational, and aggregative context in which they occur.

The current BLT ontology of types has proven practically adequate in empirical tests, but by its very nature the definitions are open to development through an iterative dialectic with empirical findings. Furthermore, adopters should be mindful that I can only vouch for this ontology as causally following from my particular social interpretive perspective that enables radical comparisons. When a disparate interest is pursued in studying the material-spatial characteristics of boundaries (edges or interfaces) that compose the built environment, other definitions might be called for even if some of the boundary theory retains its pertinence.

Chapters 6 and 7 evaluate the methodological precedent for examining urban morphology and built form originating from the disciplinary contexts of geography, history, archaeology and architecture. The preparatory and analytical processes of applying BLT Mapping are much indebted to these preceding methods, even though I conclude that none of these suits my particular social interpretive perspective on radical urban comparisons. The BLTs were put to the test in two cases captured in sharply divergent legacy datasets. The maps for Winchester and Chunchucmil together represent an array of mapping purposes: an archaeological topographical survey, historically reconstructed maps, historical cartography, and a policy-oriented contemporary urban plan. Despite inevitable limitations imposed by respectively different mapping standards, and my knowledge of what each dataset records exactly, I could demonstrate that BLTs can be applied in all these data conditions. Comparative potential is further maximised by the deliberate selection of examples of dramatically contrasting urban traditions. First, the long disappeared, indigenous tropical dispersed urbanism of ancient Maya cities, represented by Chunchucmil (Mexico). Second, the currently globalised high-density urbanism, which historically spread out of Europe, represented by Winchester (UK).

The successful application of BLT Mapping in these cases demonstrates a native ability for interpretive radical comparisons that significantly improves on existing methods and research practice, notably urban historical GIS (HGIS), (Conzenian) urban morphology, and (urban) space syntax. Nevertheless, each data source will have restrictions – spatial analysis cannot abide data gaps – which can be moderated with pragmatic rulesets in data preparation to various degrees of satisfaction (project dependent). It may come as no surprise that when working on material properties, good quality archaeological plans are naturally the least ambiguously equipped for the task. However, since archaeological preservation is not perfect, a critical and rigorous approach to filling in the unpreserved urban form and fabric is required. Historical reconstructions will usually not only be partial in how much of the urban topography is mapped, they can also suffer from the complication of historical sources, which tend to record property rather than the physical environment. Historical cartography varies greatly and some examples are unsuitable without carrying out substantive additional original research on how and what of the physical environment is mapped. The late nineteenth-century standards in the UK can surpass the detail contained on contemporary city plans, sometimes approximating archaeology for architectural precision. Yet, both the nineteenth century and contemporary standards maintain several significant ambiguities and omissions from their mapping conventions. Conjectures, therefore, are pervasive regardless of data source. Here, I prioritised topological conjectures (i.e. subdividing boundaries) over precise morphology, but varying degrees of uncertainty cannot be avoided.

When the methodological development turns to analytical measures, it must respect the GIS data structure resulting from applying BLT Mapping, as well as how any specific measure is supported by the theoretical conceptualisations and the levels of socio-spatial significance of Chapter 5. Taking this into account, Chapter 8 develops a set of visualisations and analytical measures that regularly must also acknowledge empirical precedents, or some overlap with existing methods. Ultimately, similarities are caused because the basic input for these methods, the urban built environment, is shared. Along the same line, I conclude that BLT data preparation leaves the original topography of the built environment layout intact to such an extent that methodological integration is entirely possible. Indeed, concurring with critical realist triangulation, it would be welcomed. Although there may be disagreements in theoretical foundations, BLT Mapping's interpretive agenda is complementary rather than in conflict or competition with these methods. According to its distinct objectives, I have reasoned through a number of analytical measures, as well as their interpretive value when applied synchronically and diachronically, which are particular to BLT Mapping. Many of these measures make use of an emergent deconstruction of BLT data as an analytical unit: topological segments, which are composed of BLT combinations. Topological segments act as the smallest meaningful element in the inhabited urban built environment. Their variety and occurrence are completely dependent on each case, attesting that BLT ontologies are intrinsic.

Finally, BLT Mapping makes a persuasive case for original geocomputational developments, based on requirements resulting from Chapter 8's analytical rationales and demonstrated by Chapter 9's initial analytical explorations. The quantification and visualisation of spatial analyses offer opportunities to advance the interpretive and comparative agenda of BLT Mapping, because it can make analytical measures more adaptable and data processing much more efficient. Preliminary geocomputational programming to lay the basis of a future extensive suite of tools in an *ArcGIS* plugin was carried out collaboratively (credit to Andrew Evans) during BLT Mapping's first methodological development at the University of Leeds. The initial attempt at producing readable BLT maps by manipulating how *ArcGIS* displays data in the data frame, supports various manual workarounds that allow data abstractions and selections to further scrutinise just what BLT data reveal.

Meanwhile the global statistical output from the rudimentary *ArcGIS* plugin provides immediate general contexts, based on separate BLTs and topological segments, for any small-scale exploration. Chapter 9 demonstrates beyond doubt the enormous breadth of research questions that could be addressed using Chapter 8's analytical suggestions, even though only few of these are computationally fully operational. To progress the meticulous comparative examination of intricate BLT maps, I devised the 'clock diagram' to standardise the visualisation of how spaces are constituted by topological segments regardless of morphology (here restricted to geometry of shape and size). These diagrams have proven to be a highly flexible aid in extracting quantitative patterns, and clarify more intuitive inspections of BLT maps.

Since my final aim with this book is merely to demonstrate the functionality and capability of the resultant new method, the value of the interpretative arguments in Chapter 9 is conspicuously restricted by the test case data selections. These interpretations are simply indicative of what full-fledged case studies might address, and the extensive scope for further comparative work these analyses support. At the same time, since these crude interpretations are already reproducing and confirming some existing knowledge and familiarity within the Winchester case, important proof of concept for the validity of applying BLT Mapping is also delivered. Worthwhile directions for further research are so identified, including the promise of combinations with other information sources and correlating the outcomes of multiple methods. In addition, it shows BLT Mapping is an example of successful and progressive qualitative use of vector GIS.

To close this reflection on the main results I will briefly revisit salient examples of interpretation. In Winchester, BLT Mapping concretely reflects a stage of urban development in the Victorian era from shared (in the sixteenth century) to individual plot structures. BLT Mapping also makes a strong case for the structuring socio-functional role of the medieval east gate. Diachronically, even on a minute scale, BLT Mapping gave precise expression to general processes of urban development: e.g. pressure on integration of and access to natural features, and the intensification of architecturally mediated access to increasing numbers of plots. In radical comparisons, BLT Mapping produced crystal-clear variables that indicate the actual differences between inhabiting tropical dispersed 'low-density' and compact 'high-density' urban form. The relative complexity and diversity of interaction opportunities resulting from the socio-spatial composition of both cities was contrasted in direct relation to each other. Findings particular to Chunchucmil include a much-improved appreciation of the structural properties of circulation space, and the functional differences in traversability choice and thoroughfare afforded by big open spaces. I traced how an inhabitant would be exposed to experiential changes when moving along an origin-destination path. Moreover, the disproportional stake of shared plots and open space in determining Chunchucmil's built environment structure was given an absolute expression, and internally contrasted to the more specialised socio-functional position of square-like (or plazas) architectural groups.

Future research

The future research anticipated in this final section is not absolutely new to this book. Throughout the chapters and in the above, various cases and suggestions for future research have been made. This book, I hope, will be received as much as an invitation to critically engage and adapt my concepts and theories, as that it serves as a manual both to apply BLT Mapping proper and to develop further approaches for radical comparative research based on material evidence. The current section, then, serves to emphasise, reiterate and collate such opportunities concisely.

As a comprehensive presentation of authentic methodological development, at virtually all stages, this book encourages new or alternative ways of knowledge production. The obstacles encountered in this development have been countered with workable solutions. The successful application of BLT Mapping on diverse spatial datasets, and the promising indications to both produce new interpretations and provide underpinning evidence for existing understandings of urban space, should instil confidence in readers wishing to follow the same process. For purposes here that 'same process' is double counted: first, developing case studies and comparisons based on BLT Mapping, and second, developing alternative methodological directions and associated concepts according to the overarching research process. If, after reading, neither option seems feasible or attractive, I implore the reader at least to consider my plea for radically comparative urban studies, and to contribute by better equipping comparative urban research with appropriate frames of reference.

When accepting its particular social interpretive perspective on the inhabited urban built environment, the most apparent opportunity for future research presents itself in the form of developing full-fledged case studies. Naturally, the test cases presented here, Chunchucmil and Winchester, readily hold this potential and, therefore, so does most legacy spatial data on archaeological, historical and contemporary phases of cities' built environments. Arguably, the key to proving, beyond doubt, the relevance and validity of the specific interpretive contributions BLT Mapping could make is to gradually build a body of case studies. Incrementally adding examples that cover greater variety and better representation of all urban traditions and cultural contexts provides a collection of evidence that meanwhile increases the scope for meaningful comparisons. By contrasting cases from past and contemporary urban societies and cultures of building to articulate differences, similarities, and to identify regularities to the experience of urban life and the effects of urban developments, I expect emancipating understanding will follow. Such emancipating understanding can act as a cogwheel in the multidisciplinary mechanism that informs future urban developmental scenarios and trajectories.

Until that time, when pursuing separate case studies, or even simply with additional data from selective test cases, more strictly purposive and thematically focused studies can be undertaken. Most immediately, these purposes include investigations on patterns of the socio-spatial composition of architectural complexes. In the locational and aggregative contexts their interrelated position, and how architectural complexes link up, could reveal neighbourhood effects and other socio-functional zonation. Alternatively, one might focus on disentangling the distinct socio-spatial roles of urban open space and the material properties of how circulation space connects and structures across cities. With sufficient availability of diachronic data, the opportunity is opened to assess and identify how aspects of urban form adapt and get modified, or how elements of urban form display rhythms in the changes they afford.

Subsequently, thematic foci could be reinforced by structurally linking and engaging with other information sources available for the same city. This could include locations of urban and societal service provision, such as places of production, commerce, and consumption, ecosystem services, (informal) activity areas, (natural) resources, and applying functional architectural typologies. Furthermore, one might consider the labour investment in the material construction of a city, applying stylistic architectural typologies, multisensory experience and response, and special material functions, such as defensibility, socio-cultural, symbolic or political communication (semiotics). In addition, the effects of temporary and recurrent changes of the material state of the city could be relevant, and might require running analyses in various scenarios, e.g. opening and closure times, seasonal and weather changes, or the conditions unfolding during special events. These opportunities can be operationalised by investing such information in the BLT data or associate polygons with attributes in the GIS database to create a structurally linked dialogue. BLT Mapping also supports studying more objective and subjective urban morphological variables, including metric measurements, appreciation of urban fabric, and morphological development zones. Chapter 9's example of integrating accessible area sizes in clock diagrams showed some of these combinations may be within immediate grasp.

According to the critical realist process of iterative abstraction, continued empirical engagement may result in findings that request development, intervention, or deviation from some of the current conceptual definitions this book contains, especially the BLTs themselves. Next to such inevitable conceptual succession, arbitrary research preferences, e.g. operating at other levels of detail or disparate aims, may demand the complete reformulation of a BLT-like ontology of types, or a departure from current emphases in boundary theory, while holding on to boundary principles. Simply put, the same concepts are not necessarily (causally) fit to support inferences towards theoretically unrelated hypotheses. This does not withstand that when interpretive correlations are found through working with other (complementary) sources or methods, such serendipity could also lead to new questions that invite further research to provide explanations for why that correlation may occur (cf. discourse in space syntax). Thanks to BLT Mapping's fundamentally human and optimally comparative social science, it can act as an underlabourer that merely provides thick formal socio-spatial redescriptions. That alone can forge discursive synergies with other methods and fields of knowledge.

In the case of urban morphology and space syntax, BLT Mapping is introduced at a fortuitous moment. A growing body of research is exploring synergies between these two, either maintaining them as essentially separate methods that are applied to particular cases (Griffiths et al. 2010), or developing new approaches of integrative measures (Marcus 2007, 2010; Ståhle et al. 2005). Within a GIS environment, integration is recently aided and advanced by plugins that bring space syntactic analyses to these platforms (Gil et al. 2007, 2015; Ståhle et al. 2005; Ståhle 2012). It cannot be anticipated how this integration will play out, but it is clear that rather than complicate the current state of affairs, BLT Mapping data would willingly allow all three methods to sit alongside each other in GIS. The relatively flexible and layered geographical nature of GIS, as is also exploited in HGIS, logically surfaces as a uniting computational user interface. Doing so, for these three methods, would open a dialogue to identify mutually reinforcing output and productive complementarity.

Finally, it can be foreseen that as long as BLT Mapping remains a predominantly manual interpretive mapping practice, BLT data creation can be relatively slow and laborious. This may prove an obstacle in the uptake of this new method for those with limited time resources. Naturally, the more the input data is natively suited and appropriately formatted, the speedier the data preparation process will be. Moreover, vectorisation and tracing tools in GIS are likely to keep improving too. On top of that, geocomputational development dedicated to BLT Mapping has the opportunity to make for more rewarding research prospects. While I believe the BLT definitions themselves are some way off enabling automatic identification, the propositions for analytical measures in Chapter 8 show clear pathways for hugely beneficial GIS software development. The BLT data structure challenges GIS's native abilities for spatial analysis, because it respects interpretive concepts rather than empirical observation alone. New projects could undertake work towards a comprehensive BLT toolkit by building on my projected array of propositions and defining further measures with clear interpretive value. Presently, density-intensity measures come to the fore as exceptionally high-potential. Methodologically, this potential shines through in the analytical trials in this work. The benefits to comprehension that variegating density-intensity measures would have is corroborated by the largely concealed controversy over the qualified use of high- and low-density urbanism labels. Apropos to density, the compact city paradigm is the global fashion of sustainable urban design, while Maya cities illustrate long histories of developing contrary patterns in the landscape.

Eventually, it can be expected that fulfilling the promise of BLT Mapping applications and derivative research, which is to make a significant contribution to emancipating understanding and appreciation of the processes of urban life and development manifested in all their versatility, will be a long-term affair. Protean contributions are possible, ranging incrementally from, broadly speaking, the human experience of built space, to the process of materialisation, to patterns of socio-spatial coherence, and built environments' disposition to afford and promote societal stability and social sustainability. Through radical urban comparisons, the differences and regularities between urban traditions or the outcomes of developmental strategies today, become tied to understanding our successes and failures in long-term trajectories. Such emancipatory, theoretically grounded evidence-base may then go on to inform and empower interventions, modelling, and planning in urban design, because that evidence reifies the blueprint for human inhabitation of the world.

REFERENCES

Abbott, A. 1995, Things of Boundaries, *Social Research* 62(4): 857–882.

Abed, J. and Kaysi, I. 2003, Identifying Urban Boundaries: Application of remote sensing and geographic information system technologies, *Canadian Journal of Civil Engineering* 30: 992–999.

Adanez Pavón, J., Lacadena García-Gallo, A., Ciudad Ruiz, A. and Ponce de León, M.J.I. 2009, La Identificación de Unidades Socio-Administrativas en las Ciudades Mayas Clásicas: El caso de Tikal (Petén, Guatemala), *XIX Encuentro Internacional 'Los Investigadores de la Cultura Maya'*, Universidad Autónoma de Campeche, San Francisco de Campeche.

Aimers, J.J. 2007, What Maya Collapse? Terminal Classic variation in the Maya Lowlands, *Journal of Archaeological Research* 15(4): 329–377.

Alberti, B. 2016, Archaeologies of Ontology, *Annual Review of Anthropology* 45: 163–179.

Alexander, C. 1979, *The Timeless Way of Building*, Oxford University Press, New York.

Alexander, C., Ishikawa, S., Silverstein, M., Jacobson, M., Fiksdahl-King, I., Angel, S. 1977, *A Pattern Language: Towns, buildings, construction*, Oxford University Press, New York.

Algaze, G. 2005, The Sumerian Takeoff, *Structure and Dynamics* 1(1) (http://escholarship.org/uc/item/76r673km, accessed 24-09-2013).

Amherst College 2009, *Tokyo Cityscape* (http://ats.amherst.edu/tokyodemo/, accessed 06-05-2013).

Amherst College 2010, *Paris Cityscape* (http://ats.amherst.edu/parisdemo/, accessed 06-05-2013).

Anderson, B. and Tolia-Kelly, D. 2004, Matter(s) in Social and Cultural Geography, *Geoforum* 35: 669–674.

Anderson, B. and Wylie, J. 2009, On Geography and Materiality, *Environment and Planning A* 41: 318–335.

Andersson, H. 2016, Urban or Urbanization, *Norwegian Archaeological Review* 49(1): 62–64.

Andrews, G.F. 1975, *Maya Cities: Placemaking and urbanization*, University of Oklahoma Press, Norman.

Appleton, J. 1975, *The Experience of Landscape*, John Wiley, London.

ArcGIS Resources: Identify feature changes between map editions 2012 (http://blogs.esri.com/esri/arcgis/2012/08/08/identify-feature-changes-between-map-editions/, accessed 13-08-2013).

Archer, M.S. 1995, *Realist Social Theory: The morphogenetic approach*, University of Cambridge Press, Cambridge.

Archer, J. 2005, Social Theory of Space: Architecture and the production of self, culture, and society, *Journal of the Society of Architectural Historians* 64(4): 430–433.

Arnade, P.J., Howell, M.C. and Simons, W. 2002, Fertile Spaces: The productivity of urban space in Northern Europe, *Journal of Interdisciplinary History* 32(4): 515–548.

Arnauld, M.C. Manzanilla, L.R. and Smith, M.E. (ed.) 2012, *The Neighborhood as a Social and Spatial Unit in Mesoamerican Cities*, The University of Arizona Press, Tucson.

Arnoldi, J. 2001, Niklas Luhmann: An introduction, *Theory, Culture & Society*, 18(1): 1–13.

Ashmore, W. and Sabloff, J.A. 2002, Order in Maya Civic Plans, *Latin American Antiquity* 13(2): 201–215.

Ashmore, W. and Sabloff, J.A. 2003, Interpreting Ancient Maya Civic Plans: Reply to Smith, *Latin American Antiquity* 14(2): 229–236.

Atkin, T. and Rykwert, J. (ed.) 2005, *Structure and Meaning in Human Settlement*, University of Pennsylvania Museum of Archaeology and Anthropology, Philadelphia.

Bafna, S. 2003, Space Syntax: A brief introduction to its logic and techniques, *Environment and Behavior* 35(1): 17–29.

Bakirtzis, C. 2003, The Urban Continuity and Size of Late Byzantine Thessalonike, in: Talbot, A.-M. (ed.) *Symposium on Late Byzantine Thessalonike*, Dumbarton Oaks Papers, No. 57, Dumbarton Oaks Research Library and Collection, Washington: 35–64.

Barnhart, E.L. 2003, Urbanism at Palenque, *The Pari Journal: A quarterly publication of the Pre-Columbian Art Research Institute* 4(1): 10–16.

Barnhart, E.L. 2005, *Palenque's Settlement Pattern and Social Organization Models* (http://www.mayaexploration.org/pdf/PalenqueSocialOrganization_Nov2005.pdf, accessed 15-08-2013).

Barthel, S. and Isendahl, C. 2013, Urban Gardens, Agriculture, and Water Management: Sources of resilience for long-term food security in cities, *Ecological Economics* 86: 224–234.

Bastian, R.W. 1980, Urban House Types as a Research Focus in Historical Geography, *Environmental Review: ER* 4(2): 27–34.

Batty, M. 2009, Accessibility: In search of a unified theory, *Environment and Planning B: Planning and Design* 36: 191–194.

Batty, M. and Longley, P. 1994, *Fractal Cities: A geometry of form and function*, Academic Press, London.

Batty, M. and Rana, S. 2004, The automatic definition and generation of axial lines and axial maps, *Environment and Planning B* 31: 615–640.

Bazy, D. 2011, Las Modalidades y Dinámicas de las Relaciones entre Facciones Políticas en Piedras Negras, Petén, Guatemala: El dualism politico, *Traces* 59: 59–73.

Becker, J.M. 2001, Houselots at Tikal Guatemala: It's what's out back that counts, in: Ruiz, A.C., Ponce de Leon, M.J.I. and Carmen Martinez Martinez, M. del (ed.) *Reconstruyendo la Ciudad Maya: El urbanismo en las sociedades antiguas*, Publicaciones de la SEEM, no. 6), Sociedad Española de Estudios Mayas, Madrid: 427–460.

Becker, J.M. 2004, Maya Heterarchy as Inferred from Classic-Period Plaza Plans, *Ancient Mesoamerica* 15: 127–138.

Beisaw, A.M. and Gibb, J.G. 2013, Mapping Town Formation: Precision, accuracy, and memory, presented at: *Society for Historical Archaeology annual meeting, 2013*, Leicester, UK.

Bell, C.M. 2009, *Ritual: Perspectives and dimensions*, Revised Edition, Oxford University Press, Oxford.

Bentley, R.A. and Maschner, H.D.G. (ed.) 2003, *Complex Systems and Archaeology: Empirical and theoretical applications*, Foundations of Archaeological Inquiry, University of Utah Press, Salt Lake City.

Bentley, R.A. and Maschner, H.D.G. 2009a, Complexity Theory, in: Bentley, R.A., Maschner, H.D.G. and Chippindale, C. (ed.) *Handbook of Archaeological Theories*, AltaMira Press, Lanham: 245–270.

Bentley, R.A. and Maschner, H.D.G. 2009b, Introduction: On archaeological theories, in: Bentley, R.A., Maschner, H.D.G. and Chippindale, C. (ed.) *Handbook of Archaeological Theories*, AltaMira Press, Lanham: 1–8.

Bettencourt, L.M.A. 2013, The Origin of Scaling in Cities, *Science* 340: 1438–1441.

Bevan, A., Jobbová, E., Helmke, C. and Awe, J. 2013, Directional Layouts in Central Lowland Maya Settlement, *Journal of Archaeological Science* 40(5): 2373–2383.

Biddle, M. 1976, *Winchester in the Early Middle Ages: An edition and discussion of the Winton Domesday*, Winchester Studies 1, Oxford University Press, Oxford.

Biddle, M. 2011, personal communication.

Bintliff, J. 2010, The Annales, Events, and the Fate of Cities, in: Bolender, D.J. (ed.) *Eventful Archaeologies: New approaches to social transformation in the archaeological record*, SUNY Press, Albany: 117–131.

Bintliff, J. and Pearce, M. (ed.) 2011, *The Death of Archaeological Theory?*, Oxbow Books, Oxford.

Bisschops, T. 2011, personal communication.

Bisschops, T. 2012, It Is All about Location: GIS, property records and the role of space in shaping late medieval urban life. The case of Antwerp around 1400, *Post-Classical Archaeologies* 2: 83–106.

Bissell, D. 2009, Conceptualising Differently-Mobile Passengers: Geographies of everyday encumbrance in the railway station, *Social & Cultural Geography* 10(2): 173–195.

Blake, E. 2002, Spatiality Past and Present: An interview with Edward Soja, Los Angeles, 12 April 2001, *Journal of Social Archaeology* 2(2): 139–158.

Blanton, R. 1982, Urban Beginnings: A view from anthropological archaeology, *Journal of Urban History* 8(4): 427–446.

Blaut, J.M. 1961, Space and Process, *The Professional Geographer* 13(4): 1–7.

Blaut, J.M. 1971, Space, Structure and Maps, *Tijdschrift voor Economische en Sociale Geografie* 62(1): 18–21.

Boivin, N., Brumm, A., Lewis, H., Robinson, D. and Korisettar, R. 2007, Sensual, Material, and Technological Understanding: Exploring prehistoric soundscapes in South India, *Journal of the Royal Anthropological Institute* (N.S.) 13: 267–294.

Bollnow, O.F. 1961, Lived-Space, *Philosophy Today* 5(1/4): 31–39.

Boone, M. 2002, Urban Space and Political Conflict in Late Medieval Flanders, *Journal of Interdisciplinary History* 32(4): 621–640.

Bossche Encyclopedie n.d. (http://www.bossche-encyclopedie.nl/, accessed 30-07-2013).

Bourdieu, P. 1977, *Outline of a Theory of Practice*, Cambridge University Press, Cambridge.

Bowen, W.M., Dunn, R.A. and Kasdan, D.O. 2010, What is 'Urban Studies'?: Context, internal structure, and content, *Journal of Urban Affairs* 32(2): 199–227.

Bowser, B.J. and Zedeño, M.N. (ed.) 2009, *The Archaeology of Meaningful Places*, Foundations of Archaeological Inquiry, University of Utah Press, Salt Lake City.

Briggs, X. de S. 2004, Civilization in Color: The multicultural city in three millennia, *City & Community* 3(4): 311–342.

British Historic Towns Atlas n.d. (http://www.historictownsatlas.org.uk/, accessed 06-08-2013).

Brown, C.T. and Witschey, W.R.T. 2003, The Fractal Geometry of Ancient Maya Settlement, *Journal of Archaeological Science* 30: 1619–1632.

Brown, C.T., Witschey, W.R.T. and Liebovitch, L.S. 2005, The Broken Past: Fractals in archaeology, *Journal of Archaeological Method and Theory* 12(1): 37–78.

Brughmans, T., Keay, S. and Earl, G. 2012, Complex Networks in Archaeology: Urban connectivity in Iron Age and Roman Southern Spain, *Leonardo* 45(3): 280.

Bruun, H. and Langlais, R. 2003, On the Embodied Nature of Action, *Acta Sociologica* 46(1): 31–49.

Bull, M. and Back, L. (ed.) 2003, *The Auditory Culture Reader*, Berg, Oxford.

Butzer, K.W. 2008, Other Perspectives on Urbanism: Beyond disciplinary boundaries, in: Marcus, J. and Sabloff, J.A. (ed.) *The Ancient City: New perspectives on urbanism in the Old and New World*, School for Advanced Research Press, Santa Fe: 77–92.

Byers, A.M. 2012, [review] Contradictions of Archaeological Theory, *Journal of Critical Realism* 11(4): 499–506.

Campbell, T. 1981, *Seven Theories of Human Society*, Clarendon Press, Oxford.

Carmack, R. M. 1981, *The Quiché Mayas of Utatlán: The evolution of a highland Guatemala kingdom*, University of Oklahoma Press, Norman.

Carmona, M., Tiesdell, S., Heath, T. and Oc, T. 2003, *Public Places, Urban Spaces: The dimension of urban design*, Architectural Press, Oxford.

Carter, H. 1972, *The Study of Urban Geography*, Edward Arnold, London.

Carvalho, R. and Penn, A. 2004, Scaling and Universality in the Micro-Structure of Urban Space, *Physica A* 332: 539–547.

Cataldi, G., Maffei, G.L. and Vaccaro, P. 2002, Saverio Muratori and the Italian School of Planning Typology, *Urban Morphology* 6(1): 3–14.

Certeau, M. de 1988[1984], *The Practice of Everyday Life*, University of California Press, Berkeley.

Chappell, J.E. Jr. 1991, On Realism, in Geography and Elsewhere, *The Professional Geographer* 43(2): 228–231.

Charalambous, N. and Mavridou, M. 2012, Space Syntax: Spatial integration accessibility and angular segment analysis by metric distance (ASAMeD), in: Hull, A., Silva C. and Bertolini, L. (ed.) *Accessibility Instruments for Planning Practice*, COST Office: 57–62.

Chase, D.Z., Chase, A.F., and Haviland, W.A. 1990, The Classic Maya City: Reconsidering the 'Mesoamerican Urban Tradition', *American Anthropologist* 92(2): 499–506.

Chase, D.Z., Chase, A.F. Awe, J.J., Walker, J.H. and Weishampel, J.F. 2011a, Airborne LiDAR at Caracol, Belize and the Interpretation of Ancient Maya Society and Landscapes, *Research Reports in Belizean Archaeology* 8: 61–73.

Chase, A.F., Chase, D.Z., Weishampel, J.F., Drake, J.B., Shrestha, R.L., Slatton, K.C., Awe, J.J. and Carter, W.E. 2011b, Airborne LiDAR, Archaeology, and the Ancient Maya Landscape at Caracol, Belize, *Journal of Archaeological Science* 38: 387–398.

Chase, A.F., Reese-Taylor, K., Fernandez-Diaz, J.C. and Chase, D.Z. 2016, Progression and Issues in the Mesoamerican Geospatial Revolution: An introduction, *Advances in Archaeological Practice* 4(3): 219–231.

Chiaradia, A. and Lemlij, M. 2007, *Croydon Town Centre, Croydon Council: Baseline analysis of urban structure, layout and public spaces*, Space Syntax Limited, London.

Chiaradia, A., Schwander, C., Gil, J. and Friedrich, E. 2008, Mapping the Intangible Value of Urban Layout (i-VALUL): Developing a tool kit for the socio-economic valuation of urban area, for designers and decision makers, *9th International Conference on Design & Decision Support Systems in Architecture and Urban Planning*, Eindhoven, Netherlands.

Childe, V.G. 1936, *Man Makes Himself*, Watts & Co., London.

Childe, V.G. 1950, The Urban Revolution, *Town Planning Review* 21(1): 3–17.

Christaller, W. 1933, *Die Zentralen Orte in Süddeutschland*, Gustav Fischer, Jena.

Christophersen, A. 2015, Performing Towns: Steps towards an understanding of medieval urban communities as social practice, *Archaeological Dialogues* 22(2): 109–132.

Christophersen, A. 2016, The City Is Alive – Still!, *Norwegian Archaeological Review* 49(1): 58–61.

Clark, P. (ed.) 2000, *The Cambridge Urban History of Britain, Vol. II, 1540–1840*, Cambridge University Press, Cambridge.

Clark, P. (ed.) 2013, *Oxford Handbook of Cities in World History*, Oxford University Press, Oxford.

Clarke, H. 1985, The Mapping of Medieval Dublin: A case-study in thematic cartography, in: Clarke, H. and Simms, A. (ed.) *The Comparative History of Urban Origins in Non-Roman Europe*, BAR, Vol. 2: 617–643.

Clarke, H. and Simms, A. 1985, Towards a Comparative History of Urban Origins, in: Clarke, H. and Simms, A. (ed.) *The Comparative History of Urban Origins in Non-Roman Europe*, BAR, Vol. 2: 669–714.

Clarke, N. 2012, Actually Existing Comparative Urbanism: Imitation and cosmopolitanism in north-south interurban partnerships, *Urban Geography* 33(6): 796–815.

Coe, M.D. 1961, Social Typology and the Tropical Forest Civilizations, *Comparative Studies in Society and History* 4: 65–85.

Colding, J. and Barthel, S. 2017, An Urban Ecology Critique on the "Smart City" Model, *Journal of Cleaner Production* 164: 95–101.

Conroy Dalton, R. 2007, Social Exclusion and Transportation in Peachtree City, Georgia, *Progress in Planning* 67(3): 264–286.

Conroy Dalton, R., Hölscher, C. and Turner, A. 2012, Understanding Space: The nascent synthesis of cognition and the syntax of spatial morphologies, *Environment and Planning B: Planning and Design* 36: 7–11.

Conzen, M.P. 2009, How Cities Internalize their Former Urban Fringes: A cross-cultural comparison, *Urban Morphology* 13(1): 29–54.

Conzen, M.R.G. 1960, *Alnwick, Northumberland: A study in town-plan analysis*, Transactions and Papers (Institute of British Geographers) Publication 27, George Philip, London.

Conzen, M.R.G. 1968, The Use of Town Plans in the Study of Urban History, in: Dyos, H.J. (ed.) *The Study of Urban History*, Edward Arnold, London: 113–130.

Conzen, M.R.G. 1981, The Plan Analysis of an English City Centre, in: Whitehand, J.W.R. (ed.) *The Urban Landscape: Historical development and management*, Academic Press, London: 25–53.

Conzen, M.R.G. 1988, Morphogenesis, Morphological Regions and Secular Human Agency in the Historic Townscape, as Exemplified by Ludlow, in: Denecke, D. and Shaw, G. (ed.) *Urban Historical Geography: Recent progress in Britain and Germany*, Cambridge University Press, Cambridge: 253–272.

Conzen, M.R.G. 2004, *Thinking about Urban Form: Papers on urban morphology 1932–1998*, Peter Lang, New York.

Costall, A. 2006, On Being the Right Size: Affordances and the meaning of scale, in: Lock, G. and Molyneux, B. (ed.) *Confronting Scale in Archaeology: Issues of theory and practice*, Springer, New York: 15–26.

Cowgill, G.L. 2004, Origins and Development of Urbanism: Archaeological perspectives, *Annual Review of Anthropology* 33: 525–549.

Cox, K.R. 2013a, Notes on a Brief Encounter: Critical realism, historical materialism and human geography, *Dialogues in Human Geography* 3(1): 3–21.

Cox, K.R. 2013b, The Continuing Relevance of Old Debates, *Dialogues in Human Geography* 3(1): 49–55.

Cox, K.R. and Mair, A. 1989, Levels of Abstraction in Locality Studies, *Antipode* 21(2): 121–132.

Craane, M. 2009, The Medieval Urban 'Movement Economy': Using space syntax in the study of medieval towns as exemplified by the town of 's-Hertogenbosch, the Netherlands, in: Koch, D., Marcus, L. and Steen, J. (ed.) *Proceedings of the 7th International Space Syntax Symposium*, Stockholm: KTH: 019.

Creekmore, A. III and Fisher, K. (ed.) 2014, *Making Ancient Cities: Space and place in early urban societies*, Cambridge University Press, Cambridge.

Csordas, T.J. 1990, Embodiment as a Paradigm for Anthropology, *Ethos* 18(1): 5–47.

Cutting, M. 2003, The Use of Spatial Analysis to Study Prehistoric Settlement Architecture, *Oxford Journal of Archaeology* 22(1): 1–21.

Dahlin, B.H. 2000, The Barricade and Abandonment of Chunchucmil: Implications for northern Maya warfare, *Latin American Antiquity* 11(3): 283–298.

Daunton, M.J. 1983, Public Place and Private Space: The Victorian city and the working-class household, in: Fraser, D. and Sutcliffe, A. (ed.) *The Pursuit of Urban History*, Edward Arnold, London: 212–233.

Daunton, M.J. (ed.) 2001, *The Cambridge Urban History of Britain, Vol. III, 1840–1950*, Cambridge University Press, Cambridge.

David, B. and Thomas, J. (eds) 2008, *Handbook of Landscape Archaeology*, Left Coast Press, Walnut Creek.

Dean, G. 2012a, GIS, Archaeology and Neighbourhood Assemblages in Medieval York, *Post-Classical Archaeologies* 2: 7–29.

Dean, G. 2012b, *Urban Neighbourhoods: Social and spatial development in York c.600–1600*, unpublished PhD thesis, University of York.

Dean, G. 2013, personal communication.

Dear, M. 2005, Comparative Urbanism, *Urban Geography* 26(3): 247–251.

Deleuze, G. 1984, Michel Tournier and World Without Others, *Economy and Society* 13(1): 52–71.

Deleuze, G. and Guattari, F. 1987, *A Thousand Plateaus: Capitalism and schizophrenia*, University of Minnesota Press, Minneapolis.

Delitz, H. unpublished, *Architecture as Medium of the Social: Towards a sociological theory of built space*, trans. Gorny, R. and Card, K.

Demarest, A.A. 1997, The Vanderbilt Petexbatun Regional Archaeological Project 1989–1994: Overview, history, and major results of a multidisciplinary study of the Classic Maya collapse, *Ancient Mesoamerica* 8: 209–227.

Denecke, D. 1988, Research in German Urban Historical Geography, in: Denecke, D. and Shaw, G. (ed.) *Urban Historical Geography: Recent progress in Britain and Germany*, Cambridge University Press, Cambridge: 24–33.

Denecke, D. and Shaw, G. (ed.) 1988, *Urban Historical Geography: Recent progress in Britain and Germany*, Cambridge University Press, Cambridge.

Dennehy, T.J., Stanley, B.W. and Smith, M.E. 2016, Social Inequality and Access to Services in Premodern Cities, *Archaeological Papers of the American Anthropological Society* 27(1): 143–160.

Dennis, R. and Prince, H. 1988, Research in British Urban Historical Geography, in: Denecke, D. and Shaw, G. (ed.) *Urban Historical Geography: Recent progress in Britain and Germany*, Cambridge University Press, Cambridge: 9–23.

Dervin, B. 1993, Verbing Communication: Mandate for disciplinary invention, *Journal of Communication* 43(3): 45–54.

Diederiks, H.A. and Laan, P.H.J. van der 1976, Urban History in the Netherlands: A survey of recent writings and developments, *Urban History* 3: 28–34.

Dittmar, H. 2013, Global Problems; Local Answers, *Prince's Foundation for Building Community Magazine*, Issue 23, spring: 4–5.

Doornink-Hoogenraad, M.M. 1983, *Historische Stedenatlas van Nederland: Zutfen*, Afl. 3, Delftse Universitaire Pers, Delft.

Douglas, M. 1972, Symbolic Orders in the Use of Domestic Space, in: Ucko, P.J., Tringham, R. and Dimbleby, G.W. (ed.) *Man, Settlement and Urbanism*, Research Seminar in Archaeology and Related Subjects Meeting, Institute of Archaeology, London University, 1970, Duckworth, London: 513–523.

Drennan, R.D. and Peterson, C.E. 2004, Comparing Archaeological Settlement Systems with Rank-Size Graphs: A measure of shape and statistical confidence, *Journal of Archaeological Science* 31: 533–549.

Drobnick, J. (ed.) 2006, *The Smell Culture Reader*, Berg, Oxford.

Drunen, A. van 2011, personal communication.

Duncan, S. and Savage, M. 1989, Space, Scale and Locality, *Antipode* 21(3): 179–206.

Dyos, H.J. (ed.) 1968, *The Study of Urban History*, Edward Arnold, London.

Economic Foundations of Mayapan Project (PEMY) n.d. (http://www.albany.edu/mayapan/PEMY. shtml, accessed 25-09-2013).

Edensor, T. and Jayne, M. (ed.) 2012, *Urban Theory beyond the West: A world of cities*, Routledge, London.

Elden, S. 2011, What's Shifting?, *Dialogues in Human Geography* 1(3): 304–307.

Ellen, R. 2010, Theories in Anthropology and Anthropological Theory, *Journal of the Royal Anthropological Institute* 16: 387–404.

Emberling, G. 2003, Urban Social Transformations and the Problem of the 'First City': New research from Mesopotamia, in: Smith, M.L. (ed.) *The Social Construction of Ancient Cities*, Smithsonian Institution, Washington: 254–268.

Estabrook, C.B. 2002, Ritual, Space, and Authority in Seventeenth-Century English Cathedral Cities, *Journal of Interdisciplinary History* 32(4): 593–620.

Evans, D., Pottier, C., Fletcher, R., Hensley, S., Tapley, I., Milne, A. and Barbetti, M. 2007, A Comprehensive Archaeological Map of the World's Largest Preindustrial Settlement Complex at Angkor, Cambodia, *PNAS* 104(36): 14277–14282.

Fahlander, F. 2012, Are We There Yet?: Archaeology and the postmodern in the new millennium, *Current Swedish Archaeology* 20: 109–129.

Fairclough, G. 1992, Meaningful Constructions: Spatial and functional analysis of medieval buildings, *Antiquity* 66: 348–366.

Falconer, S.E. and Savage, S.H. 1995, Heartlands and Hinterlands: Alternative trajectories of early urbanization in Mesopotamia and the Southern Levant, *American Antiquity* 60(1): 37–58.

Farkas, K. 2003, *The Threefold Cord: Mind, Body and World* by Hilary Putnam (review), *Mind, New Series* 112(448): 786–789.

Fash, W.L. 1998, Dynastic Architectural Programs: Intention and design in Classic Maya buildings at Copan and other sites, in: Houston, S.D. (ed.) *Function and Meaning in Maya Architecture*, Dumbarton Oaks Research Library and Collection, Washington: 223–270.

Faulconbridge, J.R. and Grubbauer, M. 2015, Transnational Building Practices: Knowledge mobility and the inescapable market, *Global Networks* 15(3): 275–287.

Faulkner, M. (ed.) n.d., *Mapping Medieval Chester Project* (http://www.medievalchester.ac.uk, accessed 06-05-2013).

Fedick, S. and Morrison, B. 2004, Ancient Use and Manipulation of Landscape in the Yalahau Region of the Northern Maya Lowlands, *Agriculture and Human Values* 21: 207–219.

Fernández-Götz, M. and Krausse, D. 2013, Rethinking Early Iron Age Urbanisation in Central Europe: The Heuneburg site and its archeological environment, *Antiquity* 87: 473–487.

Fesenmaier, D.R., Goodchild, M.F. and Morrison, S. 1979, The Spatial Structure of the Rural-Urban Fringe: A multivariate approach, *Canadian Geographer* 23(3): 255–265.

Fisher, K.D. 2009, Placing Social Interaction: An integrative approach to analyzing past built environments, *Journal of Anthropological Archaeology* 28: 439–457.

Fletcher, L.A. 1983, Linear Features in Zone I: Description and classification, in: Folan, W.J., Kintz, E.R. and Fletcher, L.A. (ed.) *Coba: A Classic Maya metropolis*, Academic Press, New York: 89–102.

Fletcher, L.A. and Kintz, E.R. 1983, Solares, Kitchen Gardens, and Social Status in Coba, in: Folan, W.J., Kintz, E.R. and Fletcher, L.A. (ed.) *Coba: A Classic Maya metropolis*, Academic Press, New York: 103–119.

Fletcher, R. 2008, Some Spatial Analyses of Chalcolithic Settlement in Southern Israel, *Journal of Archaeological Science* 35: 2048–2058.

Fletcher, R.J. 2004, Materiality, Space, Time and Outcome, in: Bintliff, J.L. (ed.) *A Companion to Archaeology*, Blackwell, Oxford: 110–140.

Fletcher, R.J. 2009, Low-Density, Agrarian-Based Urbanism: A comparative view, *Insights* 2(4): 1–19.

Fletcher, R.J. 2010, Shining Stars and Black Holes: Urbanism, comparison, and comparability, *Journal of Urban History* 36(2): 251–256.

Fletcher, R.J. 2012, Low-Density, Agrarian-Based Urbanism: Scale, power, and ecology, in: Smith, M.E. (ed.) *The Comparative Archaeology of Complex Societies*, Cambridge University Press, New York: 285–320.

Fogelin, L. 2007, Inference to the Best Explanation: A common and effective form of archaeological reasoning, *American Antiquity* 72(4): 603–625.

Folan, W.J., Hernandez, A.A., Kintz, E.R., Fletcher, L.A., Gonzalez Heredia, R., Hau, J.M. and Caamal Canche, N. 2009, Coba, Quintana Roo, Mexico: A recent analysis of the social, economic and political organization of a major Maya urban center, *Ancient Mesoamerica* 20: 59–70.

Fox, R.G. 1977, *Urban Anthropology: Cities in their cultural settings*, Prentice-Hall, Englewood Cliffs.

Frank, Z. 2013, *Layers, Flows, Intersections: Historical GIS for 19th-century Rio de Janeiro* (http://vimeo.com/60104031, accessed 06-05-2013).

Franz, G. and Wiener, J.M. 2008, From Space Syntax to Space Semantics: A behaviorally and perceptually oriented methodology for the efficient description of the geometry and topology of environments, *Environment and Planning B: Planning and Design* 35: 574–592.

Fraser, D. and Sutcliffe, A. (ed.) 1983, *The Pursuit of Urban History*, Edward Arnold, London.

Galinié, H., Rodier, X. and Saligny, L. 2004, Entités Fonctionnelles, Entités Spatiales et Dynamique Urbaine dans la Longue Durée, *Histoire & Mesure* 19(3/4): 223–242.

Gates, C. 2011[2003], *Ancient Cities: The archaeology of urban life in the ancient Near East and Egypt, Greece, and Rome*, 2nd edition, Routledge, Abingdon.

Gaydarska, B. 2016, The City is Dead! Long Live the City!, *Norwegian Archaeological Review* 49(1): 40–57.

Geddes, P. 1915, *Cities in Evolution: An introduction to the town planning movement and to the study of civics*, Williams & Norgate, London.

Gibson, J. 1979, *The Ecological Approach to Visual Perception*, Houghton Mifflin, Boston.

Giddens, A. 1984, *The Constitution of Society: Outline of the theory of structuration*, University of California Press, Berkeley.

Gil, J., Stutz, C. and Chiadaria, A. 2007, Confeego: Tool set for spatial configuration studies, in: Turner, A. (ed.) *New Developments in Space Syntax Software*, ITU Faculty of Architecture, Istanbul: 15–22.

Gil, J., Varoudis, T., Karimi, K. and Penn, A. 2015, The Space Syntax Toolkit: Integrating depthmapX and exploratory spatial analysis workflows in QGIS, in: Karimi, K., Vaughan, L., Sailer, K., Palaiologou, G. and Bolton, T. (ed.) *Proceedings of the 10th International Space Syntax Symposium*, Space Syntax Laboratory, The Bartlett School of Architecture, University College London, London: 148.

Gillings, M. 2012, Landscape Phenomenology, GIS and the Role of Affordance, *Journal of Archaeological Method and Theory* 19(4): 601–611.

Golden, C., Murtha, T., Cook, B., Shaffer, D.S., Schroder, W., Hermitt, E.J., Firpi, O.A. and Scherer, A.K. 2016, Reanalyzing Environmental Lidar Data for Archaeology: Mesoamerican applications and implications, *Journal of Archaeological Science: Reports* 9: 293–308.

Gordon, G. 1981, The Historico-Geographic Explanation of Urban Morphology: A discussion of some Scottish evidence, *Scottish Geographical Magazine* 79: 16–26.

Graham, E. 1996, Maya Cities and the Character of Tropical Urbanism, in: *The Development of Urbanism from a Global Perspective*, Uppsala University, Uppsala (http://www.arkeologi. uu.se/Forskning/Publikationer/Digital/Development_of_Urbanism/, accessed 25-09-2013).

Graham, E. 1999, Stone Cities, Green Cities, *Archeological Papers of the American Anthropological Association* 9(1): 185–194.

Granö, J.G. 1997[1929], *Pure Geography*, Johns Hopkins University Press, Baltimore.

Greene, K. 1999, V. Gordon Childe and the Vocabulary of Revolutionary Change, *Antiquity* 73: 97–109.

Gregory, I.N. and Ell, P.S. 2007, *Historical GIS: Technologies, methodologies and scholarship*, Cambridge University Press, Cambridge.

Griffiths, S. 2009, Persistence and Change in the Spatio-Temporal Description of Sheffield 1750–1905, in: Koch, D., Marcus, L. and Steen, J. (ed.) *Proceedings of the 7th International Space Syntax Symposium*, Stockholm, KTH: 037.

Griffiths, S. 2011, Temporality in Hillier and Hanson's Theory of Spatial Description: Some implications of historical research for space syntax, *Journal of Space Syntax* 2(1): 73–96.

Griffiths, S. 2012a, The Use of Space Syntax in Historical Research: Current practice and future possibilities, in: Greene, M., Reyes, J. and Castro, A. (ed.) *Proceedings of the 8th International Space Syntax Symposium*, Santiago de Chile, PUC: 8193.

Griffiths, S. 2012b, Still in Different Spaces?: Some implications of Hillier and Hanson's 'space syntax' for humanities research into the historical built environment, presentation at: *Assembly for Comparative Urbanisation and the Material Environment (ACUMEN)*, Leeds.

Griffiths, S. 2013, GIS and Research into Historical 'Spaces of Practice': Overcoming the epistemological barriers, in: Lünen, A. von and Travis, C. (ed.) *History and GIS: Epistemologies, considerations and reflections*, Springer, Dordrecht: 153–171.

Griffiths, S. and Quick, T. 2005, How the Individual, Society and Space Become Structurally Coupled over Time, in: Nes, A. van (ed.) *5th International Space Syntax Symposium Proceedings*, Techne Press, Amsterdam: 447–458.

Griffiths, S., Jones, C., Vaughan, L. and Hacklay, M. 2010, The Persistence of Suburban Centres in Greater London: Combining Conzenian and space syntax approaches, *Urban Morphology* 14(2): 85–99.

Groff, R. 2004, *Critical Realism, Post-positivism and the Possibility of Knowledge*, Routledge, London.

Grosso, E. 2011, *MorphAL: Outil d'analyse, version 0.1*, document version 1.0 (http://alpage.tge-adonis. fr/documents/ressources/MorphAL-0.1-guide_utilisateur-1.0.pdf, accessed 25-09-2013).

Grove, D. 1972, The Function and Future of Urban Centres, in: Ucko, P.J., Tringham, R. and Dimbleby, G.W. (ed.) *Man, Settlement and Urbanism*, Research Seminar in Archaeology and Related Subjects Meeting, Institute of Archaeology, London University, 1970, Duckworth, London: 559–565.

Grube, N. (ed.) 2000, *Maya: Divine kings of the rainforest*, Könemann, Cologne.

Guderjan, T.H. 2007, *The Nature of an Ancient Maya City: Resources, interaction, and power at Blue Creek, Belize*, The University of Alabama Press, Tuscaloosa.

Habraken, N.J. 2000[1998], *The Structure of the Ordinary: Form and control in the built environment*, MIT Press, Cambridge.

Hacıgüzeller, P. 2012, GIS, Critique, Representation and Beyond, *Journal of Social Archaeology* 12(2): 245–263.

Hägerstrand, T. 1970, What About People in Regional Science?, Presidential Address, Ninth European Congress of the Regional Science Association, Papers in Regional Science, *Journal of the Regional Science Association International* 23(1): 6–21.

Hägerstrand, T. 1975, Space, Time and Human Conditions, in: Karlqvist, A., Lundqvist, L. and Snickars, F. (ed.), *Dynamic Allocation of Urban Space*, Saxon House, Westmead: 3–14.

Hägerstrand, T. 1976, Geography and the Study of Interaction between Nature and Society, *Geoforum* 7: 329–334.

Hägerstrand, T. 1984, Presence and Absence: A look at conceptual choices and bodily necessities, *Regional Studies* 18(5): 373–379.

Hall, E.T. 1959, *The Silent Language*, Doubleday & Company Inc., Garden City, New York.

Hall, E.T. 1968, Proxemics, *Current Anthropology* 9(2-3): 83–108.

Hall, E.T. 1996, Foreword, in: Pellow, D. (ed.) *Setting Boundaries: The anthropology of spatial and social organization*, Bergin & Garvey, Westport: vii–viii.

Hamm, E. 1932, *Die Städtegründungen der Herzöge von Zähringen in Südwestdeutschland*, Veröffentliching des Alemannischen Instituts, Urban-Verlag, Freiburg im Breisgau.

Hansen, M.H. (ed.) 2000, *A Comparative Study of Thirty City-State Cultures*, Det Kongelige Danske Videnskabernes Selskab, Copenhagen.

Hansen, M.H. 2008, Analyzing Cities, in: Marcus, J. and Sabloff, J.A. (ed.) *The Ancient City: New perspectives on urbanism in the Old and New World*, School for Advanced Research Press, Santa Fe: 67–76.

Hanson, J. 1989, Order and Structure in Urban Design: The plans for the rebuilding of London after the Great Fire of 1666, *Ekistics* 56(334-335): 22–42.

Hanson, J. 2012, correspondence via the space syntax mailing list (https://www.jiscmail.ac.uk/cgi-bin/webadmin?A0=spacesyntax, accessed 25-07-2013).

Hare, T.S. and Masson, M.A. 2012, Intermediate-Scale Patterns in the Urban Environment of Postclassic Mayapan, in: Arnauld, M.C., Manzanilla, L.R. and Smith, M.E. (ed.) *The Neighborhood as a Social and Spatial Unit in Mesoamerican Cities*, The University of Arizona Press, Tucson: 229–260.

Hare, T.S., Masson, M.A. and Russell, B.W. 2014, High-Density LiDAR Mapping of the Ancient City of Mayapán, *Remote Sensing* 6(9): 9064–9085.

Harris, R. and Smith, M.E. 2011, The History in Urban Studies: A comment, *Journal of Urban Affairs* 33(1): 99–105.

Hegmon, M. 2003, Setting Theoretical Egos Aside: Issues and theory in North American archaeology, *American Antiquity* 68(2): 213–43.

Heidegger, M. 1972, *Sein und Zeit*, 12th edition, Niemeyer Verlag, Tübingen.

Heritage Gateway n.d. (http://www.heritagegateway.org.uk/gateway/, accessed 25-09-2013).

Hermon, S. and Niccolucci, F. 2002, Estimating Subjectivity of Typologists and Typological Classification with Fuzzy Logic, *Archeologia e Calcolatori* 13: 217–232.

Herva, V.-P., Ylimaunu, T., Kallio-Seppä, T., Kuokkanen, T. and Nurmi, R. 2011, Urban Boundaries, in: Lamberg, M., Hakanen, M. and Haikari, J. (ed.) *Physical and Cultural Space in Pre-Industrial Europe: Methdological approaches to spatiality*, Nordic Academic Press, Lund: 321–338.

Hetherington, K. 2003, Spatial Textures: Place, touch, and praesentia, *Environment and Planning A* 35: 1933–1944.

Hill, R.M. II and Monaghan, J. 1987, *Continuities in Highland Maya Social Organization: Ethnohistory in Sacapulas, Guatemala*, University of Pennsylvania Press, Philadelphia.

Hillier, B. 2005, Between Social Physics and Phenomenology: Explorations towards an urban synthesis?, Nes, A. van (ed.) *5th International Space Syntax Symposium Proceedings*, Techne Press, Amsterdam: 3–23.

Hillier, B. 2007[1996], *Space is the Machine: A configurational theory of architecture*, Space Syntax, London.

Hillier, B. and Hanson, J. 1984, *The Social Logic of Space*, Cambridge University Press, Cambridge.

Hillier, B. and Iida, S. 2005, Network Effects and Psychological Effects: A theory of urban movement, Nes, A. van (ed.) *5th International Space Syntax Symposium Proceedings*, Techne Press, Amsterdam: 553–564.

Hillier, B. and Penn, A. 2004, Rejoinder to Carlo Ratti, *Environment and Planning B: Planning and Design* 31: 501–511.

Hillier, B. and Vaughn, L. 2007, The City as One Thing, *Progress in Planning*, 67(3): 205–230.

Hillier, B., Hanson, J. and Graham, H. 1987, Ideas are in Things: An application of the space syntax method to discovering house genotypes, *Environment and Planning B: Planning and Design* 14: 363–385.

Hillier, B., Penn, A., Hanson, J., Grajewski, T. and Xu, J. 1993, Natural Movement: Or, configuration and attraction in urban pedestrian movement, *Environment and Planning B: Planning and Design* 20: 29–66.

Hillier, B., Turner, A., Yang, T., and Park, H. 2007, Metric and Topo-Geometric Properties of Urban Street Networks: Some convergences, divergences and new results, in: *Proceedings 6th International Space Syntax Symposium, ITU, Istanbul, Turkey, 12–15 June 2007*: 001 (http://www.spacesyntaxistanbul.itu.edu.tr/papers/longpapers/001%20-%20Hillier%20 Turner%20Yang%20Park.pdf, accessed 12-07-2017).

Hinchcliffe, S. 2003, 'Inhabiting': Landscapes and natures, in: Anderson, K., Domosh, M., Pile, S. and Thrift, N. (ed.) *Handbook of Cultural Geography*, Sage, London: 207–226.

Historic Cities Center n.d., *Historic Cities*, Department of Geography, Hebrew University of Jerusalem and Jewish National and University Library (http://historic-cities.huji.ac.il/historic_cities.html, accessed 30-07-2013).

Hodos, T. (ed.) 2017, *The Routledge Handbook of Archaeology and Globalization*, Routledge, Abingdon.

Hohmann-Vogrin, A. 2005, Space Syntax in Maya Architecture, in: Nes, A. van (ed.) *5th International Space Syntax Symposium Proceedings*, Techne Press, Amsterdam: 279–292.

Hohmann-Vogrin, A. 2006, Spatial Alignments in Maya Architecture, in: Robertson, E.C., Seibert, J.D., Fernandez, D.C., Zender, M.U. (ed.) *Space and Spatial Analysis in Archaeology*, University of Calgary Press, Alberta: 199–204.

Hoskins, 1977[1955], *The Making of the English Landscape*, Hodder and Stoughton, London.

Howes, D. 2005a, Introduction, in: Howes, D. (ed.) *Empire of the Senses: The sensual culture reader*, Berg, Oxford: 1–17.

Howes, D. (ed.) 2005b, *Empire of the Senses: The sensual culture reader*, Berg, Oxford.

Hutson, S.R. 2011, personal communication.

Hutson, S.R. 2012, personal communication.

Hutson, S.R. 2013, personal communication.

Hutson, S.R. 2012, Unavoidable Imperfections: Historical contexts for representing ruined Maya buildings, in: Pillsbury, J. (ed.) *Past Presented: Archaeological illustration and the ancient Americas*, Dumbarton Oaks, Washington: 283–316.

Hutson, S.R. 2016, *The Ancient Urban Maya: Neighborhoods, inequality, and built form*, University Press of Florida, Gainesville.

Hutson, S.R. and Welch, J. 2016, Neighborhoods at Chunchucmil, in: Hutson, S.R. *The Ancient Urban Maya: Neighborhoods, inequality, and built form*, University Press of Florida, Gainesville: 97–138.

Hutson, S.R. and Magnoni, A. 2017, Km Blocks, Transects, and Keys to Maps, digital appendix to: Hutson, S.R. (ed.) *Ancient Maya Commerce: Multidisciplinary Research at Chunchucmil*, University Press of Colorado, Boulder (http://upcolorado.com/component/k2/item/3199-ancient-maya-commerce-km-blocks-transects-and-keys-to-maps#km-blocks, accessed 18-07-2017).

Hutson, S.R., Magnoni, A., and Stanton, T.W. 2004. House rules?: The practice of social organization in classic period Chunchucmil, Yucatan, Mexico, *Ancient Mesoamerica* 15: 74–92.

Hutson, S.R., Magnoni, A., Mazeau, D. and Stanton, T. 2006, The Archaeology of Urban Houselots at Chunchucmil, Yucatan, Mexico, in: Mathews, J. and Morrison, B. (ed.) *Lifeways in the Northern Lowlands: New approaches to Maya archaeology*, University of Arizona Press, Tucson: 77–92.

Hutson, S.R., Stanton, T.W., Magnoni, A., Terry, R. and Craner, J. 2007, Beyond the Buildings: Formation processes of ancient Maya houselots and methods for the study of non-architectural space, *Journal of Anthropological Archaeology* 26: 442–473.

Hutson, S.R., Hixson, D.R., Magnoni, A., Mazeau, D. and Dahlin, B. 2008, Site and Community at Chunchucmil and Ancient Maya Urban Centres, *Journal of Field Archaeology* 33(1): 19–40.

Ingold, T. 2000, *The Perception of the Environment*, Routledge, London.

Ingold, T. 2007, Materials against Materiality, *Archaeological Dialogues* 14(1): 1–16.

Ingold, T. 2008a, Bindings against Boundaries: Entanglements of life in an open world, *Environment and Planning A* 40(8): 1796–1810.

Ingold, T. 2008b, Bringing Things to Life: Creative Entanglements in a world of materials, presented as a keynote address at: *Vital Signs: Researching Real Life Conference*, University of Manchester, UK (http://www.socialsciences.manchester.ac.uk/realities/publications/workingpapers/15-2010-07-realities-bringing-things-to-life.pdf, accessed 25-09-2013).

Ingold, T. 2011, *Being Alive: Essays on movement, knowledge and description*, Routledge, Abingdon.

Irish Historic Towns Atlas n.d. (http://www.ria.ie/Research/IHTA/European-Project, accessed 30-07-2013).

Isendahl, C. and Smith, M.E. 2013, Sustainable Agrarian Urbanism: The low-density cities of the Mayas and Aztecs, *Cities* 31: 132–143.

Jackson, P. 2000, Rematerializing Social and Cultural Geography, *Social & Cultural Geography* 1(1): 9–14.

Jacobs, J. 1969, *The Economy of Cities*, Random House, New York.

Jacobs, S. 2016, 12 Eerie Images of Huge Chinese Cities Completely Empty of People, *The Independent* (http://www.independent.co.uk/news/world/asia/12-eeries-images-of-huge-chinese-cities-completely-empty-of-people-a6932936.html, accessed 17-05-2016).

Jenkins, L. 2002, Geography and Architecture: 11, Rue du Conservatoire and the permeability of buildings, *Space and Culture* 5(3): 222–236.

Jensen, J.T. and Keyes, G. 2003, Mapping Urban History: GIS and the analysis of the urban space of nineteenth-century Aarhus, *International Association for History and Computing XVth conference in Tromsø* (http://www.rhd.uit.no/ahc/paper/jtj_gk_mapping_urban_history.pdf, accessed 06-05-2013).

Jessop, B., Brenner, N. and Jones, M. 2008, Theorizing Sociospatial Relations, *Environment and Planning D: Society and Space* 26(3): 389–401.

Jiang, B. 2007, A Topological Pattern of Urban Street Networks: Universality and peculiarity, *Physica A* 384: 647–655.

Johnston, K.J. and Gonlin, N. 1998, What Do Houses Mean? Approaches to the analysis of Classic Maya commoner residences, in: Houston, S.D. (ed.) *Function and Meaning in Classic Maya Architecture*, Dumbarton Oaks, Washington: 141–185.

Jones, C. 2015, The Marketplace at Tikal, in: King, E.M. (ed.) *The Ancient Maya Marketplace: The archaeology of transient space*, The University of Arizona Press, Tucson: 67–89.

Jones, K.S. 2003, What Is an Affordance?, *Ecological Psychology* 15(2): 107–114.

Jones, M. 2009, Phase Space: Geography, relational thinking, and beyond, *Progress in Human Geography* 33(4): 487–506.

Jones, R. 2004, What Time Human Geography?, *Progress in Human Geography* 28(3): 287–304.

Jones, R. 2009, Categories, Borders and Boundaries, *Progress in Human Geography* 33(2): 174–189.

Jones, R. 2010, The Spatiality of Boundaries, *Progress in Human Geography* 34(2): 263–267.

Jones, C., Griffiths, S., Mordechay, H. and Vaughan, L. 2009, A multi-disciplinary perspective on the built environment: Space Syntax and Cartography – the communication challenge, in: Koch, D., Marcus, L. and Steen, J. (ed.) *Proceedings of the 7th International Space Syntax Symposium*, KTH, Stockholm: 048.

Joyce, A.A. 2009, Theorizing Urbanism in Ancient Mesoamerica, *Ancient Mesoamerica* 20: 189–196.

Joyce, R.A. 2005, Archaeology of the Body, *Annual Review of Anthropology* 34(1): 139–158.

JTS Topology Suite n.d. (http://www.vividsolutions.com/jts/JTSHome.htm, accessed 26-09-2013).

Kalmring, S. 2012, The Birka Proto-Town GIS: A source for comprehensive studies of Björkö, *Fornvännen* 107: 253–265.

Kasper, C., Giseke, U., Spars, G., Heinze, M., Feiertag, P., Naismith, I.-C. and Berdouz, S. 2015. A Model Approach to Urbanizing Regions and their Rural, in: Giseke U., Gerster-Bentaya, M., Helten, F., Kraume, M., Scherer, D., Spars, G., Amraoui, F., Adidi, A., Berdouz, S., Chlaida, M., Mansour, M. and Mdafaiet, M. (ed.) *Urban Agriculture for Growing City Regions: Connecting urban-rural spheres in Casablanca*, Routledge, Abingdon: 292–303.

Keene, D. 1985, *Survey of Medieval Winchester*, Winchester Studies 2, Volume i and ii, Oxford University Press, Oxford.

Keene, D. 2011, personal communication.

Keene, D. 2012, personal communication.

Keene, D. and Harding, V. 1987, *Historical Gazetteer of London before the Great Fire: Cheapside; parishes of All Hallows Honey Lane, St Martin Pomary, St Mary le Bow, St Mary Colechurch and St Pancras Soper Lane* (http://www.british-history.ac.uk/source.aspx?pubid=8, accessed 06-05-2013).

Kent, S. (ed.) 1990, *Domestic Architecture and the Use of Space: An interdisciplinary cross-cultural study*, Cambridge University Press, Cambridge.

Kent, S. 1991, Partitioning Space: Cross-cultural factors influencing domestic spatial segmentation, *Environment and Behavior* 23(4): 438–473.

Keyser, E. 1969, *Bibliographie zur Städtegeschichte Deutschlands*, Böhlau, Cologne.

Killion, T.W., Sabloff, J.A., Tourtellot, G. and Dunning, N.P. 1989, Intensive Surface Collection of Residential Clusters at Terminal Classic Sayil, Yucatan, Mexico, *Journal of Field Archaeology* 16(3): 273–294.

Kim, W.K. and Wentz, E.A. 2011, Re-Examining the Definition of Urban Open Space Using Fuzzy Set Theory, *CAP LTER Thirteenth Annual Poster Symposium*, Arizona State University (http://caplter.asu.edu/docs/symposia/symp2011/Kim_Wentz.pdf, accessed 26-09-2013).

Knappett, C. 2004, The Affordances of Things: A post-Gibsonian perspective on the relationality of mind and matter, in: DeMarrais, E., Gosden, C. and Renfrew, C. (ed.) *Rethinking Materiality: The engagement of mind with the material world*, McDonald Institute Monographs, Cambridge: 43–51.

Knappett, C. 2007, Materials with Materiality?, *Archaeological Dialogues* 14(1): 20–23.

Knox, P.L. and Mayer, H. 2013, *Small Town Sustainability: Economic, social and environmental innovation*, Birkhäuser, Basel.

Koch, A. 2005, Autopoietic Spatial Systems: The significance of actor network theory and systems theory for the development of a system theoretical approach of space, *Social Geography* 1(1): 5–14.

Kolen, J.C.A. 2005, *De Biografie van het Landschap: Drie essays over landschap, geschiedenis en erfgoed*, academisch proefschrift, VU Amsterdam.

Kosiba, S. and Bauer, A.M. 2013, Mapping the Political Landscape: Towards a GIS analysis of environmental and social difference, *Journal of Archaeological Method and Theory*, 20(1): 61–101.

Koster, E.A. 1998, Urban Morphology and Computers, *Urban Morphology* 2(1): 3–7.

Koster, E.A. 2009, Urban Morphology and Computers 10 Years on, *Urban Morphology* 13(1): 74–76.

Kostof, S. 1991, *The City Shaped: Urban patterns and meanings through history*, Thames & Hudson, London.

Kostof, S. 1992, *The City Assembled: Elements of urban form through history*, Thames & Hudson, London.

Kowalewski, S.A. 1990, The Evolution of Complexity in the Valley of Oaxaca, *Annual Review of Anthropology*, 19: 39–58.

Kowalewski, S.A. 2003[1983], Differences in the Site Hierarchies below Monte Albán and Teotihuacán: A comparison based on the rank-size rule, in: Flannery, K.V. and Marcus, J. (ed.), *The Cloud People: Divergent evolution of the Zapotec and Mixtec civilizations*, Percheron Press, New York: 168–169.

Krier, R. 1979[1975], *Urban Space*, Academy Editions, London.

Kropf, K.S. 1993, *An Enquiry into the Definition of Built Form in Urban Morphology*, unpublished PhD thesis, 2 volumes, University of Birmingham.

Kropf, K.S. 1996, Urban Tissue and the Character of Towns, *Urban Design International* 1(3): 247–263.

Kropf, K.S. 2009, Aspects of Urban Form, *Urban Morphology* 13(2): 105–120.

Kropf, K.S. 2011, Morphological investigations: Cutting into the substance of urban form, *Built Environment* 37(4): 393–405.

Krzywinski, M., Schein, J., Birol, I., Connors, J., Gascoyne, R., Horsman, D., Jones, S.J. and Marra, M.A. 2009, Circos: An information aesthetic for comparative genomics, *Genome Research* 19(9): 1639–1645.

Kwan, M.-P. and Schwanen, T. 2009, Critical Quantitative Geographies, *Environment and Planning A* 41: 261–264.

Laan, Dom H. van der 1983, *Architectonic Space*, Brill, Leiden.

Lamont, M. and Molnár, V. 2002, The Study of Boundaries in the Social Sciences, *Annual Review of Sociology* 28: 167–195.

Larkham, P.J. 2006, The Study of Urban Form in Great Britain, *Urban Morphology* 10(2): 117–141.

Latour, B. 1992, Where Are the Missing Masses?: The sociology of a few mundane artifacts, in: Bijker, W. and Law, J. (ed.) *Shaping Technology-Building Society: Studies in sociotechnical change*, MIT Press, Cambridge: 225–259.

Lawrence, R.J. 1996, The Multidimensional Nature of Boundaries: Social classifications, human ecology, and domesticity, in: Pellow, D. (ed.) *Setting Boundaries: The anthropology of spatial and social organization*, Bergin & Garvey, Westport: 9–36.

Lawson, V.A. and Staeheli, L.A. 1990, Realism and the Practice of Geography, *The Professional Geographer* 42(1): 13–20.

Lawson, V.A. and Staeheli, L.A. 1991, On Critical Realism, Human Geography, and Arcane Sects!, *The Professional Geographer* 43(2): 231–233.

Layder, D. 1988, The Relation of Theory and Method: Causal relatedness, historical contingency and beyond, *The Sociological Review* 36(3): 441–463.

Lefebvre, B. 2009, How to Describe and Show Dynamics of Urban Fabric: Cartography and chronometry?, *Proceedings of the 37th Computer Applications and Quantitative Methods in Archaeology Conference*, Williamsburg (http://www.caa2009.org/articles/Lefebvre_Contribution224_a.pdf, accessed 26-09-2013).

Lefebvre, B. 2012, The Study of Urban Fabric Dynamics in Long Time Spans: Modelling, analysis and representation of spatio-temporal transformations, *Post-Classical Archaeologies* 2: 65–82.

Lefebvre, B., Rodier, X. and Saligny, L. 2008, Understanding Urban Fabric with the OH_FET Model Based on Social Use, Space and Time, *Archeologia e Calcolatori* 19: 195–214.

Lefebvre, H. 1991[1974], *The Production of Space*, Blackwell, Oxford.

Lefebvre, H. 2014, *Toward an Architecture of Enjoyment*, University of Minnesota Press, Minneapolis.

Lemonnier, E. 2012, Neighborhoods in Classic Lowland Maya Societies: Their identification and definition from the La Joyanca case study (northwestern Petén, Guatemala), in: Arnauld, M.C., Manzanilla, L.R. and Smith, M.E. (ed.) *The Neighborhood as a Social and Spatial Unit in Mesoamerican Cities*, The University of Arizona Press, Tucson: 181–201.

Leszczynski, A. 2009, Quantitative Limits to Qualitative Engagements: GIS, its critics, and the philosophical divide, *The Professional Geographer* 63(3): 350–365.

Lewis, E., Roberts, E. and Roberts, K. 1988, *Medieval Hall Houses of the Winchester Area*, Winchester City Museum, Winchester.

Ley, K. 2010, Understanding Urban Form as Results of a Conditioning System of Interrelated Factors: Some thoughts on the issue of morphologically defining the city, *7th Conference International Seminar on Urban Form (ISUF)*, Hamburg/Lübeck (http://darwin.bth.rwth-aachen.de/opus3/volltexte/2011/3719/pdf/3719.pdf, 26-09-2013).

Ley, K. 2012, What Is an Urban Morphologist?, *Urban Morphology* 16(1): 78–80.

Li, L. and Goodchild, M.F. 2010, Automatically and Accurately Matching Objects in Geospatial Datasets, *The International Archives of the Photogrammetry, Remote Sensing and Spatial Information Sciences* 38(2): 98–103.

Li, L. and Goodchild, M.F. 2011, An Optimisation Model for Linear Feature Matching in Geographical Data Conflation, *International Journal of Image and Data Fusion* 2(4): 309–328.

Lilley, K.D. n.d., Digital Mappings, in: Faulkner, M. (ed.) *Mapping Medieval Chester Project* (http://www.medievalchester.ac.uk, accessed 06-05-2013).

Lilley, K.D. 2000, Mapping the Medieval City: Plan analysis and urban history, *Urban History* 27(1): 5–30.

Lilley, K.D. 2011, personal communication.

Lilley, K.D. 2011a, Urban Mappings: Visualizing Late Medieval Chester in cartographic and textual form, in: Clarke, C. (ed.) *Mapping the Medieval City*, University of Wales Press, Cardiff: 19–41.

Lilley, K.D. 2011b, Geography's Medieval History: A neglected enterprise?, *Dialogues in Human Geography* 1(2): 147–162.

Lilley, K.D. 2012, Mapping Truth? Spatial Technologies and the Medieval City: A critical cartography, *Post-Classical Archaeologies* 2: 201–224.

Lilley, K.D., Lloyd, C.D. and Trick, S. 2005, *Mapping Medieval Townscapes: A digital atlas of the New Towns of Edward I* (http://archaeologydataservice.ac.uk/archives/view/atlas_ahrb_2005/, accessed 06-05-2013).

Lilley, K.D., Lloyd, C.D. and Trick, S. 2007, Designs and Designers of Medieval 'New Towns' in Wales, *Antiquity* 81: 279–293.

Liu, Q., Xu, N. and Ding, W. 2010, Study on Mapping the Urban Textural Characteristic, *7th Conference International Seminar on Urban Form (ISUF)*, Hamburg/Lübeck (http://www.isuf2010.de/Papers/Liu_Quan.pdf, accessed 26-09-2013).

Llobera, M. 2003, Extending GIS-Based Visual Analysis: The concept of visualscapes, *International Journal of Geographical Information Science* 17(1): 25–48.

Llobera, M. 2012, Life on a Pixel: Challenges in the development of digital methods within an "Interpretive" landscape archaeology framework, *Journal of Archaeological Method and Theory* 19(4): 495–509.

Llobera, M. 2015, Working the Digital: Some thoughts from landscape archaeology, in: Wylie, A. and Chapman, J. (ed.) *Material Evidence: Learning from archaeological practice*, Routledge, Abingdon: 173–188.

Lobel, M. (ed.) 1969, *Historic Towns: Maps and plans of towns and cities in the British Isles*, Lovell Johns Ltd., London.

Locating London's Past (http://www.locatinglondon.org/, accessed 26-09-2013).

Longley, P.A. and Batty, M. (ed.) 2003, *Advanced Spatial Analysis: The CASA book of GIS*, ESRI Press, Redlands.

Löw, M. 2008, The Constitution of Space: The structuration of spaces through the simultaneity of effect and perception, *European Journal of Social Theory* 11(1): 25–49.

Löw, M. 2013, The City as Experiential Space: The production of shared meaning, *International Journal of Urban and Regional Research* 37(3): 894–908.

Low, S.M. and Lawrence-Zúñiga, D.L. 2006, Locating Culture, in: Low, S.M. and Lawrence-Zúñiga, D. (ed.) *The Anthropology of Space and Place: Locating culture*, Blackwell, Oxford: 1–47.

Lünen, A. von and Travis, C. (ed.) 2013, *History and GIS: Epistemologies, considerations and reflections*, Springer, Dordrecht.

Lyman, R.L., O'Brien, M.J. and Dunnell, R.C. 1997, *The Rise and Fall of Culture History*, Plenum Press, New York.

Lynch, K. 1960, *The Image of the City*, Technology Press, Cambridge.

Lynch, K. 1981, *Good Urban Form*, MIT Press, Cambridge.

MacEachren, A.M. 2004, *How Maps Work: Representation, visualization and design*, The Guilford Press, New York.

Magnoni, A. 2007, Population Estimates at the Ancient Maya City of Chunchucmil, Yucatán, Mexico, in: Clark, J.T. and Hagemeister, E.M. (ed.) *Proceedings of 34th Computer Applications and Quantitative Methods in Archaeology Conference*, Fargo: 160–167.

Magnoni, A., Hutson, S. and Dahlin, B. 2012, Living in the City: Settlement patterns and the urban experience at Classic period Chunchucmil, Yucatan, Mexico, *Ancient Mesoamerica* 23(2): 313–343.

Magnoni, A., Ardren, T., Hutson, S. and Dahlin, B. 2014, The Production of Space and Identity at Classic Period Chunchucmil, Yucatán, Mexico, in: Creekmore, A. III and Fisher, K. (ed.) *Making Ancient Cities: Space and place in early urban societies*, Cambridge University Press, Cambridge: 148–180.

Manzanilla, L., Barba, L. 1990, The Study of Activities in Classic Households: Two case studies from Coba and Teotihuacan, *Ancient Mesoamerica* 1: 41–49.

Marcus, L. 2007, Spatial Capital and How to Measure It: An outline of an analytical theory of the social performativity of urban form, *Proceedings of the 6th International Space Syntax Symposium*, Istanbul: 005 (http://www.spacesyntaxistanbul.itu.edu.tr/papers.htm, accessed 26-09-2013).

Marcus, L. 2010, Spatial Capital: A proposal for an extension of space syntax into a more general urban morphology, *Journal of Space Syntax* 1(1): 30–40.

Marcus, J. and Sabloff, J.A. (ed.) 2008, *The Ancient City: New perspectives on urbanism in the Old and New World*, School for Advanced Research Press, Santa Fe.

Marshall, S. 2016, *The Self-Organising Built Environment* (https://naturbanism.wordpress.com/, accessed 31-05-2017).

Marston, S.A. 2000, The Social Construction of Scale, *Progress in Human Geography* 24(2): 219–242.

Massey, D. 2005, *For Space*, Sage, London.

Massey, D. 2007, *World City*, Polity, Cambridge.

Mavridou, M. 2012, Perception of Three-Dimensional Urban Scale in an Immersive Virtual Environment, *Environment and Planning B: Planning and Design* 36: 33–47.

MayaArch3D n.d. (http://www.mayaarch3d.org/language/en/mayaarch3d-digital-collections/, accessed 24-07-2017).

McAnany, P.A., Sabloff, J.A., Lamoureux St-Hilaire, M. and Iannone, G. 2016, Leaving Classic Maya Cities: Agent-based modeling and the dynamics of diaspora, in: Emberling, G. (ed.)

Social Theory in Archaeology and Ancient History: The present and future of counternarratives, Cambridge University Press, New York: 259–288.

McCafferty, G.G. and Peuramaki-Brown, M. 2007, Ancient Cities of Mesoamerica, *Western Humanities Review* 61(3): 100–111.

McCann, E. and Ward, K. (ed.) 2011, *Mobile Urbanism: Cities and policymaking in the global age*, University of Minnesota Press, Minneapolis.

McEwan, D.G. and Millican, K. 2012, In Search of the Middle Ground: Quantitative spatial techniques and experiential theory in archaeology, *Journal of Archaeological Method and Theory* 19(4): 491–494.

Meijers, E. 2007, From Central Place to Network Model: Theory and evidence of a paradigm change, *Tijdschrift voor Economische en Sociale Geografie* 98(2): 245–259.

Mekking, A. 2009, The Architectural Representation of Reality: The built environment as the materialization of mental construct, in: Mekking, A. and Roose, E. (ed.) *The Global Built Environment as a Representation of Realities: Why and how architecture should be the study of worldwide comparison*, Pallas Publications, Amsterdam: 23–49.

Merton, R.K. 1936, The Unanticipated Consequences of Purposive Social Action, *American Sociological Review* 1(6): 894–904.

Miller, D. (ed.) 1998, *Material Cultures: Why some things matter*, University of Chicago Press, Chicago.

Miller, D. (ed.) 2005, *Materiality*, Duke University Press, Durham.

Min, D., Zihlin, L. and Xiaojong, C. 2007, Extended Hausdorff Distance for Spatial Objects in GIS, *International Journal of Geographical Information Science* 21(4): 459–475.

MIS Quarterly, 2013, special issue: Critical realism in IS research, 34(3).

Mises, L. von 1998[1949], *Human Action: A treatise on economics*, The Scholar's Edition, The Ludwig von Mises Institute, Auburn.

Monmonier, M. 1996, *How to Lie with Maps*, 2nd edition, University of Chicago Press, Chicago.

Moore, J.D. 1992, Pattern and Meaning in Prehistoric Peruvian Architecture: The architecture of social control in the Chimu state, *Latin American Antiquity* 3(2): 95–113.

Morton, S.G., Peuramaki-Brown, M.M., Dawson, P.C. and Seibert, J.D. 2012a, Civic and Household Community Relationships at Teotihuacan, Mexico: A space syntax approach, *Cambridge Archaeological Journal* 22(3): 387–400.

Morton, S.G., Peuramaki-Brown, M.M., Dawson, P.C. and Seibert, J.D. 2012b, The Dynamic Maya City: Methods for modelling pedestrian movement in ancient urban centres, presented at: *17th European Maya Conference*, University of Helsinki.

Morton, S.G., Peuramaki-Brown, M.M., Dawson, P.C. and Seibert, J.D. 2014, Peopling the Past: Interpreting models for pedestrian movement in ancient civic-ceremonial centres, in: Rau, S. and Schönherr, E. (ed.) *Mapping Spatial Relations, their Perceptions and Dynamics: The City Today and in the Past*, Lecture Notes in Geoinformation and Cartography, Springer International: 25–44.

Moudon, A.V. 1997, Urban Morphology as an Emerging Interdisciplinary Field, *Urban Morphology* 1: 3–10.

Mould, O. 2016, A Limitless Urban Theory? A response to Scott and Storper's 'The Nature of Cities: The scope and limits of urban theory', *International Journal of Urban and Regional Research* 40(1): 157–163.

Mumford, L. 1961, *The City in History: Its origins, its transformations, and its prospects*, Secker & Warburg, London.

Narvaez, L., Penn, A. and Griffiths, S. 2012, Creating Urban Place: Re-thinking the value of residential and commercial use in urban street networks, *Spaces and Flows: An International Journal of Urban and ExtraUrban Studies* 2(3): 149–168.

National Heritage List for England n.d. (http://www.english-heritage.org.uk/professional/protection/process/national-heritage-list-for-england/, accessed 25-09-2013).

National Library of Scotland: Town plans n.d. (http://maps.nls.uk/towns/, accessed 26-09-2013).

National Library of Scotland: OS abbreviations n.d. (http://maps.nls.uk/os/abbrev/, accessed 26-09-2013).

Nes, A. van 2011, Measuring Spatial Visibility, Adjacency, Permeability and Degrees of Street Life in Pompeii, in: Laurence, R. and Newsome, D. (ed.) *Rome, Ostia, Pompeii: Movement and space*, Oxford University Press, Oxford: 100–117.

Nes, A. van (in prep.), *Space Syntax in Urban Studies: An introduction*, Sage.

Nes, A. van and López, M.J.J. 2007, Micro Scale Spatial Relationships in Urban Studies: The relationship between private and public space and its impact on street life, in: *Proceedings of the
6th International Space Syntax Symposium*, Istanbul: 023 (http://www.spacesyntaxistanbul.
itu.edu.tr/papers.htm, accessed 26-09-2013).

Newman, P. and Thornley, A. 2011, *Planning World Cities: Globalisation and urban politics*, Palgrave
Macmillan, Basingstoke.

Nichols, D.L. 2006, Shining Stars and Black Holes: Population and preindustrial cities, in: Storey,
G.R. (ed.) *Urbanism in the Preindustrial World: Cross-cultural approaches*, University of
Alabama Press, Tuscaloosa: 330–340.

Nijman, J. 2007, Introduction: Comparative urbanism, *Urban Geography* 28(1): 1–6.

Noizet, H. and Costa, L. (ed.) n.d., *Alpage (AnaLyse diachronique de l'espace urbain PArisien: approche
GEomatique)* (http://alpage.tge-adonis.fr/en/, accessed 26-09-2013).

Noizet, H. and Grosso, E. 2011, The ALPAGE Project: Paris and its suburban area at the intersec-
tion of history and geography (9th–19th century), in: *Proceedings of the 25th International
Cartographic Conference (ICC)*, Paris (http://halshs.archives-ouvertes.fr/docs/00/66/84/00/
PDF/aci_2011_ALPAGE_project.pdf, accessed 06-05-2013).

Oliver, R. 1993, *Ordnance Survey Maps: A concise guide for historians*, The Charles Close Society, London.

Omer, I. and Zafrir-Reuven, O. 2010, Street Patterns and Spatial Integration of Israeli Cities,
Journal of Space Syntax 1(2): 280–295.

OS Mastermap® Topography Layer: User Guide and Technical Specification, v1.3, July 2007, Ordnance
Survey, Southampton.

Ostwaldt, M.J. 2011, The Mathematics of Spatial Configuration: Revisiting, revising and critiquing
justified plan graph theory, *Nexus Network Journal* 13(2): 445–470.

Paasi, A. 1991, Deconstructing Regions: Notes on the scales of spatial life, *Environment and
Planning A* 23: 239–256.

Paasi, A. 2002, Place and Region: Regional worlds and words, *Progress in Human Geography*
26(6): 802–811.

Palaiologou, G. and Vaughan, L. 2012, Urban Rhythms: Historic housing and sociospatial boundaries, in: Greene, M., Reyes, J. and Castro, A. (ed.) *Proceedings of the 8th International Space
Syntax Symposium*, Santiago de Chile, PUC: 8161.

Paliou, E. and Knight, D.J. 2013, Mapping the Senses: Perceptual and social aspects of Late Antique
liturgy in San Vitale, Ravenna, in: Contreras, M., Farjas, M. and Melero, F.J. (ed.) *Proceedings of
the 38th Annual Conference on Computer Applications and Quantitative Methods in Archaeology,
Granada*: 229–236.

Paliou, E., Corsi, C. and Vermeulen, F. 2012, The Whole Is More than the Sum of its Parts: Geospatial
data integration and analysis at the Roman site of Ammaia (Marvão, Portugal), presented at: *40th
Computer Applications and Quantitative Methods in Archaeology Conference*, Southampton.

Paliou, E., Lieberwirth, U. and Silvia, P. (ed.) 2014, *Spatial Analysis and Social Spaces: Interdisciplinary approaches to the interpretation of prehistoric and historic built environments*, Topoi
18, Berlin Studies of the Ancient World, Walter de Gruyter, Berlin.

Palliser, D.M. (ed.) 2000, *The Cambridge Urban History of Britain, Vol. I, 600–1540*, Cambridge
University Press, Cambridge.

Parmington, A. 2011, *Space and Sculpture in the Classic Maya City*, Cambridge University Press,
New York.

Parr, J.B. 2005, Perspectives on the City-Region, *Regional Studies* 39(5): 555–566.

Parr, J.B. 2007, Spatial Definitions of the City: Four perspectives, *Urban Studies* 44(2): 381–392.

Peck, J. 2015, Cities beyond Compare, *Regional Studies* 49(1): 160–182.

Peiró Vitoria, A. 2015, *La Estructura Urbana de las Ciudades Mayas del Periodo Clásico*, Tesis
Doctoral, Tomo I–III, Universitat Politècnica de València.

Pellow, D. (ed.) 1996, *Setting Boundaries: The anthropology of spatial and social organization*,
Bergin & Garvey, Westport.

Penn, A. 2003, Space Syntax and Spatial Cognition: Or why the axial line?, *Environment and
Behavior* 35: 30–65.

Peuquet, D.J. 1994, It's about Time: A conceptual framework for the representation of temporal
dynamics in geographic information systems, *Annals of the Association of American Geographers*
84(3): 441–461.

Peuquet, D.J. 2001, Making Space for Time: Issues in space-time data representation,
GeoInformatica 5(1): 11–32.

Peuramaki-Brown, M. 2013, Identifying Integrative Built Environments in the Archaeological Record: An application of New Urban Design Theory to ancient urban spaces, *Journal of Anthropological Archaeology* 32: 577–594.

Pierce, K.B. and Weiss, A.D. 2010, Hydrodiff: An ArcGIS/Python polyline comparison tool, presented at: *WAURISA conference*, Tacoma (http://www.waurisa.org/conferences/2010/presentations/317_Kenneth_Pierce_Quantifying_Differences_Hydrodiff.pdf, accessed 26-09-2013).

Pinho, P. and Oliviera, V. 2009a, Different Approaches to Urban Form, *Journal of Urbanism: International research on placemaking and urban sustainability* 2(2): 103–125.

Pinho, P. and Oliveira, V. 2009b, Cartographic Analysis in Urban Morphology, *Environment and Planning B: Planning and Design* 36: 107–127.

Pleho, J. and Avdagic, Z. 2008, Fuzzy Model in Urban Planning, in: Dimitrov, D.P., Mladenov, V., Jordanova, S. and Mastorakis, N. (ed.) *FS'08 Proceedings of the 9th WSEAS International Conference on Fuzzy Systems*, World Scientific and Engineering Academy and Society (WSEAS), Stevens Point: 156–160.

Poehler, E. n.d., *Pompeii Bibliography and Mapping Project* (http://digitalhumanities.umass.edu/pbmp/, accessed 26-09-2013).

Pollard, H.P. 1977, An Analysis of Urban Zoning and Planning at Prehispanic Tzintzuntzan, *Proceedings of the American Philosophical Society* 121(1): 46–69.

Pollock, H.E.D., Roys, R., Proskouriakoff, T. and Ledyard Smith, A. 1962, *Mayapan, Yucatan, Mexico*, Carnegie Institution of Washington, Publication 619, Washington.

Pratt, A.C. 1995, Putting Critical Realism to Work: The practical implications for geographical research, *Progress in Human Geography* 19(1): 61–74.

Pratt, A.C. 2013, '… The Point is to Change it': Critical realism and human geography, *Dialogues in Human Geography* 3(1): 26–29.

Pred, A.R. 1977, The Choreography of Existence: Comments on Hägerstrand's time-geography and its usefulness, *Economic Geography, Planning-Related Swedish Geographic Research* 53(2): 207–221.

Pred, A.R. 1981, Social Reproduction and the Time-Geography of Everyday Life, *Geografiska Annaler, series B, Human Geography* 63(1): 5–22.

Pred, A.R. 1984, Place as Historically Contingent Process: Structuration and the time-geography of becoming places, *Annals of the Association of American Geographers* 74(2): 279–297.

Pred, A.R. 1986, *Place, Practice and Structure: Social and spatial transformation in southern Sweden: 1750–1850*, Polity Press, Cambridge.

Pugh, T.W. 2003, A Cluster and Spatial Analysis of Ceremonial Architecture at Late Postclassic Mayapán, *Journal of Archaeological Science* 30: 941–953.

Putnam, H. 1981, *Reason, Truth and History*, Cambridge, Cambridge University Press.

Putnam, H. 1990, *Realism with a Human Face*, Harvard University Press, Cambridge.

Raja, R. 2016, Becoming Urban, *Norwegian Archaeological Review* 49(1): 76–78.

Raja, R. 2017, *Network Evolutions: Abstract from the conference* (http://urbnet.au.dk/events/2017/networkevolutions/, accessed 16-05-2017).

Rapoport, A. 1988, Levels of Meaning in the Built Environment, in: Poyatos, F. (ed.) *Cross-Cultural Perspectives in Non Verbal Communication*, C.J. Hogrefe, Toronto: 317–336.

Rapoport, A. 1990[1982], *The Meaning of the Built Environment: A nonverbal communication approach*, University of Arizona Press, Tucson.

Rapoport, A. 1994, Spatial Organization and the Built Environment, in: Ingold, T. (ed.) *Companion Encyclopedia of Anthropology: Humanity, culture and social life*, Routledge, London: 460–502.

Rapoza, K. 2015, What will become of China's Ghost Cities? *Forbes* (https://www.forbes.com/sites/kenrapoza/2015/07/20/what-will-become-of-chinas-ghost-cities/#1a3da3242e7b, accessed 17-05-2016).

Ratti, C. 2004a, Urban Texture and Space Syntax: Some inconsistencies, *Environment and Planning B: Planning and Design* 31: 487–499.

Ratti, C. 2004b, Rejoinder to Hillier and Penn, *Environment and Planning B: Planning and Design* 31: 513–516.

Raue, J.J. 1982, *De Stad Delft: Vorming en ruimtelijke ontwikkeling in de late Middeleeuwen: Interpratie van 25 jaar binnenstadsonderzoek*, Delftse Universitaire Pers, Delft.

Read, D.W. 1989, Intuitive Typology and Automatic Classification: Divergence or full circle?, *Journal of Anthropological Archaeology* 8: 158–188.

Renfrew, C. 2008, The City through Time and Space: Transformations of Centrality, in: Marcus, J. and Sabloff, J.A. (ed.) *The Ancient City: New perspectives on urbanism in the Old and New World*, School for Advanced Research Press, Santa Fe: 29–51.

Rice, D.S. 2006, Late Classic Maya Population: Characteristics and implications, in: Storey, G.R. (ed.) *Urbanism in the Preindustrial World: Cross-cultural approaches*, University of Alabama Press, Tuscaloosa: 252–276.

Rice, D.S. and Culbert, T.P. 1990, Historical Contexts for Population Reconstruction in the Maya Lowlands, in: Culbert, T.P. and Rice, D.S. (ed.) *Precolumbian Population History in the Maya Lowlands*, University of New Mexico Press, Albuquerque: 1–36.

Rice Humanities Research Centre 2016, *imagineRio* (http://imaginerio.org/, accessed 06-07-2017).

Richardson, M. 2006, Being-in-the-Market versus Being-in-the-Plaza: Material culture and the construction of social reality in Spanish America, in: Low, S. M. and Lawrence-Zúñiga, D. (ed.) *The Anthropology of Space and Place: Locating culture*, Blackwell, Oxford: 74–91.

Richards-Rissetto, H. 2012, Social Interaction at the Maya Site of Copán, Honduras: A least cost approach to configurational analysis, in: White, D.A. and Surface-Evans, S.L. (ed.) *Least Cost Analysis of Social Landscapes: Archaeological case studies*, University of Utah Press, Salt Lake City: 109–129.

Richards-Rissetto, H. and Landau, K. 2014, Movement as a Means of Social (Re)Production: Using GIS to measure social integration across urban landscapes, *Journal of Archaeological Science* 41: 365–375.

Rietschel, S. 1897, *Markt und Stadt in ihrem rechtlichen Verhältnis: Ein Beitrag zur Geschichte der Deutschen Stadtverfassung*, Veit & comp., Leipzig.

Robinson, J. 2004, In the Tracks of Comparative Urbanism: Difference, urban modernity and the primitive, *Urban Geography* 25(8): 709–723.

Robinson, J. and Roy, A. 2016, Debate on Global Urbanisms and the Nature of Urban Theory, *International Journal of Urban and Regional Research* 40(1): 181–186.

Rodier, X., Saligny, L, Lefebvre, B. and Pouliot, J. 2009, ToToPI (Topographie de Tours Pré-Industriel): A GIS for understanding urban dynamics based on the OH_FET model (Social Use, Space and Time), in: *Proceedings of the 37th Computer Applications and Quantitative Methods in Archaeology Conference*, Williamsburg.

Rodman, M. and Cooper, M. 1996, Boundaries of Home in Toronto Housing Cooperatives, in: Pellow, D. (ed.) *Setting Boundaries: The anthropology of spatial and social organization*, Bergin & Garvey, Westport: 91–110.

Rörig, F. 1928, *Hansische Beiträge zur deutschen Wirtschaftsgeschichte: Mit einem Plan des Marktes von Lübeck*, F. Hirt, Breslau.

Rose, M. 2012, Dwelling as Marking and Claiming, *Environment and Planning D: Society and Space* 30: 757–771.

Rose, M. and Wylie, J. 2006, Animating Landscape, *Environment and Planning D: Society and Space* 24: 475–479.

Rotenberg, R. 1996, Tearing Down the Fences: Public gardens and municipal power in nineteenth-century Vienna, in: Pellow, D. (ed.) *Setting Boundaries: The anthropology of spatial and social organization*, Bergin & Garvey, Westport: 55–70.

Russell, B.W. 2008, *Postclassic Maya Settlement on the Rural-Urban Fringe of Mayapán, Yucatán, Mexico*, unpublished PhD thesis, 2 volumes, University at Albany, State University of New York.

Rutte, R. 2008, Bouwstenen voor Vergelijkende Analyse?: Stedenatlassen en het stadshistorisch onderzoek in Nederland, *Stadsgeschiedenis* 3(1): 71–86.

Rutte, R. 2011, personal communication.

Samuels, I. 2010, Understanding place?, *Urban Morphology* 14(2): 122–123.

Sanders, W.T. and Webster, D. 1988, The Mesoamerican Urban Tradition, *American Anthropologist, New Series* 90(3): 521–546.

Savage, S.H. 1997, Assessing Departures from Log-Normality in the Rank-Size Rule, *Journal of Archaeological Science* 24: 233–244.

Sayer, A. 1979, Understanding Urban Models versus Understanding Cities, *Environment and Planning A* 11: 853–862.

Sayer, A. 1981, Abstraction: A realist interpretation, *Radical Philosophy* 28: 6–15.

Sayer, A. 1985, The Difference that Space Makes, in Gregory, D. and Urry, J. (ed.), *Social Relations and Spatial Structures*, Macmillan, Basingstoke: 49–66.

Sayer, A. 1993, Postmodernist Thought in Geography: A realist view, *Antipode* 25(4): 320–344.

Sayer, A. 2000, *Realism and Social Science*, Sage Publications, London.

Sayer, A. 2013, Looking forward to New Realist Debates, *Dialogues in Human Geography* 3(1): 22–25.

Schaffter, M., Fall, J.J. and Debarbieux, B. 2010, Unbounded Boundary Studies and Collapsed Categories: Rethinking spatial objects, *Progress in Human Geography* 34(2): 254–262.

Scheer, B.C. and Ferdelman, D. 2001, Inner-City Destruction and Survival: The case of Over-the-Rhine, Cincinnati, *Urban Morphology* 5(1): 15–27.

Schiffer, M.B. 1987, *The Formation Processes of the Archaeological Record*, University of New Mexico Press, Albuquerque.

Schütz, A. 1967, *The Phenomenology of the Social World*, Northwestern University Press, Evanston.

Schwerdtfeger, F.W. 1972, Urban Settlement Patterns in Northern Nigeria (Hausaland), in: Ucko, P.J., Tringham, R. and Dimbleby, G.W. (ed.) *Man, Settlement and Urbanism*, Research Seminar in Archaeology and Related Subjects Meeting, Institute of Archaeology, London University, 1970, Duckworth, London: 547–556.

Scobie, G.D., Zant, J.M. and Whinney, R. 1991, *The Brooks, Winchester: A preliminary report on the excavations, 1987–88*, Archaeology Report 1, Winchester Museums Service, Winchester.

Scott, A.J. and Storper M. 2015, The Nature of Cities: The scope and limits of urban theory, *International Journal of Urban and Regional Research* 39(1): 1–15.

Seamon, D. n.d.[2000], *Phenomenology, Place, Environment, and Architecture: A review* (http://www.arch.ksu.edu/seamon/Seamon_reviewEAP.htm, accessed 26-09-2013).

Seamon, D. 2012, Place, Place Identity, and Phenomenology: A triadic interpretation based on J.G. Bennett's systematics, in: Casakin, H., Romice, O. and Porta, S. (ed.) *The Role of Place Identity in the Perception, Understanding, and Design of the Built Environment*, Betham Science Publishers, London: 3–21.

Sharer, R.J. and Traxler, L.P. 2005, *The Ancient Maya*, 6th edition, Stanford University Press, Stanford.

Silverstein, J.E., Webster, D., Martinez, H. and Soto, A. 2009, Rethinking the Great Earthwork of Tikal: A hydraulic hypothesis for the Classic Maya polity, *Ancient Mesoamerica* 20: 45–58.

Sima, Y. and Zhang, D. 2009, Comparative Precedents on the Study of Urban Morphology, in: Koch, D., Marcus, L. and Steen, J. (ed.) *Proceedings of the 7th International Space Syntax Symposium*, KTH, Stockholm: 103.

Simon, D. and Adam-Bradford, A. 2016, Archaeology and Contemporary Dynamics for More Sustainable, Resilient Cities in the Peri-Urban Interface, in: Maheshwari, B., Singh, V.P. and Thoradeniya, B. (ed.) *Balanced Urban Development: Options and strategies for liveable cities*, Water Science and Technology Library, Vol. 72, Springer International Publishing, Cham: 57–83.

Sinclair, P.J.J., Nordquist, G., Herschend, F. and Isendahl, C. (ed.) 2010, *The Urban Mind: Cultural and environmental dynamics*, African and Comparative Archaeology, Department of Archaeology and Ancient History, Uppsala University, Uppsala.

Sjoberg, G. 1960, *The Preindustrial City: Past and present*, The Free Press, New York.

Slater, T.R. (ed.) 1990, *The Built Form of Western Cities: Essays for M.R.G. Conzen on the occasion of his eightieth birthday*, Leicester University Press, Leicester.

Slater, T.R. 1996, The European Historic Towns Atlas, *Journal of Urban History* 22(6): 739–749.

Smith, A.T. 2001, The Limitations of Doxa: Agency and subjectivity from an archaeological point of view, *Journal of Social Archaeology* 1(2): 155–171.

Smith, A.T. 2003, *The Political Landscape: Constellations of authority in early complex polities*, University of California Press, Berkeley.

Smith, B. 2001, Fiat Objects, *Topoi* 20(2): 131–148.

Smith, B. and Varzi, A.C. 1997, Fiat and Bona Fide Boundaries: Towards an ontology of spatially extended objects, in: Hirtle, S. and Frank, A.U. (ed.) *Spatial Information Theory: A Theoretical Basis for GIS*, Springer, Berlin: 103–119.

Smith, B. and Varzi, A.C. 2000, Fiat and Bona Fide Boundaries, *Philosophy and Phenomenological Research* 60(2): 401–420.

Smith, C. and Cochrane, E.E. 2011, How Is Visibility Important for Defence?: A GIS analysis of sites in the western Fijian Islands, *Archaeology in Oceania* 46: 76–84.

Smith, H.S. 1972, Society and Settlement in Ancient Egypt, in: Ucko, P.J., Tringham, R. and Dimbleby, G.W. (ed.) *Man, Settlement and Urbanism*, Research Seminar in Archaeology and Related Subjects Meeting, Institute of Archaeology, London University, 1970, Duckworth, London: 705–720.

Smith, M.E. 1989, Cities, Towns, and Urbanism: Comment on Sanders and Webster, *American Anthropologist, New Series* 91(20): 454–460.

Smith, M.E. 2003, Can We Read Cosmology in Ancient Maya City Plans? Comment on Ashmore and Sabloff, *Latin American Antiquity* 14(2): 221–228.

Smith, M.E. 2005, Did the Maya Build Cosmograms?, *Latin American Antiquity* 16(2): 217–224.

Smith, M.E. 2006, The Founding of Cities in the Ancient World: Review of concepts, unpublished translation by author, originally in: Ponce de León, M.J.I., Valencia Rivera, R. and Ciudad Ruiz, A. (ed.) *Nuevas Ciudades, Nuevas Patrias: Fundación y relocalización de ciudades en Mesoamérica y el Meditterráneo antiguo*, Sociedad Española de Estudios Mayas, Madrid: 11–23.

Smith, M.E. 2007, Form and Meaning in the Earliest Cities: A new approach to ancient urban planning, *Journal of Planning History* 6(1): 3–47.

Smith, M.E. 2008, *Aztec City-State Capitals*, University of Florida Press, Gainesville.

Smith, M.E. 2009a, V. Gordon Childe and the Urban Revolution: A historical perspective on a revolution in urban studies, *Town Planning Review* 80(1): 3–29.

Smith, M.E. 2009b, Just How Comparative Is Comparative Urban Geography? A perspective from archaeology, *Urban Geography* 30(2): 113–117.

Smith, M.E. 2010a, Sprawl, Squatters and Sustainable Cities: Can archaeological data shed light on modern urban issues?, *Cambridge Archaeological Journal* 20(2): 229–253.

Smith, M.E. 2010b, The Archaeological Study of Neighborhoods and Districts in Ancient Cities, *Journal of Anthropological Archaeology* 29: 137–154.

Smith, M.E. 2011a, Empirical Urban Theory for Archaeologists, *Journal of Archaeological Methods and Theory* 18: 167–192.

Smith, M.E. 2011b, Classic Maya Settlement Clusters as Urban Neighborhoods: A comparative perspective on low-density urbanism, *Journal de la Société des Américanistes* 97(1): 51–73.

Smith, M.E. 2012, The Role of Ancient Cities in Research on Contemporary Urbanization, *UGEC Viewpoints* 8: 15–19.

Smith, M.E. 2016, How Can Archaeologists Identify Early Cities: Definitions, types, and attributes, in: Fernández-Götz, M. and Krausse, D. (ed.) *Eurasia at the Dawn of History: Urbanization and social change*, Cambridge University Press, New York: 153–168.

Smith, M.E. and Peregrine, P. 2012, Approaches to Comparative Analysis in Archaeology, in: Smith, M.E. (ed.) *The Comparative Archaeology of Complex Societies*, Cambridge University Press, New York: 4–20.

Smith, M.E., Feinman, G.M., Drennan, R.D., Earle, T. and Morris, I. 2012, Archaeology as a Social Science, *PNAS Early Edition*: 1–5 (doi:10.1073/pnas.1201714109).

Smith, M.L. 2003a, Introduction: The Social Construction of Ancient Cities, in: Smith, M.L. (ed.) *The Social Construction of Ancient Cities*, Smithsonian Institution, Washington: 1–36.

Smith, M.L. (ed.) 2003b, *The Social Construction of Ancient Cities*, Smithsonian Institution, Washington.

Smith, M.L. 2008, Urban Empty Spaces: Contentious places for consensus-building, *Archaeological Dialogues* 15(2): 216–231.

Soja, E.W. 2010, Cities and States in Geohistory, *Theory and Society* 39(3-4): 361–376.

Space Syntax Ltd. n.d., *Space Syntax: The science of human behaviour for cities, urban places & buildings* (http://www.spacesyntax.com/, accessed 25-07-2013).

Space Syntax Network n.d., *Software* (http://www.spacesyntax.net/software/, accessed 12-07-2017).

Spatial Morphology Group n.d., *Place Syntax Tool* (https://www.smog.chalmers.se/pst, accessed 12-07-2017).

Speet, B.M.J. 1982, *Historische Stedenatlas van Nederland: Haarlem*, Afl. 1, Delftse Universitaire Pers, Delft.

Speet, B.M.J. 1983, *Historische Stedenatlas van Nederland: Amersfoort*, Afl. 2, Delftse Universitaire Pers, Delft.

Speet, B.M.J. 2006, *Historische Atlas van Haarlem: 1000 jaar Spaarnestad*, SUN, Amsterdam.

Šprajc, I. 2000, Astronomical alignments at Teotihuacan, Mexico, *Latin American Antiquity* 11: 403–415.

ST_HausdorffDistance n.d. (http://postgis.net/docs/ST_HausdorffDistance.html, accessed 26-09-2013).

Ståhle, A. 2012, Place Syntax Tool (PST), in: Hull, A., Silva, C. and Bertolini, L. (ed.) *Accessibility Instruments for Planning Practice*, COST Office, Brussels: 173–178.

Ståhle, A., Marcus, L. and Karlström, A. 2005, Place Syntax: Geographic accessibility with axial lines in GIS, in: Nes, A. van (ed.) *5th International Space Syntax Symposium Proceedings*, Techne Press, Amsterdam: 131–144.

Stanley, B.W., Stark, B.L., Johnston, K.L. and Smith, M.E. 2012, Urban Open Spaces in Historical Perspective: A transdisciplinary typology and analysis, *Urban Geography* 33(8): 1089–1117.

Stanley, B.W., Dennehy, T., Smith, M.E., Stark, B.L, York, A., Cowgill, G., Novic, J. and Ek, J. 2015, Service Access in Premodern Cities: An exploratory comparison of spatial equity, *Journal of Urban History* 42(1): 121–144.

Stanton, T.W. and Hutson, S.R. 2012, Patrones de Crecimiento Urbano: Albarradas y grupos domésticos en el Clásico Temprano en Chunchucmil, Yucatán, in: Acosta Ochoa, G. (ed.) *VII Coloquio Pedro Bosch Gimpera*, UNAM, Mexico City: 299–316.

Star, S.L. 2010, This Is Not a Boundary Object: Reflections on the origin of a concept, *Science, Technology & Human Values* 35(5): 601–617.

Steadman, P. 2004, Developments in Space Syntax, *Environment and Planning B: Planning and Design* 31: 483–486.

Steadman, S.R. 2016, *Archaeology of Domestic Architecture and the Human Use of Space*, Routledge, Abingdon.

Stöger, J. 2011, *Rethinking Ostia: A spatial enquiry into the urban society of Rome's imperial port-town*, PhD thesis, Leiden University Press, Leiden (https://openaccess.leidenuniv.nl/handle/1887/18192, accessed 26-09-2013).

Stoob, H. 1985, The Historic Town Atlas: Problems and working methods, in: Clarke, H. and Simms, A. (ed.) *The Comparative History of Urban Origins in Non-Roman Europe*, BAR, Vol. 2: 583–615.

Storey, G.R. (ed.) 2006, *Urbanism in the Preindustrial World: Cross-cultural approaches*, University of Alabama Press, Tuscaloosa.

Tang, M. and Yang, D. 2008, *Urban Paleontology: Evolution of urban forms*, Universal Publishers, Boca Raton.

Tang, J., Wang, L. and Yao, Z. 2007, Spatio-Temporal Urban Landscape Change Analysis Using the Markov Chain Model and a Modified Genetic Algorithm, *International Journal of Remote Sensing* 28(15): 3255–3271.

Taverne, E. 2008, Terug naar Dorestad: Op zoek naar vroege stedelijke stelsels in de noordelijke delta, in: Rutte, R. and Engen, H. van (ed.) *Stadswording in de Nederlanden: Op zoek naar overzicht*, Uitgeverij Verloren, Hilversum: 171–186.

Taylor, P. 2012, Extraordinary Cities: Early 'city-ness' and the origins of agriculture and states, *International Journal of Urban and Regional Research* 36(3): 415–447.

Teklenburg, J.A.F., Timmermans, H.J.P. and Wagenberg, A.F. van 1993, Space Syntax: Standardised integration measures and some simulations, *Environment and Planning B: Planning and Design* 20: 347–357.

Thaler, U. 2005, Narrative and Syntax: New perspectives on the Late Bronze Age palace of Pylos, Greece, in: Nes, A. van (ed.) *5th International Space Syntax Symposium Proceedings*, Techne Press, Amsterdam: 323–339.

Thrift, N.J. 1983, On the Determination of Social Action in Space and Time, *Environment and Planning D: Society and Space* 1(1): 23–57.

Thrift, N.J. and Pred, A.R. 1981, Time-Geography: A new beginning, *Progress in Human Geography* 5: 277–286.

Tilley, C.Y. 1994, *A Phenomenology of Landscape: Places, paths and monuments*, Berg, Oxford.

Tilly, C. 1967, The State of Urbanization, *Comparative Studies in Society and History* 10(1): 100–113.

Tilly, C. 1996, What good is Urban History?, *Journal of Urban History* 22(6): 702–719.

Tilly, C. 2008, *Explaining Social Processes*, Paradigm Publishers, Boulder.

Tourtellot, G. III 1988, *Excavations at Seibal, Department of Peten, Guatemala: Peripheral survey and excavation, settlement and community patterns*, Volume 16, Part 1, Peabody Museum of Archaeology and Ethnology, Harvard University, Cambridge.

Trancik, R. 1986, *Finding Lost Space: Theories of urban design*, John Wiley & Sons, Hoboken.

Trigger, B. 1972, Determinants of Growth in Pre-Industrial Societies, in: Ucko, P.J., Tringham, R. and Dimbleby, G.W. (ed.) *Man, Settlement and Urbanism*, Research Seminar in Archaeology and Related Subjects Meeting, Institute of Archaeology, London University, 1970, Duckworth, London: 575–599.

Trigger, B. 1989, *A History of Archaeological Thought*, Cambridge University Press, Cambridge.

Trigger, B. 2003, *Understanding Early Civilizations: A comparative study*, Cambridge University Press, New York.

Tuan, Y.-F. 1976, Humanistic Geography, *Annals of the Association of American Geographers* 66: 266–276.

Tuan, Y.-F. 1977, *Space and Place: The perspective of experience*, University of Minnesota Press, Minneapolis.

Tuan, Y.-F. 1979, Space and Place: Humanistic perspective, in: Gale, S. and Olsson, G. (ed.) *Philosophy in Geography*, Theory and Decision Library, Volume 20, D. Reidel Publishing Company, Dordrecht: 387–427.

Turner, V. 1969, *The Ritual Process: Structure and anti-structure*, Aldine de Gruyter, New York.

Turner II, B.L. and Sabloff, J.A. 2012, Classic Period Collapse of the Central Maya Lowlands: Insights about human–environment relationships for sustainability, *PNAS* 109(35): 13908–13914.

Tuzcu, N., 2017, *Istanbul Urban Database* (http://www.istanbulurbandatabase.com/, accessed 06-07-2017).

UCL Space Syntax 2017, *Representations of Space* (http://otp.spacesyntax.net/applying-space-syntax/urban-methods-2/representations-of-space/, accessed 12-07-2017).

Ünlü, T. 2013, Thinking about Urban Fringe Belts: A Mediterranean perspective, *Urban Morphology* 17(1): 5–20.

Valente, V. 2012, Space Syntax and Urban Form: The case of late medieval Padua, *Post-Classical Archaeologies* 2: 147–166.

Vannieuwenhuyze B. and Lisson, J. 2012, De Stadsplannen van Jacob van Deventer: Een schitterende bron voor de stads en dorpsgeschiedenis, *Bladwijzer: Wegwijs met Heemkunde Vlaanderen* 4 (onderzoek): 3–16.

Varzi, A.C. 2012, Mereology, in: Zalta, E.N. (ed.) *The Stanford Encyclopedia of Philosophy*, Winter 2012 edition (http://plato.stanford.edu/archives/win2012/entries/mereology/, accessed 26-09-2013).

Vaughan, L, Jones, C.E., Griffiths, S. and Haklay, M. 2010, The Spatial Signature of Suburban Town Centres, *Journal of Space Syntax* 1(1): 77–91.

Vaughn, S. and Crawford, T. 2009, A Predictive Model of Archaeological Potential: An example from northwestern Belize, *Applied Geography* 29: 542–555.

Verbruggen, R. 2007, The World City Network in Europe between 1250 and 1640: From Chrisaller to Braudel, presented at: *First International Conference for Young Urban Researchers (FICYUrb)*, CIES, Centre for Research and Studies in Sociology, Lisbon (http://conferencias.iscte.pt/viewpaper.php?id=138&cf=3, accessed 26-09-2013).

Vetch, P., Clarke, C. and Lilley, K.D. 2011, Between Text and Image: Digital renderings of a Late Medieval City, *New Technologies in Medieval and Renaissance Studies* 3: 365–396.

Vis, B.N. 2009, *Built Environments, Constructed Societies*, Sidestone Press, Leiden.

Vis, B.N. 2012, Bintliff, J. and Pearce, M., *The Death of Archaeological Theory?* (book review), *Antiquity* 86: 274–275.

Vis, B.N. 2013, Establishing Boundaries: A conceptualisation for the comparative social study of built environment configurations, *Spaces & Flows: An International Journal of Urban and ExtraUrban Studies* 2(4): 15–29.

Vis, B.N. 2014a, Boundary Concepts for Studying the Built Environment: A framework of socio-spatial reasoning for identifying and operationalising comparative analytical units in GIS, in: Earl, G. et al. (ed.) *Proceedings of CAA 2012 Southampton*, Amsterdam University Press, Amsterdam: 820–838 (http://dare.uva.nl/aup/en/record/500958, accessed 1-06-2016).

Vis, B.N. 2014b, Mapping Socio-Spatial Relations in the Urban Built Environment through Time: Describing the socio-spatial significance of inhabiting urban form, in: Rau, S. and Schönherr, E. (ed.) *Mapping Spatial Relations, their Perceptions and Dynamics: The city today and in the past*, Lecture Notes in Geoinformation and Cartography, Springer International: 45–93.

Vis, B.N. 2016, The Material Logic of Urban Space, *Journal of Space Syntax* 6(2): 271–274.

Vis, J. 2010, *Ondernemend Waarderen: Waarderend Ondernemen: De subjectiviteit van het begrip economische waarde*, Maklu Uitgevers, Apeldoorn.

Visser, J.C., Elsing, T.M., Henderikx, P.A. and Wegner, J.G. 1990, *Historische Stedenatlas van Nederland: Schoonhoven en Nieuwpoort*, Afl. 5, Delftse Universitaire Pers, Delft.

Volchenkov, D. and Blanchard, Ph. 2008, Scaling and Universality in City Space Syntax: Between Zipf and Matthew, *Physica A* 387: 2353–2364.

Wagner, R. 2008, On the Metric, Topological and Functional Structures of Urban Networks, *Physica A* 387: 2120–2132.

Wallace, S. 2011, *Contradictions of Archaeological Theory: Engaging critical realism and archaeological theory*, Routledge, Oxford.

Walker, R.A. 2016, Why Cities? A response, *International Journal of Urban and Regional Research* 40(1): 164–180.

Ward, K. 2010, Towards a Relational Comparative Approach to the Study of Cities, *Progress in Human Geography* 34(4): 471–487.

Weber, M. 1979[1909], *The Agrarian Sociology of Ancient Civilizations*, New Left Books, London.

Webmoor, T. 2007, What about 'One More Turn after the Social' in Archaeological Reasoning?: Taking things seriously, *World Archaeology* 39(4): 563–578.

Webmoor, T. and Witmore, C.L. 2008, Things Are Us!: A commentary on human/things relations under the banner of a 'social' archaeology, *Norwegian Archaeological Review* 41(1): 53–70.

Webster, D., Murtha, T., Silverstein, J., Martinez, H., Terry, R.E. and Burnett, R. 2007, The Great Tikal Earthwork Revisited, *Journal of Field Archaeology* 32: 41–64.

Weller, R.J., Hoch, C. and Huang, C. 2017, *Atlas for the End of the World* (http://atlas-for-the-end-of-the-world.com, accessed 27-07-2017).

Whatmore, S. 2006, Materialist Returns: Practising cultural geography in and for a more-than-human world, *Cultural Geographies* 13: 600–609.

Wheatley, P. 1969, *City as Symbol*, University College London, H.K. Lewis, London.

Wheatley, P. 1972, The Concept of Urbanism, in: Ucko, P.J., Tringham, R. and Dimbleby, G.W. (ed.) *Man, Settlement and Urbanism*, Research Seminar in Archaeology and Related Subjects Meeting, Institute of Archaeology, London University, 1970, Duckworth, London: 601–637.

Wheatley, D. and Gillings, M. 2000, Vision, Perception and GIS: Some notes on the development of enriched approaches to the study of archaeological visibility, in: Lock, G. (ed.) *Beyond the Map: Archaeology and spatial technologies*, Nato Science Series A: Life Sciences, IOS Press, Amsterdam: 1–27.

Whitehand, J.W.R. 1977, The Basis for an Historico-Geographical Theory of Urban Form, *Transactions of the Institute of British Geographers* 2(3): 400–416.

Whitehand, J.W.R. 1981a, Background to the Urban Morphogenetic Tradition, in: Whitehand, J.W.R. (ed.) *The Urban Landscape: Historical development and management*, Academic Press, London: 1–24.

Whitehand, J.W.R. (ed.) 1981b, *The Urban Landscape: Historical development and management*, Academic Press, London.

Whitehand, J.W.R. 2001, British Urban Morphology: The Conzenian tradition, *Urban Morphology* 5(2): 103–109.

Whitehand, J.W.R. 2007, Conzenian Urban Morphology and Urban Landscapes, in: *Proceedings of the 6th International Space Syntax Symposium*, Istanbul: ii (http://www.spacesyntaxistanbul.itu.edu.tr/papers.htm, accessed 26-09-2013).

Whitehand, J.W.R. 2009, The Structure of Urban Landscapes: Strengthening research and practice, *Urban Morphology* 13(1): 5–27.

Whitehand, J.W.R. 2010a, The Problem of Separate Worlds, *Urban Morphology* 14(2): 83–84.

Whitehand, J.W.R. 2010b, Minding the Gap: Linking different approaches to built-form studies, *Journal of Space Syntax* 1(2): 361–363.

Whitehand, J.W.R. 2012, Issues in Urban Morphology, *Urban Morphology* 16(1): 55–65.

Whitehand, J.W.R. and Larkham, P.J. 1992a, The Urban Landscape: Issues and perspectives, in: Whitehand, J.W.R. and Larkham, P.J. (ed.) *Urban Landscapes: International perspectives*, Routledge, London: 1–19.

Whitehand, J.W.R. and Larkham, P.J. (ed.) 1992b, *Urban Landscapes: International perspectives*, Routledge, London.

Whitehand, J.W.R. and Morton, N.J. 2004, Urban Morphology and Planning: The case of fringe belts, *Cities* 21(4): 275–289.

Wilson, A. 2012, Geographical Modeling for Archaeology and History: Two case studies, *Advances in Complex Systems* 15(1-2): 1–14.

Wilson, A. and Dearden, J. 2011, Phase Transitions and Path Dependence in Urban Evolution, *Journal of Geographical Systems* 13: 1–16.

Wirth, L. 1938, Urbanism as a Way of Life, *The American Journal of Sociology* 44(1): 1–24.

Wiseman, R. 2011, What Theory Could Do for the Field, presented at: *33rd Theoretical Archaeology Group annual meeting*, University of Birmingham.

Witschey, W.R.T. and Brown, C.T. 2010, *The Electronic Atlas of Ancient Maya Sites: A Geographic Information System (GIS)* (http://mayagis.smv.org/, accessed 29-08-2013).

Wood, D. 1992, *The Power of Maps*, The Guilford Press, New York.

Woodward, K. and Jones, J.P. III 2005, On the Border with Deleuze and Guattari, in Houtum, H. van, Kramsch, O.T. and Zierhofer, W. (ed.) *B/ordering Space*, Ashgate, Burlington: 235–248.

Wunderlich, A.L. and Hatcher, R.D. Jr. 2009, Rescuing Legacy Digital Data: Maps stored in Adobe Illustrator™ format, in: Soller, D.R. (ed.) *Digital Mapping Techniques 08-Workshop Proceedings*, U.S. Geological Survey Open-File Report 2009: 1298 (http://pubs.usgs.gov/of/2009/1298/, accessed 08-05-2013).

Wylie, J. 2005, A Single Day's Walking: Narrating self and landscape on the South West Coast Path, *Transactions of the Institute of British Geographers* 30: 234–247.

Yaneva, A. 2012, *Mapping Controversies in Architecture*, Ashgate: Farnham.

Yeung, H.W. 1997, Critical Realism and Realist Research in Human Geography: A method or a philosophy in search of a method? *Progress in Human Geography* 21(1): 51–74.

Yoffee, N. 2009, Making Ancient Cities Plausible, *Reviews in Anthropology* 38: 264–289.

York, A.M., Smith, M.E., Stanley, B.W., Stark, B.L., Novic, J., Harlan, S.L., Cowgill, G.L. and Boone, C.G. 2011, Ethnic and Class Clustering through the Ages: A transdisciplinary approach to urban neighbourhood social patterns, *Urban Studies* 48(11): 2399–2415.

Yusuf, S.A., Georgakis, P. and Nwagboso, C. 2010, Review of Modelling, Visualisation and Artificial Intelligent Methodologies for Built Environment Applications, *The Built & Human Environment Review* 3: 12–41.

Zacharias, J. 1997, The Impact of Layout and Visual Stimuli on the Itineraries and Perceptions of Pedestrians in a Public Market, *Environment and Planning B: Planning and Design* 23: 23–35.

Zedeño, M.N. and Bowser, B.J. 2009, The Archaeology of Meaningful Places, in: Bowser, B.J. and Zedeño, M.N. (ed.) *The Archaeology of Meaningful Places*, Foundations of Archaeological Inquiry, University of Utah Press, Salt Lake City: 1–14.

Zierhofer, W. 2002, Speech Acts and Space(s): Language pragmatics and the discursive constitution of the social, *Environment and Planning A* 34: 1355–1372.

Zimmermann, K. 2012, Eigenlogik of Cities: Introduction to the themed section, *Urban Research & Practice* 5(3): 299–302.

Abridged BLT Definitions

Boundary Line Type (BLT)	Empirically identifiable principle	Social relation to interaction opportunities	Indicative contemporary urban example
1 Closing boundaries R: 115 G: 76 B: 0 C: 12 M: 47 Y: 100 K: 60 R: 235 G: 228 B: 190 C: 7 M: 8 Y: 31 K: 0	Operates on the basis of seclusion of a continuous spatial arrangement from the surrounding configuration with the material property that the boundary can be closed off towards its outside, thus making it a dominant. It is also a solid (i.e. no internal arrangement of outlines)	Interaction opportunities are quite stringently internalised as distinct from the outside, though there is a mutual (in)direct orientation between the solid dominant and the surrounding configuration	These boundaries typically circumscribe buildings of any sort or size
2 Facing boundaries R: 170 G: 255 B: 0 C: 41 M: 0 Y: 100 K: 0	Operates on the principle of the orientation for soliciting interaction from the surrounding configuration	Is the site of solicitation of interaction with a dominant	These boundaries represent the doorways or entrance ways into a building
3 Associative boundaries R: 230 G: 0 B: 0 C: 0 M: 92 Y: 100 K: 0	Operates on the basis of dependence on a single dominant that it is directly associated with and, in a conjunction including possible other (in)directly associated boundaries, with which it forms an adjoining configurative complex	Interaction opportunities are mediated between the openness of the surrounding configuration and the related dominant	These boundaries are typically associated with gardens or any plots and surfaces belonging to a specific building
4 Extended facing boundaries R: 56 G: 168 B: 0 C: 69 M: 0 Y: 100 K: 0	Operates on the principle of orientation in an uninterrupted connection to a facing boundary by dependence on any boundary associated with a proceeding dominant	Is the site of indirect solicitation of interaction with a dominant, proceeding is no necessity	These boundaries are typically associated with garden gates or courtyard entrances, etc.
5 Directing boundaries R: 0 G: 92 B: 230 C: 91 M: 76 Y: 0 K: 0	Operates on the basis that it directs interaction along opportunities for further boundary crossings in parallels	Interaction opportunities are directed along the boundary crossings that constitute its sides, connecting all sorts of bounded spaces	These boundaries are associated with the street network, access and pathways
6 Disclosing boundaries R: 255 G: 170 B: 0 C: 0 M: 40 Y: 100 K: 0	Operates on the basis of guiding interaction towards opportunities for further boundary crossings in multiple directions rather than a single particular direction with necessary (in)direct connections to solid dominants	Interaction opportunities are freely organised, yet directed in multiple directions which in several cases will eventually lead to soliciting interaction with solid dominants	These boundaries are associated with square-like spaces in well integrated urban situations with several associated buildings
7 Enclosing boundaries R: 255 G: 255 B: 0 C: 3 M: 0 Y: 93 K: 0	Operates on the basis of seclusion from the surrounding configuration with the material property that the boundary can be closed off towards its outside, making it a dominant while containing solid dominants	Interaction opportunities are restricted by solicitation between the openness of the integration within the boundary configuration and the configuration with solid dominants that it circumscribes	These boundaries are typically associated with city walls and gated communities

Abridged BLT Definitions

Boundary Line Type (BLT)	Empirically identifiable principle	Social relation to interaction opportunities	Indicative contemporary urban example
8 Mutual boundaries R: 169 G: 0 B: 230 C: 67 M: 99 Y: 0 K: 0	Operates on the principle that it is simultaneously associated with, or encompassing, a distinct subset of several solid dominants with which it forms a configurative complex	Interaction opportunities are indirectly directed to several solid dominants and mediated between the openness of thoroughfare	These boundaries are associated with a specific group of buildings without any preference as to which it provides access such as shared porches, cul-de-sacs and communal space in gated communities
9 Opening boundaries R: 230 G: 0 B: 169 C: 24 M: 95 Y. 0 K: 0	Operates on the principle that it creates open, accessible connections towards its outside, while being an integrated part of the configuration	Interaction opportunities are freely organised, with no prerequisites for boundary contexts and the possibility of thoroughfare	These boundaries can be described as park-like spaces, e.g. garden plots, urban fallow, parking surfaces
10 Neutral boundaries R: 204 G: 204 B: 204 C: 22 M: 16 Y: 16 K: 2	Operates on the principle of neutrality, which results from ambiguity and the absence of singular associations, and can occur in virtually any context	Due to the absence of an unambiguous relation to a residing socio-spatial system, crossing the boundary creates no difference from the surrounding non-dominant configuration	These boundaries tend to be the left over areas in less optimally used built environment configurations and also some delimited functional areas connected to streets (e.g. electricity supply)
11 Man-made boundaries of unoccupiability R: 156 G: 156 B: 156 C: 38 M: 30 Y. 30 K: 13	Operates on the basis of negativity, can occur in most contexts	Negativity means there is no residing socio-spatial system, in this case because an area cannot be occupied by human beings	Structures that create an unoccupiable surface area, such as ponds, canals, architectural talus, narrow gaps, etc.
12 Not man-made boundaries of unoccupiability R: 104 G: 104 B: 104 C: 55 M: 45 Y. 44 K: 35	Operates on the basis of negativity, can occur in most contexts	Negativity means there is no residing socio-spatial system, in this case because an area cannot be occupied by human beings	Steep slopes, natural bodies of water, etc., which are contained in the built environment
13 Not man-made negative boundaries R: 0 G: 0 B: 0 C: 0 M: 0 Y: 0 K: 100	Operates on the basis of negativity, can occur in most contexts	Negativity means there is no residing socio-spatial system, in this case because it marks the end of the built environment	'Nature': wild or not fully cultivated areas
V Virtual boundaries R: 190 G: 232 B: 255 C: 28 M: 0 Y: 0 K: 0	Sites of distinction afforded by extant physical distinctions, human beings would have understood and/or experienced to be a crossing from subdivision into subdivision without clear material markers imposed onto the surface	Can in principle be part of any BLT that is not closable or negatively defined	Locations of crossings from space to space are in principle unimpeded and predominantly unmarked, such as openings in dry stone walls circumscribing fields, or a cul-de-sac connecting to a street with similar surface

Index

human-environment relationship 12, 38
human experience 31, 361
human fiat 118–19, 123
human geography 14–15, 47–53, 57,
    169, 172
human phenomenon of urban life 10, 22, 57
human processes 12–13
Hutson, Scott 211, 213, 221–2
hypothesis-testing 71, 192, 271, 287, 349,
    353, 359
hypothetical measures 9

ideal types 19–20, 35
ideation 4, 6–7, 10, 44, 103–4, 113, 117–8,
    120–1, 125, 160
identifying BLTs 8, 260–1, 266–8, 334–5, 339,
    also see boundary line types
identity 35, 38, 103, 177, 221
identity points 221
ideograms 310
ideographic representations 16, 147
immanent critique 60–1, 74, 352
indigenous responses 1, 11, 354
indirect co-presence 91, 195
individual human *being* 90–1
Industrial Revolution 17
inertia 55, 107
informality 145, 148, 153–4, 276, 291, 359
infrastructure 14, 30, 265, 322–3, 335
Ingold, Tim 52, 80–3, 87, 96
inhabitation, processes of 3, 12–13, 24,
    26, 38, 43, 45–6, 54, 57–8, 73–4, 78–9,
    84–8, 96–101, 108, 110, 115, 120–1, 129,
    137, 160, 177, 272, 288
'inhabited built environment' concept
    96–9, 109, 352
inherited outlines 187
inside-outside distinctions 88, 94, 96, 99, 105,
    112, 114–5, 132–3, 135, 261, 263, 283–4
institutions 92–93, 96, 118
integration measures 196, 287
integration, of data 170–1,
intelligibility 6, 81, 85–8, 106, 111, 196
intensity 21, 26, 89, 186, 206, 219, 314,
    348, 360
intentionality 32, 35, 40, 54–5, 57, 92, 99,
    101, 114, 188, 256, 280, 290
interaction opportunities 31, 39, 65, 101, 113,
    121, 160–1, 198, 279, 281–2, 285–6, 294,
    323, 357
inter-city comparisons 10, 18, 349
interdisciplinarity 6, 352
interfaces 96–8, 128, 280, 286, 320
interior design 125, 136
'internal realism' (Putnam) 47–8, 60
International Seminar on Urban Form
    (ISUF) 177
interpersonal distance 92
interpretive insights 10–11
intersections, in the built environment 146–7,
    218, 299
intersubjectivity 31, 56, 77–9, 90–1
interventions 3, 11, 149, 221, 231, 271,
    359, 361
intervisibility 195, 306
intra-city comparisons 18, 31, 42, 349

intramural 212, 219, 298
intrinsic logic 30, 99, 132
intrusive interactions 135, 242
inventories 268, 274, 278
inverse distance weighting 276
Islam 206
isovists 192, 272–4
iterative abstraction 46, 66–74, 138–9, 184,
    252, 353, 359

J-graphs 193–4
junctions 146–7, 249, *see also* intersections

Keene, Derek 174, 216, 220, 231, 233
Khmer 22
knowledge, endurance of 60
Kropf, Karl 14, 34, 36, 130, 139, 177–8, 199

Laan, Dom van der 88, 136
labour 48, 66, 288, 338, 350, 359
land use 105, 186, 188, 195–8, 227, 287, 293
land-value 196
Latour, Bruno 135
layers, of (geo)data 202, 217–8, 221, 224–5,
    234, 239–41, 245, 251, 260, 263, 265–6,
    307–9, 360, *see also* overlays
layman's terms 40, 161, *see also* commonplace
    terms
least-cost path (LCP) analysis 306
Lefebvre, Henri 29, 169, 174–6
legacy data 8–9, 125, 203–5, 209, 354, 358
lens distortion 217
levels of meaning (*low*, *middle* and *high*)
    38–43
levels of socio-spatial significance 4, 9, 158,
    161–2, 258, 271–4, 296, 354–5
life-paths 57, 78, 81, 92–5, 287
life-worlds 38, 43, 46, 51, 54, 75, 79
light detection and ranging (LiDAR)
    209–14, 307
Lilley, Keith 172–3, 178, 180, 183,
    188, 207–8
linked data 173
live subjects 53, 58
lived experience 23, 75–6, 81, 84–9, 127–8
localising effects 323
locational context 159–61, 280–2, 285,
    288, 291
long-term, of developmental processes 3,
    11–2, 38, 55, 60–2, 108, 166, 172, 188,
    205–6, 270, 361
longue durée 15Lowland Maya 138
low-level interpretive approaches 5, 17, 23,
    30, 43, 46, 69
low-level meaning 37–8, 41
low order concepts 69
Ludlow 184
Lynch, Kevin 40, 68, 199

macro-scale 115, 290
making-habitable 6, 88
man–environment paradigm 3, 190
man-made and *not-man-made* boundaries
    154–8
MapInfo Professional 224
mapped representation 40, 127, 137–8

rationality 32, 76, *see also* ordinal decisions
realism 6, 46–55, 59–61, 65–70, 76, 141, 192,
    252, 352, *see also* social empirical reality
realist ontology 58, 70
realms of the social 65, 131
recentism 14–15
reconstruction, cartographic 173, 208–9
reductionism 45
reflexive research practice 214, 237, 251
regal ritual 28
regressive sequence mapping 173
regularity 64, 108, 346
relational approaches 18, 29–30, 49–54, 61,
    66, 97, 104, 109–10, 116, 124, 133,
    159–60, 193, 205, 281
'relational realism' (Tilly) 61
relative frequency and diversity 324
relativism 47, 49, 70
religious complexes 27
relocation 28–9
remote sensing 204, 209–10, 231, 276, 307
representational thinking 33, 38, 41, 104,
    169, 188
representativeness, of samples 301, 307, 311,
    316, 348–9
reproduction 28, 71, 93, 113–15, 349
residential structures 237
residents 26, 103, 171, 189
residuals 87, 187
resilience 3, 29, 106, 273, 346
resistance 57, 64, 77, 89, 108, 114
resolution 22, 31, 34, 42, 57, 122, 124, 182,
    199, 216–17, 226, 228–9, 236, 239–40
resources (natural and social) 25, 36, 160–1,
    285–288, 338, 359, *see also* time-space
    resources and restrictions
restricting and enabling 33, 51, 54, 64,
    160, 280
retroduction 67
rhythm 83, 124, 162, 174, 176, 268, 271, 291,
    294, 311, 326, 346, 359
Rice Humanities Research Centre 171
ring roads 186
Rio de Janeiro 171
rivers 157
RMS error 218, 226
road centre lines 193, 316
road crossing 341
roller scanners 217
Roman Empire 205–6
'rubbersheeting' 221
rules of thumb 215, 217, 255

St. Mary's Abbey, Winchester 340
Sayer, Andrew 48, 60–70, 132
scaffolding 333
scanning 217, *see also* digitisation
Schütz, Alfred 62, 68, 77, 132
science and technology studies (STS) 51
'scientification' of research 108
screen walls 237–8
Sea, the 156
seclusion 40, 113, 115, 127–36, 140–2,
    148, 151, 159, 162, 178, 193, 353
segment analysis 193
self-referential understanding 91

self-selection 254
semiotics 51, 359
sense of place 38
senses 61, 77–8, 86, 91, 192, 359
sequence mapping 208–9
settlement patterns 13, 17–19, 22, 168,
    206, 297
settling, process of 13, 16, 24, 34, 36, 40, 55,
    73–4, 188
seventh century 211
sheds 246, 254
shelter 82, 136
's–Hertogenbosch 208
shopping 95, 97–8
signatures: of inhabitation 7, 159;
    socio-spatial 162, 271, 275, 297–8
simultaneity 127, *see also* atomicity
sites of difference 7, 114–15, 119, 123, 131,
    267, 287, 292, 353
situated understanding 48
sixteenth century 174, 207, 305, 335–8, 342,
    348, 357
sixth century 8, 213, 222, 346
Sjöberg, Gideon 15
slopes 83, 155–6, 261
smallest meaningful element 262, 275, 298,
    311, 355
'smart cities' 11
Smith, Barry 116–20, 137, 353
Smith, Michael E. 13–14, 18–19, 21,
    24, 38, 43, 61, 127
snapping 221, 233–4, 239, 241
social action 29, 116
social aspects of city life 2, 11
social empirical reality 7, 175, 188, 199, 262
social functioning, of cities 3, 207, 301,
    306, 330
social information 171
Social Logic of Space, The 129, 189–91
social opportunities 270, 349
social practice 25–32, 37, 43–4
    and the definition of a city 25–9
social problems 189
social relationships 28, 61–6, 71,
    78, 92–4, 121, 198
social science 24, 48–50, 52, 56, 108, 168,
    350, 353, 359
social systems 72, 94–7, *see also* socio-spatial
    systems
social theory 55, 190, 192, 197
sociality 27
socially positioned spatiality 40
societal organisation 2, 19, 28, 92, 180, 332
societal realm, the 65–6, 90, 96, 188
society-space relations 3, 15, 40, 198, 269, 352
socio-cultural context 2, 100, 130, 169
socio-functional context 14, 348, 357–8
socio-spatial systems 6–11, 37–40, 46, 73,
    78–9, 94 *et seq*
sociology 30, 90
software development 9, 263, 307, 360
soliciting interaction 142–53, 157, 286, 319,
    328, 330, 348
solids 88, 136, 148, 186, *see also* built volumes
solid dominants *see* boundary line types
source effect (bias) 176

Lightning Source UK Ltd.
Milton Keynes UK
UKHW020642110619
344177UK00002B/10/P